Inscribed for

Ralph Draughon, Jr.,

a good friend, true
Southern gentleman (Alabama
Division), indispensable prop
of the Stratford Seminar, and master
orator on eagles and the Lees,
with esteem,

Daniel P. Jordan
March 2, 1984

A Richmond Reader, 1733–1983

Special Acknowledgment

This book is being published with the
generous financial assistance of the
Mary Wingfield Scott Publication Fund of
the Valentine Museum and of corporate
grants from the Charles E. Culpeper Foundation, Incorporated, and the Continental
Financial Services Company.

Edited, with Introductory Notes,

by Maurice Duke and Daniel P. Jordan

With an Introduction by Louis D. Rubin, Jr.

The University of North Carolina Press

Chapel Hill and London

A
Richmond
Reader
1733-1983

© 1983 by The University of North Carolina Press

All rights reserved

Manufactured in the United States of America

Library of Congress Cataloging in Publication Data

Main entry under title:

A Richmond reader, 1733–1983.

  Bibliography: p.
  Includes index.
  1. Richmond (Va.)—History—Sources. 2. Richmond
(Va.)—Social life and customs—Sources. 3. Richmond
(Va.)—Popular culture—Sources. I. Duke, Maurice.
II. Jordan, Daniel P.
F234.R545R52 1983 975.5′451 82-21921
ISBN 0-8078-1546-2

Contents

II. § THE PEOPLE AND THEIR CULTURAL TRADITION

Preface

A Richmond Reader is based on a wide diversity of documentary and literary material, much of which has not been available in the twentieth century because it has been either inaccessible, out of print, or both. The selections presented here represent roughly one-fourth of what we originally examined, and the compilation itself is designed to appeal to a variety of audiences, from the scholar searching for original sources to the general reader seeking both knowledge and enjoyment. It is our hope that the items as selected, edited, and introduced will depict in a new way the historic, cultural, and ethnic experience of two and a half centuries of Richmond. We further hope that the book will stand as a tribute to the city and its residents.

In preparing *A Richmond Reader* we have attempted to present an extended document that would reflect a broad, humanistic view of the past by blending the city's historic and cultural traditions. To accomplish this we have organized the selections into two distinct categories. In the first category, "The Times as Seen from the Times," we assembled eyewitness accounts of many of the major events in Richmond's past. In the second category, "The People and Their Cultural Tradition," we focused on the central personalities who have been active in the city's life, but we excluded individuals such as Arthur Ashe, Bill "Bojangles" Robinson, and Shirley MacLaine, for example, who were natives but whose accomplishments were made on stages larger than the ones afforded them at home. We have also presented selections, some of them fictional, that we thought best reflected the ways in which Richmonders have lived their day-to-day lives since the mid eighteenth century. Above all, we sought to include here items that are readable, interesting, and sufficiently significant to stand on their own. Therefore, each selection in the pages that follow tells its own story about some single aspect of Richmond and thus can be read either in isolation or as complementary to the other pieces in the book.

Each decade in the past two centuries is represented by an entry that we hope captures the spirit of its particular era. Further, each selection is preceded by an introduction, the purpose of which is to place the item in its appropriate historical context. The appendix is an exhaustive and annotated bibliography of books about Richmond, with recommended titles asterisked.

Some of the selections presented here were taken from academic sources and were originally documented in the customary scholarly fashion. To facilitate easier reading, we have omitted footnotes and their accompanying references. The interested reader, however, will find a short-title reference at the end of each entry indicating the source for the selection itself, which is cited completely at the end of the book. The symbol *q.v.*, which occurs in a number of the introductory notes, indicates that the word preceding the symbol has an individual entry elsewhere in the text. Finally, we have silently corrected obvious spelling errors in the original materials, but no other emendations have been made.

This book would not have been possible without the collaboration of many people. Some gave of their time to acquire funding, and others evaluated the manuscript in its various stages. Still others made valuable suggestions, which undoubtedly have strengthened the volume.

John G. Zehmer, Jr., director of the Valentine Museum, supported the project with enthusiasm from its inception. Sarah Shields, curator of the library at the Valentine, assisted in a variety of ways and was particularly helpful in selecting the illustrations, all of which come from the museum's collection.

The Publications Committee at the Valentine Museum also deserves our sincere gratitude. Members Mrs. T. Braxton Horsley, Louis H. Manarin, and Wallace Stettinius aided in the project, while thanks go to Mrs. John H. Moon, chairman, John Stewart Bryan III, and S. Douglas Fleet, all of whom gave extra time and effort in order to make *A Richmond Reader, 1733–1983* a reality.

A word of appreciation is also due the trustees of the Mary Wingfield Scott Publication Fund, who lent financial assistance to the project, as did Helen Johnson, of the Charles E. Culpeper Foundation, Inc., and J. Robert Nolley, Jr., of the Continental Financial Services Company.

A number of persons read and criticized the entire manuscript. Through their efforts, headnotes have been made clearer, errors corrected, and weak entries replaced by stronger ones. These people include Mrs. Ralph T. Catterall, Virginius Dabney, Agnes Bondurant Marcuson, Louis D. Rubin, Jr., Sarah Shields, Lynn L. Sims, and Emory M. Thomas.

Persons who suggested specific selections include Elsa B. Brown, Michael B. Chesson, Virginius Dabney, Daryl C. Dance, Louis H.

Manarin, Louis D. Rubin, Jr., Philip J. Schwarz, L. Winston Smith, and Brent Tarter.

Charles Saunders, head librarian at Richmond Newspapers, Inc., merits our thanks, as do Pattie J. Scott, of the Richmond Public Library, and Daniel Yanchisin, special collection librarian at Virginia Commonwealth University. Dennis F. Robison, librarian at the University of Richmond, generously provided working space during an entire summer.

Help in preparing the original manuscript was given by Elizabeth Duke, and valuable clerical assistance was provided by Wanda P. Clary, Peggy J. Cook, and Maureen T. Levins.

Encouragement has come from a number of people, among them Lynn Z. Bloom, Edward J. Kopf, George C. Longest, James T. Moore, and J. Harvie Wilkinson III. Keenly interested observers included Lewellyn S. Jordan, Daniel P. Jordan III, Grace D. Jordan, and Katherine L. Jordan.

Maurice Duke and Daniel P. Jordan
Richmond, Virginia, April 1982

Introduction
by Louis D. Rubin, Jr.

When I was growing up in Charleston, South Carolina, in the late 1920s and 1930s, the city of Richmond, Virginia, occupied a place in my imagination that was quite extraordinary. Not only was it the city where my mother's family lived—my grandparents, my aunts and uncles, my cousins. It was a *big* city. It had department stores with real escalators to ride up and down on. It had a professional baseball team. It had duckpin alleys and drive-ins. It had five-and-ten-cent stores with toy counters of a magnificence that put those in Charleston to shame. In Byrd Park there was a fountain with floodlights that transformed the plumes of white spray into all manner of colors. It had double-sized trolley cars, far larger than the little cars that I rode on in Charleston. It had a university on a real campus—with hills and walkways and numerous buildings. It had not one but two large railroad stations, and another small one over in South Richmond. It had an amusement park with ferris wheels, merry-go-rounds, rides, and concessions—one that remained there permanently, not merely for a week in the autumn when the fair was in town. It had also been the wartime capital of the Confederacy, and was thus just about the only city that I knew whose historical renown could possibly rival that of Charleston.

A trip to Richmond, therefore, was an event to be anticipated long in advance of departure. One saved money—or intended to do so—from one's weekly allowance to spend while there (though once I arrived, my various uncles and aunts could be relied upon to bestow largesse frequently and liberally). To get there one drove up to North Charleston and boarded the day-coach of an Atlantic Coast Line passenger train that was so long and so important that it did not even deign to come down into the peninsula of downtown Charleston. The train was air-conditioned. It had vendors on it—selling, among other things, Hershey bars of unparalleled size that cost as much as fifteen cents. It had two dining cars, back to back—even though one did not dare venture into them, but subsisted upon the sandwiches, fried chicken, and fruit that one brought along, supplemented by hourly purchases from the vendors. Not until long after dark did the train finally arrive in Richmond, and then it rolled into a huge railroad station with tracks and platforms underneath the building and, upstairs, a spacious waiting room with ornate marble columns and a lofty, domed ceiling. Outside the station there were taxicabs—not merely automobiles painted yellow, but genuine Yellow Cabs, just like in the movies; and right across from the station was a hotel that was many stories high. A few blocks down Broad Street one passed a building atop which was an illuminated sign the likes of which one had never before witnessed, made up of thousands of colored light bulbs, forming a huge container of Sauer's Extract that actually poured, or at any rate seemed to. And what a vast thoroughfare was this Broad Street! Down its center was a double row of trolley car tracks, while on each side was pavement along which automobiles might move two abreast.

A city, too, of enormous sophistication. To think of going with one's cousins over to the Byrd Theater on Saturday morning and viewing an entire program consisting of nothing but animated cartoons. And then proceeding into a confectionary (what a delicious word!) with real pinball machines in it that paid off in dimes. And living in houses that had not mere enclosed basements but actual cellars, dug down into the ground, musty and mysterious and with the faint odor of bituminous coal. And, when riding over to South Richmond, actually driving through an underground tunnel, dark inside, and with the daylight a long way off at the far end. And going with one's grandfather to a live stage show at a theater, with skits and songs and acrobats and comedians telling jokes—the jokes didn't seem very funny, even if sometimes the adults in the audience laughed immoderately. That didn't matter, however, not so long as one's seat was convenient to a popcorn machine and a candy dispenser, and one was with one's grandfather.

Such was the way that the city of Richmond appeared to a youthful visitor from further south: a place of metropolitan splendors and sybaritic delights, the very last word in up-to-date innovations, a veritable spa of wonders, where the downtown air was permeated with the fragrant bouquet of raw tobacco. To the modern-day Richmonder the memories that I have described are of a city that now must seem very quaint, old-fashioned, and difficult to recall when driving through the endless suburbs and huge shopping centers and along the interstate highways of the modern industrial metropolis that Richmond has become.

It is a place difficult for me, too, to remember when I am there, for I came later to spend a good deal of my life in the city of Richmond, going to college there, working for the Associated Press and later for the afternoon newspaper, and thereafter returning frequently to visit my parents. Few places seem to me to have changed more than Richmond—though what I have long since come to realize is that Richmond was always changing and always growing, that almost from the beginning it was a *city*, not a town, and that if it seemed very urban and metropolitan to me as a child, the impression was quite correct.

In the decades before the War Between the States, Richmond was a prosperous manufacturing community, with a population that in presidential election years was solidly Whig—and not the States Rights', Planter style of Whig, either, but the manufacturing, protectionist, pro-Internal Improvements variety. That John Marshall lived in Richmond was no mere accident. It is my hunch that if the outbreak of the War could have been postponed for another decade, Richmond, and therefore Virginia, might not have seceded from the Union at all. And after it was wracked by three years of siege and the center of the city left in ashes, it rebuilt swiftly and efficiently, regaining its prosperity within a relatively few years and thereafter functioning as an industrial and commercial center in important respects more akin to the Middle States than to the Deep South.

When one thinks of Richmond's role in history, of course, one thinks of the Confederacy. It was the Lost Cause that kept Richmond a Southern city for so long after the war. In sketching the appearance that the city had for me as a child, I should have mentioned the monuments. J. E. B. Stuart, Robert E. Lee, Stonewall Jackson, all on horseback, raised upon pedestals high above the traffic along Monument Avenue; Jefferson Davis; Matthew Fontaine Maury; at the intersection of Hermitage Road and Laburnum Avenue, A. P. Hill—here was a pantheon of heroes for any young citizen of the South to marvel at. The Confederate Museum downtown at the onetime White House, with its fascinating collection of actual wartime relics, including the jacket, stained brown from blood, that Doctor Hunter McGuire was wearing when treating the wounded Jackson after Chancellorsville. Battle Abbey, with its flags and the magnificent portraiture of the High Command. The late Douglas Southall Freeman, saluting General Lee's statue each day on the way downtown to his work on Fourth Street, and then returning to his study to rehearse in impassioned prose, properly anchored with footnotes, the indisputable evidence of heroic valor.

I happened to be temporarily resident in Richmond, where my father was recuperating from an operation, in June of 1932, when the last Confederate reunion was held. I was eight years old and had little idea of what was involved, but I remember that the newspapers came out with a special edition, filled with articles and photographs and—as is the way of newspaper supplements—numerous congratulatory advertisements celebrating the reunion. I was taken with one particular advertisement, recounting how a local citizen had gone off to fight in the war, then had returned afterward to burnt-out Richmond, established a little bakery (I think Broome's) among the ruins, and through hard work and patriotic devotion had risen with the city into renewed prosperity. For some reason that item exerted an uncommonly powerful appeal upon my eight-year-old imagination. I thought about it recurrently for years, until finally in 1957 I went back into the file room of the *News-Leader*, of which I was then associate editor, located the bound volume for that period, and searched for the advertisement. My memory had envisioned it as a full-page display, proudly ostentatious in its celebration of the noble past that the bakery and city had shared. To my surprise, however, I found that it was only a small notice, no more than a few inches in size. Such are the ways that the quirks of memory can play tricks.

There was a grand parade, commencing downtown and moving westward along Monument Avenue past the statues of the dead chieftains. My father took me to see it; we joined a large crowd that lined the sidewalks a block or two west of the Boulevard. Presently the procession drew near, prefaced by an impressively noisy vanguard of motorcycle police. Then came the armed forces—the Army, the Navy, the Marine Corps, the National Guard units, and numerous marching bands, including one drum-and-bugle aggregation, from an American Legion post in Norfolk, I think, resplendent in scarlet tunics, khaki pants and leggings, and shining chrome doughboy helmets.

At last came the culmination, for which we had all been waiting: the Confederate veterans themselves. To my surprise and my dismay, instead of columns of soldiers in gray, marching along in serried ranks, what I saw was a line of open touring cars, each containing some very old men, wearing gray uniforms to be sure, but white-haired and bent with age, waving canes and nodding feebly to the crowds. For a minute there was silence (or so I remember). Then my father said, "Give the old boys a hand!," and as he spoke, not in response to it but because he had said what all were thinking, there came a tremendous roar of applause and acclamation, rolling along the avenue, an ear-splitting testimony of affection and loyalty to the aged survivors of the Lost Cause from the citizenry of the capital they had once defended. Though I was very young I must have recognized something of what was involved, for I have never forgotten it (and once used it, transplanted to Fort Sumter in Charleston Harbor for the occasion, in a novel).

But that was almost half a century ago in its own right, and it is doubtful that the Confederate allegiance counts for much in Richmond anymore (or anywhere else in the South, especially after the centennial got upstaged by the civil rights movement). All the same, part of what Richmond now is, is the result of that Confederate heritage—and both for better and for worse. I like to think that in the long run it will be almost all for the better, that as its more deleterious effects continue to yield to ameliorative change, it will be seen at last to have helped to create and maintain what is so necessary in modern industrial society: a genuine human community.

Reading through the selections that the editors have chosen for inclusion in this anthology, I am impressed with the richness and variety of the human experience that has taken place in the city of Richmond. I am glad that the editors did not restrict themselves to the customary documents and accounts that might have been expected to fill the pages of a book such as this, but instead have moved, obviously as a matter of editorial policy, to encompass additional kinds of experience, by a variety of elements of the city's population, that do not ordinarily get into the history books and tourist guides.

I was surprised and delighted, for example, to find what appears to be the transcript of a taped interview with an uncle of mine, the late Joseph Joel, the husband of my mother's older sister. The experience he describes—of an immigrant Jewish family in the late decades of the nineteenth century—seems far removed from the kind of cultural milieu in which I was raised, in part I suppose because Richmond was a large enough city so that its immigrant groups could retain a cultural identity of their own instead of being swiftly assimilated into the American mainstream, and in part too because my father's people, among whom I grew up in South Carolina, were in temperament and interests quite different from my mother's.

In the course of his reminiscences Joseph Joel describes the advent of a relative, one Israel Weinstein, from the old country, and his subsequent marriage to a young woman from Baltimore. They were my mother's parents, my grandfather and grandmother. Israel Weinstein and another cousin, he says, came to the United States in order to avoid military service. If one were a Jew and lived in the ghettos of Galicia, one doubtless had little desire to serve in a conscripted army in which Jews were treated with less than entire regard for their religious sensibilities. But in the United States of America, and in Richmond, Virginia, it was a different matter. When needed, one could willingly fight for what was now indeed one's *country*. Thus when a few decades after that same Israel Weinstein arrived in Richmond there was a world war, one of his sons was wounded in action during the fighting in the Argonne Forest. And in a second and vaster war his grandson, Major Milton Joel of the U.S. Army Air Corps, the only son of Joseph Joel, gave up his life in the sky over Bremen while leading his squadron of P-38s in fighter support of a daylight bombing raid on Nazi Germany.

And that, too, is what I remember about Richmond, Virginia.

Here, then, is not merely a Richmond reader, but a Richmond treasury—writings about Richmond, writings by Richmonders, writings about Richmonders. May those who cherish the old city find in it reminders of things both familiar and felicitous. May those who do not yet know Richmond-on-the-James find this book an introduction to a place that, to quote from a 1907 guidebook, "in natural and historic interest . . . ranks . . . among the very first cities of the country, with a reputation far surpassing that of many other places superior to her in population and wealth."

I § The Times as Seen from the Times

"Cities in the Air": William Byrd Founds Richmond (1733–1742)

William Byrd II, whose famous house Westover still stands on the north bank of the James River below the city, founded Richmond, which he named for Richmond, England. The geography of the two locales, he noted, seemed similar to him. The decision to found the city was made by Byrd in 1733. The town was actually laid out by his friend Major Mayo in 1737 and incorporated by the General Assembly in 1742.

One of the most learned men in Virginia, at that time extending half way across the continent, Byrd had inherited the land on which the city was to be built from his father, who had died in 1705. A life-long public servant who represented the colony in England on numerous occasions, Byrd was born in 1674 near the fall line of the present city. He was educated abroad, being a resident of the Middle Temple, at which he studied law. He also surveyed the line between Virginia and North Carolina and served on the Governor's Council. In addition, he was at one time a member of the House of Burgesses.

In many ways, Byrd typifies the colonial planter at his best. From his diaries we know that he read Latin, Greek, Hebrew, and French. Additionally, he was a prolific author, although few of his writings were published during his lifetime. Moreover, his personal library in excess of three thousand volumes was one of the finest in the colonies. Byrd was as much at home in London society as on the streets of rustic Williamsburg, being friends with leading men on both sides of the Atlantic in his day. When he died in 1744 at the age of seventy, having spent half his life abroad, he left behind a legacy in his writings. He also left Richmond, the tiny trading hamlet that he founded and named, part of which his profligate son William Byrd III would attempt to dispose of by lottery in 1768.

The following three selections, the first written by Byrd, the second from a newspaper advertisement placed by him, and the third from early Virginia law, tell of the beginnings of the city.

§I

When we got home, we laid the foundation of two large cities: one at Shacco's, to be called Richmond, and the other at the point of Appomattox River, to be named Petersburg. These Major Mayo offered to lay out into lots without fee or reward. The truth of it is, these two places, being the uppermost landing of James and Appomattox rivers, are naturally intended for marts where the traffic of the outer inhabitants must center. Thus we did not build castles only, but also cities in the air. [1733]

Byrd, *Prose Works*, ed. Wright (1966), p. 338

§II

This is to give Notice, That on the North Side of James River, near the Uppermost Landing, and a little below the Falls, is lately laid off by Major Mayo, a Town, called Richmond, with Streets 65 Feet wide, in a pleasant and healthy Situation, and well supply'd with Springs of good Water. It lies near the Publick Warehouse at Shoccoe's, and in the midst of great Quantities of Grain, and all kind of Provisions. The Lots will be granted in Fee Simple, on Condition only of building a House in Three Years Time, of 24 by 16 Feet, fronting within 5 Feet of the Street. The Lots to be rated according to the Convenience of their Situation, and to be sold after this April General Court, by me,

William Byrd.

Virginia Gazette, April 1737,
quoted in Weddell, *Richmond* (1932), p. 3

§III

An Act, for establishing the Town of Richmond, in the county of Henrico; and allowing fairs to be kept therein.

II. *Be it enacted, by the Lieutenant Governor, Council, and Burgesses, of this present General Assembly, and it is hereby enacted, by the authority of the same,* That the said piece or parcel of land, lately belonging, or now belonging, to the said William Byrd, esquire; lying and being at the falls of James river, on the north side of the said river, in the county of Henrico aforesaid, be and is hereby constituted, appointed, erected, and established, a town, in the manner it is already laid out, or shall be laid out, by the said William Byrd, in lots, and streets, to be called by and retain the name of Richmond: And that the freeholders of the said town, shall, forever hereafter, enjoy the same rights and privileges, which the freeholders of other towns erected by act of Assembly, in this colony, have and enjoy. And that the said William Byrd, and his heirs, stand seized in fee-simple, of the lands lying and being between the present southern bounds of the said town, and the river, bounded to the eastward by a line, to be run a strait course, from the present extreme bounds of the said town to strike the river; and on the westward, by a line, to be run from the end of the present westward street, beyond the lot numbered [1] a straight course, to strike Shoccoe's creek, thence down the said creek to the River, and then by the river: to remain and be, as and for a common, for the use and benefit of the inhabitants of the said town, for ever.

III. And whereas allowing fairs to be kept in the said town of Richmond, will be very commodious to the inhabitants of that part of this colony, *Be it further enacted, by the authority aforesaid*, For the future, two fairs shall and may be annually kept and held, in the said town of Richmond, on the second Thursday in May, and the second Thursday in November, in every year; each to continue for the space of two days, for the sale and vending of all manner of cattle, victuals, provisions, Goods, wares and merchandises whatsoever: On which fair days, and on two days next before, and two days next after each of the said fairs, all persons coming to, being at, or going from the same, together with their cattle, goods, wares, and merchandizes, shall be exempt and privileged from all arrests, attachments, and executions, whatsoever, except for capital offences, breaches of the peace, or for any controversies, suits, and quarrels, that may arise and happen, during the said time; in which cases process may be immediately issued, and proceedings thereupon had, in the same manner as if this act had never been made: Anything herein before contained, or any law, custom, or usage, to the contrary thereof, in any wise, notwithstanding.

Hening, *Statutes at Large* (1819–23), 5:191–93

"Removal of the Seat of Government": Richmond Becomes the Capital (1779–1780)

The removal of the seat of government to Richmond, perhaps the most significant event in the city's history, began with a blank space. As a member of the first House of Delegates in 1776, Thomas Jefferson (1743–1826) introduced a bill to relocate the capital from Williamsburg, but he left a vacant line for the General Assembly to

designate the site of its choice. Three years later the legislature selected "Richmond, in the county of Henrico, which is more safe and
central than any other town situated on navigable water"—thus re-
jecting the claims of such rivals as Hanovertown on the Pamunkey
River. In April 1780, two years before the city was incorporated, the
physical transferral took place; the temporary capitol, on the corner
of Fourteenth and Cary streets (presently a parking lot), was "a small
frame building . . . used also on occasion, with change of scene, for
balls and public banquets." Overseeing the move and first governor
to reside in the city was Jefferson himself, whose enabling legislation, slightly revised from 1776, is produced below, along with an act
passed in 1780 specifying Shockoe Hill as the location for the Commonwealth's new public structures.

§ An Act for the Removal of the Seat of Government

I. WHEREAS great numbers of the inhabitants of this commonwealth must frequently and of necessity resort to the seat of government where general assemblies are convened, superior courts are
held, and the governour and council usually transact the executive
business of government; and the equal rights of all the said inhabitants require that such seat of government should be as nearly central
to all as may be, having regard only to navigation, the benefits of
which are necessary for promoting the growth of a town sufficient for
the accommodation of those who resort thereto, and able to aid the
operations of government: And it has been also found inconvenient
in the course of the present war, where seats of government have
been so situated as to be exposed to the insults and injuries of the publick enemy, which dangers may be avoided and equal justice done to
all citizens of this commonwealth by removing the seat of government
to the town of Richmond, in the county of Henrico, which is more
safe and central than any other town situated on navigable water: *Be it
therefore enacted by the General Assembly*, That six whole squares of
ground surrounded each of them by four streets, and containing all
the ground within such streets, situate in the said town of Richmond,
and on an open and airy part thereof, shall be appropriated to the use
and purpose of publick buildings: On one of the said squares shall be
erected, one house for the use of the general assembly, to be called
the capitol, which said capitol shall contain two apartments for the use
of the senate and their clerk, two others for the use of the house of
delegates and their clerk, and others for the purposes of conferences,

committees and a lobby, of such forms and dimensions as shall be adopted to their respective purposes: On one other of the said squares shall be erected, another building to be called the halls of justice, which shall contain two apartments for the use of the court of appeals and its clerk, two others for the use of the high court of chancery and its clerk, two others for the use of the general court and its clerk, two others for the use of the court of admiralty and its clerk, and others for the uses of grand and petty juries, of such forms and dimensions as shall be adopted to their respective purposes; and on the same square last mentioned shall be built a publick jail: One other of the said squares shall be reserved for the purpose of building thereon hereafter, a house for the several executive boards and offices to be held in: Two others with the intervening street, shall be reserved for the use of the governour of this commonwealth for the time being, and the remaining square shall be appropriated to the use of the publick market. The said houses shall be built in a handsome manner with walls of brick or stone, and porticoes where the same may be convenient or ornamental, and with pillars and pavements of stone. There shall be appointed by joint ballot of both houses of assembly, five persons to be called the directors of the publick buildings, who, or any three of them shall have power to make choice of such squares of ground, situate as before directed, as shall be most proper and convenient for the said publick purposes, to agree on plans for the said buildings, to employ proper workmen to erect the same, to superintend them, to procure necessary materials by themselves or by the board of trade, and to draw on the treasurer of this commonwealth, from time to time, for such sums of money as shall be wanting; the plans and estimates of which shall be submitted to the two houses of assembly whensoever called for by their joint vote, and shall be subjected to their control. . . .

II. And whereas it may be expedient to enlarge the said town of Richmond, by laying off a number of lots to be added thereto, and it may also happen that some of the lands adjacent to the said town may be more convenient for the publick uses: *Be it therefore enacted*, That the said directors cause two hundred additional lots or half acres, with necessary streets to be laid off adjacent to such parts of the said town as to them shall seem most convenient, and they shall also be at liberty to appropriate the six squares aforesaid, or any part of them, either from among the lots now in the said town, or those to be laid off as before directed, or of the lands adjacent to the said former or latter lots, and the said six squares and two hundred lots shall thenceforth be a part of the said town. And the said directors shall return into the clerk's office of the said county of Henrico, there to be recorded a full and distinct report under their hands and seals of the lots and squares of land added by them to the said town, or appropriated to the publick uses, together with the plan thereof. The rights of the several owners and tenants of the lots of land so to be added to the town and not appropriated to the publick uses, are nevertheless saved to them.

III. But whereas from the great expence attending the just and necessary war this commonwealth is at present engaged in, the difficulties of procuring the materials for building, and the high price for labour, it will be burthensome to the inhabitants if the said publick buildings be immediately erected: *Be it therefore enacted*, That the directors aforesaid shall, with all convenient speed, cause to be erected or otherwise provide some proper and temporary buildings for the sitting of the general assembly, the courts of justice, and the several boards before described.

IV. And whereas the present jail of the county of Henrico, now within the said town of Richmond, if enlarged may be made sufficient for a publick jail until a more commodious one can be built; the said directors are hereby empowered to enlarge the same. . . .

§ An Act for Locating the Publick Squares, to Enlarge the Town of Richmond, and for Other Purposes

BE it enacted by the General Assembly, That the ground to be appropriated to the purpose of building thereon a capitol, halls of justice, state house for the executive boards, and an house for the governour, shall be located on Shockoe hill; and those to be appropriated to the use of the publick market, shall be below the said hill, on the same side of Shockoe creek; which location shall be made immediately; and where the nature of the ground shall render other form more eligible for the said uses than a square, it shall be lawful for his excellency Thomas Jefferson, esquire, Archibald Cary, Robert Carter Nicholas, Richard Adams, Edmund Randolph, Turner Southall, Robert Goode, James Buchanan, and Samuel DuVall, esquires, directors, or a majority of them, to lay off in such form, and of such dimensions as shall be convenient and requisite. The said directors shall cause the several tenements of irregular shape and size included within the limits of the town of Richmond, to be laid off into regular squares with intervening streets at such intervals as in the other parts of the town, unless by varying the said intervals more favourable ascents may be procured

up the hill. They shall cause all the streets on Shockoe hill to be en-
largened to a breadth, not less than eighty, or more than one hundred
and twenty feet, of which breadth also shall be such new streets as
shall be laid off below the hill as before directed; and whereby such
enlargement or laying off new streets, or from any other circumstances, any house already erected shall happen to be in a street, it
shall be lawful for the said house to be continued twenty years, and no
longer. They shall also lay off, in the most easy direction, whether
straight or curved, so many streets for ascending and traversing with
facility, the several hills in the said town as may be thought necessary
in any supposed state of future increase and population, and at such
intervals as shall be convenient, making them to communicate with
the streets above the brow, and below the foot of each hill.

Hening, *Statutes at Large* (1819–23), 10:85–89, 317–18

"Richmond . . . Was Their Object":
Benedict Arnold's Raid (1781)

Although destined to wear a capital's crown, Richmond at the time
of the Revolution was little more than a frontier trading hamlet, "a
village of muddy streets and small frame houses." The population for
1775, the year that Patrick Henry made his famous Give-Me-Liberty
speech at what is now St. John's Church, has been "roughly calculated" at six hundred persons, almost half of whom were black.
Important as a supply and recruiting center even before it became the
seat of government, Richmond—and Virginia for that matter—had
largely escaped the ravages of war before 1780. That tranquil condition changed dramatically in late 1779 with the sudden arrival of a
British force under Benedict Arnold, "the greatest of all traitors"
in Jefferson's opinion, but also one of the most intrepid and expert
commanders of the time. Moving with characteristic skill and alacrity,
Arnold reached Richmond on January 5, faced perhaps "a single
volley" of local resistance, and spent about twenty-four hours selectively destroying property in and near the town. The city would be
raided again during the Revolution—a prelude to its beleaguered
status some eighty years afterward—but Arnold's attack stands as a
particularly humiliating episode. Governor Jefferson was greatly

criticized for it (somewhat unjustly), and one can sense his own feeling of helplessness as he reported the dark events a few days later
in a Richmond newspaper.

§ Benedict Arnold's Invasion of Richmond as Reported by Thomas Jefferson in the *Virginia Gazette*

RICHMOND, January 13 [1781]
A narrative of the late incursion made by the enemy to this place.

On the 31st of December, a letter from a private Gentleman to
General Nelson reached this place, notifying that in the morning of
the preceding day, twenty seven sail of vessels had entered the Capes,
and from the tenor of the letter, there was reason to expect within
a few hours farther intelligence whether they were friends or foes,
their force, and other circumstances. General Nelson went immediately into the lower country, with powers to call on the militia in that
quarter, or to act otherwise as exigencies should require. The call of
the militia from the middle and upper counties was not made till intelligence could be received that the fleet was certainly hostile. No
farther intelligence came till the second instant, when the former was
confirmed; it was ascertained that they were enemies, and had advanced up James river to Warrasqueak bay. All arrangements were
immediately taken for calling in a sufficient body of militia for opposition. In the night of the third, advice was received that they were at
anchor opposite Jamestown, Williamsburg was then supposed to be
their object; the wind however, which had hitherto been unfavour-
able, shifted fair, and the tide being also in their favour, they ascended
the river to Kennon's that evening, and with the next tide came up
to Westover, having on their way taken possession of the battery at
Hoods, by which two or three of their vessels had received some damage, but which was of necessity abandoned by the small garrison of
fifty men placed there on the enemy's landing to invest the works.
Intelligence of the enemy's having quitted the station at James-town,
from which it was supposed they meant to [land at] Williamsburg, and
that they had got in the evening to Kennon's, reached this place at five
o'clock in the morning of the fourth, this was the first indication of
their meaning to penetrate towards Richmond or Petersburg. As the
orders for drawing the militia hither had been given but two days, no
opposition was in readiness. Every effort was therefore necessary to
withdraw the arms and other military stores, records, &c. from this

place: Every effort was accordingly exerted to convey them to the foundery and labaratory, till about sunset of that day, when intelligence was received that the enemy had landed at Westover: From this it appeared that Richmond, and not Petersburg, was their object; it became necessary to remove every thing which remained here, across the river, as well as what had been carried to the foundery and labaratory; which operation was continued till the enemy approached very near. They marched from Westover at 2 o'clock in the afternoon of the 4th, and entered Richmond at one o'clock in the afternoon of the 5th. A regiment of infantry and about fifty horse continued on without halting to the foundery, they burnt that, the boring mill, the magazine, and two other houses, and proceeded to Westham, but nothing being in their power there, they retired to Richmond. The next morning they burnt some buildings of publick and some of private property, with what stores remained in them; destroyed a great quantity of private stores and about 12 o'clock retired towards Westover, where they encamped within the neck the next day. The loss sustained is not yet accurately known. At this place about 300 muskets, some soldiers clothing to a small amount, sulphur, some quarter masters stores, of which 120 sides of leather was the principal article, part of the artificers tools, and 3 waggons; besides which five brass 4 pounders, which had been sunk in the river, were discovered to them, raised and carried off. At the foundery about 5 tons of powder was thrown into the canal, of which there will be a considerable saving by remanufactoring it. Part of the papers belonging [to] the Auditors office, and the books and papers of the Council office, which were ordered to Westham, but in the confusion carried by mistake to the foundery, were also destroyed. The roof of the foundery was burnt, but the stacks of chimnies and furnaces not at all injured. Within less than 48 hours from the time of their landing and 19 from our knowing their destination they had penetrated 33 miles, done the whole injury, and retired. Our militia, dispersed over a large tract of country can be called in but slowly. On the day the enemy [march]ed to this place, two hundred only were [embodi]ed, they were of this town and neighbour[hood] and were too few to do any thing effectual. The enemy's forces are commanded by the parricide Arnold.

Jefferson, *Papers*, ed. Boyd (1950–), 4:269–70

"Of Coaches There Were None":
A German Traveler Visits the Emerging City
at the Falls (1783)

As the new capital of America's largest state and as a growing town easily accessible by water and by the primary stage route along the east coast, Richmond attracted its share of that post-Revolutionary phenomenon—the curious, well-educated, ever-observant traveler from Europe. One of the first and most insightful was Dr. Johann David Schöpf (1752–1800), formerly a Hessian surgeon with the British army during the war. Schöpf, a learned man and "child of the Enlightenment," passed through Richmond in late 1783 as part of his grand tour of the United States. A trained scientist, he quite naturally noted the "great and pleasing" falls of the James, remarked on their pervasive noise and water sprays, and speculated on the river's salubrious impact on the physical and economic well-being of the city. Schöpf also expressed a European's skepticism about Richmond's rough democracy, as he observed it in the legislative chambers, tavern life, and society in general.

Richmond stands on the hilly banks of the James River, over against the falls of this stream which is here perhaps half a mile wide. The houses of this town, a short time since of little consequence, are almost wholly of wood and scattered irregularly on two heights, divided by the Shokoes (*sic*), a small brook; the number of them is not large* nor are they in themselves of a handsome appearance. What gives the place fame and regard is the falls of the James River, in addition to its being the seat of the Virginia government.

The falls of the river were the first object of my curiosity. The lower terminus of these is next [to] the town; but their whole breadth or extent is 7 miles upstream to Westham, a small place, and in this distance the total perpendicular fall of the water is only 71 ft., according to an exact measurement said to have been made. Hence the falls are of themselves inconsiderable, and one looks in vain for high rock-walls over which the water plunges straight down; but a vast number of great and small fragments of rock fill the bed of the river as far as the eye can see, and through these the current, with foaming uproar,

---

*Recently the number of the houses of Richmond was estimated at 280, and that of the inhabitants at about 2,000.

makes its way. What with the help of devious banks and the forests on both sides, the impression from a view of the whole is great and pleasing. The noise of the falls, especially at night, is heard not only throughout the town but, before the wind, for several miles around. These falls are occasioned by the granite ledge, so often mentioned, which runs along the eastern coast of North America for the most of its extent, and gives rise to most of the falls, to those at least found near the ocean. . . .*

The James River, up from its mouth in the Bay, is one of the greatest and most beautiful of American streams, and on account of the profitable tobacco-trade which it facilitates and furthers, one of the richest. It is navigable for large merchantmen as far up as three miles below Richmond, that is, below the falls. The tide comes up to the falls. From Westham on beyond the falls only flat-boats and canoes may be navigated, and that no farther than to another falls in the South Mountains. The James rises in the Alleghany Mountains under the name of the Fluviana (*sic*), and receives a considerable addition from the South Mountain, in the Riviana (*sic*). . . .

The falls, incessantly churning the water and throwing it up to the air, are thought to be the occasion of the clouds, which are more frequent here, it is said, than at other places where circumstances are dissimilar; on this ground also it is claimed further that Richmond is not so healthy as, from its situation in other respects, it might well be supposed to be but is very subject to autumn and intermittent fevers. But these diseases being general along the coast the falls of the river cannot be regarded as the especial occasion, any more than the universal use of swine flesh, which I remarked above; with more reason the cause may be taken to be the swamps and the amount of standing water in the country.

Richmond has not always had the honor, which fell to it four years since, of being the seat of government of the state of Virginia. Before the founding of Williamsburg, Jamestown, now in ruins, was the capital of the province. But after the settlement of the interior progressed more and more, it was found convenient to desert Williamsburg also and to establish the seat of government at Richmond, 60 miles to the west. . . .

*Recently there have been set on foot plans to remove the obstacles to inland navigation in the James River, and to establish a connection between it and the Great Kenhaway (*sic*) river, to the west of the mountains, these two streams being separated by a land-passage of only 23 miles. In this way an easy communication will be opened between the James and the Ohio. And General Washington has also proposed a further connecting of the Potowmack (*sic*) and the James (presumably by means of the Shannandore [*sic*]).

The Assembly had just now come together for its half-yearly winter session; a small frame building serves the purpose, used also on occasion, with change of scene, for balls and public banquets. It is said of the Assembly: It sits; but this is not a just expression, for these members show themselves in every possible position rather than that of sitting still, with dignity and attention. An assembly of men whose object is the serious and important one of making laws, should at least observe a certain *decorum*, but independence prevails even here. During the visits I made I saw this estimable assembly quiet not 5 minutes together; some are leaving, others coming in, most of them talking of insignificant or irrelevant matters, and to judge from the indifference and heedlessness of most of their faces it must be a trifling business to make laws. At the open door of the hall stands a door-keeper, who is almost incessantly and with a loud voice calling out for one member after another. In the ante-room there is a tumult quite as constant; here they amuse themselves zealously with talk of horse-races, runaway negroes, yesterday's play, politics, or it may be, with trafficking. Nor must it be expected that this illustrious assembly shall be seen dressed as in other countries etiquette, in like circumstances, would demand. In the same clothes in which one goes hunting or tends his tobacco-fields, it is permissible to appear in the Senate or the Assembly. There are displayed boots, trousers, stockings, and Indian leggins; great-coats, ordinary coats, and short jackets, according to each man's caprice or comfort, and all equally honorable. . . .

As in all other public and private societies there are certain men who lead the debate, and think and speak for the rest, so it is also in these Assemblies. Among the orators here is a certain Mr. Henry who appears to have the greatest influence over the House. He has a high-flown and bold delivery, deals more in words than in reasons, and not so long ago was a country schoolmaster. Men of this stamp, either naturally eloquent or become so through their occupation, as, e.g., lawyers, invariably take the most active and influential part in these Assemblies; the other members, for the most part farmers without clear and refined ideas, with little education or knowledge of the world, are merely there to give their votes, which are sought, whenever the House is divided into parties, by the insinuations of agreeable manners and in other ways. . . .

The want of hard money is felt not only in commercial affairs but also in the collection of the public revenues, and the government has been obliged to pass an act proclaiming that tobacco, hemp, flour, grain, and skins are to be accepted of the people in payment of their taxes. For this purpose special magazines have been established and inspectors appointed, whereby the state is subject to additional expense. And the government, having to set up as a merchant, and pay the costs of ware-houses, inspectors &c., must therefore exact more of the citizen who cannot pay cash money, or suffer loss itself.

Richmond has only one public sheet, issued twice a week: and so far as I know this is the only newspaper in all Virginia. Nevertheless it is inferior in every respect to the sorriest of the Philadelphia sheets, and in comparison with these, seldom contains any articles of importance; and in general this province is poor in literary productions. Inquiring, I could hear only of a Mr. Jefferson, at this time a member of the Congress, as the author of several excellent political brochures, with the contents of which nobody seemed familiar. The constitution of Virginia, indeed, mentions liberty of the press as one of its cardinal principles; but at the beginning of the Revolution there was a law of the state forbidding anything whatever to be said or written against independence. However, if little is written in Virginia, there is all the more of speaking, for the Virginians are very conversable. They boast that among all the American colonies the English language is with them preserved purest and most complete, and one cannot altogether deny them. But here and there a few negroisms have crept in, and the salmagundy of the English language has here been enriched even by words of African origin, and some of these are regarded as really meritorious additions, e.g., the negro expression "*toat*," to carry something on the shoulder, for which there is no word in the English.

There is but one church at Richmond, one small church, but spacious enough for all the pious souls of the place and the region. If the Virginians themselves did not freely and openly admit that zeal for religion, and religion generally, is now very faint among them, the fact might easily be divined from other circumstances. Considering the extent of the state, one sees not only a smaller number of houses of worship than in the other provinces, but what there are in a ruinous or ruined condition; and the clergy for the most part dead or driven away and their places unfilled. . . .

No matter if special privileges are denied the churchly order, and in general an equality of all ranks is promoted and defended, the ladies here are not the more inclined to part with any advantage of position to which they fancy themselves entitled through the offices held by their husbands. News of the definitive treaty just arrived in America was the occasion at Richmond of illuminations, fire-works, banquetings, and finally, a ball, at which the honor of the first dance fell by lot to the very honorable daughter of a very honorable shoemaker. That the distinction should have been awarded by lot was the cause of great displeasure to the ladies of the Governor's family and his relatives, and the incident was the subject of every conversation the next day, but the unanimous opinion was that the lot should be valid as against any claims of rank, and that no exception to the generally allowed equality should be granted even the fair sex beyond that due personal merit and accomplishment.

According to the principles of a general equality was the behavior at our tavern, which in its arrangements was very like an eastern caravansery [sic]. Mr. Formicola, a Neapolitan by birth, was the landlord here. The entire house contained but two large rooms on the ground-floor, and two of the same size above, the apartments under the roof furnished with numerous beds standing close together, both rooms and chambers standing open to every person throughout the day. Here, no less than in most of the other public-houses in America, it is expected that rooms are to be used only as places for sleeping, eating and drinking. The whole day long, therefore, one is compelled to be among all sorts of company and at night to sleep in like manner; thus travellers, almost anywhere in America, must renounce the pleasure of withdrawing apart (for their own convenience or their own affairs), from the noisy, disturbing, or curious crowd, unless it may be, that staying at one place for some time, a private apartment is to be rented. The Assembly meeting at this time was the occasion of a great gathering of strangers and guests at Richmond, and every evening our inn was very full. Generals, Colonels, Captains, Senators, Assembly-men, Judges, Doctors, Clerks, and crowds of Gentlemen, of every weight and calibre and every hue of dress, sat all together about the fire, drinking, smoking, singing, and talking ribaldry. There is in this no great ground of complaint, because such a company at other times may be very agreeable, entertaining, and instructive; but the indelicate custom of having so many beds together in one room is the more surprising, since elsewhere in America there is much store set by decorum and neatness, which by such an arrangement as this must often be dispensed with.

The coming together of so many gentlemen from all parts of the province brought hither a great number of very fine horses. One could almost fancy it was an Arabian village; there were to be seen the whole day long saddled horses at every turn, and a swarming of riders in the few and muddy streets, for a horse must be mounted, if only to fetch a prise of snuff from across the way; but of coaches there were none, which in the larger towns elsewhere jolt through all the streets. Horses are a prime object with the Virginians; but they give their attention chiefly to racers and hunters, of which indubitably they have the finest in America, their custom formerly being to keep up and improve the strain by imported English stallions and mares. The pedigree of their horses is carried out with great exactitude. . . .

On the south side of the James River, exactly opposite Richmond, stands a small town called Manchester. Between the two places the river is not wide, and in crossing one scarcely observes whence the current comes; the numerous rocks and small islands in and about the falls seeming at a distance to make up one continuous whole. A circumstance which it has been proposed to make use of in the construction of a bridge over the falls; for these rocks have an owner, who bought in for a few hundred pounds the lower part of the falls together with a narrow strip along either bank, and he is now working at the project of a large and fine bridge, which would be the first and only one of the sort in America, if the projector can but secure permission of the Assembly and the right to make of this a toll-bridge.

Schöpf, *Travels in the Confederation*, trans. and ed. Morrison
(1911), pp. 49–52, 55–57, 61–67

"Yielding to No One of the Beautiful Monuments": Mr. Jefferson Designs a Capitol (1785–1786)

As governor of Virginia, Thomas Jefferson played a central role in Richmond's early history, but perhaps his greatest contribution to the city came while he was three thousand miles away serving as America's minister to France. The directors of public buildings for the Commonwealth had requested his assistance with plans for a capitol and other structures—and had given him a mere thirty days to respond. Forced by the state's parsimony to concentrate on a single building, he chose as his ideal an ancient Roman temple, the Maison Carrée, in Nîmes, France, a ruin he confessed to "gazing whole hours at . . . like a lover at his mistress." Jefferson failed to meet his deadline, however, and a foundation on Shockoe Hill was already underway when he dispatched a model (purchased for fifteen guineas), "designs . . . simple and sublime," and a host of cogent arguments. As the following correspondence, centering on the capitol, indicates, he carried the day, and in the process, as historian Dumas Malone summarizes it, "provided a monumental setting for the government of his own Commonwealth, brought the support of classic authority

to American republicanism, and started the classic revival in the
United States insofar as any single person could."

§I

SIR   Richmond March 20th. 1785
The active part which you took before your departure from Virginia, as a director of the public buildings, leads us to believe, that it
will not be now unacceptable to you, to cooperate with us as far as
your engagements will permit.

We foresee, that in the execution of our commission, the Commonwealth must sustain a heavy expence, and that we can provide no
shield so effectual against the censures which await large disburse-
ments of public money, as the propriety of making them. For this
purpose we must intreat you to Consult an able Architect on a plan fit
for a Capitol, and to assist him with the information of which you
are possessed.

You will recollect, Sir, that the first act directed separate houses for
the accommodation of the different departments of government. But
fearing that the Assembly would not countenance us in giving sufficient magnificence to distinct buildings, we obtained leave to con-
solidate the whole under one roof, if it should seem advisable. The
inclosed draught will show that we wish to avail ourselves of this li-
cence. But, altho it contains many particulars it is not intended to
confine the architect except as to the number and area of the rooms.

We have not laid down the ground, it being fully in your power to
describe it, when we inform You that the Hill on which Gunns yellow
house stands and which you favoured as the best situation, continues
to be preferd by us and that we have allocated 29 half acre lots, including Marsdon's tenement, and Minzies' lots in front of Gunns. The
Legislature have not limited us to any sum; nor can we, as yet at least,
resolve to limit ourselves to a precise amount. But we wish to unite
œconomy with elegance and dignity. At present the only funds submitted to our order are nearly about £10,000 Virga. Currency.

We have already contract'd with Edward Voss of Culpepper, for the
laying of 1500 thousand Bricks. He is a workman of the first reputation here, but skilful in plain and rubbed work alone. We suppose he
may commence his undertaking by the beginning of August, and have
therefore stipulated with him to be in readiness by that time. This circumstance renders us anxious for expedition in fixing the plans,

especially too as the foundation of the Capitol will silence the enemies of Richmond in the next October Session.

Should an assistant be thought necessary whose employment will be either independant of Voss or subordinate to him, we will pay him.

We shall send to Europe for any Stone which may be wanted.

The roof will be covered with lead, as we conceive that to be better than Copper or tiles.

In the remarks, which accompany the plan, we have requested a draught for the Governor's house and prison. But we hope that the Capitol will be first drawn and forwarded to us, as there is no hurry for the other buildings.

We trust Sir, you will excuse the trouble which we now impose on you, and will ascribe it to our belief of your alacrity to serve your Country on this occasion. We have the honour to be very respectfully Sir Your most obt. hble. Servts.,

JAMES BUCHANAN
WM. HAY
on Behalf of the Directors

§II

To James Madison   Paris Sept. 20, 1785
DEAR SIR

... I received this summer a letter from Messrs. Buchanan and Hay as directors of the public buildings desiring I would have drawn for them plans of sundry buildings, and in the first place of a Capitol. They fixed for their receiving this plan a day which was within one month of that on which their letter came to my hand. I engaged an Architect of capital abilities in this business. Much time was requisite, after the external form was agreed on, to make the internal distribution convenient for the three branches of government. This time was much lengthened by my avocations to other objects which I had no right to neglect. The plan however was settled. The gentlemen had sent me one which they had thought of. The one agreed on here is more convenient, more beautiful, gives more room and will not cost more than two thirds of what that would. We took for our model what is called the Maison quarrée of Nismes, one of the most beautiful, if not the most beautiful and precious morsel of architecture left us by antiquity. It was built by Caius and Lucius Caesar and repaired by

Louis XIV. and has the suffrage of all the judges of architecture who have seen it, as yielding to no one of the beautiful monuments of Greece, Rome, Palmyra and Balbec which late travellers have communicated to us. It is very simple, but it is noble beyond expression, and would have done honour to our country as presenting to travellers a morsel of taste in our infancy promising much for our maturer age. I have been much mortified with information which I received two days ago from Virginia that the first brick of the Capitol would be laid within a few days. But surely the delay of this piece of a summer would have been repaid by the savings in the plan preparing here, were we to value its other superiorities as nothing. But how is a taste in this beautiful art to be formed in our countrymen, unless we avail ourselves of every occasion when public buildings are to be erected, of presenting to them models for their study and imitation? Pray try if you can effect the stopping of this work. I have written also to E. R. on the subject. The loss will be only of the laying the bricks already laid, or a part of them. The bricks themselves will do again for the interior walls, and one side wall and one end wall may remain as they will answer equally well for our plan. This loss is not to be weighed against the saving of money which will arise, against the comfort of laying out the public money for something honourable, the satisfaction of seeing an object and proof of national good taste, and the regret and mortification of erecting a monument of our barbarism which will be loaded with execrations as long as it shall endure. The plans are in good forwardness and I hope will be ready within three or four weeks. They could not be stopped now but on paying their whole price which will be considerable. If the Undertakers are afraid to undo what they have done, encourage them to it by a recommendation from the assembly. You see I am an enthusiast on the subject of the arts. But it is an enthusiasm of which I am not ashamed, as its object is to improve the taste of my countrymen, to increase their reputation, to reconcile to them the respect of the world and procure them it's praise.

I shall send off your books, in two trunks, to Havre within two or three days to the care of Mr. Limozin, American agent there. I will advise you as soon as I know by what vessel he forwards them. Adieu. Your's affectionately,   TH: JEFFERSON

§III

GENTLEMEN Paris Jan. 26. 1786.
I had the honour of writing to you on the receipt of your orders to procure draughts for the public buildings, and again on the 13th. of August. In the execution of those orders two methods of proceeding presented themselves to my mind. The one was to leave to some architect to draw an external according to his fancy, in which way experience shews that about once in a thousand times a pleasing form is hit upon; the other was to take some model already devised and approved by the general suffrage of the world. I had no hesitation in deciding that the latter was best, nor after the decision was there any doubt what model to take. There is at Nismes in the South of France a building, called the Maison quarrée, erected in the time of the Caesars, and which is allowed without contradiction to be the most perfect and precious remain of antiquity in existence. Its superiority over any thing at Rome, in Greece, at Balbec or Palmyra is allowed on all hands; and this single object has placed Nismes in the general tour of travellers. Having not yet had leisure to visit it, I could only judge of it from drawings, and from the relation of numbers who had been to see it. I determined therefore to adopt this model, and to have all it's proportions justly observed. As it was impossible for a foreign artist to know what number and sizes of apartments would suit the different corps of our government, nor how they should be connected with one another, I undertook to form that arrangement, and this being done, I committed them to an Architect (Monsieur Clérisseau) who had studied this art 20. years in Rome, who had particularly studied and measured the Maison quarrée of Nismes, and had published a book containing 4 most excellent plans, descriptions, and observations on it. He was too well acquainted with the merit of that building to find himself restrained by my injunctions not to depart from his model. In one instance only he persuaded me to admit of this. That was to make the Portico two columns deep only, instead of three as the original is. His reason was that this latter depth would too much darken the apartments. Œconomy might be added as a second reason. I consented to it to satisfy him, and the plans are so drawn. I knew that it would still be easy to execute the building with a depth of three columns, and it is what I would certainly recommend. We know that the Maison quarrée has pleased universally for near 2000 years. By leaving out a column, the proportions will be changed and perhaps the effect may be injured more than is expected. What is good is often spoiled by trying to make it better.

The present is the first opportunity which has occurred of sending the plans. You will accordingly receive herewith the ground plan, the elevation of the front, and the elevation of the side. The architect having been much busied, and knowing that this was all which would be necessary in the beginning, has not yet finished the Sections of the building. They must go by some future occas[ion] as well as the models of the front and side which are making in plaister of Paris. These were absolutely necessary for the guide of workmen not very expert in their art. It will add considerably to the expence, and I would not have incurred it but that I was sensible of it's necessity. The price of the model will be 15 guineas. I shall know in a few days the cost of the drawings which probably will be the triple of the model; however this is but my conjecture. I will make it as small as possible, pay it, and render you an account in my next letter. You will find on examination that the body of this building covers an area but two fifths of that which is proposed and begun; of course it will take but about one half the bricks; and of course this circumstance will enlist all the workmen, and people of the art against the plan. Again the building begun is to have 4 porticos; this but one. It is true that this will be deeper than those were probably proposed, but even if it be made three columns deep, it will not take half the number of columns. The beauty of this is ensured by experience and by the suffrage of the whole world; the beauty of that is problematical, as is every drawing, however well it looks on paper, till it be actually executed; and tho I suppose there is more room in the plan begun, than in that now sent, yet there is enough in this for all the three branches of government and more than enough is not wanted. This contains 16. rooms, to wit, 4. on the first floor, for the General court, Delegates, Lobby, and Conference; eight on the 2d. floor for the Executive, the Senate, and 6 rooms for committees and [juri]es, and over 4. of these smaller rooms of the 2d floor are 4. Mezzanines or Entresoles, serving as offices for the clerks of the Executive, the Senate, the Delegates and the court in actual session. It will be an objection that the work is begun on the other plan. But the whole of this need not be taken to pieces, and of what shall be taken to pieces the bricks will do for inner work. Mortar never becomes so hard and adhesive to the bricks in a few months but that it may easily be chipped off. And upon the whole the plan now sent will save a great proportion of the expence.

Hitherto I have spoken of the Capitol only. The plans for the prison also accompany this. They will explain themselves. I send also the plan of the prison proposed at Lyons which was sent me by the architect, and to which we are indebted for the fundamental idea of ours.

You will see that of a great thing a very small one is made. Perhaps you may find it convenient to build at first only two sides, forming an L. But of this you are the judges. It has been suggested to me that fine gravel mixed in the mortar prevents the prisoners from cutting themselves out, as that will destroy their tool. In my letter of Aug. 13. I mentioned that I could send workmen from hence. As I am in hopes of receiving your orders precisely in answer to that letter I shall defer actually engaging any till I receive them. In like manner I shall defer having plans drawn for a Governor's house &c. till further orders, only assuring you that the receiving and executing these orders will always give me a very great pleasure, and the more should I find that what I have done meets your approbation. I have the honour to be, with sentiments of the most perfect esteem, Gentlemen your most obedient and most humble servant, TH: JEFFERSON

§ IV

To James Currie
DEAR SIR   Paris Jan. 28. 1786
. . . I send by this conveiance designs for the Capitol. They are simple and sublime. More cannot be said. They are not the brat of a whimsical conception never before brought to light, but copied from the most precious the most perfect model of antient architecture remaining on earth; one which has received the approbation of near 2000 years, and which is sufficiently remarkable to have been visited by all travellers. It will be less expensive too than the one begun. . . .

TH: JEFFERSON

Jefferson, *Papers*, ed. Boyd (1950–), 8:48–49, 534–35;
9:220–22, 240

"Gaming Is the Ruling Passion":
A French Nobleman's Observations (1796)

La Rochefoucault-Liancourt (1747–1827) could claim the standing of peerage but preferred the cause of democratic reform. To Louis XVI's description of the turbulence of 12 July 1789 as a revolt, La Rochefoucault-Liancourt responded with the classic summation, "Non, sire, c'est une révolution." A scientific farmer, political economist, and champion of various medical advances, the nobleman traveled extensively in America in the mid-1790s, always alert to topics close to his own interests. He came to Richmond in the early summer of 1796 and was particularly observant, as the following excerpt indicates, of matters mercantile and moral.

§ Journey to Richmond

. . . In the space of sixty miles which I yesterday travelled from Williamsburg to Richmond, I did not see twenty houses; and such as I saw were mean and wretched. . . .

§ Town of Richmond

The position of Richmond is truly agreeable. The lower town, which is situated along the bank of James-River, lies between that river and a tolerably high hill: but the greater part of the houses—those indeed of almost every person who is not engaged in trade—are built on the hill, which commands a prospect of the river, and whence the view embraces at once the island formed by its waters, the extensive valley through which it flows, and the numerous falls by which its stream is broken. On the opposite side of the river, the country rises in a gentle acclivity; and the little but well-built town of Manchester, environed by cultivated fields which are ornamented by an infinite number of trees and dotted with scattered houses, embellishes the sweet, variegated, agreeable, and romantic perspective. . . .

The population of Richmond amounts to six thousand persons, of whom about one third are negroes. This town has prodigiously increased during the years which have elapsed since the legislature chose it for the place of their sittings: but within the last two or three years it has remained stationary. A few years back, a conflagration consumed almost all the lower part of the town. This accident induced the inhabitants to rebuild in brick not only the houses consumed, which had been of wood, but also several others which the owners' fears wished to preserve from the same calamity. At present there are few wooden houses at Richmond.

The trade of this town consists in the purchase of the country productions, the number of which is confined to wheat, Indian corn, and tobacco—and in selling at second hand the articles of domestic consumption, which are generally procured from England. The number of merchants who carry on a direct commerce with Europe is inconsiderable: they keep their ships at Norfolk; the river not being navigable for those of large size higher up than City-Point, at the distance, by water, of sixty-six miles below Richmond. They therefore send the produce of the country in smaller vessels to Norfolk, where they easily find opportunities of completing their cargo, if needful. The generality of these merchants are only the agents or partners of English houses: the others hardly carry on any other than the commission trade, which may be considered as the real business of the place.

It is from the merchants of Richmond or Petersburg that those of Norfolk most commonly purchase the grain, flour, and tobacco, which the latter export, and which the former have purchased at first hand. The country produce is paid for by the merchants in ready money or at short credit: they even frequently obtain it on cheaper terms by furnishing the planters with an advance of money on their crop. The Richmond merchants supply all the stores through an extensive tract of back country. As they have a very long credit from England, they can allow a similar indulgence of six, nine, or twelve months to the shopkeepers whom they supply, and from whom they always derive a considerable profit, which is still further increased when they exact payment in country produce.

Almost all the merchants of Richmond have shops for the retail-trade. They all deal in bills of exchange on Europe; a trade which often proves extremely profitable to them.

There are few opulent merchants at Richmond; still fewer in easy circumstances; and it is no difficult matter to find good notes at four and five per cent per month. But people have not here, as in the principal towns of America, the resource of putting these notes into the bank; accordingly this kind of traffic is here much more lucrative. The legal interest of money, which is only five per cent per annum, together with the scarcity of specie and the general want of confidence, render it difficult to obtain money on loan.

§ Richmond Canal

The falls of James-River, which obstructed its navigation from the distance of seven miles above Richmond, heretofore imposed a necessity of employing land-carriage for that space. At present a canal, running parallel with the course of the river for those seven miles, connects the communication by water, and opens a navigation which extends without interruption two hundred miles above Richmond. This canal, already nearly finished, will be entirely completed during the present year, excepting the basin, which the directors propose to form at the entrance of the town, and of a much greater size than seems necessary for the trade of Richmond on any reasonable supposition of its future encrease. The locks at the opening of the canal are erected: they are simple, and the gates are easily managed by one or two men, but might be rendered still more easy in their movement. These, being three in close succession, raise the boats to an elevation of seventeen feet. Others will be required, if it be intended to carry the canal as far as Rockets, a mile below the town, beyond which point vessels of forty tons cannot come up on the Richmond side: on the other side vessels even of greater burden can come up almost opposite to the town. The extension of the canal to Rockets has for its object to facilitate the direct transportation of the back-country produce to City-Point, and so on to Norfolk. By this mean, those commodities, which otherwise would find no market except at Richmond, might reach Norfolk, and, by exciting a competition between the merchants of both towns, might probably cause an encrease of profit to the planters. But the expence of these additional locks would be very considerable. The fund of two hundred and forty thousand dollars, raised by a subscription of seven hundred shares, is already exhausted and a loan of twenty-one thousand dollars, made by the trustees of the canal under the authority of the state, and secured by a mortgage of the tolls that have already begun to be received on the part which is finished, has been proved scarcely sufficient to complete the execution of the original plan. It appears that the great expence which would attend the addition furnishes the holders of the canal shares with a pretext for opposing it, and that the Richmond merchants use that as a cloak to cover their wish to remain the sole purchasers of the produce of the back country, which is the real motive of their opposition to the further extension of the canal. . . .

§ Manners and Laws

Society here displays the characteristics of simplicity and honesty: nevertheless it is not linked in the bond of unity. The men who belong to opposite parties seldom visit each other: but, when they happen to meet, they treat each other with all the politeness and civility of well-bred people.

The party opposed to government—that is to say, the party wishing for a change in the existing constitution, a restriction in the executive power—has here many zealous adherents. This party would prefer to their own the new French constitution such as it is: and, from the permanency of that constitution in France, they derive encouragement to effect a change in the constitution of the United States. . . .

The profession of a lawyer is here, as in every other part of America, one of the most profitable. But, though the employment be here more constant than in Carolina, the practitioner's emoluments are very far from being equally considerable. Mr. Marshall does not from his practice derive above four or five thousand dollars per annum, and not even that sum every year. In Virginia the lawyers usually take care to insist on payment before they proceed in a suit: and this custom is justified by the general disposition of the inhabitants to pay as little and as seldom as possible. I have heard physicians declare that they do not annually receive one-third of what is due to them for their attendance; that they have some of these debts of five and twenty years standing; that their claims are frequently denied; and that, in order to recover payment, they are obliged to send writs, carry on lawsuits, &c. &c. &c.

The derangement of affairs occasioned by expenses exceeding the bounds of income, and especially by gaming—and, above all, the want of delicacy resulting from that derangement and from the habit of thinking lightly of debts—are the causes of this immoral order of things; and it is in some degree encouraged by the laws of the state, which do not allow the seizure of lands or other immovable property for the payment of debts. This law, which the Virginians say they originally derived from England, has been preserved by them in all the reforms which they have made in their legal code, and has been preserved by them alone. Slaves and movable property are seizable: but whoever is acquainted with the manners of the country may readily conceive how great the facility of making a feigned sale of them: and then, by holding them as hired, they are placed beyond the reach of seizure.

Gaming is the ruling passion of the Virginians: at pharo, dice, billiards, at every imaginable game of hazard, they lose considerable sums. Gaming-tables are publicly kept in almost every town, and particularly at Richmond. Yet a law of the state, enacted no longer ago than in December 1792 [?] expressly prohibits all games of hazard, all wagers at horse-races or cock-fights, of which the Virginians are passionately fond—forbids the losing of more than twenty dollars at cards within four and twenty hours—places all the holders of banks on the footing of vagabonds—orders the justices of the peace, on the slightest information, to enter the places where they are held, to break the tables, seize the money, &c. &c. Nevertheless, to the present hour, the greater number of those who enacted that law—of the present legislators, the justices of the peace, and the other magistrates —are assiduous in their attendance at those seats of gambling. The bank-holders are everywhere received and acknowledged as "gentlemen"; and their profession is envied, as being a very lucrative one. The part of this law which is said to be the most punctually executed is that which cancels the debts contracted at the gaming-table, and prohibits the payment of them.

It is not uncommon to witness scenes of bloodshed at these gaminghouses. Since my arrival here, a young man, of a family of consequence in Virginia, fancying, in his impatient heat at a billiard-party, that he had reason to be dissatisfied with the behaviour of a marker whom he thought deficient in due respect to him,—after discharging a volley of abuse on the man who with much difficulty bore it—thrust him through the body with a kind of cutlass which he wore by his side. The marker did not die in consequence of the wound: but, even if he had, the young man would have equally escaped prosecution. The latter has quitted the town for a few days, and will shortly reappear, and resume his usual pursuits, as if he had been absent only on account of ill health; although nobody denies the commission of that public act, or attempts to palliate it. . . .

Perfect freedom of religion is allowed by the laws of Virginia: but few nations are less addicted to religious practices than the Virginians. At Richmond there is no church. Prayers are sometimes read in the Capitol, in one of the halls destined for the legislature: and then they are read by an episcopalian clergyman, because those who call themselves members of that profession are more numerous than the others. Meetings of anabaptists, methodists, and even quakers, are more regularly held, but in private houses, as none of those sects have any public buildings.

La Rochefoucault-Liancourt, *Travels . . . 1795, 1796, and 1797* (1799), 3:53, 60, 63–68, 73–74, 76–79, 99

"To Fight the White People for Their Liberty": The Prosser Revolt (1800)

The best-known slave insurrection of the antebellum South occurred in 1831 in Southampton County, Virginia, under the leadership of Nat Turner, but thirty-one years earlier Richmond had been the focal point for what Virginius Dabney (q.v.) calls "the greatest slave plot in U.S. history." Against the backdrop of seething antagonisms and an awareness of both the rhetoric of the American Revolution and the deeds of black revolutionaries in Santo Domingo, a broad conspiracy developed among slaves in central Virginia in the summer of 1800. Foremost among the leaders were "the Main Spring & Chief Mover," Gabriel Prosser, and Jack Bowler, a giant black believed to be "perhaps as Strong a man as any in the State." Committed to the overthrow of white rule, hundreds and perhaps thousands of blacks knew of the insurrection. It was set to begin at midnight August 30 but was foiled by the alarms of loyal slaves and a violent storm. Governor James Monroe led the white populace in mass arrests of the rebels. Prosser and Bowler, among the last apprehended, were tried and executed along with over thirty of their co-conspirators, as revealed in the extracts from the court proceedings. The year 1800 marked this abortive slave revolt—but also the birth of Nat Turner and John Brown.

Henrico County Court sentences Jack Bowler, a negro man slave, the property of Wm. Bowler of the County of Caroline, to death on the charge of conspiracy and insurrection, and orders him to be hung on the second Friday in November next.

§ Substance of the Testimony Given in the Trial of Jack Bowler

Prosser's Ben—The witness deposes that Gabriel informed him that the prisoner was the first person from whom he received information of the insurrection intended by the negroes, which was to centre at William Young's. The prisoner said at the Blacksmith shop, in which the witness worked, that he would raise and enlist men and contend for command with Gabriel.

The prisoner came to the shop at sundry times, and had frequent conversations and mentioned at repeated times there, that he had procured six or seven pounds of powder for the purpose of fighting the white people: The prisoner agreed (in hearing of the witness) together with Gabriel and Solomon, to commence the fight with scythe blades, until they could procure arms from the white people. He saw the prisoner at his Master's great-house on the Saturday night appointed for the commencement of the insurrection, in company with Gabriel and Solomon, who said and concluded that the excessive bad weather would prevent the people from meeting that night, and appointed the ensuing Sunday night as the time of meeting at his Master's tobacco house; he also saw them together on the Sunday morning following.

Mrs. Prices John—I saw the prisoner at Mr. Young's spring, in company with Gabriel: he enlisted with Gabriel and engaged to get as many men to join as he could, and meet in three weeks from that time for the purpose of fighting the white people. Prosser's Tavern being appointed the place of Rendezvous, the prisoner enquired of Gabriel what he was to do for arms: the prisoner applied to many who had agreed to engage in the insurrection, to give him the voice for General. But upon the votes being taken, Gabriel had by far the greater number. Whereupon, it was concluded that the prisoner should be second in command, to-wit, a captain of light horse. The prisoner and Gabriel had secret conversations. That the meeting was interrupted by the appearance of Mr. Young's overseer, and thereupon the people dispersed, having previously agreed to meet at Mr. Moore's schoolhouse, where a final conclusion on the business should be had.

Prosser's Sam—This witness was a run-away at the time the affair was to have happened: On the Tuesday night of the week appointed for the meeting of the negroes, the prisoner fell in company with a negro by name Frank: the prisoner enquired of the deponent, if he had heard that the negroes were going to rise in arms and fight for their liberty (being the first knowledge he had of the insurrection) and the prisoner said the business would certainly commence on Saturday night then next ensuing, if it did not rain hail stones. The prisoner said they intended to seize on some arms deposited at Priddy's Tavern: a negro by name Charles having promised to conduct them to the spot where they were kept. In a conversation with the prisoner in the corn field, he remarked that he had procured as much ammunition as two persons could carry, and throwing his arms around Lewis, another negro present, said we have as much right to fight for our liberty as any men: and that on Saturday night they would kill the white people: that they would first kill Mr. Prosser and the neighbors, and then proceed to Richmond. . . .

At a Court of Oyer and Terminer held for the county of Henrico on Monday, the sixth day of October, 1800, for the trial of Gabriel, a negro man slave, the property of Thomas Henry Prosser, of the said county, charged with conspiracy and insurrection, the said Gabriel was convicted and condemned to execution on Tuesday, the seventh day of October, 1800.

§ The Trial of Gabriel

Prosser's Ben—Gabriel was appointed Captain at first consultation respecting the Insurrection, and afterwards when he had enlisted a number of men was appointed General. That they were to kill Mr. Prosser, Mr. Mosby, and all the neighbors, and then proceed to Richmond, where they would kill everybody, take the treasury, and divide the money amongst the soldiers: after which he would fortify Richmond and proceed to discipline his men, as he apprehended force would be raised elsewhere to repel him. That if the white people agreed to their freedom they would then hoist a white flag, and he would dine and drink with the merchants of the city on the day when it should be agreed to.

Gabriel enlisted a number of negroes. The prisoner went with the witness to Mr. Young's to see Ben Woolfolk, who was going to Caroline to enlist men there. He gave three shillings for himself and three other negroes, to be expended in recruiting men.

The prisoner made the handles of the swords, which were made by Solomon. The prisoner shewed the witness a quantity of bullets, nearly a peck, which he and Martin had run, and some lead then on hand, and he said he had ten pounds of powder which he had purchased. Gabriel said he had nearly 10,000 men; he had 1,000 in Richmond, about 600 in Caroline, and nearly 500 at the Coal pits, besides others at different places, and that he expected the poor white people would also join him, and that two Frenchmen had actually joined, whom he said Jack Ditcher knew, but whose names he would not mention to the witness. That the prisoner had enlisted nearly all the negroes in town as he said, and amongst them had 400 Horsemen. That in consequence of the bad weather on Saturday night, an agreement was made to meet at the Tobacco House of Mr. Prosser the ensuing night. Gabriel said all the negroes from Petersburg were to join him after he had commenced the Insurrection.

Mr. Price's John—He saw the prisoner at a meeting, who gave a general invitation to the negro men to attend at the Spring to drink grog. That when there he mentioned the Insurrection, and proposed that all present should join them in the same, and meet in 3 weeks for the purpose of carrying the same into effect, and enjoined several of the negroes then present to use the best of their endeavors in enlisting men, and to meet according to the time appointed.

Ben Woolfolk—The prisoner was present at the meeting at Mr. Young's, who came to get persons to join him to carry on the war against the white people. That after meeting they adjourned to the Spring and held a consultation, when it was concluded that in 3 weeks the business should commence. Gabriel said he had 12 dozen swords made, and had worn out 2 pair of bullet moulds in running bullets, and pulling a third pair out of his pocket, observed that was nearly worn out. That Bob Cooley and Mr. Tinsley's Jim was to let them into the Capitol to get the arms out. That the lower part of the Town towards Rocketts was to be fired, which would draw forth the citizens (that part of the town being of little value); this would give an opportunity to the negroes to seize on the arms and ammunition, and then they would commence the attack upon them. After the assembling of the negroes near Prosser's, and previous to their coming to Richmond, a company was to be sent to Gregorie's Tavern to take possession of some arms there deposited. The prisoner said, at the time of meeting the witness at Mr. Young's, that he had the evening before received six Guns—one of which he had delivered to Col. Wilkinson's Sam. That he was present when Gabriel was appointed General and Geo. Smith second in command. That none were to be spared of the whites except Quakers, Methodists, and French people. The prisoner and Gilbert concluded to purchase a piece of silk for a flag, on which they would have written "death or Liberty," and they would kill all except as before excepted, unless they agreed to the freedom of the Blacks, in which case they would at least cut off one of their arms. That the prisoner told the witness that Bob Cooley had told him if he would call on him about a week before the time of the Insurrection he would untie the key of the room in which the arms and ammunition were kept at the Capitol and give it to him, or if he did not come, then on the night of the Insurrection being commenced, he would hand him arms out as fast as he could arm his men, and that he had on a Sunday previous to this, been shown by Cooley every room in the Capitol.

Palmer, ed., *Calendar of Virginia State Papers* (1875–95),
9:159–60, 164–65

"Impressed on My Childhood, Perhaps on My Imagination": Richmond in the Early 1800s

Samuel Mordecai (1786–1865) was one of Richmond's first historians, and his *Virginia, Especially Richmond, in By-Gone Days* has for more than a century been a source of delight and information about the early days of the capital and its inhabitants. Born in New York City, Mordecai was brought to Richmond as an infant by his parents, Jacob and Judith Myers Mordecai. An apprentice to his uncle, Samuel Myers, Mordecai was later a commission merchant in the city and in Petersburg. Sometime during the period that he was writing *Richmond in By-Gone Days*, a statue was made of Mordecai by the famous Richmond sculptor Edward V. Valentine. Although he was not a professional historian in the modern sense of the word, Mordecai had a sharp eye for detail and a subtle understanding of human nature. After reading *Richmond in By-Gone Days*, Washington Irving, who had visited the city during the trial of Aaron Burr, wrote the following to Mordecai: "Every page of your volume brought up some delightful recollection of scenes and characters long since passed away; for at Richmond, at the time of my visit, there was a rare assemblage of the talent and beauty of Virginia. . . ."

There are few residents of Richmond whose reminiscence of its localities, &c., have a more remote retrospection than mine; impressed on my childhood, perhaps on my imagination; and as the latter may occasionally prevail, I will not venture to assert that my descriptions and anecdotes are literally correct—they are so, as the qualification in court goes, "to the best of my knowledge and belief." As far back as the year 1792, I think I remember the *market-house* occupying the site of the one just rebuilt (1855) on Main and Seventeenth streets. The first edifice was an open shed supported on wooden posts, and the slope from it down to *Shockoe Creek* was a green pasture, and considered a common, much used by laundresses whereon to dry the clothes which they washed in the stream. A spring of cool water arose in the common on the south side of Main street, but the spot is now occupied by a building where fountains of *fire-water* are substituted for the natural and pure element, and, I fear, it may be added, that the combined elements attract more thirsty bodies than the simple one did of yore; although the thirst is more apt to be increased than allayed by the fiery substitute.

The creek was crossed by foot passengers on a narrow bridge, raised a few feet above the surface of the water, but horses cooled *their* feet by fording it. When freshets occurred, the planks were removed from the bridge and a ferry-boat was substituted, which conveyed vehicles, as well as man and horse, across the wide and sometimes deep stream.

At the mouth of the creek, where the gas holders now rise and fall, was a wharf, built around a broad, flat rock (which has been blasted to accommodate the gas), and this place was called the *Rock Landing*, where oyster boats and small craft resorted.

Along the then elevated bank of the river, from about the rear of the present Union Hotel, a grassy walk, shaded by elm and other trees, extended for a considerable distance, down to where *Foster's rope-walk* afterwards stood, and this was the fashionable promenade. Of late years, the clay which nourished those trees has been converted into bricks, the surface lowered many feet, and a large portion of it covered with buildings. Below this bank was a narrow branch of the river, separated from the main stream by a narrow strip of land, an island, on which grew a few large sycamore trees, about the site of the present dock. I remember a vessel, grounded probably in a freshet, in this narrow stream, and converted into a place of refreshment, which was reached by a platform from the shore, and resorted to by promenaders. Its position was peculiarly favorable for obtaining and disposing of oysters.

The eastern end of this shaded walk terminated in a high and steep cliff, overhanging the river, which washed its base at high water, but at low tide admitted of a narrow walk on the sands. On the occasion of a severe ice freshet once, a great deposit of drift-wood, soil and sand formed a small island some hundred feet from this cliff. A German, named Widewilt, procured a land warrant and located it on this new-found land, and, to secure it against becoming a floating island, he drove stakes all around his slippery domain, and wattled them so that future freshets might add further deposits; and thus *Widewilt's Island* became a possession of some value as a fishery and sand mart. The island remained above water longer than its founder did above ground; but a similar accident to that which formed the island recurred, and destroyed the work of its predecessor. An ice freshet consolidated the river, and so obstructed the current that the ice borne over the Falls continued to accumulate in height until it rose to the level of Mayo's Bridge. An unfrozen current flowed underneath, but was not visible for many miles. The immense mass of ice slowly disappeared, and with it disappeared Widewilt's Island. . . .

The Rock Landing has had a singular succession of occupants. When vessels of some size could no longer float there, and when even the oyster boats had to abandon it in favor of a wharf, which was extended to deeper water, a shot-tower was erected on it, or, according to modern parlance, was *being erected*. Although founded on a rock, it had not attained to its full attitude, when it fell to the ground, proving that bad bricks and weak mortar were unfit for high pressure, or perhaps the rock on which it was based may not have been dressed to a true level, and the tall structure slid off sidewise. The materials served to form a less aspiring structure, to use a gentle term, for a block of buildings in the Valley not always in very good repute.

Thus dead to any useful purpose, the Rock Landing was buried under the accumulating mass of earth and rubbish, which was carted from foundations for houses and from less pure sources. After many years interment it was exhumed, and like some other subjects, whose graves are violated, its still firm body was dislocated, and the members scattered abroad or used in the erection of the huge monument which covers its grave, but a bright and subtle spirit arises from it, which serves to enlighten our citizens in the most benighted times.

"*The Cage*" is, I believe, a term peculiar to Richmond, as applied to the receptacle for offenders. It originated from a structure so called, erected at the north-east end of the market bridge, some fifty years ago, when it terminated close to the market-house; its long parapet-wall of brick, surmounted by a capping of free-stone. This cage, of octagonal form, had open iron gratings on three sides, about ten feet above the street, and the floor of this open prison was arranged amphitheatrically, so that each occupant could see, and, what was worse, be seen from the street.

Here were encaged (when caught) the unfeathered night-hawks that prowl for prey, and screeching owls that make night hideous, and black birds, who had flown from their own nests, to nestle elsewhere, like cuckoos; and some birds, both black and white, who had no nests at all, were brought to roost here until that official ornithologist, the police master, should examine into their characters. This was a somewhat convenient arrangement to the citizen, who, on rising in the morning, missed the attendant on his household comforts, and who, as he went to market, had only to look into the cage for his flown bird.

A structure made memorable to future ages by the author of Hudibras, stood in rear of the cage.

> "_____In all the fabrick
> You shall not see one stone or brick,

But all of wood, by powerful spell
Of magic, made impregnable:
There's neither iron bar, nor gate,
Portcullis, chain, nor bolt, nor grate:
And yet men durance there abide,
In dungeon, scarce three inches wide,
With roof so low, that under it
They never stand, but lie or sit;
And yet so foul that whoso is in,
Is to the middle-leg in prison;
In circle magical confin'd,
With wall of subtile air and wind;
Which none are able to break thorough,
Until they're freed by the head-borough."

This mystical prison—the *stocks*—surmounted the *whipping-post*, and was an awful warning to the foul birds; some of whom were occasionally condemned to roost in the upper part and others to become acquainted with the twigs in the lower. . . .

§ The Capitol and the Square

The *Capitol Square* was originally as rugged a piece of ground as many of our hill-sides in the country exhibit, after a ruinous course of cultivation. Deep ravines furrowed it on either side, and May and James-town weeds decorated and perfumed it in undisturbed luxuriance. On either side of the capitol was a long horse-rack, for the convenience of the public and to diversify the odor. In front of the portico stood an unpainted wooden belfry, somewhat resembling the dairies we see at good farm-houses. The portico might then be reached by a narrow, winding stone stairway, now closed, which gave to the goats and kids, who sported in numbers about the grounds, a convenient access to the portico, where they found shelter in wet weather. A few of the original forest trees, oaks and pines, which had escaped the barbarous refinement of clearing away native growths to be supplanted by exotics, constituted the only relief to the dismal aspect of the grounds, except a few chinquepin bushes, which served to prick the fingers of boys in due season, and a copious and luxuriant growth of thistles, whose down, in a good breeze, resembled a snow storm.

Between the Governor's house and the Capitol was a high stone wall, near the line of the street, built to close the upper end of an immense ravine (now a shady dell), and over this wall, after a heavy fall of rain, flowed a great body of water, forming a fine rose-tinted cascade.

The *Guard-house* and belfry, now rather disfiguring the square, was preceded by a much uglier edifice: a shabby, old second-hand wooden house, occupied as barracks by the Public Guard, under the command of Captain Quarrier. The grounds immediately around it were bedecked with the shirts of the soldiers and the chemises of their wives, which flaunted on clothes-lines, and pigs, poultry and children enlivened the scene.

The *Capitol* itself, not then stuccoed, exposed its bare brick walls between the columns or pilasters. The roof was once flat, if I mistake not, and paved with tiles, and, like Noah's Ark, "was pitched without, with pitch." But as a hot sun caused the pitch to flow down the gutters, and the rains to enter the halls, an elevated roof was substituted. In process of time, the attic thus formed was converted into an arsenal, the building and the fire-arms being perhaps considered fire-proof, or the risk not considered at all. Even at this day, a most valuable deposit, the *State Library*, is at risk in the combustible upper part of the Capitol, and the inestimable statue of *Washington*, by *Houdon*, may one day be destroyed as was Canova's splendid one at Raleigh, N.C. A handsome fire-proof building should be erected for the preservation of both, and of other objects of value.*

The *Governor's House* preceding the present one, was a very plain wooden building of two stories, with only two moderate sized rooms on the first floor. It was for many years unconscious of paint, and the furniture was in keeping with the republican simplicity of the edifice, and of its occupants, from Henry and Jefferson down to Monroe and Page. The palings around the yard were usually in a dilapidated condition, and the goats that sported on the steep hill-sides of the Capitol Square, claimed and exercised the liberty of grazing on his Excellency's grounds.

The cows are now endeavoring to establish a similar claim to the grass and onions on the public square in the very face of the sentry.†

The old residence of the Governors of Virginia might usually have

---

*Governor Wise has followed up this suggestion and wisely recommended the erection of such an edifice (1857), but to no purpose.

†Since writing the above, posts have been planted at each gate, about twelve inches apart, which, while they exclude the cows, may also practically exclude fashionable ladies from the Capitol Square, now that the *Eugénie hoops* have become in vogue, and are adopted indiscriminately by those who have or have not the same motive that in-

boasted that, if it had in itself no claims to distinction, its occupants had many.

Two articles of furniture of the colonial times are extant in the Capitol, namely: the *Speaker's chair* of the House of Burgesses, originally decorated with the royal arms; this was removed from Williamsburg, and is now, though shorn of its regal emblems, occupied by the Speaker of the House of Delegates:—and secondly, the tall *stove* which warmed those colonial and independent halls, in succession, for about sixty years, and for the last twenty-five has served to warm the central hall, in which stands Houdon's statue of Washington. This stove, a work of note, bears the old Virginia colonial arms and other embellishments in relief, and they remain perfect, being as indestructible as the structure they decorate, for the stove is truly a structure of three stories.

The founder of it, Buzaglo, was proud of his work, and when it was shipped from London, he thus writes to "My Lord" (Botetourt), dated August 15th, 1770: *"The elegance of workmanship does honour to Great Britain. It excels in grandeur anything ever seen of the kind, and is a masterpiece not to be equalled in all Europe. It has met with general applause, and could not be sufficiently admired."!!!* The reader is advised to draw a long breath, and pause awhile, till his admiration subsides.

This "warming machine," as Buzaglo called it, this master-piece of art and science, doomed to carry his name to posterity, was presented to the House of Burgesses by the Duke of Beaufort. It has survived three British monarchs, and been contemporaneous with three kingly monarchies, two republics and two imperial governments in France —but of only one constellation of republics in the United States,—I hope and trust *"one and indivisible, now and forever!"*

The grounds of the Capitol Square were originally laid out by Mons. Godefroï, a French gentleman of skill and taste, according to the formal style, where

> "Grove nods at grove, each alley has its brother,
> And half the terrace just reflects the other."

He certainly reduced chaos to order, and made the grounds very handsome, and wonderfully uniform; considering their original irregularity. But now "half the terrace" does not "reflect the other"; The west side has been modernized according to an irregular plan,

---

duced the Empress to introduce them. It is impracticable for a fashionable hoop, without considerable coaxing, to pass between the barriers which are placed to obstruct the entrance of the cows. 1856.

adapted to it by Mr. Notman, of Philadelphia. Some dozen flights of stone steps are dispensed with; the straight lines of trees are being gradually thrown into disorder. But the east side, like a prim old maid, retains its formality for the present, and serves to show the contrast between the formal and the picturesque styles.* But the great and striking embellishment of the square will be the Washington Monument,† now ready for the erection of the statuary on their pedestals.

The succeeding generation will have no idea of the original surface of Richmond, from that which will be presented to their view. Besides the changes noted elsewhere, there existed a few years ago a complete barrier to the progress of man and horse, north of Leigh street from Fourth to Fourteenth, by the intervention of a deep ravine, which has now (1860) been filled up on Fourth and Fifth, and is being filled on the higher numbers. Another ravine cut off the communication between Clay and Leigh streets from Sixth to Fourteenth or further. The intercourse is now opened on Sixth, Seventh, Eighth and Ninth, and a stack or chimney (for water, not fire), about 100 feet high, is now being erected on Tenth, down which the water will flow from Clay and from Leigh streets, when the chasm between them shall be filled. Marshall street, a few years ago, was closed at Twelfth by a profound ravine, which is now overcome as far as College street—but the heaviest work yet executed, has been the present easy connection of Shockoe hill with Church hill along the line of Broad street, which seemed almost impracticable. The extension of Franklin street from Fourteenth to Seventeenth along precipices and deep gullies is another strong case. It would be wearisome, if not so already, to describe the changes south of Broad street. In a word, the city was all hills, valleys and deep ravines, and had a most forbidding aspect. This page is written for readers in Richmond in 1900.

In the days of my boyhood springs of cool water flowed from various spots at the base of Shockoe hill, along its whole extent from Fifth to Fourteenth streets, and the number of them was considerable, as was their utility. It is but a few years ago that one which discharged itself on Thirteenth street, below the Governor's house, was condemned to flow under the pavement into the culvert; one of the two in the Capitol Square is permitted to discharge its waters near the Court house, far from the spot where they formerly rose. Its brother on the west side of the Capitol was condemned a few years ago and

---

*The east side has also been changed and beautified.
†The incomparable equestrian statue of Washington, by Crawford, was erected and inaugurated February 22d, 1858.

buried alive. On almost every square (west of the Capitol) that sloped to the foot of the hill there was a spring—Hay's, Blair's, Dobie's, Graham's and Hay's again. They all continue to flow in obscurity, no doubt, but the kindness of Nature in bestowing them on thirsty man and beast, and on the arid earth, is no longer estimated—like benefactors whose gifts are forgotten, when no longer enjoyed. . . .

§ Manufactures and Mills

. . . The first grist mill in Richmond was built, I am told, near the spot where *Haxall's mills* now stand, or run. It was a mere wooden shanty, built on the rocks in the river, and approached by planks laid from one rock to another. The machinery was a common tub wheel, propelled by a natural rapid, and gave motion to a pair of mill stones, which served to grind corn for the inhabitants. Twenty-two pair now grind eight hundred barrels of flour per day, more or less, according to circumstances; and from the extensive additions to the buildings recently made, perhaps some ten or twenty pair more may be added to the establishment.

In the long interval between the erection of the shanty and of Haxall's mills, the site of the latter was occupied by *Ross's mills*, which were swept off by a freshet and rebuilt. They then acquired celebrity as *Gallego's mills*, the first of the name, and resisted the floods to fall a victim to the flames, as did the next generation of mills on the same spot.

The Gallego mills changed their locality to a site on the canal, some miles above the city, and these twice shared the fate of their predecessors. Then was erected a much larger establishment on the basin, which after a few years was also destroyed by fire. The enterprising owners however, nothing daunted, rebuilt them on even a more extended scale, and are now erecting another building of similar dimensions, machinery in which can, if introduced, be propelled by the same water-power repeated—constituting probably the largest mills in the world.

A portion of the *Armory* has been converted (like the sword to a ploughshare), into a flour mill; but I believe the State is not a partner, and may permit it on the ground that it is better to manufacture food than fire-arms. A large flour mill has been erected at Tredegar, a short distance above the armory, and here grain is ground and cannons are cast in close proximity. This, however, as well as two flour mills, *Taliaferro's* and *Bragg's*, on the *Manchester* side, are all of recent construction, and do not belong to bygone days; but those do which preceded them and occupied the same ground. *Cunningham's*, afterwards *Rutherford's* mill, and also a distillery and a tan-yard, stood where the *Tredegar Iron Works* are. The mill was burnt and rebuilt, and burned again, if I mistake not; and Mr. Rutherford built a mill higher up the canal, which suffered the fate of Sebastopol, by bombardment, in the process of blasting rock to widen the canal.

To a stranger, a walk along the banks of the canal is well compensated by a view of the Armory, the Tredegar Iron Works, the mills, the Water Works, Belle Isle (where there are also Iron Works) and the Rapids; and though last, not least, the Hollywood Cemetery.

§ Tobacco Warehouses

Where *Tobacco* is in almost every one's mouth, either for mastication, fumigation, inhalation, or discussion, and where it constitutes one of the most important commercial staples; it seems proper to notice it, though I fear that my fair readers, if I have any, may turn up their pretty noses at it, instead of turning it up their pretty noses, against which latter turn I enter my protest, as well as against the practice of *dipping*, which I will not explain, lest an Eve-like, and evil curiosity might induce some now sweet lips to try the experiment, and I won't play the serpent to tempt them.

Tobacco is now an universal medium of introduction among those who are addicted to its use; but in the early days of Virginia, and until the last seventy or eighty years, it was a *circulating medium* in the place of money. Even the parson's salary and fees were rated at so many pounds of tobacco, estimated at two pence per pound.

The *Tobacco Warehouses* or Inspections in Richmond, fifty years ago, were *Shockoe*, a mere cluster of wooden sheds; *Byrd's*, of brick, opposite to the present Exchange hotel; and *Rockets*, of which a portion of the walls is now standing, their aspect from the river having the appearance of an old fortification. The two latter ceased their vocation long since, as has also one of later date, below Rockets, called *Powhatan*, from being built near the wigwam of that King. It is now converted into a number of dwellings, and serves to shelter other heads than hogs-heads. In later years, the *Public warehouse* on the Basin became an Inspection and *Seabrook's* was built in the valley.

In old times a furnace stood near each warehouse, and tobacco unfit for export was treated as heretics were at an *auto-da-fé*, as being unfit for salvation—both were burned; and now both are suffered to pass for what they are worth.

The primitive mode of transporting tobacco to market was curious. The cask containing it, was actually rolled to market on its own periphery, through mud and stream. A long wooden spike driven into the centre of each end, and projecting a few inches beyond it, served for an axletree, a split sapling was fitted to it for shafts, and extended in rear of the cask, they were there connected by a hickory withe; a few slabs were nailed to these, in front of the cask, forming a sort of foot board, or box, in which were stowed a middling or two of bacon, a bag of meal, a frying pan, a hoe, an axe, and a blanket, for the bipeds; the whole covered to some height with fodder, for the quadrupeds. If the distance to market was moderate, the hogshead was rolled on its hoops, which were stout and numerous; but if fifty to a hundred miles, or more, were to be overcome, rough felloes were spiked on at each end, or quarter of the cask, and these rude tires served to protect it from being worn through. Rough fellows also were the conductors.

The *tobacco roller*, as the driver (often the owner) was called, sought no roof for shelter, during his journey, sometimes of a week's duration and severe toil; but at nightfall he kindled a fire in the woods by the road side, baked a hoe cake, fried some bacon, fed his team (I omitted to mention the bag of corn), rolled his blanket around him, and slept by the fire, under the lee of his cask.

When he reached the warehouse, his tobacco was inspected, a note or receipt expressing the weight, etc., was handed to him, and he then sallied forth into the streets in search of a purchaser; calling out as he entered a store, "Mister, do you buy tobacco?" When he had found the right "Mister," and obtained his money, and a few articles to carry to his "old woman," he strapped the blanket on one of his horses and rode home. These men generally travelled in small parties, and if the weather and roads were good, had a merry time of it; if bad, they assisted each other, when obstacles occurred.

The journey from beyond Roanoke, which then consumed six days, is now performed in as many hours, and for the labor of two hundred and fifty horses, and almost as many men and boys (for a boy usually accompanied each man) during ten days going and returning, is now substituted a train of railroad cars, with some four or five men, for half a day, and at one-fourth of the expense.

It were superfluous to draw the contrast of those days with the present. Tobacco rollers are an extinct species. Instead of them, tobacco buyers throng the warehouses. Manufactories of the weed have sprung up in every direction. The largest buildings in the city are, with few exceptions, tobacco factories, and I may venture to say that more tobacco is manufactured in Richmond, than in any other place in the world. Such vulgar terms as *negro-head* and *pig-tail* are discarded, and the most fanciful ones substituted, "*Honey-dew*," "*Christian's-comfort*," "*Heart's-delight*," "*Perfect-love*," "*Rose-bud*," and "*Cousin-Sally*," are adopted. Artists are employed to design and execute embellishments for the packages, and various sweets, spirits, spices, and essences, are used to give flavor or to conceal it.

Italy, Spain, and France, furnish thousands of boxes of Liquorice and of Olive Oil to sweeten, and to brighten the quid—but they do not accept a *quid pro quo*, by permitting the importation of "Christian's-comfort," or "Heart's-delight," or any other of the consolations prepared abroad, for the lovers of tobacco.

NOTE—The following advertisement, which does not exclude Liquorice, Rum, Olive Oil, and Sugar, will give an idea of the condiments used in preparing tobacco for mastication.
"To Tobacconists—500 lbs. large black Angustura Tongue Beans; 200 lbs. Oil of Cinnamon, Cloves, Peppt., &c.; 1,000 lbs. good Gum Arable, in bales, low priced; 25 bottles English Essential Oil Bitter Almonds; 1,000 lbs. Cloves, Allspice, Nutmegs, Cassia, &c.; Oil of Sweet-Flag Root; Branding Paint, red and blue; a large assortment of copper bound Branding Brushes, Varnish; Spirits Turpentine, and every article used about a factory, at low prices."

Mordecai, *Virginia, Especially Richmond, in By-Gone Days* (1860), pp. 17–20, 22–24, 71–78, 259, 265–73

"A Wanton Insult": Aaron Burr Dines with Justice Marshall as Washington Irving Enjoys Local Hospitality during a Trial for Treason (1807)

Early in the year 1807, Aaron Burr—former vice-president of the United States and slayer of Alexander Hamilton in a duel—came to Richmond to be tried for treason under the gavel of Chief Justice John Marshall (q.v.) in the Virginia State Capitol. The dramatic proceedings lasted from late March through August and attracted to the city such notables as Andrew Jackson, Winfield Scott, and young Washington Irving (1783–1859). The latter is famous today for "Rip

Van Winkle" and "The Legend of Sleepy Hollow," but in his time
he rose to the distinction of being the first American literary figure
widely read and admired in Europe. Irving had come as a young
reporter to cover the trial for a New York newspaper, only to find
himself "absolutely enchanted with Richmond." Burr likewise enjoyed
local hospitality, including that of his attorney, the elegant John
Wickham, in the presence of Wickham's neighbor and fellow Fed-
eralist, presiding Judge Marshall. It was an episode, as the following
letters show, that enraged the city's Republicans. The drama of the
case and the prestige of the rival attorneys were in a sense overshadowed by the concurrent battle between Marshall and his cousin-
adversary President Jefferson. The jury's verdict?—a most unusual
"Not proved to be guilty . . . by any evidence submitted to us," which
Marshall ordered registered as "Not Guilty."

§ I

In the Argus of the 7th, it is stated, and the fact is now too generally
notorious to be doubted, that the chief justice Marshall has dined with
Aaron Burr at Mr. Wickham's, since he himself solemnly decided, that
there was probable cause to believe Burr guilty of a high misdemeanor
against his country. The story has indeed excited some surprise in
Richmond, but none of those sentiments of lively indignation, which a
stranger from the country would naturally have expected.

As to Burr himself, I feel towards him the same sentiment I feel
towards every man charged with a crime—the wish, that he may have
a fair and impartial trial; that if guilty, he may be punished, if innocent, acquitted. His efforts, to whatever end directed, have not as yet
been attended with consequences, which can excite in the bosom of
a patriot any thing like personal resentment. I heard with pleasure,
that Burr on his arrival in Richmond, was readily furnished with the
supplies necessary to his comfort: I thought it a signal proof of the
generosity of my countrymen. I heard with pleasure, how zealously
and ably his counsel had defended him: I thought such exertions
honorable to our bar. That his counsel should admit him to the freest
communion of a professional nature, and that such intercourse should
be conducted on their part with civility and tenderness, even tho' they
may think him guilty, I am not disposed to deny; but I insist, that no
situation should (God forbid, that the profession of the law should!)
excuse a man, for wanting the ordinary feelings of a citizen towards

the violators of the law. And truly, my surprise would have equalled my indignation, had Burr been admitted to the familiarity of private friendship, much more to the house and table, of any man, but Mr. Wickham. . . .

I have never had the least confidence in the political principles of the chief justice. I have never discovered in his public (for I am ignorant of his private) character, any of that noble candor, which his friends have made the theme of such extravagant eulogium. I cannot discern in him, for my soul, those splendid and even godlike talents, which many of all parties ascribe to him: his book certainly displays none such. But I have always been informed, and 'till now have believed, that he was a man of excellent judgement, most consummate prudence, and of a deportment highly decorous and dignified. I took his merits upon trust, and bountifully gave him credit for good qualities I find he does not possess.

Let me inform the conscience of the chief justice, that the public do not view his dining with Burr, as a circumstance so trivial as he himself may incline to consider it. It is impossible to separate the judge from the man. We regard such conduct as a willful prostration of the dignity of his own character, and a wanton insult he might have spared his country. How has Burr entitled himself to be the social companion of the chief justice? Is he not still suspected of the blackest crimes? How has he manifested his innocence? Has he even thrown off that cloak of mystery, which truth, innocence, and virtue were never known to wear, and in which all his words and actions have been enveloped?

What will the people of Virginia, who yet regard the name of John Marshall with a kind of parental fondness, and too faintly condemn the fatal errors, or impious ambition, that led him to defeat them— what will the people of the union, who look up to the chief justice, as the head of the third great co-ordinate branch of government, too high to be ambitious, and supported against any fall from dignity by his very elevation (for such is the impracticable theory of our independent judiciary)—what will they think, how will they feel, when they learn, that the chief justice has feasted at the same convivial board with Aaron Burr?—with whom?—With the very man, of whom that very chief justice has declared, that there is probable cause to believe him guilty of a high misdemeanor against the U. States; at whose trial the chief justice is himself to preside; who is suspected to have plotted schemes hostile to the happiness, the liberty and integrity of the union, schemes which would have rendered the chief justice an alien to his own father; who is charged on the evidence of a gentleman, on whom his country have bestowed many testimonies of esteem, I mean Mr. Eaton—with having entertained the abominable design, or at least imagination, of assassinating the president, dissolving the congress, disrobing the chief justice himself of his ermine, overturning all our sacred institutions, state and federal, and erecting an execrative despotism on the ruins of freedom. Whether Burr will be able to repell these charges or not, I shall not pretend to decide; for I do not mean to prejudge him; but I do say, that the evidence they rest on, is sufficient to render him an unfit companion for the chief justice.

I have searched in vain in my own mind, for some apology for conduct so grossly indecent. Perhaps, it may be thought that my understanding is not likely to be very acute on such a subject; but indeed I have heard no excuse offered by any other person. . . .

But it may be said, Mr. Wickham's was a friend's house, and surely the chief justice may visit at a friend's house with any person whom that friend may think to invite. Indeed! Suppose that that "unfortunate gentleman," Thomas Logwood, lately consigned to the penitentiary had been bailed, as he might have been had his friends been as zealous as Burr's—and suppose that pending the prosecution, Mr. Edmund Randolph had thought fit to give his client an entertainment (though I ought to bespeak Mr. Randolph's pardon for even supposing such a case)—and suppose Mr. Randolph had invited the chief justice to be of the party; how would he have felt? How acted? Would he have laughed at the folly, or burned at the insolence, which must have induced such an invitation? Yet, where is the man, so ignorant of the nature and consequences of crimes, as to compare that of Logwood, to the misdemeanor, for which the chief justice has declared that Burr ought to be tried; much more to the treason of which he is suspected? Or is it only the grandeur and sublimity of the crime, which redeems the character of the criminal and exalts him to a level with a federal judge?

Has the chief justice forgotten or neglected the maxim, which is in the mouth of every tyro of the law—*that the administration of justice should not only be pure but unsuspected?* I warn him to have it constantly in his remembrance, and to beware how he inconsiderately betrays motives which may expose him to further scrutiny.

I doubt not, this will be deemed a very singular publication. The style of it is, indeed, little consonant to that which prevails too generally throughout this superb and courtly metropolis. But the sentiments, as well as the manner in which they are expressed, are suitable to my own temper, & sanctioned by my own judgment; and I am not very anxious to obtain the approbation of those, who approve the conduct which I have here condemned.

A STRANGER FROM THE COUNTRY.
Richmond *Enquirer*, 10 April 1807

§ II

[To Mrs. Hoffman]   Richmond, June 4, 1807
. . . You expected that the trial was over at the time you were writing; but you can little conceive the talents for procrastination that have been exhibited in this affair. Day after day have we been disappointed by the non-arrival of the magnanimous Wilkinson; day after day have fresh murmurs and complaints been uttered; and day after day are we told that the next mail will probably bring his noble self, or at least some accounts when he may be expected. We are now enjoying a kind of suspension of hostilities; the grand jury having been dismissed the day before yesterday for five or six days, that they might go home, see their wives, get their clothes washed, and flog their negroes. As yet we are not even on the threshold of a trial; and, if the great hero of the South does not arrive, it is a chance if we have any trial this term. I am told the Attorney-General talks of moving the Court next Tuesday for a continuance and a special Court, by which means the present grand jury (the most enlightened, perhaps, that was ever assembled in this country) will be discharged; the witnesses will be dismissed; many of whom live such a distance off that it is a chance if half of them will ever be again collected. The Government will be again subjected to immense expense, and Col. Burr, besides being harassed and detained for an additional space of time, will have to repeat the enormous expenditures which this trial has already caused him. I am very much mistaken, if the most underhand and ungenerous measures have not been observed towards him. He, however, retains his serenity and self-possession unshaken, and wears the same aspect in all times and situations. I am impatient for the arrival of this Wilkinson, that the whole matter may be put to rest; and I never was more mistaken in my calculations, if the whole will not have a most farcical termination as it respects the charges against Col. Burr. . . .

§ III

Dear James: Richmond, June 22, 1807
. . . I can appoint no certain time for my return, as it depends entirely upon the trial. Wilkinson you will observe has arrived; the bets were against Burr that he would abscond, should W. come to Richmond; but he still maintains his ground, and still enters the Court every morning with the same serene and placid air that he would show were he brought there to plead another man's cause, and not his own.

The lawyers are continually entangling each other in law points, motions, and authorities, and have been so crusty to each other, that there is a constant sparring going on. Wilkinson is now before the grand jury, and has such a mighty mass of words to deliver himself of, that he claims at least two days more to discharge the wondrous cargo. The jury are tired enough of his verbosity. The first interview between him and Burr was highly interesting, and I secured a good place to witness it. Burr was seated with his back to the entrance, facing the judge, and conversing with one of his counsel. Wilkinson strutted into Court, and took his stand in a parallel line with Burr on his right hand. Here he stood for a moment swelling like a turkey-cock, and bracing himself up for the encounter of Burr's eye. The latter did not take any notice of him until the judge directed the clerk to swear Gen. Wilkinson; at the mention of the name Burr turned his head, looked him full in the face with one of his piercing regards, swept his eye over his whole person from head to foot, as if to scan its dimensions, and then coolly resumed his former position, and went on conversing with his counsel as tranquilly as ever. The whole look was over in an instant; but it was an admirable one. There was no appearance of study or constraint in it; no affectation of disdain or defiance; a slight expression of contempt played over his countenance, such as you would show on regarding any person to whom you were indifferent, but whom you considered mean and contemptible. Wilkinson did not remain in Court many minutes.

§ IV

[To Miss Mary Fairlie]   Washington City, July 7, 1807.
. . . I am now scribbling in the parlor of Mr. Van Ness, at whose house I am on a visit; having, as you plainly perceive, torn myself from Richmond. I own the parting was painful, for I had been treated there with the utmost kindness, and having become a kind of old inhabitant

of the place, was permitted to consult my own whims, inclinations, and caprices, just as I chose; a privilege which a stranger has to surrender on first arriving in a place. By some unlucky means or other, when I first made my appearance in Richmond, I got the character, among three or four novel-read damsels, of being an *interesting young man*; now of all characters in the world, believe me, this is the most intolerable for any young man, who has a will of his own to support; particularly in warm weather. The tender-hearted fair ones think you absolutely at their command; they conclude that you must, of course, be fond of moonlight walks, and rides at daybreak, and red-hot strolls in the middle of the day (Fahrenheit's Thermom. 98½ in the shade) and "melting-hot—hissing-hot" tea parties, and what is worse, they expect you to talk sentiment and act Romeo, and Sir Charles, and King Pepin all the while. 'Twas too much for me; had I been in love with any one of them, I believe I could have played the dying swain, as eloquently and foolishly as most men; but not having the good luck to be inspired by the tender passion, I found the slavery insupportable; so I forthwith set about ruining my character as speedily as possible. I forgot to go to tea-parties; I overslept myself of a morning; I protested against the moon, and derided that blessed planet most villainously. In a word, I was soon given up as a young man of most preposterous and incorrigible opinions, and was left to do e'en just as I pleased. Yet, believe me, I did, notwithstanding, admire the fair damsels of Richmond exceedingly; and, to be candid at once, the character of the whole sex, though it has ever ranked high in my estimation, is still more exalted than ever. I have seen traits of female goodness while at Richmond, that have sunk deeply in my heart—not displayed in one or two individual instances, but frequently and generally manifested; I allude to the case of Col. Burr. Whatever may be his innocence or guilt, in respect to the charges alleged against him (and God knows, I do not pretend to decide thereon) his situation is such as should appeal eloquently to the feelings of every generous bosom. Sorry am I to say, the reverse has been the fact—fallen, proscribed, prejudged, the cup of bitterness has been administered to him with an unsparing hand. It has almost been considered as culpable to evince towards him the least sympathy or support; and many a hollow-hearted caitiff have I seen, who basked in the sunshine of his bounty, when in power, who now skulked from his side, and even mingled among the most clamorous of his enemies. The ladies alone have felt, or at least had candor and independence sufficient to express, those feelings which do honor to humanity. They have been uniform in their expressions of compassion for his misfortunes, and a hope for his acquittal; not a lady, I believe, in Richmond, whatever may be her husband's sentiments on the subject, who would not rejoice on seeing Col. Burr at liberty. It may be said that Col. Burr has ever been a favorite with the sex; but I am not inclined to account for it in so illiberal a manner; it results from that merciful, that heavenly disposition, implanted in the female bosom, which ever inclines in favor of the accused and the unfortunate. You will smile at the high strain in which I have indulged; believe me, it is because I feel it; and I love your sex ten times better than ever. The last time I saw Burr was the day before I left Richmond. He was then in the Penitentiary, a kind of State prison. The only reason given for immuring him in this abode of thieves, cutthroats, and incendiaries, was that it would save the United States a couple of hundred dollars (the charge of guarding him at his lodgings) and it would insure the security of his person. This building stands about a mile and a half from town, situated in a solitary place among the hills. It will prevent his counsel from being as much with him as they deemed necessary. I found great difficulty in gaining admission to him, for a few moments. The keeper had orders to admit none but his counsel and his witnesses—strange measures these! That it is not sufficient that a man against whom no certainty of crime is proved, should be confined by bolts, and bars, and massy walls in a criminal prison; but he is likewise to be cut off from all intercourse with society, deprived of all the kind offices of friendship, and made to suffer all the penalties and deprivations of a condemned criminal. I was permitted to enter for a few moments, as a special favor, contrary to orders. Burr seemed in lower spirits than formerly; he was composed and collected as usual; but there was not the same cheerfulness that I have hitherto remarked. He said it was with difficulty his very servant was allowed occasionally to see him; he had a bad cold, which I suppose was occasioned by the dampness of his chamber, which had lately been white-washed. I bid him farewell with a heavy heart, and he expressed with peculiar warmth and feeling his sense of the interest I had taken in his fate. I never felt in a more melancholy mood than when I rode from his solitary prison. Such is the last interview I had with poor Burr, and I shall never forget it. I have written myself into a sorrowful kind of a mood, so I will at once desist, begging you to receive this letter with indulgence, and regard, with an eye of Christian charity, its many imperfections.

Believe me, truly and affectionately,

Your friend,
WASHINGTON IRVING.
Irving, *Life and Letters* (1862), 1:191–95, 200–203

"Their Clothes Took Fire and They Perished": The Theater Fire (1811)

Like most cities accessible by water in the early history of the United States, Richmond had a thriving theater in which was produced Shakespeare, popular European plays, and occasional American works. As early as the 1780s, according to Martin Staples Shockley, historian of Richmond's stage, troupes probably came from Williamsburg to act in the new capital. By the early nineteenth century, Richmond had its own theater, and on the night after Christmas 1811 it burned when scenery was accidentally ignited. Some six hundred playgoers were crowded into the building when the fire broke out, claiming seventy-two lives, including that of the governor of Virginia. The remains of those who perished were placed in a common grave where the theater had been; Parsons Blair (q.v.) and John Buchanan (q.v.) officiated at the burial ceremony.

After a period of mourning, Richmonders proceeded with the idea of constructing a church on the site of the tragedy. Accordingly, Monumental Episcopal Church, a memorial to those who lost their lives, still stands on Virginia Commonwealth University's east campus as a major example of early Classic Revival architecture. Designed by American architect Robert Mills, who also designed the national Treasury Building and the Washington Monument, the church is one of the first in the country to follow the "auditorium" theory, instituted because of changing practices in church services during the era.

The conflagration is graphically described by a survivor—Thomas R. Joynes (1789–1858), a distinguished lawyer and public servant from Accomack County—in the following letter to his brother.

Dʳ Brother,   Richmond December 27th 1811
I have now taken my pen to relate to you a circumstance which occurred in this City last night, at the recollection of which my heart is chilled with horror. It was a scene the horrors of which the most fruitful imagination cannot conceive and much less can any person describe its tragical aspect—

Last night there was a Play performed at this place and such a crowded audience was never before witnessed at the Richmond Theatre. There were not less than seven Hundred persons. About half past ten o'clock several pieces of fire fell from the top of the Theatre down on the stage amongst the Actors and in an instant it was discovered that the whole house was envelloped in flames. Then commenced a scene of horror and misery, than which one more tragical perhaps never happened. The Shrieks of women and children, the cries of men in search of an affectionate wife, a tender child, or an aged parent, presented to view a scene of woe and misery which I can scarcely mention without my blood chilling in my veins.

When it was discovered that the house was on fire, I was, with a great many others, in the third story in a situation extremely remote from the door, and I have abundant reason to thank Heaven for my escape from that abyss in destruction in which so many perished. When the fire was discovered I rushed to the stair-case, and with Considerable difficulty I made my way through the door entirely unhurt. When I got to the ground the whole roof was an entire volume of flame. A few minutes after I got out, the whole stair-case was in flames which prevented persons from escaping in that way, and there was no alternative but to jump out at the windows. Hundreds flocked to the windows in the second and third stories and precipitated themselves down on the ground. Some got killed in the fall and some got their legs and arms broken and some few escaped unhurt. But the most melancholy tale remains yet to be told. More than one Hundred persons of every age and sex perished in the flames! I myself saw a crowd standing at one of the windows when they were well surrounded by the flames, their clothes took fire and they perished in the general conflagration. I saw two wretched men, frantic for the loss of an affectionate wife, and dear relatives and connections, after they were themselves safe on the ground rush impetuously into the flames and share the fate of those who were dearer to them than life. I have this moment returned from the place of this melancholy catastrophe, where great quantities of human carcases are to be seen which were not entirely consumed by the fire. The precise number who perished is not ascertained, but no person thinks there was less than one hundred and some compute the number at 150 persons.

Amongst the unhappy sufferers we have to lament the death of some of the most respectable citizens. Amongst whom are George Wm Smith Esqr., who was recently elected Governor of this Commonwealth, who having saved his wife perished in an attempt to save his child—Abraham B. Venable Ex-president of the Virginia Bank—Benjamin Botts Esqr Attorney at Law and his wife—Mrs Thomas Wilson the mother-in-law of Littleton Upshur Esqr of Northampton and numbers of others of equal respectability might be enumerated. Severn E. Parker and his wife were both sitting in the same row of seats with me, though at some distance apart—Mr. Parker took his wife in his arms and carried her, over the heads of the crowd, to a window in the second story, from whence they both leaped out. Mr. Parker escaped unhurt. Mrs. Parker got considerably injured, though I believe not dangerously, but the extent of the injury I cannot ascertain as I have not seen Mr. Parker this morning.

It was supposed when the fire was first discovered, that the house was intentionally set on fire, and that it was only the precursor of scenes still more tragical than the one which has happened. It was supposed by many to have been the signal for *insurrection*, and that those who escaped the fury of the flames, might have to encounter an enemy more destructive than fire itself. But there is now no doubt but that these fears were groundless. If there had been any intention of that kind, it would have been carried into effect when the flames were at their height, and all the inhabitants were collected there. It has been, I believe, satisfactorily ascertained, that the fire was accidentally communicated by a lamp to the scenery, and in a few seconds after it first took fire the whole scenery and indeed the whole house was in flames.

When the house was tumbling in, and the unhappy victims were suffering the pangs of death, the miserable survivors of departing connections were frantically running to and fro, and exclaiming to every person they met with, "Have you seen my dear wife?" "Have you seen my husband?" "Have you seen my dear son or daughter?" "Have you seen my brothers, sisters, father or mother?" The subject is too shocking to dwell on.

All the members of the Assembly from the Eastern Shore escaped unhurt, and it is not yet ascertained whether any members of the Assembly were killed.

You will please communicate to my dear mother and all my connections my fortunate escape from destruction. The enclosed letter you will please forward immediately, as it may prevent the anxiety and uneasiness which would be occasioned by the reading of the newspaper account without hearing from me.

I shall write to you again in a few days, when spirits bec [torn] giving you information on other subjects

I remain y^r affectionate brother
Tho R. Joynes

"Burning of the Richmond Theatre, 1811," *Virginia Magazine of History and Biography*, July 1943, pp. 297–300

"The Nation's Guest":
The City Welcomes Lafayette (1824)

One of only two men—the other being John D. Rockefeller, Jr.—to be named an honorary citizen of the Commonwealth, Marie-Joseph-Paul-Yves-Roch-Gilbert du Motier, Marquis de Lafayette (1757–1834) had a firm hold on Virginia's affections for his youthful military service in the state during the Revolution. In the early 1820s, as the country entered an "Era of Good Feelings" and as the fiftieth anniversary of the Great Declaration drew near, President James Monroe and Congress invited the marquis for an extended visit to the republic his sacrifices had helped to establish.

Accompanied by a secretary and by his son (George Washington Lafayette), the French nobleman arrived in New York in August 1824 and for a year became "The Nation's Guest." His stay in the Old Dominion caused a patriotic and nostalgic extravaganza as locales vied with one another to honor the aging general and his former comrades in arms. On two occasions, he came to Richmond. Samuel Mordecai, who saw many grand moments in a long life, confessed "the greatest popular enthusiasm I ever witnessed was excited by the *visit of Lafayette*"—a sentiment fully conveyed in the following accounts from the contemporary Richmond press.

§ La Fayette in Richmond

The reception of *"The Nation's Guest"* in Richmond has called forth those deep-toned sentiments of gratitude and joy which he has every where inspired. His presence seems to operate as a spell. All regular business is suspended—crowds rush from all parts to see him—and the most rapturous welcomes burst from every lip.

The appearance of La Fayette had been anticipated with the most intense curiosity in this City; arrangements had been long maturing for his reception; and on Tuesday last, our anxious fellow-citizens were gratified by his presence.

On Monday night, he had attended a splendid ball in the Borough of Norfolk; and its Managers, with a courtesy which received the thanks of our deputation, had consented to have their supper at 10 o'clock, to enable him to depart at an early hour. At 11, he took leave and embarked with his numerous suite on board the steam-boat

Petersburg for this City. He was expected to arrive here about 2 o'clock, and every preparation was made to receive him in form. But, the morning was very inclement; and the Mayor determined to suspend the procession until the following day.

At an early hour in the morning, however, four gentlemen of the Committee of Arrangement proceeded in carriages to Osborne's, where it was intended that he should be escorted to Richmond; but when the steam boat hove in sight about 12 o'clock, at the intended point of landing, and the Committee had gone aboard and communicated with the General, it was determined to send the carriages back to Rocketts—and to conduct the General to that point by the steam boat. About 2 o'clock the boat reached the wharf at Rocketts; and notwithstanding the Procession had been in the mean while put off until the following day yet so intense was the anxiety of our citizens to see him, that the wharves and the heights were filled by eager spectators on foot and on horseback. The Volunteer troops had turned out to honor him. Every imaginable respect was paid him on landing; and he was conducted to his carriage amid the cheerings of an immense multitude. The procession set out with an escort of the Fayette Guards in front—next, the barouche with Gen. La Fayette, Mr. Secretary Calhoun and two of the Members of the City [Committee] of Arrangement; next, the other carriage, drawn by four elegant greys, with Mr. G. W. La Fayette, the Secretary Mr. de Vasseur, and two other members of the Committee of Arrangement.—In the other carriages were Messrs. Scion, and G. Hay; Gen. McComb; Gen. W. Jones, and his staff; Gen. Cocke; Com. Barron and Capt. Elliott of the U. S. Navy; Colonel McLane; Col. Roberdeau of the Engineer Corps; Captain Mountfort; Maj. Mercer, and Lieut. Ringgold; Mr. C. F. Mercer, member of the H. of R.—Cols. Harvie and Peyton, the Governors aids, and other gentlemen.

The procession advanced up E or main street; followed by an immense mass of people, who were mounted on horseback or lined the footways. The troop of Horse followed behind the Carriages—then the Artillery company—the Light Infantry Blues, Rifle Rangers, the Junior Volunteers; and the pretty looking company of small boys, dressed in hunting shirts, and styling themselves the Morgan Legion. —At the intersection of various cross streets, carriages were stationed, filled with ladies. The rain had subsided; joy and animation were exhibited in every countenance; and the welkin rang with strains of music and salutes of the artillery.—The fair sex expressed their feelings by the waving of handkerchiefs, as the procession passed every window. When it arrived opposite to the Union Hotel, it halted for a moment under the double arch which was erected at that spot by the citizens of the neighbourhood, and was tastefully embellished with wreaths of evergreens. At each of the four basements of this double arch, a young lady was stationed. As soon as the cheerings of the immense multitude had ceased, the procession marched on up the main street, until it halted at the Eagle Hotel, which had been selected for the quarters of the General, his suite, all the invited guests, embracing of course the officers of the Revolutionary army. Tho' Gen. La Fayette had been conducted to his levée room, yet the crowd still continued hovering in the street. Their intense curiosity was not yet satisfied. Many citizens were introduced to La Fayette—but none were so much entitled to a reception, none received a warmer welcome, than his old associates in arms.

The introduction of the Revolutionary Officers, here, as well as at York, was, perhaps, the most interesting and affecting scene to which his visit among us has given rise. These aged and venerable men, amounting to 40 in number, were presented to their old Companion in Arms, in the spacious and elegant drawing room appropriated to his use, on Tuesday evening, very soon after his arrival. He received them in the most cordial and affectionate manner; evincing the deepest sympathy with them in their recollections of the hardships and dangers through which they had mutually passed, and the proud results of their joint labors. The old soldiers were themselves, variously affected. Some of them saluted in silence with the most profound and heartfelt respect. Others welcomed him among us in every expression of sincerity and kindness.

At 5 o'clock Gen. La Fayette sat down to a dinner, at which his suite, the gentlemen who had attended him from Norfolk, the officers of the Revolution, the officers of the General, State, and City Governments, and the Members of the Committee of Arrangement, attended. Mr. Leigh acted as President of the one table; Dr. John Brockenbrough at the other; assisted by Messrs. Fitzwhylsonn, T. Brockenbrough, R. G. Scott and W. Roane, as Vice Presidents. Gen. La Fayette, the Chief Justice [John Marshall, who resided in Richmond], Mr. Calhoun, at the right of Mr. Leigh; the Governor, Judge Brooke, at his left; and on both sides, and in front, were stationed the Revolutionary officers.—The following toasts were given:

By Mr. Leigh: The memory of the great and good Washington.

The health of our generous friend, our gallant General, our beloved guest and fellow citizen.

By Gen. La Fayette: The State of Virginia and the City of Richmond

—And may their joint share in the prosperity of America, be equal to the Virginian's share in the beginning of the revolutionary struggle, and in the campaign which terminated the contest.

By Governor Pleasants: The State of Virginia: Her sons and daughters; though last not least in love to the Nation's Guest.

By Chief Justice Marshall: Rational liberty—The cause of mankind. Its friends cannot despair when they behold its champions.

By Judge Brooke: The gratitude of a free people, to the apostle of liberty in both hemispheres. It fills the hearts of kings and princes with the fear of change.

By Mr. Secretary Calhoun: The cause of '76. We have this day witnessed, that age has not diminished the ardor of its defenders, no art, no power, nor time itself can deprive the world of the benefits of their glorious example.

By Mr. G. W. La Fayette: The share my countrymen had the honor to have in the decisive battle at Yorktown; may they, whenever they shall fight for the cause of liberty be as successful as they were that day.

[Here follows forty-five additional toasts.]

§ Order of the Day

"The inclemency of the weather, yesterday, having interrupted the arrangements which were designed for the reception of General La Fayette into the City, the Procession (as arranged for yesterday,) will take place this morning, at 11 o'clock. It will commence at the Eagle Hotel; the right of the Procession will be at the Hotel, extending westwardly, and march by E street to 5th; thence pursuing 5th street to H street; thence down H street to the City Hall; where he will be addressed by the Mayor.

Thence he will be conducted by the Committee of Arrangement, under the La Fayette Arch, to the Temple of Independence, where he will be addressed by the Chief Justice Marshall, on behalf of the Officers of the Revolutionary Army. Thence to the Marquee, where he will receive the Ladies; thence, under the Greene Arch, to the corner of 9th and H streets, where he will review the Troops; on the conclusion of which ceremony, he will be conducted to his quarters.

At 7 o'clock in the evening the Marquee will be open to Citizens of both sexes, where suitable refreshments will be provided; the arches will be illuminated, and, at intervals, fire works will be exhibited.

No intoxicated or colored person will be permitted to enter the Square.

At the conclusion of the fire works, General La Fayette has consented to attend the Theatre."

At an early hour, the Mayor waited upon the General at his own quarters [Lafayette's] and was privately introduced to him in his room.

In pursuance of the preceding arrangement, the procession was formed in front of the Eagle [Hotel] between 11 and 12 o'clock. The crowd collected before the house was immense. He appeared more than once at the window to gratify their curiosity; but it was when he mounted his barouche, that the voice of eager congratulation burst from the multitude. The Procession marched up E street, until it reached 5th street—thence down that street into H street—thence down H street until it arrived at the City Hall. The crowd was very great; but the utmost order characterised the whole.—Col. Lambert acted as the Chief Marshall of the day; assisted by other gentlemen in Uniform.

The ceremony of a public presentation of the General to the Mayor was to take place in the City Hall. The moment had arrived for this purpose—and Gen. La Fayette, with his suite and the Committee of Arrangement entered the North door of the Hall—the gallery was found filled with ladies; the Mayor alone was seated upon the bench. The guests being now also arranged upon the bench, the doors were thrown open, and the area of the Hall was immediately filled. On one side of the bench was placed the portrait of Washington by Warrell; and on the other, the portrait of La Fayette himself, when a young man, by Petticolas.—After a short pause, the Mayor addressed our distinguished guest in the following manner:

In approaching General La Fayette, the united corporate bodies of the City of Richmond salute a fellow citizen of Virginia and a brother by adoption; one, whom we have never ceased to love for his exalted virtues, to admire for his great military skill and to venerate with overflowing gratitude for the exercise of that skill and those talents in defence of the lives and fortunes of our fathers, when assailed by a devouring enemy.—A brother in whose noble efforts in support of the cause of rational liberty in his native country, we greatly rejoiced, and in whose general prosperity and happiness we have and still feel the most anxious solicitude.

By these endearing ties we welcome the return to our city of our friend and benefactor, after an absence of forty years; and by a feeling not less connected with our warmest affections, we make him twice welcome as the adopted Son and confidential friend of our much loved and illustrious Washington.

In the choice of such gratifications as might be most acceptable to Gen. La Fayette, or which might do most honour to our own feelings, we could imagine none more promising of success, than the presence of his former companions in arms, "that Band of Brothers," by whose toils, privations and mighty efforts, the fair fabric of this republican government has been reared, and will we trust forever stand, on the firm basis of virtue, on which it was erected.

These veteran worthies regardless of distance, age and infirmity, have cheerfully obeyed the call to meet their much loved General; they are assembled and await his coming with the most ardent affection; and with the most youthful impatience. In obedience to their anxious wishes, we should not cause a longer separation; but let us detain our *Guest* for a moment longer, by offering the entreaty in the name of the citizens of Richmond, whom we have the honour to represent on this august occasion, that he will not hasten his departure from our City, and that he will favour us with his company as long as may be consistent with his other engagements.

General La Fayette made the following reply:

My recollections and feelings so intimately connected with the State of Virginia and its Metropolis would have sufficed, sir, to render this meeting most gratifying to me; but your kind and flattering reception, Mr. Mayor, and gentlemen of both councils, the affectionate welcome of the citizens and the wonderful improvements which I have witnessed in your city, complete my grateful satisfaction. Indeed, sir, my visits to this city have often been eventful moments in my life. In the last one, near forty years ago, I met here our beloved military chief, my paternal friend, the illustrious son of Virginia.—Now you are pleased to announce a meeting with many of my surviving companions in arms; and while I hasten to follow you, Mr. Mayor, to the place of the happy rendezvous, I beg you, and the gentlemen of both councils to receive my respectful and devoted acknowledgements to the citizens of Richmond, and their honored representatives.

A solemn silence reigned through the assembly; but the addresses could not be distinctly heard; the Mayor spoke with great sensibility; and the Gen. in a low tone of voice.—This ceremony over, the General was conducted to the South portico, where many a hoary veteran, and one or two countrymen of his own, shook him warmly by the hand. —A line was formed, and he was conducted through the North gate of the Capitol Square, under the La Fayette Arch, to the central Arch; the interior of which bore the inscription of The Temple of Independence. Here stood an ornamented quadrangular pedestal, on the top of which was intended to place the marble bust of La Fayette in the Capitol. Around the pedestal were arranged the old officers of the Revolutionary army, many distinguished officers in the army and navy of the United States, and private citizens.—The Chief Justice of the United States stood ready to receive him and address him in the following terms:

GENERAL: The surviving officers of our Revolutionary Army, who are inhabitants of the state of Virginia, Welcome you to her Metropolis with feelings which your own heart will best tell you how to estimate. We have been the more gratified by the offering of respect and affection from a whole people, spontaneously flowing from sincere gratitude for estimable services, and a deep sense of your worth, because we believe that to a mind like yours, they will compensate for the privations you sustain, and the hazards and fatigues you have encountered in re-visiting our country.—So long as Americans remember that noble struggle which drew you first to their shores, that deep gloom which overshadowed their cause when you embraced it, they cannot forget the prompt, the generous, the gallant, and the important part you took in the conflict. [Here follows a lengthy oration by Lafayette.]

Congratulations between La F. and the officers were then exchanged through the whole circle—and he was conducted to the marquee, to be introduced to the Ladies. The scene which now ensued to the moment of his departure from the Square, it is impossible for us to describe. Hundreds of ladies flocked around him in the marquee to enjoy the satisfaction of grasping his hand. The same enthusiasm pervaded the whole of the long and dense line of citizens of both sexes, which was formed from the marquee to the Western gate. Each one pressed forward anxious to grasp his hand—and some time elapsed before he was able to reach the gate.

The scene at this time on the square baffles all powers of description. It "thronged with a living multitude." The numbers defy all estimate. We must content ourselves with saying, that they exceeded all previous anticipations; and that their enthusiasm was as extraordinary as their numbers. At the western gate, the General and suite mounted their carriages, and proceeded to H. Street, where in the porch of Mr. James Lyons's house, he reviewed the passing troops. At the close of this scene, he was escorted to his quarters, where the volunteers passed him twice, marching down and up the street. La Fayette standing at the window was saluted by the officers of the companies and the huzzas of the assembled citizens.

He dined at the Governor's, in company with many of the Revolutionary officers, and other citizens. He did not arrive on the square until near 9 o'clock.—A considerable multitude had assembled to see him, as well as to witness the illumination of the Obelisks and the Pedestal, the fire-works, &c. and to partake of the refreshments which were distributed among all without exception. About 9 o'clock, the General visited the Theatre.

The House received him with a thunder of applause. And when the whole Company came out to sing "Auld Lang Syne" with new Verses sung to the honor of La Fayette [new verses not recorded] the applause was "loud and long," and many an eye was filled with tears.

Brandon, comp. and ed., *Lafayette* (1957), 3:102–5

"To Behold Those Venerable Men . . . Was to Feel the Whole History of Virginia": The Great Convention of 1829–1830

Richmond has been the scene of numerous memorable conventions, but none equalled that of late 1829 and early 1830 when the luminaries of an American era came to town to examine for revision the state constitution of 1776. That conclave has been called by one modern authority "the last of the great constituent assemblies in American history . . . unexcelled as an arena of ideological encounters . . . [and] the acme of Virginia fame." Its members included Chief Justice Marshall (q.v.), former presidents Madison and Monroe, future president Tyler, and a host of "governors, Senators, judges, past, present, and future"—as well as "without exception the character that attracts most attention . . . John Randolph of Roanoke." Political reformers, largely from the western portion of the Commonwealth, felt betrayed by the modest revision and received little consolation from the participation of the eminent statesmen, whose personalities are etched in the following selection by pioneer historian Hugh Blair Grigsby (1806–81), himself a delegate to the convention of giants.

When the General Assembly of Virginia, during the winter of 1828–9, passed the act calling a Convention, to be composed of four delegates from each senatorial district, and required it to assemble in the city of Richmond on the fifth of October following, the attention of the people was soon directed to the choice of delegates to so important a body. Federal politics were laid aside; and public worth and eminent abilities were the only standards in the selection of its members. Actual residence was overlooked, and the unusual sight was presented of one district selecting its representatives from another and a distant one. What was rarer still, the opinions of many of persons voted for were unknown, and in a comparatively few instances did any candidate address the people from the hustings.

A body of men, selected under such circumstances, might well attract attention at home and abroad; and the period of its assembling drew towards Richmond a large concourse of intelligent persons from various parts of the Union. Young men came on horseback from Kentucky, Tennessee, and other Southern States. Statesmen, men of mature years, who had already earned for themselves a title to the public regard, ministers of foreign powers, who wished to see men whose names had become historical, educated men of every profession and class, came, many of them with their families, to behold the gathering, and listen to the discussions of the body. The citizens of Virginia, who came to Richmond from within her own borders and from abroad, would alone have formed an auditory, which any speaker would have been proud to address.

It was about ten o'clock of the fifth of October, 1829, a morning as lovely and auspicious as could have been chosen, that hundreds of persons, of all ages, were seen thronging the public square, and walking through the apartments of the Capitol, now halting about the statue of Washington, which was soon to look down on some of the patriots and sages who had upheld the living original in the field and in the cabinet, then moving towards the library, then recently established, which was thrown open to public inspection. As the hour of twelve drew near, and the members elect began to assemble in the hall of the House of Delegates, and exchange salutations, the crowd gravitated toward the gallery and the lobby, and filled every place from which it was possible to see or hear. At twelve, the house was called to order by JAMES MADISON, who nominated JAMES MONROE as President of the Convention, and was seconded by JOHN MARSHALL. That the nomination of such a man, made by such men, was unanimously confirmed, is known to all.

Here let us pause, and contemplate the members who then filled the seats in that hall. To behold those venerable men—to listen to their names as they fell distinctly and deliberately from the lips of the accomplished clerk, was to feel the whole history of Virginia from the memorable session of 1765 to that moment flash full upon you. . . .

When Mr. Madison took his seat in the Convention, he was in the seventy-ninth year of his age; yet, though so far advanced in life, and entitled alike by age and position to ease, he attended the meetings of the body during a session of three months and a half without the loss, so far as I now remember, of more than a single day. That he was entitled to the chair, and that the universal expectation was that he should receive that honor, none knew better, or could have acknowledged more gracefully, than did Mr. Monroe. He spoke but two or three times, when he ascertained that his voice was too low to be heard; possibly, too, he might have been averse from mingling too closely in the bitter strifes of a new generation. When he rose to speak, the members, old as well as young, left their seats, and, like children about to receive the words of wisdom from the lips of an aged father, gathered around him. . . .

I have said that Mr. Madison rarely took part in the proceedings of the Convention then sitting. It was in conversation that he made the strongest impression on the hearts of all who sought him. A severe student in early life, he never forsook his first love, and the accuracy and freshness of his literary and political reminiscences astonished the admiring listener. . . . His wife, whose elegance diffused a lustre over his public career, and who was the light of his rural home, accompanied him to Richmond, and, as you left their presence, it was impossible not to rejoice that Providence had allotted to such a couple an old age so lovely.

But, prominent as was Mr. Madison in that Convention, none would allow sooner than he that he was among equals. . . . What Edmund Randolph said of himself is quite as applicable to John Marshall,— that he was a child of the Revolution. . . .

The personal appearance of Judge Marshall, and his manner of speaking, will be known to posterity from the descriptions of Wirt, and the British Spy is in every hand. He spoke but seldom in the Convention, and always with deliberation. I would say that an intense earnestness was the leading trait of his manner. . . .

In the domestic relations of life, which, as they ever afford the true test of intrinsic worth, become the crowning grace of an illustrious character, he was beyond all praise. Great in intellect he undoubtedly was, but he was as good as he was great; and those who knew him longest and best, found it hard to say whether they regarded him most with veneration or love.

But, however eminent as a debater, a statesman, and a jurist, it is in the garb of an historian that he will appear most frequently before the generations to come, and it is the only garb that sets ungracefully upon him. . . .

No two eminent contemporaries appear at the first glance to have fewer points of friendly contact and connexion, if not of resemblance, than James Madison and John Marshall. In their persons, dress, manners and mind, they appear to be in strong contrast. Madison, from infancy to age, was of a delicate constitution, small in stature, scrupulously attentive to his dress, and, though accessible and easy of approach, and in the highest degree courteous, was, like most delicate men, naturally reserved. Marshall enjoyed robust health in his early years, was six feet high, was ordinarily regardless of his personal appearance, and was hearty in his address, retaining to the last the downright cordiality of the camp. Madison was extremely social in his feelings, but these were exhibited in his parlour from the walls of which the works of the first masters of painting were looking down upon him, or in his library in the midst of his cherished books, with far more zest than under the freshening influences of physical exertion. If he sought exercise, it was on a well-broken horse, or from a drive in his carriage. He had no taste or strength for the rougher modes of muscular exertion. Marshall never lost his youthful habits of early rising, of walks over hill and moor, which he had taken with a musket on his shoulder and a knapsack on his back at the darkest hour of the Revolution, and of contests of personal strength. He would enjoy with as much relish a triumph on the quoit ground as at the bar, or on the bench. If Madison had lived in a city, he would have despatched every morning to market a well-dressed servant, with a tidy basket on his arm, and supplied his table through him. Marshall did his own marketing, and not unfrequently brought it home with his own hands. The grounds of Madison's town-residence would have exhibited a specimen of landscape gardening, and a view *in petto* of the Virginian Flora. Marshall, like Stephen Girard, had no opinion of a plant or a tree that did not bear something for the support of human life; and would have had a bed of fine cabbages or an orchard of delicious fruit. Madison spent his youth at Nassau Hall, as a student and resident graduate. Marshall had few opportunities of acquiring knowledge in his boyhood, and was engaged in the labors of the farm. Madison, who was four years older than Marshall, chose the cabinet; Marshall took the battlefield and the bar. These diversities lie on the surface, and strike the attention at once. Yet it will appear that there were points of friendly contact and communion between these eminent men from the beginning to the end of their lives. . . . [These two prominent] men moved in different orbits, but were bound by a common law and a common sympathy. Both possessed minds of the highest order—*magis pares quam similes*—and peculiarly adapted to their respective spheres. Both were distinguished for their generous humanity, the strength of their friendships, and the moral beauty of their lives. And, fortunately, both were summoned by their country to afford their aid in revising the constitution of their native State; and here—in this city—where it had begun fifty years before, and which had been uninterrupted by a solitary act or word of unkindness toward each other, both closed their long and illustrious political career.

Among the names of this epoch which demand something more than a passing notice, is that of WILLIAM BRANCH GILES. . . . In all things but in the vigor of his intellect, he was but the shadow of his former self. He could neither move nor stand without the aid of his crutches, and, when on the conclusion of his able speech on the basis question, the members pressed their congratulations upon him, he seemed to belong rather to the dead than the living. His face was the face of a corpse. Although he was four years younger than Monroe, seven younger than Marshall, and eleven younger than Madison, his personal appearance had suffered more from disease than that of any of his early contemporaries. To behold his rugged face and beetling brows, such as are now preserved in the portrait by Ford, it was difficult to believe that he was the handsome young man, radiant with health and arrayed in the rich costume of the last century, that is represented in one of the finest portraits from the easel of Stuart. . . .

Of all the members of the Convention Mr. [John] Randolph excited the greatest curiosity. Not a word that fell from his lips escaped the public ear, not a movement the public eye. When he rose to speak, the empty galleries began to fill, and when he ended, and the spell was dissolved, the throng passed away. It was on the 14th of November he made his first speech. Mr. Stanard had just concluded his speech, and the question on the amendment of Judge Green to the resolution of the Legislative committee basing the representation in the House of Delegates on white population exclusively was about to be taken, when he rose to address the chair. The word passed through the city in an instant that Randolph was speaking, and soon the house, the lobby, and the gallery, were crowded almost to suffocation. He was evidently ill at ease when he began his speech, but soon recovered himself when he saw the telling effect of every sentence that he uttered. He spoke nearly two hours, and throughout that time every eye was fixed upon him, and among the most attentive of his hearers were Mr. Madison and Mr. Monroe, who had not heard him before since his rupture with the administration of their predecessor in the Presidency. From that day he addressed the body with perfect self-possession, and although he did not at any subsequent time speak at length, he frequently mingled with marked ability in debate; and it was easy to tell from the first sentence that fell from his lips when he was in fine tune and temper, and on such occasions the thrilling music of his speech fell upon the ear of that excited assembly like the voice of a bird singing in the pause of the storm. It is difficult to explain the influence which he exerted in that body. He inspired terror to a degree that even at this distance of time seems inexplicable. He was feared alike by East and West, by friend and foe. The arrows from his quiver, if not dipped in poison, were pointed and barbed, rarely missed the mark, and as seldom failed to make a rankling wound. He seemed to paralyse alike the mind and body of his victim. What made his attack more vexatious, every sarcasm took effect amid the plaudits of his audience. He called himself on one occasion a tomahawker and a scalper, and, true to the race from which he sprung, he never explained away or took back any thing; and, as he knew the private as well as the public history of every prominent member, it was impossible for his opponents to foresee from what quarter and on whom his attacks would fall. He also had political accounts of long standing to settle with sundry individuals, and none could tell when the day of reckoning would arrive. And when it did come, it was a stern and fearful one. What unnerved his opponents was a conviction of his invulnerability apparent or real; for, unconnected as he was by any social relation, and ready to fall back on a colossal fortune, he was not on equal terms with men who were struggling to acquire a competency, and whose hearts were bound by all the endearing ties of domestic love. Moreover, it was impossible to answer a sneer or a sarcasm with an argument. To attempt any thing of the kind was to raise a laugh at one's expense. Hence the strong and the weak in a contest with him were upon the same level.

　In early youth the face of Mr. Randolph was beautiful, and its lineaments are in some degree preserved in his portrait by Stuart; but, as he advanced in life, it lost its freshness, and began to assume that aspect which the poet Moore described in his diary as a young-old face, and which is so faithfully portrayed by Harding. His voice, which was one of the great sources of his power, ranged from tenor to treble. It had no base notes. Its volume was full at times; but, though heard distinctly in the hall and the galleries, it had doubtless lost much of the sweetness and roundness of earlier years. Its sarcastic tones were on a high key. He was, too, though he had the art to conceal his art from common observers, a consummate actor. In the philosophy of voice and gesture, and in the use of the pause, he was as perfect an adept as ever trod the boards of Covent Garden or Drury Lane. When he described Chapman Johnson as stretching his arm to intercept and clutch the sceptre as it was passing over Rockfish Gap, or when he rallied him for speaking not "fifteen minutes as he promised, but two hours, not by Shrewsbury clock, but by as good a watch as can be made in the city of London," and, opening the case of his hunting watch, held it up to the view of the chairman; or, when seeking to deride the length of Johnson's speech, he said: "The gentleman said yesterday, or the day before, or the day before that," Garrick or Kean would have crowned his acting with applause. No weight of character, no grade of intellect, afforded a shield impenetrable by his shafts. Probably the committee to which was referred near its close all the resolutions of the Convention with a view of having them drawn in the form of a constitution, was the most venerable in years, in genius, in all the accomplishments of the human mind, and in length and value of public service, that ever sat on this side of the Atlantic. Madison, Marshall, Tazewell, Doddridge, Watkins Leigh, Johnson, and Cooke were the seven members who composed it. Yet Mr. Randolph, almost without an effort, raised a laugh at their expense. It appears, if I am not mistaken, that some qualification of the right of suffrage, which was embraced in the resolutions, was not to be found in the reported draft, and to this omission Mr. Randolph called the attention of the house. Mr. Leigh observed that, if Mr. Randolph's views were carried out, it would virtually leave the entire regulation of the right of suffrage to the General Assembly. Randolph replied with all his peculiar emphasis and gesture: "Sir, I would as soon trust the house of burgesses of the commonwealth of Virginia as the committee of *seven.*" I followed his finger, and amid the roar of laughter which burst forth, I saw Mr. Madison and Mr. Leigh suddenly and unconsciously bow their heads. He idolised Shakspear, and cherished a taste for the drama; and in this department of literature as well as in that of the older English classics from Elizabeth to Anne, and indeed, in all that was embraced by the curiosity and taste of a scholar, his library was rich. He spoke and wrote the English language in all its purity and elegance, and his opponents had at least the gratification of knowing that they were abused in good English. Indeed Madison could not vie with him in a full and ready control over the vocabulary or the harmony of the English tongue. His later speeches exemplify this remark in a more striking manner than his earlier ones. In his speech on Retrenchment delivered in the House of Representatives in 1828, one meets with sentences of great beauty, and it may be observed, that toward the close of that speech is one of the few pathetic touches to be found in his productions. Yet it may well be doubted whether his speeches will hold a high place in after times. His sayings will be quoted in the South, and some of his speeches will undoubtedly be read; but they will hardly emerge beyond Mason and Dixon's line, and never reach even within that limit the dignity of models. What Sir James McIntosh observed to an American respecting one of his speeches will probably convey, when oral tradition grows faint, the impression which they make on impartial minds,—that there was a striving after effect—a disposition to say smart or hard things beyond the ability. On the score of argument they were beneath criticism. It is but just, however, to say that Mr. Randolph protested against the authenticity of most of the speeches attributed to him. Those in the published debates of the Convention are undoubtedly authentic, and must have received his revisal. But of his eloquence thus much may fairly be said, that it fulfilled its office in its day and generation; for it is unquestionably his praise that above all his contemporaries he was successful in fixing the attention of his audience of every class and degree throughout his longest speeches. The late Timothy Pitkin, a competent judge, who had known Randolph many years in Congress, observed, at a time when it was fashionable to compare Tristram Burgess with him, that you may as well compare the broadsword of a mosstrooper with the scymitar of Saladin. When it is remembered that Mr. Randolph, at all times infirm, was sometimes during the winter of the Convention in his own opinion at the point of death, it is a fact of great import, that at no other period of his career did he speak with more judgment and acuteness, nor on any other occasion did he so entirely gain the regards of the people of Eastern Virginia, or his genius excite greater admiration than by his exhibition in that body.

As we began this division of our subject with the name of Madison, we may not unfitly close it with a name which has been intimately associated with his for half a century, and which, though it has been prominently put forth already, calls for, at least so far as the Convention is concerned, a few passing remarks. The name of JAMES MONROE has yet to receive the exalted appreciation which it deserves, and which posterity will surely award. . . .

When Mr. Madison nominated Mr. Monroe for the chair of the Convention, he was aware of his physical inability to perform any laborious service; but he might have remembered that Pendleton, who presided in the Virginia federal convention, was in appearance more of an invalid than Monroe, and had performed the duties of the office with the recorded approbation of the body. But the nature of the two bodies was wholly dissimilar. In the federal convention, the main object of which was to consider a constitution ready made, and which must be accepted or rejected as a whole, the discussions were conducted in the committee of the whole altogether, and the president was only called upon to occupy the chair for a few moments at the beginning and at the close of the daily session. Of the twenty-seven days during which the convention held its sittings, Pendleton probably did not preside three entire days. The ayes and noes were called but three times during the session. The Convention of 1829–30 presented a very different scene. Here was no constitution ready made and to be ratified or rejected as a whole, but a constitution was to be made under circumstances of extraordinary delicacy. There was hardly a prominent member who had not a plan of his own on paper or in his brain, or, if his scheme did not embrace an entire system, it fastened on one of the great departments. Others came charged with a reformation of the County Courts, the abolition of the Council, and the regulation of the right of suffrage. The members on the most important question of the day had made up their minds, and one great division of the state was arrayed against the other. To preside in such a body required not only a critical knowledge of the law of parliaments, and the utmost readiness in its application, but a capacity of physical endurance which is not often possessed by men who have passed the prime of life. It is true that much was done in committee of the whole; but the final battle on every question must be fought in the house. For such a station, which required such a rare ability of mind and body, it is not uncourteous to say that Mr. Monroe, who was never much conversant with public assemblies, and was more infirm than either Madison or Marshall, was wholly unfit. Fortunately, before the day of severe trial came, he withdrew from the house, and left the toil and the honor of his responsible position to another. Yet, while he remained a member, he engaged more than once in discussion; and, though, at that period of intense excitement, his speech on the basis was listened to more as a means of knowing on which side of a question which was ultimately decided in a house of ninety-six members by two votes his vote would be cast, rather than from any regard of its matter or its manner of delivery, he spoke more readily, and with greater self-possession, than might have been anticipated from one so advanced in life and so long retired from popular bodies. His animated description of the murder of a member in the midst of the French National Convention by a mob which marched among the members with the severed head of their victim stuck upon a pole; a murder which was perpetrated in his presence while he was the minister near the Republic, and which, though he had described it in his speech in the House of Delegates twenty years before, was heard by most of the members for the first time, made a strong impression. The resignation of the chair and of his seat was received with the deepest respect, and there was a shade of sorrow on every face when it was officially stated that his venerable form would be seen in that hall no more, and that so great and so good a name would no longer adorn the records of the house. . . .

It was on the fifteenth day of January, 1830, that the convention, which then held its sessions in the Baptist church below the Monumental, met for the last time. The enrolled bill of the constitution was signed by the president, when, after the transaction of some business strictly official, Mr. Randolph rose to offer a resolution in honor of the president (who had called Mr. Stanard to the chair) and spoke with a pathos in delightful unison with the occasion; and when the president resumed the chair, and, before pronouncing the final adjournment, addressed the body with a glow and grace that seemed beyond the reach of his peculiar powers, many a tear was seen to fall from eyes unused to the melting mood. The tide of party ran strong and full during a session of more than three months, and every one in and out of the convention felt more or less the intensity of the excitement. But the time was come, when old and young, friends and enemies, were about to part to meet no more. No eye could have discovered the cloud of death that hung black above them; for none thought of the young and vigorous so soon to fall; but every eye was fixed on a few old men of exalted worth who would soon leave us forever; and when the body adjourned, all pressed to shake by the hand for the last time these venerable men of the past age. When the president concluded his address, he declared the final adjournment, and the convention of 1829–30 became among the things that were. And, although the structure of their hands has been re-modeled by those for whom it was reared, and most of those master-builders in the science of constitutional architecture, as they were termed by the president, have passed away, I trust that the office of pronouncing their names on the ear of the busy world—an office which I sincerely wish had been consigned to more competent hands—may not be without its use in stimulating the youth of Virginia to cherish the memory of their wisdom and worth, and emulate the glory which they have bequeathed them.

Grigsby, *Virginia Convention of 1829–30* (1854), pp. 4–6, 9,
11–12, 14–16, 20–23, 41–45, 47–49, 98–99

"At Last We Were Off":
A Trip on the Kanawha Canal (1830s)

George William Bagby (1828–83) was at various times a journalist, essayist, humorist, and medical doctor. Born in Buckingham County and educated at the University of Pennsylvania, he was copublisher of the Lynchburg *Express* and was a Washington correspondent for several newspapers before becoming editor of the prestigious *Southern Literary Messenger* in Richmond. The experience of which Bagby writes was common to Richmonders, as well as other residents of the state, in the early nineteenth century. Because the railroad had not yet become a force in American life, the natural, and sometimes man-made, waterways of the country were the common means of transportation. According to Mordecai, the Kanawha Canal was the first "commenced in the United States." This slim waterway, a portion of whose restored locks can be seen today, was proposed by George Washington, who journeyed to Richmond in November 1784 to promote it. The original plan was for the canal to be the first in a series of man-made links that would hook the James River to the Ohio, and ultimately to the Mississippi. Had the project been completed, the history of Richmond would doubtlessly have been quite different. Travel by canal, as the following section indicates, was rich in social ambience.

Among my earliest recollections is a trip from Cumberland County to Lynchburg, in 1835, or thereabouts. As the stage approached Glover's tavern in Appomattox County, sounds as of a cannonade aroused my childish curiosity to a high pitch. I had been reading Parley's History of America, and this must be the noise of actual battle. Yes; the war against the hateful Britishers must have broken out again. Would the stage carry us within range of the cannon balls? Yes, and presently the red-coats would come swarming out of the woods. And—and—General Washington was dead; I was certain of that; what would become of us? I was terribly excited, but afraid to ask questions. Perhaps I was scared. Would they kill an unarmed boy, sitting peaceably in a stage coach? Of course they would; Britishers will do anything! Then they will have to shoot a couple of men first—and I squeezed still closer between them.

My relief and my disappointment were equally great, when a casual remark unfolded the fact that the noise which so excited me was only the "blasting of rock on the Jeems and Kanawha Canell." What was "blasting of rock"?

What was a "canell"? and, above all, what manner of thing was a "Jeems and Kanawha Canell"? Was it alive?

I think it was; more alive than it has ever been since, except for the first few years after it was opened.

Those were the "good old days" of batteaux—picturesque craft that charmed my young eyes more than all the gondolas of Venice would do now. True, they consumed a week in getting from Lynchburg to Richmond, and ten days in returning against the stream, but what of that? Time was abundant in those days. It was made for slaves, and we had the slaves. A batteau on the water was more than a match for the best four or six horse bell team that ever rolled over the red clay of Bedford, brindle dog and tar-bucket included.

Fleets of these batteaux used to be moored on the river bank near where the depot of the Virginia and Tennessee Railroad now stands; and many years after the "Jeems and Kanawha" was finished, one of them used to haunt the mouth of Blackwater Creek above the toll-bridge, a relic of departed glory. For if ever man gloried in his calling—the negro batteauman was that man. His was a hardy calling, demanding skill, courage and strength in a high degree. I can see him now striding the plank that ran along the gunwale to afford him footing, his long iron-shod pole trailing in the water behind him. Now he turns, and after one or two ineffectual efforts to get his pole fixed in the rocky bottom of the river, secures his purchase, adjusts the upper part of the pole to the pad at his shoulder, bends to his task, and the long, but not ungraceful bark mounts the rapids like a seabird breasting the storm. His companion on the other side plies the pole with equal ardor, and between the two the boat bravely surmounts every obstacle, be it rocks, rapids, quicksands, hammocks, what not. A third negro at the stern held the mighty oar that served as a rudder. A stalwart, jolly, courageous set they were, plying the pole all day, hauling in to shore at night under the friendly shade of a mighty sycamore, to rest, to eat, to play the banjo, and to snatch a few hours of profound, blissful sleep.

The up-cargo, consisting of sacks of salt, bags of coffee, barrels of sugar, molasses and whiskey, afforded good pickings. These sturdy fellows lived well, I promise you, and if they stole a little, why, what was their petty thieving compared to the enormous pillage of the modern sugar refiner and the crooked-whiskey distiller? They lived well. Their cook's galley was a little dirt thrown between the ribs of the boat at the stern, with an awning on occasion to keep off the rain, and what they didn't eat wasn't worth eating. Fish of the very best, both salt and fresh, chickens, eggs, milk and the invincible, never-satisfying ash-cake and fried bacon. I see the frying-pan, I smell the meat, the fish, the Rio coffee!—I want the batteau back again, aye! and the brave, light-hearted slave to boot. What did he know about the State debt? There was no State debt to speak of. Greenbacks? Bless, you! the Farmers Bank of Virginia was living and breathing, and its money was good enough for a king. Readjustment, funding bill, tax-receivable coupons—where were all these worries then? I think if we had known they were coming, we would have stuck to the batteaux and never dammed the river. Why, shad used to run to Lynchburg! The world was merry, buttermilk was abundant; Lynchburg a lad, Richmond a mere youth, and the great "Jeems and Kanawha canell' was going to—oh! it was going to do everything.

This was forty years ago and more, mark you.

In 1838, I made my first trip to Richmond. What visions of grandeur filled my youthful imagination! That eventually I should get to be a man seemed probable, but that I should ever be big enough to live, actually live, in the vast metropolis, was beyond my dreams. For I believed fully that men were proportioned to the size of the cities they lived in. I had seen a man named Hatcher from Cartersville, who was near about the size of the average man in Lynchburg, but as I had never seen Cartersville, I concluded, naturally enough, that Cartersville must be equal in population. Which may be the fact, for I have never yet seen Cartersville, though I have been to Warminster, and once came near passing through Bent-Creek.

I went by stage.

It took two days to make the trip, yet no one complained, although there were many Methodist ministers aboard. Bro. Lafferty had not been born. I thought it simply glorious. There was an unnatural preponderance of preacher to boy—nine of preacher to one of boy. That boy did not take a leading part in the conversation. He looked out of the window, and thought much about Richmond. And what a wonderful world it was! So many trees, such nice rocks, and pretty ruts in the red clay; such glorious taverns, and men with red noses; such splendid horses, a fresh team every ten miles, and an elegant smell of leather, proceeding from the coach, prevailing everywhere as we bowled merrily along. And then the stage horn. Let me not speak of it, lest Thomas and his orchestra hang their heads for very shame. I wish somebody would tell me where we stopped the first night, for I have quite forgotten. Anyhow, it was on the left-hand side coming down, and I rather think on the brow of a little hill. I know we got up mighty soon the next morning.

We drew up at the Eagle Hotel in Richmond. Here again words, and time too, fail me. All the cities on earth packed into one wouldn't look as big and fine to me now as Main Street did then. If things shrink so in the brief space of a lifetime, what would be the general appearance, say of Petersburg, if one should live a million or so of years? This is an interesting question, which you may discuss with yourself, dear reader.

Going northward, I remained a year or two, and on my return the "canell" was finished. I had seen bigger places than Richmond, but had yet to have my first experience of canal travelling. The packet-landing at the foot of Eighth Street presented a scene of great activity. Passengers on foot and in vehicles continued to arrive up to the moment of starting. I took a peep at the cabin, wondering much how all the passengers were to be accommodated for the night, saw how nicely the baggage was stored away on deck, admired the smart waiters, and picked up a deal of information generally. I became acquainted with the names of Edmond & Davenport in Richmond, and Boyd, Edmond & Davenport in Lynchburg, the owners of the packet-line, and thought to myself, "What immensely rich men they must be! Why, these boats cost ten times as much as a stage-coach, and I am told they have them by the dozen."

At last we were off, slowly pushed along under the bridge on Seventh Street; then the horses were hitched; then slowly along till we passed the crowd of boats near the city, until at length, with a lively jerk as the horses fell into a trot, away we went, the cut-water throwing up the spray as we rounded the Penitentiary hill, and the passengers lingering on deck to get a last look at the fair City of Richmond, lighted by the pale rays of the setting sun.

As the shadows deepened, everybody went below. There was always a crowd in those days, but it was a crowd for the most part of our best people, and no one minded it. I was little, and it took little room to accommodate me. Everything seemed as cozy and comfortable as [a] heart could wish. I brought to the table—an excellent one it was—a school-boy's appetite, sharpened by travel, and thought it was "just splendid."

Supper over, the men went on deck to smoke, while the ladies busied themselves with draughts or backgammon, with conversation or with books. But not for long. The curtains which separated the female from the male department were soon drawn, in order that the steward and his aids might make ready the berths. These were three deep, "lower," "middle," and "upper," and great was the desire on the part of the men not to be consigned to the "upper." Being light as cork, I rose naturally to the top, clambering thither by the leathern straps with the agility of a monkey, and enjoying as best I might the trampling overhead whenever we approached a lock. I didn't mind this much, but when the fellow who had snubbed the boat jumped down about four feet, right on my head as it were, it was pretty severe. Still I slept the sleep of youth. We all went to bed early. A few lingered, talking in low tones; the way-passengers, in case there was a crowd, were dumped upon mattresses, placed on the dining-tables.

The lamp shed a dim light over the sleepers, and all went well till some one—and there always was some one—began to snore. *Sn-a-a-aw—aw-aw-poof!* They would turn uneasily and try to compose themselves to slumber again. No use. *Sn-a-a-aw—poof!* "D—— that fellow! Chunk him in the ribs, somebody, and make him turn over. Is this thing to go on forever? Gentlemen, are you going to stand this all night? If you are, I am not. I am going to get up and dress. Who is he, anyhow? No gentleman would or could snore in that way!"

After a while silence would be restored, and all would drop off to sleep again, except the little fellow in the upper berth, who, lying there, would listen to the *trahn-ahn-ahn-ahn* of the packet-horn, as we drew nigh the locks. How mournfully it sounded in the night! what a doleful thing it is at best, and how different from the stage-horn, with its cheery, ringing notes! The difference in the horns marks the difference in the two eras of travel; not that the canal period is doleful —I would not say that, but it is less bright than the period of the stage-coach.

To this day you have only to say, within my hearing, *trahn-ahn-ahn*, to bring back the canal epoch. I can see the whole thing down to the snubbing-post, with its deep grooves which the heavy rope had worn. Indeed, I think I could snub a boat myself, with very little practice, if the man on deck would say "*hup!*" to the horses at the proper time.

We turned out early in the morning, and had precious little room for dressing. But that was no hardship to me, who had just emerged from a big boarding-school dormitory. Still, I must say, being now a grown and oldish man, that I would not like to live and sleep and dress for twenty or thirty years in the cabin of a canal-packet. The ceremony of ablution was performed in a primitive fashion. There were the tin basins, the big tin dipper with the long wooden handle. I feel it vibrating in the water now, and the water a little muddy generally; and there were the towels, a big one on a roller, and the little ones in a pile, and all of them wet. There were discomforts, it is true, but, pshaw! one good, big, long, deep draught of pure, fresh morning air—one glimpse of the roseate flush above the wooded hills of the James, one look at the dew besprent bushes and vines along the canal bank—one sweet caress of dear mother nature in her morning robes, made ample compensation for them all. Breakfast was soon served, and all the more enjoyed in consequence of an hour's fasting on deck; the sun came out in all his splendor; the day was fairly set in, and with it there was abundant leisure to enjoy the scenery, that grew more and more captivating as we rose, lock after lock, into the rock-bound eminences of the upper James. This scenery I will not attempt to describe, for time has sadly dimmed it in my recollection. The wealth of the lowlands, and the upland beauty must be seen as I have seen them, in the day of their prime, to be enjoyed.

The perfect cultivation, the abundance, the elegance, the ducal splendor, one might almost say, of the great estates that lay along the canal in the old days have passed away in a great measure. Here were gentlemen, not merely refined and educated, fitted to display a royal hospitality and to devote their leisure to the study of the art and practice of government, but they were great and greatly successful farmers as well. The land teemed with all manner of products, cereals, fruits, what not! negroes by the hundreds and the thousands, under wise directions, gentle but firm control, plied the hoe to good purpose. There was enough and to spare for all—to spare? aye! to bestow with glad and lavish hospitality. A mighty change has been wrought. What that change is in all of its effects mine eyes have happily been spared the seeing; but well I remember—I can never forget—how from time to time the boat would stop at one of these estates, and the planter, his wife, his daughters, and the guests that were going home with him, would be met by those who had remained behind, and how joyous the greetings were! It was a bright and happy scene, and it continually repeated itself as we went onward.

In fine summer weather, the passengers, male and female, stayed most of the time on deck, where there was a great deal to interest, and naught to mar the happiness, except the oft-repeated warning, "*braidge!*" "*low braidge!*" No well-regulated packet-hand was ever allowed to say plain "bridge"; that was an etymological crime in canal ethics. For the men, this on-deck existence was especially delightful; it is *such* a comfort to spit plump into the water without the trouble of feeling around with your head, in the midst of a political discussion, for the spittoon.

As for me, I often went below, to devour Dickens's earlier novels, which were then appearing in rapid succession. But, drawn by the charm of the scenery, I would often drop my book and go back on deck again. There was an islet in the river—where, exactly, I cannot tell—which had a beauty of its own for me, because from the moment I first saw it, my purpose was to make it the scene of a romance, when I got to be a great big man, old enough to write for the papers. There is a point at which the passengers would get off, and taking a near cut across the hills, would stretch their legs with a mile or two of walking. It was unmanly, I held, to miss that. Apropos of scenery, I must not forget the haunted house near Manchester, which was pointed out soon after we left Richmond, and filled me with awe; for though I said I did not believe in ghosts, I did. The ruined mill, a mile or two farther on, was always an object of melancholy interest to me; and of all the locks from Lynchburg down, the Three-Mile Lock pleased me most. It is a pretty place, as every one will own on seeing it. It was so clean and green, and white and thrifty-looking. To me it was simply beautiful. I wanted to live there; I ought to have lived there. I was built for a lock-keeper—have that exact moral and mental shape. Ah! to own your own negro, who would do all the drudgery of opening the gates. Occasionally you would go through the form of putting your shoulder to the huge wooden levers, if that is what they call them, by which the gates are opened; to own your own negro and live and die calmly at a lock! What more could the soul ask? I do think that the finest picture extant of peace and contentment—a little abnormal, perhaps, in the position of the animal—is that of a sick mule looking out of the window of a canal freight-boat. And that you could see every day from the porch of your cottage, if you lived at a lock, owned your own negro, and there was no great rush of business on the canal (and there seldom was), on the "Jeems and Kanawhy," as old Capt. Sam Wyatt always called it, leaving out the word "canal," for that was understood. Yes, one ought to live as a pure and resigned lock-keeper, if one would be blest, really blest.

Now that I am on the back track, let me add that, however bold and picturesque the cliffs and bluffs near Lynchburg and beyond, there was nothing from one end of the canal to the other to compare with the first sight of Richmond, when, rounding a corner not far from Hollywood, it burst full upon the vision, its capitol, its spires, its happy homes, flushed with the red glow of evening, . . . made your State greatest among all her sisters, and which seemed concentrated in yourself. Be your maturity what it may, it can never be brighter than this.

To return to the boat. All the scenery in the world—rocks that

Salvator would love to paint, and skies that Claude could never limn —all the facilities for spitting that earth affords, avail not to keep a Virginian away from a julep on a hot summer day. From time to time he would descend from the deck of the packet and refresh himself. The bar was small, but vigorous and healthy. I was then in the lemonade stage of boyhood, and it was not until many years afterward that I rose through porterees and claret-punches to the sublimity of the sherry cobbler, and discovered that the packet bar supplied genuine Havana cigars at fourpence-ha'penny. Why, eggs were but sixpence a dozen on the canal bank, and the national debt wouldn't have filled a teacup. Internal revenue was unknown; the coupons receivable for taxes inconceivable, and forcible readjustment a thing undreamt of in Virginian philosophy. Mr. Mallock's pregnant question, "Is life worth living?" was answered very satisfactorily, methought, as I watched the Virginians at their juleps: "Gentlemen, your very good health"; "Colonel, my respects to you"; "My regards, Judge. When shall I see you again at my house? Can't you stop now and stay a little while, if it is only a week or two?" "Sam" (to the barkeeper), "duplicate these drinks."

Bagby, "Canal Reminiscences," *The Old Virginia Gentleman*, ed. Page (1910), pp. 230–42

"Where Slavery Was": Charles Dickens Visits the City (1842)

The reader familiar with the life of Charles Dickens (1812–70) will understand why he found Richmond to be an unpleasant place, as indicated by the following selection, when he visited it in 1842. The son of an English government clerk who spent time in debtors' prison, Dickens as a youth dreamed of riches as he worked as a bottle labeler and wrapper in a London warehouse. Because he had no money for luxuries, as a youngster he spent his spare time walking the streets of his native city and observing the characters who would later populate the pages of his brilliant socially oriented novels. At the age of twenty, Dickens went to work as a reporter for one of the major London newspapers. Quickly becoming skilled as a writer, he soon turned to fiction, winning worldwide fame and riches. Owing to his impoverished youth, however, he retained a lifelong hatred of the exploitation of others as well as of those who made up society's elite. Because he considered himself to be a self-styled champion of the oppressed, he naturally deplored the social caste system that he found in Richmond, with slaves at the bottom and the wealthy property owners at the top. In addition, Dickens felt that those who entertained him and touted his accomplishments while he was in the city had little appreciation for literature. Dickens's next book after his return home, the novel *Martin Chuzzlewit* (1843–44), further dramatized his negative view of America.

The tract of country through which [the railway makes its course to Richmond] was once productive: but the soil has been exhausted by the system of employing a great amount of slave labor in forcing crops, without strengthening the land: and it is now little better than a sandy desert overgrown with trees. Dreary and uninteresting as its aspect is, I was glad to the heart to find anything on which one of the curses of this horrible institution has fallen; and had greater pleasure in contemplating the withered ground than the richest and most thriving cultivation in the same place could possibly have afforded me.

In this district, as in all others where slavery sits brooding (I have frequently heard this admitted, even by those who are its warmest advocates), there is an air of ruin and decay abroad, which is inseparable from the system. The barns and outhouses are mouldering away; the sheds are patched and half roofless; the log-cabins (built in Virginia with external chimneys made of clay or wood) are squalid in the last degree. There is no look of decent comfort anywhere. The miserable stations by the railway side; the great wild woodyards, whence the engine is supplied with fuel; the negro children rolling on the ground before the cabin doors, with dogs and pigs; the biped beasts of burden slinking past: gloom and dejection are upon them all.

In the negro car belonging to the train in which we made this journey were a mother and her children who had just been purchased; the husband and father being left behind with their old owner. The children cried the whole way, and the mother was misery's picture. The champion of Life, Liberty, and the Pursuit of Happiness, who had bought them, rode in the same train; and, every time we stopped, got down to see that they were safe. The black in Sinbad's Travels, with one eye in the middle of his forehead which shone like a burning coal, was nature's aristocrat compared with this white gentleman.

It was between six and seven o'clock in the evening when we drove to the hotel: in front of which, and on the top of the broad flight of steps leading to the door, two or three citizens were balancing themselves on rocking-chairs, and smoking cigars. We found it a very large and elegant establishment, and were as well entertained as travellers need desire to be. The climate being a thirsty one, there was never, at any hour of the day, a scarcity of loungers in the spacious bar, or a cessation of the mixing of cool liquors: but they were a merrier people here, and had musical instruments playing to them o' nights, which it was a treat to hear again.

The next day, and the next, we rode and walked about the town, which is delightfully situated on eight hills overhanging James River; a sparkling stream, studded here and there with bright islands, or brawling over broken rocks. . . . In a low ground among the hills is a valley known as "Bloody Run," from a terrible conflict with the Indians which once occurred there. It is a good place for such a struggle, and, like every other spot I saw associated with any legend of that wild people now so rapidly fading from the earth, interested me very much.

The city is the seat of the local Parliament of Virginia; and, in its shady legislative halls, some orators were drowsily holding forth to the hot noonday. By dint of constant repetition, however, these constitutional sights had very little more interest for me than so many parochial vestries; and I was glad to exchange this one for a lounge in a well-arranged public library of some ten thousand volumes, and a visit to a tobacco manufactory, where the workmen were all slaves.

I saw in this place the whole process of picking, rolling, pressing, drying, packing in casks, and branding. All the tobacco thus dealt with was in course of manufacture for chewing; and one would have supposed there was enough in that one storehouse to have filled even the comprehensive jaws of America. In this form the weed looks like the oilcake on which we fatten cattle; and, even without reference to its consequences, is sufficiently uninviting.

Many of the workmen appeared to be strong men, and it is hardly necessary to add that they were all laboring quietly then. After two o'clock in the day they are allowed to sing, a certain number at a time. The hour striking while I was there, some twenty sang a hymn in parts, and sang it by no means ill; pursuing their work meanwhile. A bell rang as I was about to leave, and they all poured forth into a building on the opposite side of the street to dinner. I said several times that I should like to see them at their meal; but, as the gentleman to whom I mentioned this desire appeared to be suddenly taken rather deaf, I did not pursue the request. Of their appearance I shall have something to say presently.

On the following day I visited a plantation or farm, of about twelve hundred acres, on the opposite bank of the river. Here again, although I went down with the owner of the estate, to "the quarter," as that part of it in which the slaves live is called, I was not invited to enter into any of their huts. All I saw of them was, that they were very crazy, wretched cabins, near to which groups of half-naked children basked in the sun, or wallowed on the dusty ground. But I believe that this gentleman is a considerate and excellent master, who inherited his fifty slaves, and is neither a buyer nor a seller of human stock; and I am sure, from my own observation and conviction, that he is a kindhearted, worthy man.

The planter's house was an airy, rustic dwelling, that brought Defoe's description of such places strongly to my recollection. The day was very warm, but the blinds being all closed, and the windows and doors set wide open, a shady coolness rustled through the rooms, which was exquisitely refreshing after the glare and heat without. Before the windows was an open piazza, where, in what they call the hot weather—whatever that may be—they sling hammocks, and drink and doze luxuriously. I do not know how their cool refections may taste within the hammocks, but, having experience, I can report that, out of them, the mounds of ices and the bowls of mint-julep and sherry-cobbler they make in these latitudes, are refreshments never to be thought of afterwards, in summer, by those who would preserve contented minds.

There are two bridges across the river: one belongs to the railroad, and the other, which is a very crazy affair, is the private property of some old lady in the neighborhood, who levies tolls upon the townspeople. Crossing this bridge on my way back, I saw a notice painted on the gate, cautioning all persons to drive slowly: under a penalty, if the offender were a white man, of five dollars; if a negro, fifteen stripes.

The same decay and gloom that overhang the way by which it is approached, hover above the town of Richmond. There are pretty villas and cheerful houses in its streets, and Nature smiles upon the country round; but jostling its handsome residences, like slavery itself going hand in hand with many lofty virtues, are deplorable tenements, fences unrepaired, walls crumbling into ruinous heaps. Hinting gloomily at things below the surface, these, and many other tokens of the same description, force themselves upon the notice, and are remembered with depressing influence, when livelier features are forgotten.

To those who are happily unaccustomed to them, the countenances in the streets and laboring places, too, are shocking. All men who know that there are laws against instructing slaves, of which the pains and penalties greatly exceed in their amount the fines imposed on those who maim and torture them, must be prepared to find their faces very low in the scale of intellectual expression. But the darkness —not of skin, but mind—which meets the stranger's eye at every turn; the brutalizing and blotting out of all fairer characters traced by Nature's hand; immeasurably outdo his worst belief. That travelled creation of the great satirist's brain, who, fresh from living among horses, peered from a high casement down upon his own kind with trembling horror, was scarcely more repelled and daunted by the sight than those who look upon some of these faces for the first time must surely be.

I left the last of them behind me in the person of a wretched drudge, who, after running to and fro all day till midnight, and moping in his stealthy winks of sleep upon the stairs between-whiles, was washing the dark passages at four o'clock in the morning; and went upon my way with a grateful heart that I was not doomed to live where slavery was, and had never had my senses blunted to its wrongs and horrors in a slave-rocked cradle.

It had been my intention to proceed by James River and Chesapeake Bay to Baltimore; but one of the steamboats being absent from her station through some accident, and the means of conveyance being consequently rendered uncertain, we returned to Washington by the way we had come (there were two constables on board the steamboat, in pursuit of runaway slaves), and, halting there again for one night, went on to Baltimore next afternoon.

Dickens, *American Notes* (1842), 2:194–99

"Many Difficulties . . . Obviated":
The First African Baptist Church (1842)

Richmond's First Baptist Church was built in 1803 at the intersection of the present-day streets of College and East Broad. As was typical of antebellum times, the church had both white and black members, but for reasons noted below, a separation by races occurred in the early 1840s. The white congregation moved nearby into an architectural gem designed by Thomas U. Walter. The blacks remained in the original building under the denomination of the First African Baptist Church, with the noted white minister and educator Robert Ryland as their pastor. The launching of this unique church reflects many of the prevailing racial values of that era, as recounted by the Reverend Jeremiah Bell Jeter (1802–80), a prominent Baptist clergyman, a founder of what is now the University of Richmond, and a longtime editor of the *Religious Herald*.

When I came to Richmond the First church contained about 2,000 colored members, and the number was considerably augmented while they were under my charge. They were a heavy burden on the white members of the church. Beside the expense of providing for their instruction, much time and labor were devoted to the exercise of discipline among them.

There were several important reasons for organizing them into a separate and independent church. The space allotted for their use in the house of worship was utterly insufficient for their accommodation. The style of preaching demanded by the white congregation was not well adapted to the instruction of the colored people. Besides, it was quite impossible for the pastor, with a large white congregation under his care, to pay much attention to the necessities of the colored portion of his flock. A pastor who should devote his whole time, or the chief part of it, to their interests seemed to be imperatively demanded.

There were, however, very serious difficulties in the way of organizing a colored church. A house of worship, of no inconsiderable extent, would be needed for their accommodation, and the means of procuring it could not be easily obtained. There was, however, a more formidable obstacle to the enterprise than the lack of money. Public sentiment was opposed to it. The unfortunate Southampton insurrection had led to the enactment of stringent laws in regard to the assembling of negroes for religious worship or any other purpose. They were forbidden to meet in any considerable number except in the presence and under the supervision of white persons. The abolition excitement at the North was producing a most unpleasant counter-excitement at the South. All efforts for meliorating the condition of the slaves were opposed by many on the ground that they favored the designs of the abolitionists. Many pious people looked with distrust, if not with hostility, on all new measures for the religious instruction of the negroes. All classes of irreligious persons—sceptics, gamblers, bar-keepers, and the like, of whom Richmond at that time had her full share—were bitter and fierce in their opposition to the proposed organization. They were hostile, indeed, to all religion, but as the white churches were too well fortified by public sentiment to be safely attacked, they concentrated their opposition against the proposed African church, and appealed to the fears excited by the recent insurrection, and to the feeling of indignation prevailing against the abolitionists, to prevent the execution of the scheme.

The church, after much anxious consultation, resolved to purchase a lot, build a new house, and make arrangements for the exclusive occupancy of the old house by the colored portion of the church. To this resolution we are indebted for the spacious and solid building now known as the First Baptist church, at the corner of Broad and Twelfth streets, and for the still more capacious edifice called the First African church, standing on the ground long occupied by the old and venerable Baptist church, in which sat for a time the distinguished Convention of 1829–'30, which remodeled the State Constitution, and on whose floor were laid the dead and dying at the time of the memorable conflagration of the theatre. The new house was built by great exertions and great sacrifices, in which the noble sisters bore a conspicuous part. Deacons James Sizer and Archibald Thomas, by their liberality and their personal attentions, contributed largely to the completion and excellent arrangements of the building. It is proper, too, to say that to Mr. James Thomas, Jr., then just commencing his successful financial career, more than to any other man, living or dead, have the colored people been indebted for the valuable house which they long occupied, and which has been succeeded by their present edifice, undoubtedly the largest house of worship in the State. The old house and lot were valued by impartial judges, the church made a contribution of $3,000 to secure the property for the use of the colored people, and the owners of slaves were solicited to aid in the enterprise. The personal application to them for help was assigned to Mr. Thomas, and right nobly and most successfully did he perform his task. His acquaintance with the tobacco merchants and manufacturers gave him advantage for the work which few possessed and which only he was willing to employ.

The African church was organized in the year 1842. Many difficulties had to be obviated in its organization. It was deemed wise to conform the church to the State laws and the municipal regulations. Its meetings were held only in the day time, and in the presence of white persons. The discipline of the church was lodged in their own hands, but owing to their inexperience in ecclesiastical government it was deemed better that an appeal should be granted to aggrieved members to a strong white committee appointed by the mother church —a privilege which was probably never exercised. The law required that the religious instructor should be a white man, but if there had been no such restriction it would probably have been impossible to find a colored man suited for the office.

After some delay and much earnest inquiry, Rev. Robert Ryland, president of Richmond College, was elected to the office. His official duties were not onerous, and as his afternoons (Saturdays and Sundays) were unoccupied, and the pastorate would make no great draft on his intellectual powers, he was unanimously selected for the important post. Of all men he was best suited for it. Deriving his support from his college services, he demanded but a small salary of the church, and that he devoted to the promotion of their interests. The colored people were emotional, fond of excitement, and would have been pleased with a declamatory and superficial preacher. Dr. Ryland —not then Doctor, but he soon received the title—was an eminently plain, instructive, and practical preacher, dealing chiefly with the conscience rather than the passions. His aim was to make his hearers think rather than to feel, and to act rather than to speculate. His ministry was precisely adapted to correct the errors and to repress the extravagances into which his hearers were prone to run.

The pastorate of Dr. Ryland was eminently successful. The colored people soon became convinced that he was their sincere friend, seeking not theirs, but them, and endeavoring by all means to promote their best interests. Great numbers were converted by his ministry and baptized by him. He stated that other pastors had difficulty in persuading their hearers to be baptized, but that his greatest trouble was to prevent his hearers from being baptized prematurely. He continued his labors among his flock until, at the close of the late war, when the negroes were freed, our social and civil institutions were overthrown, and it was supposed by those who assumed to be the leaders of the colored people that they needed a pastor more in sympathy with the new order of things, and the Doctor quietly retired from the post which he had so long and so usefully filled. Multitudes of negroes here remember the faithful and disinterested labors of their old pastor with profound gratitude, and hold his name in the highest veneration.

The labors of Dr. Ryland contributed largely to the almost unparalleled religious prosperity of the colored people in this city. They have five large houses of worship and a membership of over 13,000;

this number, however, is nominal rather than exact. It is not possible for the churches, in the homeless condition and with the migratory habits of their members, to keep exact registers of them. Still they approximate the number stated, and their progress in knowledge and efficiency is truly remarkable and gratifying. The organization of the First African church marks an era in the history of the evangelization of the colored people in this city. It may be proper to state that there were prosperous African churches in Norfolk and Petersburg, and perhaps other places, before one was formed here.

The reader may desire to know what was the result of the opposition to the organization of the African church. It led to no violence, but continued for years to display itself in constant watching for violations of the laws, complaints, and reproaches. The high character of Dr. Ryland and his prudent course gradually, among all pious, and even considerate people, quelled opposition and secured their confidence in the wisdom and usefulness of the measure. Attempts were made to have its active supporters indicted by the grand jury, but they failed.

I desire to repeat a fact in honor of Rev. William S. Plumer which I have several times published. While the formation of the African church was in contemplation, as I was desirous to have the sympathy and countenance of the Protestant pastors in the enterprise, I consulted some of them on the subject, and was advised to call a meeting of the clergy and ask their advice. When I mentioned the matter to Dr. Plumer, then pastor of the First Presbyterian church of this city, and a very popular preacher, he said: "Don't do it. The clergy may decide against your plan, but it is right. The law is in your favor. Go forward in the work, and if you have trouble I will stand by you." When he heard that an effort was being made to secure an indictment from the grand jury against the persons who had the meetings of the church in charge, the Doctor came to me and said: "I wish you to understand that in any difficulties you may have concerning the African church I am to go halves with you." It was a noble offer, and as honest and firm as it was noble. There were other ministers, I had reason to suspect, who would, from sectarian influence, have been quite pleased if the enterprise had ended in defeat and reproach.

Jeter, *Recollections* (1891), pp. 209–13

"The People of Richmond Are a Peculiar People": Another Traveler's View (1846)

Although a native of Scotland, the lawyer-journalist Alexander MacKay (1808–52) had for years resided in Canada and had toured often in the United States. As a correspondent for a London newspaper he visited much of America in 1846–47, including Richmond in late May 1846. His account of the city varies in some important particulars from the earlier selections by Schöpf and La Rochefoucault-Liancourt. Like other travelers, MacKay paid homage to the James —but from the portico of the capitol where, in those pristine days, one could enjoy a largely unobstructed view of the historic river. He also noted the significance of tobacco—a commodity received, processed, and shipped from Richmond—and the fact that the town's flour mills had by the 1840s become "the largest . . . in the United States." Finally, MacKay observed the emergence of local pride (perhaps adolescent in its defensive quality) and of a "code of honour . . . so exceedingly strict that it requires the greatest circumspection to escape its violation." The latter comment came in the wake of a tragic event in which the editor of the Richmond *Enquirer* had killed the editor of the Richmond *Whig* in a duel.

Richmond, the capital of Virginia, is a small, but certainly a very pretty town, if its people would only content themselves with having it so. It is a weakness of theirs to be constantly making the largest possible drafts upon the admiration of the visitor, by extorting his assent to the fidelity of comparisons which would be amongst the very last to suggest themselves to his own mind. He is reminded, for instance, that the prospect which it commands is very like the view obtained from the battlements of Windsor Castle; and to those who have never been at Windsor, or who, having been there, have never seen Richmond, the comparison may certainly hold good; but such as have seen both are far more indebted to their imagination than to the reality for the resemblance. He is also given to understand that it occupies more hills than imperial Rome ever sat upon; and if the number of hills on which the capital rested was an essential element of Roman greatness, this is one way of proving Richmond superior to Rome.

But notwithstanding these excusable partialities, Richmond is a beautiful place. There is a high and a low town; the former crowning the summit of an abrupt sandy bank, which hems in the latter between

it and the northern margin of the James River, a stream so justly celebrated in the early colonial history of the continent. The town itself
has not much to recommend it, consisting as it does of one good street
and a number of indifferent ones. The portion of it between the main
street and the river, in which the wholesale business is chiefly transacted, reminds one very much, in closeness and dinginess, of the
neighbourhood of Watling-street or Blackfriars. It is in its adjuncts
that the beauty of Richmond is to be sought and found; its suburbs in
the upper town being both elegant and airy, and the view obtained
from them by no means uninteresting. The best point, perhaps, from
which to ascertain the position of Richmond, is the portico of the
Capitol, a plain, unpretending building, which overhangs the lower
town. It contains within its walls, however, one of the finest, and decidedly the most interesting, of the specimens of art in America. In its
principal lobby is a full-length marble statue of Washington; not in
the garb of the warrior, but in the plain costume of the country gentleman, with his staff in his hand, instead of his sword by his side. It is
the most faithful portrait of the incorruptible patriot of which the
country is possessed, the features being modelled from a cast taken of
him during life. Time and again did I return to gaze at that placid
face, that mild yet intelligent expression, that serene yet thoughtful
brow. No portrait or bust that I had ever before seen had conveyed to
me an idea of Washington which satisfied me. But there he was to the
life, just as he appeared to his contemporaries after the turmoil of the
great contest was over, in which he played so important and honourable a part. I never think of Washington now without picturing him as
represented by that marble statue.

From the portico the scene is both extensive and varied. In the
immediate foreground is the town, the greater portion of which is so
directly underneath you that it almost seems as if you could leap into
it. Before you is the James River, tumbling in snowy masses over successive ledges of rock, its channel being divided by several islands,
which are shrouded in foliage, and imbedded in foaming rapids. To
the south of the river, an extensive vista opens up, spreading far to
the right and left, cleared in some places, but, generally speaking,
mantled in the most luxuriant vegetation. The scene is one over which
the stranger may well linger, particularly on a bright summer's day,
when his cheek is fanned by the cooling breezes, which come gaily
skipping from the distant Alleghenies, carrying the fragrant perfume
of the magnolia and the honeysuckle on their wings, and his spirit
is soothed by the incessant murmur of the rapids, which, from the
height at which he stands, steals gently to his ear.

The site of Richmond was selected chiefly with a view to the water power which is afforded it by the rapids of the James. These commence a considerable distance above the city, and terminate immediately in front of it. The fall which thus gradually takes place in the channel of the river, is altogether about eighty feet, the formation of the banks on either side being such as to render the great power thus afforded perfectly available. It has, as yet, been but partially taken advantage of. Opposite the city, on the southern bank, is the small village of Manchester, aspiring, I suppose, to that name, from the fact of its comprising two cotton factories, which, indeed, with their adjuncts, form its sum total. It is approached from Richmond by means of bridges thrown across the rapids from the mainland on either side, to the islands; but the chief industry of the spot is centred in the city itself, which derives its water power from the basin of the James River, and Kanawha canal, designed to unite the Virginian sea-board with the great valley of the West. The canal is here fed from the upper level of the river, and as it approaches the town, the difference of level between it and the falling stream becomes greater and greater, until at length a fall of eighty feet is obtained from the canal basin to the river. Here the water may be easily used three times over in changing its level; a little further up it can only be used twice, and still further up again, only once. As yet fully three-fourths of the power thus available is unemployed. The manufactures of Richmond are various, comprising woollen and cotton goods, tobacco factories, and some very large iron and steel works; but its chief feature in this respect is the manufacture of flour, the largest flour-mills in the United States being found here, one of which, when in full play, can turn out from 750 to 1,000 barrels of flour per day. It is from Richmond that the South American market is chiefly supplied with this necessary of life; the wheat of Virginia, when ground, being better adapted for tropical voyages than the produce of any other part of the country, including Ohio and Genesee wheat.

Richmond is also one of the first tobacco markets of the country, the produce of the State being concentrated upon it both for export and manufacture. The tobacco, after having been dried, as it now is, chiefly in the fields, is closely packed into hogsheads, in which state it is forwarded to Richmond, where such portion of it (the greater) as cannot be disposed of by private sale is stored in public warehouses, to await the auction sales, which take place within certain hours of the day. When a hogshead is to be put up, it is unhooped, and the compact mass, as yet but raw material, exposed to view. One of the inspectors on duty, then, by means of a crow-bar, forcibly separates it in three different places, from which a few leaves are taken to form the sample of the bulk, which is then sold according to its quality as thus ascertained. The staves are then put together again, the hogshead receives the purchaser's mark, and it is left in store until he chooses to take it away. The quantity of tobacco which is thus sometimes accumulated upon Richmond, is only exceeded by that which is generally to be found in bond at the London Docks.

Much of the tobacco thus disposed of is purchased for local manufacture, Richmond containing several large establishments for the conversion of the crude tobacco into a form fit for chewing. Over the most extensive of these I was kindly piloted by one of the owners, where I witnessed all the processes which the weed underwent in its passage from dry leaves to the marketable shape of Cavendish tobacco, in which form it was packed in small cakes, in oblong boxes, labelled with the seductive name of "Honeydew." In all the departments of the factory the labour was performed by slaves, superintended by white overseers. They appeared to be very contented at their work, although the utmost silence was observed amongst them, except within certain hours of the day, when they were permitted to relieve their toil by singing, performing a succession of solos, duets, glees, &c., &c., in a way that was truly surprising, considering that they were entirely self-taught. Having heard them sing, I was permitted to see them eat; their noon-day meal consisting of corn-bread and beef; the males and females occupying different apartments, and each appearing to have as much to eat as he or she could possibly enjoy. The factory was so complete as to be provided even with its own tailor, who was engaged, whilst I was there, in cutting out the summer suits of the workmen, from thick cotton cloth, tolerably well bleached, and of a close and by no means very coarse texture.

In a street contiguous to the public warehouses, I encountered piles of boxes filled with a very coarse liquorice, and which were being disposed of in lots by auction. The liquorice was purchased that it might be mixed with a portion of the tobacco, in the process of its manufacture, the poison being thus sweetened, to render it palatable to the uninitiated.

The neighborhood of Richmond is rich in mineral resources. The coal strata are not only abundant, but in some places approach so near the surface as to be worked at but little cost. The largest coal company is that called the English company; the coal, when raised, being carried from its pits, by means of a private railway, to the port of Richmond, a few miles below the city, whence it is shipped to the different markets of the Union. There is also a good deal of iron in the vicinity; but either from the difficulty of mining it, or from the hold which English and Pennsylvania iron has got of the market, it is as yet but little worked.

The people of Richmond are a peculiar people. They are proud and sensitive to a degree. They are proud, in the first place, of their State, and in the next, of its capital; in addition to which, they are not a little satisfied with the moral superiorities to which they lay claim. Their code of honour is so exceedingly strict that it requires the greatest circumspection to escape its violation. An offence which elsewhere would be regarded as of homeopathic proportions, is very apt to assume in Richmond the gravity of colossal dimensions; even a coolness between parties is dangerous, as having a fatal tendency speedily to ripen into a deadly feud. Once arrived at this point, a personal encounter is inevitable, unless, to avoid it, one party or the other is induced to quit the city. It is curious enough to witness the cool and matter-of-course way in which even the ladies will speculate upon the necessities for, and the probabilities of, a hostile meeting between such and such parties, and in which, when they hear of a duel, they will tell you that they long foresaw it, and that it could not be avoided. After all, this state of things, although it may indicate less of a healthy habit than of a morbid sensibility, gives to Richmond society a chivalrous and romantic cast, which is rarely to be met with in matter-of-fact America. It is seldom, indeed, that they imitate, in their personal warfare, the savage brutalities of the south-western States; their quarrels, generally speaking, taking some time to mature, and the parties, when the day of reckoning at length comes, fighting like gentlemen, instead of like tigers or hyenas.

The society of Richmond adds the warmth and fervour of the south to that frank and ready hospitality which is characteristic of American society in general. It is rarely that the stranger, in his social contact with the Americans, has to encounter the frigid influences of formalism. In Virginia, convention is, perhaps, more than any where else subjugated by the heart. It is astonishing how soon each party in an assembly appears in his or her real character. Entering a drawing-room at Richmond is like entering a theatre with the curtain up, when there is no ugly, green-baize screen between you, the scenery, and the performers. In no other place has it ever appeared to me that life was so little disfigured by masquerade. The thoughts are accorded a freedom of utterance, which is never abused, and dislikes and partialities come equally to the surface; the one not being smothered, the other not concealed. He must look into himself for the cause, who does not feel himself at once at home with his frank and hospitable friends.

The ladies of Richmond partake of that easy grace, the causes of
which, as a characteristic of Virginian society, I shall presently trace.

MacKay, *Western World* (1849), pp. 251–55

"May God Spare You from Enduring What I Then Endured": A Daring Escape from Slavery (1848)

Slavery in the antebellum South conjures up the image of blacks
toiling in the sun amid fields of cotton or tobacco, but there was con-
currently an urban, industrial slavery in Richmond. The city's bur-
geoning factories relied heavily on black labor, some of it free, some
owned by the manufacturer, and some "hired" from willing masters
who accepted—and sometimes shared—wages for their chattels'
labor. Though the traveler MacKay reported favorably on slave life in
a Richmond tobacco plant, a sharply contrasting picture emerges
from the writings of Henry Box Brown (1816–?). Following his spectacular escape in 1848, Brown lectured on the abolitionist circuit and
published his graphic autobiography. The volume, actually written
by Charles Stearns, became part of the genre of slave narratives, often
subsidized by critics of the "peculiar institution" as propaganda de-
vices, but nonetheless offering a unique vantage point for viewing
the slave domain—namely, from that of the slave himself.

As time passed along, I began to think seriously of entering into the
matrimonial state, as much as a person can, who can "make no contract whatever," and whose wife is not his, only so far as her master
allows her to be. I formed an acquaintance with a young woman by
the name of Nancy—belonging to a Mr. Lee, a clerk in the bank, and
a pious man; and our friendship having ripened into mutual love, we
concluded to make application to the powers that ruled us, for *permission* to be married, as I had previously applied for permission to
join the church. I went to Mr. Lee, and made known to him my wishes,
when he told me, he never meant to sell Nancy, and if my master
would agree never to sell me, then I might marry her. This man was a
member of a Presbyterian church in Richmond, and pretended to
me, to believe it wrong to separate families; but after I had been mar-

ried to my wife one year, his conscientious scruples vanished, and she was sold to a saddler living in Richmond, who was one of Dr. Plummer's church members. Mr. Lee gave me a note to my master, and they afterwards discussed the matter over, and I was allowed to marry the chosen one of my heart. Mr. Lee, as I have said, soon sold my wife, contrary to his promise, and she fell into the hands of a very cruel mistress, the wife of the saddler above mentioned, by whom she was much abused. This woman used to wish for some great calamity to happen to my wife, because she stayed so long when she *went to nurse her child*; which calamity came very near happening afterwards to herself. My wife was finally sold, on account of the solicitations of this woman; but four months had hardly elapsed, before she insisted upon her being purchased back again.

During all this time, my mind was in a continual agitation, for I knew not one day, who would be the owner of my wife the next. O reader, have you no heart to sympathize with the injured slave, as he thus lives in a state of perpetual torment, the dread uncertainty of his wife's fate, continually hanging over his head, and poisoning all his joys, as the naked sword hung by a *hair*, over the head of an ancient king's guest, as he was seated at a table loaded with all the luxuries of an epicure's devising? This sword, unlike the one alluded to, did often pierce my breast, and when I had recovered from the wound, it was again hung up, to torture me. This is slavery, a natural and concomitant part of the accursed system!

The saddler who owned my wife, whose name I suppress for particular reasons, was at one time taken sick, but when *his minister*, the Rev. (so called) Dr. Plumer came to pray with him, he would not allow him to perform that rite, which strengthened me in the opinion I entertained of Dr. Plumer, that he was *as wicked a man* as this saddler, and you will presently see, how bad a man he was. The saddler sent for *his slaves to pray* for him, and afterwards for me, and when I repaired to his bed-side, he beseeched me to pray for him, saying that he would live a much better life than he had done, if the Lord would only spare him. I and the other slaves prayed *three nights* for him, after our work was over, and we needed rest in sleep; but the earnest desire of this man, induced us to forego our necessary rest; and yet one of the first things he did after his recovery, was to *sell my wife*. When he was reminded of my praying for his restoration to health, he angrily exclaimed, that it was "all d——d lies" about the Lord restoring him to health in consequence of the negroes praying for him, —and that if any of them mentioned that they had prayed for him, he "would *whip them for it*."

The last purchaser of my wife, was Mr. Samuel S. Cartrell, also a member of Dr. Plumer's church.* He induced me to pay him . . . in order to assist him in purchasing my companion, so as to prevent her being sold away from me. I also paid him $50 a year, for her time, although she would have been of but little value to him, for she had young children and could not earn much for him,—and rented a house for which I paid $72, and she took in washing, which with the remainder of my earnings, after deducting master's "lion's share," supported our family. Our bliss, as far as the term bliss applies to a slave's situation, was now complete in this respect, for a season; for never had we been so pleasantly situated before; but, reader, behold its cruel termination. O the harrowing remembrance of those terrible, terrible scenes! May God spare you from ever enduring what I then endured.

It was on a pleasant morning, in the month of August, 1848, that I left my wife and three children safely at our little home, and proceeded to my allotted labor. The sun shone brightly as he commenced his daily task, and as I gazed upon his early rays, emitting their golden light upon the rich fields adjacent to the city, and glancing across the abode of my wife and family, and as I beheld the numerous companies of slaves, hieing their way to their daily labors, and reflected upon the difference between their lot and mine, I felt that, although I was a slave, there were many alleviations to my cup of sorrow. It was true, that the greater portion of my earnings was taken from me, by the unscrupulous hands of my dishonest master,—that I was entirely at his mercy, and might at any hour be snatched from what sources of joy were open to me—that he might, if he chose, extend his robber hand, and demand a still larger portion of my earnings,—and above all, that intellectual privileges were entirely denied me; but as I imprinted a parting kiss upon the lips of my faithful wife, and pressed to my bosom the little darling cherubs, who followed me saying, their childish accents, "Father, come back soon," I felt that life was not all a blank to me; that there were some pure joys yet my portion. O, how my heart would have been riven with unutterable anguish, if I had then realized the awful calamity which was about to burst upon my unprotected head! Reader, are you a husband, and can you listen to my sad story, without being moved to cease all your connection with that stern power, which stretched out its piratical arm, basely robbed me of all dear to me on earth!

*Reader, do you wonder at abolitionists calling such churches the brotherhood of thieves?   C.S.

The sun had traced his way to mid-heaven, and the hour for the laborers to turn from their tasks, and to seek refreshment for their toil-worn frames,—and when I should take my prattling children on my knee,—was fast approaching; but there burst upon me a sound so dreadful, and so sudden, that the shock well nigh overwhelmed me. It was as if the heavens themselves had fallen upon me, and the ever-lasting hills of God's erecting, like an avalanche, had come rolling over my head! And what was it? "Your wife and smiling babes are gone; in prison they are locked, and to-morrow's sun will see them far away from you, on their way to the distant South!" . . .

The next day, I stationed myself by the side of the road, along which the slaves, amounting to three hundred and fifty, were to pass. The purchaser of my wife was a *Methodist* minister, who was about starting for North Carolina. Pretty soon five waggon-loads of little children passed, and looking at the foremost one, what should I see but a little child, pointing its tiny hand toward me, exclaiming, "There's my father; I knew he would come and bid me good-bye." It was my eldest child! Soon the gang approached in which my wife was chained. I looked, and beheld her familiar face; but O, reader, that glance of agony! may God spare me ever again enduring the excruciating hor-ror of that moment! She passed, and came near to where I stood. I seized hold of her hand, *intending* to bid her farewell; but words failed me; the gift of utterance had fled, and I remained speechless. I fol-lowed her for some distance, with her hand grasped in mine, as if to save her from her fate, but I could not speak, and I was obliged to turn away in silence.

. . . The first thing that occurred to me, after the cruel separation of my wife and children from me, and I had recovered my senses, so as to know how to act, was, thoughts of freeing myself from slavery's iron yoke. I had suffered enough under its heavy weight, and I de-termined I would endure it no longer; and those reasons which often deter the slave from attempting to escape, no longer existed in refer-ence to me, for my family were gone, and slavery now had no miti-gating circumstances, to lessen the bitterness of its cup of woe. It is true, as my master had told me, that I could "get another wife"; but no man, excepting a brute below the human species, would have pro-posed such a step to a person in my circumstances; and . . . I was not such a degraded being.

I went to Mr. Allen, and requested of him permission to refrain from labor for a short time, in consequence of a disabled finger; but he refused to grant me this permission, on the ground that my hand was not lame enough to justify him in so doing. Nothing daunted by this rebuff, I took some oil of vitriol, intending to pour a few drops upon my finger, to make it sufficiently sore, to disable me from work, which I succeeded in, beyond my wishes; for in my hurry, a larger quantity than it was my purpose to apply to my finger, found its way there, and my finger was soon eaten through to the bone. The overseer then was obliged to allow me to absent myself from business, for it was impossible for me to work in that situation. But I did not waste my precious furlough in idle mourning over my fate. I armed myself with determined energy, for action, and in the words of one of old, in the name of God, "I leaped over a wall, and run through a troop" of difficulties. After searching for assistance for some time, I at length was so fortunate as to find a friend, who promised to assist me, for one half the money I had about me, which was one hundred and sixty-six dollars. I gave him eighty-six, and he was to do his best in forwarding my scheme. Long did we remain together, attempting to devise ways and means to carry me away from the land of separation of families, of whips and thumb-screws, and auction blocks; but as often as a plan was suggested by my friend, there would appear some difficulty in the way of its accomplishment. Perhaps it may not be best to mention what these plans were, as some unfortunate slaves may thereby be prevented from availing themselves of these methods of escape.

At length, after praying earnestly to Him, who seeth afar off, for assistance, in my difficulty, suddenly, as if from above, there darted into my mind these words, "Go and get a box, and put yourself in it." I pondered the words over in my mind. "Get a box?" thought I; "what can this mean?" But I was "not disobedient unto the heavenly vision," and I determined to put into practice this direction, as I considered it, from my heavenly Father. I went to the depot, and there noticed the size of the largest boxes, which commonly were sent by the cars, and returned with their dimensions. I then repaired to a carpenter, and induced him to make me a box of such a description as I wished, informing him of the use I intended to make of it. He assured me I could not live in it; but as it was dear liberty I was in pursuit of, I thought it best to make the trial.

When the box was finished, I carried it, and placed it before my friend, who had promised to assist me, who asked me if that was to "put my clothes in"? I replied that it was not, but to "*put Henry Brown in*"! He was astonished at my temerity; but I insisted upon his placing me in it, and nailing me up, and he finally consented.

After corresponding with a friend in Philadelphia, arrangements were made for my departure, and I took my place in this narrow prison, with a mind full of uncertainty as to the result. It was a critical period of my life, I can assure you, reader; but if you have never been deprived of your liberty, as I was, you cannot realize the power of that hope of freedom, which was to me indeed, "an anchor to the soul, both sure and steadfast."

I laid me down in my darkened home of three feet by two, and like one about to be guillotined, resigned myself to my fate. My friend was to accompany me, but he failed to do so; and contented himself with sending a telegraph message to his correspondent in Philadelphia, that such a box was on its way to his care.

I took with me a bladder filled with water to bathe my neck with, in case of too great heat; and with no access to the fresh air, excepting three small gimblet holes, I started on my perilous cruise. I was first carried to the express office, the box being placed on its end, so that I started with my head downwards, although the box was directed, "this side up with care." From the express office, I was carried to the depot, and from thence tumbled roughly into the baggage car, where I *happened* to fall "right side up," but no thanks to my transporters. But after a while the cars stopped, and I was put aboard a steamboat, *and placed on my head.* In this dreadful position, I remained the space of an hour and a half, it seemed to me, when I began to feel of my eyes and head, and found to my dismay, that my eyes were almost swollen out of their sockets, and the veins on my temple seemed ready to burst. I made no noise however, determining to obtain "*victory or death,*" but endured the terrible pain, as well as I could, sustained under the whole by the thoughts of sweet liberty. About half an hour afterwards, I attempted again to lift my hands to my face, but I found I was not able to move them. A cold sweat now covered me from head to foot. Death seemed my inevitable fate, and every moment I expected to feel the blood flowing over me, which had burst from my veins. One half hour longer and my sufferings would have ended in that fate, which I preferred to slavery; but I lifted up my heart to God in prayer, believing that he would yet deliver me, when to my joy, I overheard two men say, "We have been here *two* hours and have travelled twenty miles, now let us sit down, and rest ourselves." They suited the action to the word, and turned the box over, containing my soul and body, thus delivering me from the power of the grim messenger of death, who a few moments previously, had aimed his fatal shaft at my head, and had placed his icy hands on my throbbing heart. One of these men inquired of the other, what he supposed that box contained, to which his comrade replied, that he guessed it was the mail. "Yes," thought I, "it is a *male*, indeed, although not the *mail* of the United States."

Soon after this fortunate event, we arrived at Washington, where I was thrown from the wagon, and again as my luck would have it, fell on my head. I was then rolled down a declivity, until I reached the platform from which the cars were to start. During this short but rapid journey, my neck came very near being dislocated, as I felt it crack, as if it had snapped asunder. Pretty soon, I heard some one say, "there is no room for this box, it will have to remain behind." I then again applied to the Lord, my help in all my difficulties, and in a few minutes I heard a gentleman direct the hands to place it aboard, as "it came with the mail and must go on with it." I was then tumbled into the car, my head downwards again, as I seemed to be destined to escape on my head; a sign probably, of the opinion of American people respecting such bold adventurers as myself; that our heads should be held downwards, whenever we attempt to benefit ourselves. Not the only instance of this propensity, on the part of the American people, towards the colored race. We had not proceeded far, however, before more baggage was placed in the car, at a stopping place, and I was again turned to my proper position. No farther difficulty occurred until my arrival at Philadelphia. I reached this place at three o'clock in the morning, and remained in the depot until six o'clock, A.M., at which time, a waggon drove up, and a person inquired for a box directed to such a place, "right side up." I was soon placed on this waggon, and carried to the house of my friend's correspondent, where quite a number of persons were waiting to receive me. They appeared to be some afraid to open the box at first, but at length one of them rapped upon it, and with a trembling voice, asked, "Is all right within?" to which I replied, "All right." The joy of these friends was excessive, and like the ancient Jews, who repaired to the building of Jerusalem, each one seized hold of some tool, and commenced opening my grave. At length the cover was removed, and I arose, and shook myself from the lethargy into which I had fallen; but exhausted nature proved too much for my frame, and I swooned away.

After my recovery from this fainting fit, the first impulse of my soul, as I looked around, and beheld my friends, and was told that I was safe, was to break out in a song of deliverance, and praise to the most high God, whose arm had been so signally manifest in my escape. Great God, was I a freeman! Had I indeed succeeded in effecting my escape from the human wolves of Slavery? O what extatic joy thrilled through every nerve and fibre of my system! My labor was accomplished, my warfare was ended, and I stood erect before my equal fellow men; no longer a crouching slave, forever at the look and nod of a whimsical and tyrannical slave-owner.

Stearns, *Narrative of Henry Box Brown* (1849),
pp. 47–51, 55–56, 58–63

"Thank God, the Scene Did Not End There": The Saving of a Slave Family (1850s)

In the period prior to the Civil War, Richmond's economy had come to be closely tied to the slave trade. In addition to the large numbers of slaves owned by the city government and by factories and industries, slaves from the outlying regions were usually brought to auction houses in Richmond to be sold when land changed hands,when owners died and their estates were liquidated, or when there simply was a need for ready cash.

Most of the slave trade in Richmond centered in the area between Fourteenth and Fifteenth streets on Franklin. On the north side of the street at that location could be found the business of Pulliam and Betts, which advertised itself as "Auctioneers for the Sale of Negroes." In the same area was Hector Davis, who advertised both the public and private sale of slaves. He further informed his clientele that he had "a safe and commodious jail, where he will board all Negroes intended for his sales at 30 cents per day."

Doubtless there must have been scenes of heartbreak and anguish when friends of many years were parted by the drop of the auctioneer's hammer, or, more painfully, when families were torn asunder, under the approbation of the law of the land.

Given the fact that legal human bondage is of itself inhumane, there nevertheless were many deep and permanent bonds established between whites and blacks, both free and enslaved, in the antebellum era. The following selection, which describes the way Richmond's slave auctions were run and at the same time tells a story in which tragedy was averted, might well have led to one such bond.

A member of one of Richmond's leading families, though originally from Virginia's eastern shore, John Sergeant Wise, author of the following selection, served with distinction in the Civil War and later became a lawyer, politician, and author. An ardent sportsman who fought several duels (q.v.) before helping to stamp out that practice, he was narrowly defeated in his bid for governor in 1885.

. . . The occupations of my father and brother left their visitor to find his own amusements until the evening hour, and he diverted himself at such times by reading or sight-seeing, or in diversions with the children, of whom he was very fond.

One Saturday, thus left alone with me, the subject of "Uncle Tom's Cabin" came up. He asked if I had ever seen a slave sale. "No," said I, all alert, for since I saw the play I had resolved that I would some time see a slave auction; "but I know where they sell them. I saw the sign a few days ago. Let us go and see what it is like." So off we started. Out of the beautiful grounds and past the handsome residences we went, turning down Franklin Street towards the great Exchange Hotel, which was at that time the principal public place of Richmond. Beyond it we passed a church, still used as such, although the locality had been deserted by residences, and stables and little shops surrounded it. As we proceeded, the street became more and more squalid and repulsive, until at last we reached a low brick warehouse, with its end abutting on the street and running far back. Over the place was the sign, with the name of an owner and the words "Auction House" conspicuously painted. At the door hung a red flag, with an advertisement pasted on its side, and up and down the street a mulatto man walked with another flag, ringing a large bell, and shouting, "Oh, yea! Oh, yea! Oh, yea! Walk up, gentlemen. The sale of a fine, likely lot of young niggers is now about to begin." To these he added, in tones which were really merry, and with an expansive smile, that they were "all sorts of niggers, belonging to the estate of the late——, sold for no fault, but to settle the estate;" and that the lot embraced all kinds, "old ones and young ones, men and women, gals and boys."

About the door, and on the inside, a few men were grouped, some in their shirt-sleeves. For the most part, they had the appearance of hostlers. The place itself looked like a livery stable within the building. For a long distance back from the street, there were no side-lights or skylights. In the rear only was it light, where the structure projected beyond those on either side of it, and there the light was ample, and the business in hand was to be transacted.

We moved cautiously through the dark front of the building, and came at last to the rear, where a small platform occupied the centre of the room, and chairs and benches were distributed about the walls.

Another large mulatto man appeared to act as usher, standing near a door, through which from time to time he furnished a fresh supply of slaves for sale. A large man, with full beard, not a bad-looking fellow but for the "ratty" appearance of his quick, cold, small black eyes, acted as auctioneer. A few negroes sat on the bench by the door, they being the first "lot" to be disposed of. The purchasers stood or sat about, smoking or chewing tobacco, while the auctioneer proceeded to read the decree of a chancery court in the settlement of a decedent's estate, under which this sale was made. The lawyers representing different interests were there, as were also the creditors and distributees having interests in the sale. Besides these were ordinary buyers in need of servants, and slave-traders who made a living by buying cheap and selling for a profit. We took seats, and watched and listened intently.

After reading the formal announcement authorizing the sale, the auctioneer became eloquent. He proceeded to explain to his auditors that this was "no ordinary sale of a damaged, no-'count lot of niggers, whar a man buyin' a nigger mout or mout not git what he was lookin' fur, but one of those rar' opperchunities, which cum only once or twice in a lifetime, when the buyer is sho' that fur every dollar he pays he's gittin' a full dollar's wuth of raal genuine nigger, healthy, well-raised, well-mannered, respectful, obejunt, and willin'." "Why," said he, "gentlemen, you kin look over this whole gang of niggers, from the oldest to the youngest, an' you won't find the mark of a whip on one of 'em. Colonel——, for whose estate they is sold, was known to be one of the kindest marsters, and at the same time one of the best bringers-up of niggers, in all Virginia. These here po' devils is sold for no fault whatever, but simply and only because, owin' to the Curnel's sudden death, his estate is left embarrassed, and it is necessary to sell his niggers to pay his debts, and for distributin' some reddy monny amongst numrus 'aars. Of these facts I assure you upon the honor of a gentleman."

Having thus paved the way for good prices, he announced that among the slaves to be offered were good carriage-drivers, gardeners, dining-room servants, farm hands, cooks, milkers, seamstresses, washerwomen, and "the most promisin', growin', sleek, and sassy lot of young niggers he had ever had the pleasure of offerin'."

The sale was begun with some "bucks," as he facetiously called them. They were young, unmarried fellows from eighteen to twenty-five. Ordered to mount the auction-block, they stripped to the waist and bounced up, rather amused than otherwise, grinning at the lively bidding they excited. Cautious bidders drew near to them, examined their eyes, spoke with them to test their hearing and manners, made them open their mouths and show their teeth, ran their hands over the muscles of their backs and arms, caused them to draw up their trousers to display their legs, and, after fully satisfying themselves on these and other points, bid for them what they saw fit. Whenever a sale was concluded, the successful bidder was announced, and the announcement was greeted by the darkeys themselves with broad grins, and such expressions as "Thank Gord," or "Bless de Lord," if it went as they wished, or in uncomplaining silence if otherwise. It was surprising to see how thoroughly they all seemed to be informed concerning the men who were bidding for them.

The scenes accompanying the sales of young women were very similar to those with the young men, except that what was said to them and about them was astonishingly plain and shocking. One was recommended as a "rattlin' good breeder," because she had already given birth to two children at seventeen years of age. Another, a mulatto of very comely form, showed deep embarrassment when questioned about her condition.

They brought good prices. "Niggers is high" was the general comment. Who bought them, where they went, whether they were separated from father, mother, brother, or sister, God knows. Let us hope the result was as humane as possible.

"I am now goin' to offer you a very likely young chile-barin' woman," said the auctioneer. "She is puffectly helthy, and without a blemish. Among the family, she is a universal favorite. I offer her with the privilidge of takin' her husban' and two chillen with her at a very rejuced price, because it is the wish of all concerned to keep 'em together, if possible. Get up here, Martha Ann." A large-framed, warm, comfortable-looking, motherly soul, with a fine, honest face, mounted the block. "Now, gentlemen," said he, continuing, "ef you'll cast yo' eyes into that corner, you will see Israel, Martha Ann's husband, and Cephas and Melindy, her two children. Israel is not what you may call a raal able-bodied man. He broke his leg some years ago handlin' one of the Curnel's colts, and he ain't able to do heavy work; but I am asshoed by everybody on the place that Israel is a most valuable servant about a house for all kind of light work, and he can be had mighty cheap."

"Yes, sir," spoke up Israel eagerly, "I kin do as much ez ennybody; and, marsters, ef you'll only buy me and de chillun with Martha Ann, Gord knows I'll wuk myself to deth fur you."

The poor little darkeys, Cephas and Melinda, sat there frightened and silent, their white eyes dancing like monkey-eyes, and gleaming in the shadows. As her husband's voice broke on her ear, Martha Ann, who had been looking sadly out of the window in a pose of quiet dignity, turned her face with an expression of exquisite love and gratitude towards Israel. She gazed for a moment at her husband and at her children, and then looked away once more, her eyes brimming with tears.

"How much am I offered for Martha Ann with the privilidge?" shouted the auctioneer. The bidding began. It was very sluggish. The hammer fell at last. The price was low. Perhaps, even in that crowd, nobody wanted them all, and few were willing to do the heartless act of taking her alone. So she sold low. When the name of her purchaser was announced, I knew him. He was an odd, wizened, cheerless old fellow, who was a member of the Virginia legislature from one of the far-away southside counties adjoining North Carolina. Heaven be praised, he was not a supporter of father, but called himself an Old-line Whig, and ranked with the opposition. He seemed to have no associates among the members, and nobody knew where he lived in the city. He was notoriously penurious, and drew his pay as regularly as the week rolled around.

"Mr. —— buys Martha Ann," said the auctioneer. "I congratulate you, Mr. ——. You've bought the cheapes' nigger sold here to-day. Will you take Israel and the young uns with her?"

Deep silence fell upon the gathering. Even imperturbable Martha Ann showed her anxiety by the heaving of her bosom. Israel strained forward, where he sat, to hear the first word of hope or of despair. The old man who had bid for her shuffled forward, fumbling in his pockets for his money, delaying his reply so long that the question was repeated. "No—o," drawled he at last; "no—o, I'm sorry for 'em, but I railly can't. You see, I live a long way from here, and I ride down to the legislatur', and, when I get here, I sell my horse and live cheap, and aims to save up enough from my salary to buy another horse and a 'chile-barin' woman' when the session's done; and then I takes her home, ridin' behind me on the horse. Thar ain't no way I could provide for gittin' the man and the young uns home, even if they was given to me. I think I'm doin' pretty well to save enough in a session to buy one nigger, much less a whole fambly." And the old beast looked up over his spectacles as he counted his money, and actually chuckled, as if he expected a round of applause for his clever business ability.

A deep groan, unaccompanied by any word of complaint, came from the dark corner where Israel sat. Martha Ann stepped down from the platform, walked to where he was, the tears streaming down her cheeks, and there, hugging her children and rocking herself back and forth, she sobbed as if her heart was breaking.

My companion and I looked at each other in disgust, but neither spoke a word. I was ready to burst into tears. The old creature who had bought the woman lugged out his hoarded money in sundry packages of coin and paper, and, as he counted it, said, "Martha Ann, cheer up; you'll find me a good marster, and I'll get you a new husband." He might well have added, "and the more children you have, the better I'll like you."

Thank God, the scene did not end there. The silence was oppressive. The veriest savage on earth could not have witnessed it without being moved. "Let us go away," I whispered. At last the suspense was broken. A handsome, manly fellow, one of the lawyers in the case, exlaimed, "By ——! I can't stand this. I knew Colonel —— well. I know how he felt towards Israel and Martha Ann and their children. This is enough to make him turn in his grave. I am unable to make this purchase; but sooner than see them separated, I'll bankrupt myself. Mr. ——, I will take Martha Ann off your hands, so as to buy her husband and children, and keep them together."

"Well, now, you see," drawled the old fellow, pausing in his work, with trembling hand, "if you feel that way, the time to speak was when the gal was up for sale." His eye glittered with the thought of turning the situation to advantage. "You see she's mine now, and I consider her a very desirable and very cheap purchase. Moreover, if you want her, I think you ought to be willin' to pay me something for the time and trouble I've wasted here a-tryin' to git her."

The proposition was sickening. But the old creature was so small himself that his demand of profit was likewise small, and the matter was soon arranged. Whether he remained and bought another "chile-barin'" woman is unknown; for, sick at heart at the sights we had witnessed, we withdrew, and walked slowly back in the glorious sunlight, past the neighboring church, and up to the happy abodes of Virginia's best civilization, little inclined to talk of the nightmare we had been through. From that hour, the views of both of us concerning slavery were materially modified. Throughout the day, the horrors we had witnessed came back and back again to me; and, recuperative as I was, I was very, very unhappy.

Wise, *The End of an Era* (1899; 1965), pp. 80–87

"Delighted Beyond All Bounds with the Grand Work of Art": Washington's Monument (1858)

A snowstorm notwithstanding, the citizens of Richmond gathered on Capitol Square at noon on 22 February 1858 for a long-awaited ceremony. After Masonic rites and a series of orations, Thomas Crawford's equestrian statue of George Washington was unveiled "amidst the inspiriting shouts of the admiring multitude mingled with martial music and the boom of cannon." Town fathers had originally planned for a monument large enough to house the last remains of the Washingtons—and indeed the visitor today can see the iron-gated opening to the crypt in the base of the statue. The family disagreed, however, and the caskets remain at Mount Vernon. Despite this setback, the project continued, and the cornerstone was laid on 22 February 1850 in the company of President Zachary Taylor, former President John Tyler, and a crowd of ten thousand.

Crawford's imposing work was not the only reminder in 1858 that Richmonders were also Americans. That same year saw a national agricultural exposition in what was then the state fair grounds (now Monroe Park and environs) and the reinterment of James Monroe in Hollywood Cemetery, the body having been transported from New York by a militia honor guard from that state. Few in the city would have predicted that only three years away was a southern, not an American future. The symbols of 1858 remained, ironically, as Washington's statue embellished the great seal of the Confederacy, the fairgrounds became a military training camp, and Monroe in time would be joined in Hollywood by the bodies of over eighteen thousand Confederate dead.

§ The Twenty-Second in Richmond

The twenty-second of February, so eagerly expected by the tens of thousands of persons who were present in Richmond on Monday to witness the ceremonies, and participate in the pageantry of the day, dawned upon us drearily. The sky was overcast with leaden clouds; not a ray of sunshine smiled through the fast falling flakes of a most dispiriting snow storm. Nevertheless, the great day had commenced; a half a dozen brass guns on the Capitol Square announced its advent.

At the appointed hour the procession moved through the streets in imposing array, presenting a spectacle varied, beautiful and grand.

An immense assemblage of citizens and soldiers soon congregated on the Capitol Square, and between twelve and one o'clock the ceremonies at the Monument began. The Masonic forms and rites concluded, and an impressive prayer offered up, an oration replete with eloquence and pathos was delivered on the part of the Masons, by Ro. G. Scott, Esq. Governor Wise then arose, amid spontaneous plaudits of the multitude, that told the sincerity and enthusiasm of the hearts from which they came. His address, which we publish today, is characteristic of its author—fervid in eloquence and in patriotism, strong, sententious and suggestive in thought. At the conclusion of the Governor's remarks, Jno. R. Thompson, Esq., was introduced, and the initial ode, which, we regret, is unavoidably excluded from our columns to day, was pronounced, and received with marked evidences of enthusiastic admiration.—Senator Hunter, the orator of the day, was then presented to the audience. And in an oration appropriate, eloquent, interesting and instructive, he reflected credit upon himself and on the State which was honored in honoring him.—James Barron Hope, Esq., then delivered the terminal ode, which was *worthy the occasion.* This is saying much. It would indeed be impossible to say more, for, in the whole history of Virginia, there is not now, and perhaps there will never be recorded the incidents of a day demanding loftier thoughts or more heroic poetry than the twenty-second of February, 1858. Mr. Hope having concluded, the equestrian statue was unveiled amidst the inspiriting shouts of the admiring multitude mingled with martial music and the boom of cannon.

It was indeed a scene to be witnessed once and never forgotten. Notwithstanding the snow storm, there were hundreds of ladies on the ground. The windows of the capitol were filled; and on balcony or housetop or wherever a view could be obtained, there were spectators to be seen. At six o'clock there was a sumptuous dinner served up in the new post office, where interesting addresses were delivered by several of the distinguished guests. At night a splendid ball at the Ballard House, and a brilliant illumination, which extended throughout the city, closed the joyous festivities and patriotic offerings of perhaps the greatest day our city shall ever see.

We lay before our readers Senator Hunter's address and feel assured that it will be universally admired. To-morrow, we will publish Mr. Thompson's ode which we have no doubt will be read with as much interest as it was heard. It is a production of which he may well be proud.

§ The Inauguration

The procession arrived on Capitol Square about 12 o'clock. After some difficulty in getting the stand cleared the ceremonies commenced.

A prayer was offered by the Rev. Francis J. Boggs, Chaplain of the Grand Lodge of the State of Virginia. Then followed the return of Implements to the Grand Master by the Architect, and the Most Worthy Grand Master's reply. Then the public grand honors, and the Ode by the Masonic Fraternity.

A gun was here fired, and then followed the following admirable address of Robert G. Scott, Esq., Grand Past Master of Masons in Virginia. . . .

The cannon, in thundering tones, announced the wished for event, and the

STATUE WAS UNVEILED.

The air was rent with the cheers of the multitude, who were delighted beyond all bounds with the grand work of art. There was Crawford's Equestrian Group, and there was the throng offering its homage to the glorious conception of a mind now stilled in death. It was indeed a most enthusiastic demonstration, and long will it linger in the memories of those who witnessed the pageant and the attendant ceremonies.

Richmond *Enquirer*, 24 February 1858

"An Ordinance Concerning Negroes": The Richmond Black Code (1859)

The census of 1860 accorded Richmond a population of almost thirty-eight thousand—making the city the South's third largest, after New Orleans and Charleston, respectively. Over a third of the inhabitants of 1860 were black: 11,699 were listed as slaves, and 2,576 as free persons of color. The latter category is even today little recognized or understood. In point of fact, the free black community dated from the earliest origins of the town, and through the years it had developed rich traditions, institutions, and values. One thinks of great churches and of such organizations as the Burying Ground Society of the Free People of Color of the City of Richmond (ca.

1815). Numerous free blacks owned property, some virtually monopolized certain trades, and many resided in what is now Jackson Ward. They were free, yet not free, and they suffered from a panoply of legal restrictions and modes of racial discrimination, as is manifestly apparent in the following City Ordinances.

§ An Ordinance concerning Negroes

1. Who are deemed negroes.
2. Slave absent from home, how punished.
3. What pass to designate, who to give it, when to be endorsed.
4. When fine may be instead of stripes.
5. Persons signing or endorsing pass without authority, how punished.
6. When slave not to ride in hack or carriage.
7. What places slaves not to walk in.
8. Where slaves not to smoke.
9. Negro not to keep a cook-shop or eating house.
10. Negro not to carry a cane at night.
11. Negroes standing or passing on sidewalks.
12. Not to organize secret societies or attend them.
13. Slave not to rent room or house.
14. Slave not to hire himself out or board himself. Owner or hirer to provide him with board, and give list of slaves boarded to mayor.
15. Free negro not to permit slave to remain on his lot.
16. Not to sell ardent spirits to slaves.
17. Free negroes to have copy of register.
18. Not to be employed without copy of register.
19. Slave not to be hired without consent of master.
20. Negro to be punished for provoking language, gestures, or indecent exposure.
21. White person not to give or sell weapons to negro. Negro not to keep them.
22. Not to sell medicine to slave. Slave or free negro not to administer medicine.
23. Negro engaging in riot, &c., or committing a trespass, how punished.
24. What an unlawful assembly of negroes about churches.
25. What an unlawful assembly of negroes upon lot.
26. How negroes in such assembly arrested and punished. Person allowing such assembly fined.
27. Persons beating slaves, how punished.

1. *Be it ordained by the council of the city of Richmond,* That in this ordinance, and in any future ordinance of this city, the word "negro" shall be construed to mean mulatto as well as negro.

2. If two hours after sunset of any day a slave be found in this city absent from his owner's or employer's tenement without such pass in writing as is herein after mentioned, he may be punished with stripes.

3. The pass shall designate the particular place or places to which, or the purpose for which the slave may go, and if it designate more than one, it shall be good only for a single night; but if it designate a single house to which the slave may go before 11 o'clock at night, it may be given for any time not exceeding one month, provided the assent of the occupier of such house, to the slave's staying there, be signified by his signing his name on the back of the pass; and if during the continuance of such pass for one month the slave be detained by his owner or employer after 11 o'clock at night, there must be a special pass stating that fact.

4. Whenever under the preceding sections a slave is punishable, the justice before whom the offence is tried may, in his discretion, commute the punishment of stripes on the payment instanter of a fine not exceeding five dollars.

5. When a slave absent at night from his owner's or employer's tenement has a writing designed to show that his absence is by the permission of his owner or employer, if such writing be signed by any other person than his owner or employer, or a member of his family, or by some other person authorized by the owner or employer to sign the same; or when a writing designates a house to which a slave may go at night for one month, if the name on the back of such writing be signed by any other person than the occupant of such house, or a member of his family, the *person* signing such writing, or signing such name on the back of such writing, if white, may for every such offence be fined not exceeding twenty dollars; and if a free negro, shall be punished with stripes, and the slave may also be punished with stripes.

6. If a slave shall ride in a licensed hack or carriage without the written consent of his owner or employer, or some white member of his family, or the guardian or committee of the owner of such slave, the owner or keeper of such hack or carriage, if a white person, shall be fined not less than five nor more than twenty dollars; and if a negro, punished by stripes, at the discretion of the justice who may try him for the offence, not exceeding thirty-nine at any one time.

7. No negro shall walk or be in the Capitol Square, or in the grounds adjacent to the City Spring or City Hall, or be thereupon, or be within

the enclosure of any of the places known as city grounds, unless to attend a white person, being an infant, or sick, or infirm, or to serve their owner or employer; nor shall a negro walk or be within the walls of any public burying ground for white persons, unless to attend the funeral of his owner or employer, or of some of his family, or to serve his owner or employer, or by permission of the keeper thereof.

8. No negro shall smoke tobacco in any place mentioned in the preceding section, or in any public street or other public place.

9. No negro shall keep a cook shop or eating house, unless he be licensed to keep an ordinary or house of entertainment.

10. No negro shall in the night time carry a cane, unless because of his age or infirmity, or for his owner or employer.

11. Not more than five negroes shall at any one time stand together on a side-walk at or near the corner of a street or public alley. And negroes shall not at any time stand on a side-walk to the inconvenience of persons passing by. A negro meeting or overtaking, or being overtaken by a white person on a side-walk, shall pass on the outside; and if it be necessary to enable such white person to pass, shall immediately get off the side-walk. Any negro violating this or either of the three preceding sections, may be punished with stripes.

12. If any negro shall organize, or attempt to organize, or form any secret society of negroes, for any purpose whatsoever, or shall attend or be present at any such society, he shall be punished by stripes, not exceeding thirty-nine at any one time.

13. If any free person rent or hire a house, lot or tenement, or any part thereof to a slave, for any purpose whatever, he shall, if a white person, be fined not less than five, nor more than ten dollars for every day that the same shall be held or occupied by such slave; and if he be a free negro, may be punished by stripes, not exceeding thirty-nine for every day such house shall be occupied or held, or fined as a white person committing the like offence, at the discretion of the justice trying the offence.

14. The owner, hirer or other employer of a slave in the city of Richmond, shall not permit such slave to hire himself out, or receive the price of his hire, nor shall he permit such slave to engage or pay for his own board or to board himself; nor shall he give to such slave money or food in place of his board. But it shall be the duty of every owner, hirer or other employer of a slave in the city of Richmond, to provide food and lodging for such slaves upon his own premises, or by engaging board and lodging for them with some free person, and paying the price thereof to such person, except when the slave has a wife living in the city, and he stays with her at the house of her master.

And it shall be the duty of the owners, hirers, or other employers of slaves in the city of Richmond, having slaves which are not fed and lodged by themselves on their own premises, to make out a list of slaves boarded out by him and the place where each one is boarded, and deliver the said list to the mayor of the city; and as often as he buys, hires or employs another slave, or as often as one of the slaves changes his boarding house, he shall within one week inform the mayor of the fact, and state the place where such slave is boarded. And if the said owners, hirers, or other employers of slaves in the city of Richmond shall do any act herein forbid, or shall fail for one week to do what he is herein required to do, he shall for each week pay a fine of not less than five nor more than twenty dollars.

15. If any free negro shall knowingly suffer or permit any slave to be and remain upon his lot or tenement, or upon any lot or tenement held or occupied by him more than one hour in the day time, or for any time at night, without the consent in writing of the owner or employer of such slave, he shall be punished by stripes, not exceeding thirty-nine.

16. If any person shall sell by retail to a slave ardent spirits, or a mixture thereof, or any wine to be drunk at the place where sold, he shall be fined not less than five nor more than twenty dollars. If any free negro shall commit the like offence, he shall be fined in like manner, or be punished by stripes in the discretion of the justice trying the offence.

17. If any free negro above the age of twenty-one years, resident in this city, shall be found going at large without an attested copy of his register, as is required by law, he may be punished by stripes, not exceeding thirty-nine, or may be fined not exceeding ten dollars, at the discretion of the justice trying the offence. And all free negroes coming into the city from any county or corporation within the State, and who shall habitually remain in the city more than two months without being registered in the hustings court of said city, and obtaining an attested copy of such register, shall be considered, treated and punished as resident free negroes going at large without a register.

18. If any free person shall employ any such free negro as is mentioned in the preceding section, he shall be fined five dollars for every day that he shall so employ such free negro.

19. If any white person shall, without the written consent of his master or owner, employ a slave, he shall be fined not less than five nor more than twenty dollars. And if any free negro commit the like offence, he shall, in the discretion of the justice trying the offence, pay the like fine, or be punished by stripes not exceeding thirty-nine.

20. If any negro use provoking language, or use or make insolent or menacing gestures to a white person, or speak aloud any blasphemous or indecent word, or make any loud or offensive noise by conversation or otherwise, in any street or other public place, or shall indecently expose his person, or any part thereof, to public view in this city, he shall, if a slave, be punished by stripes, or if a free negro, either by stripes, or be fined not less than one nor more than twenty dollars, at the discretion of the justice trying the offence.

21. If any person shall give, lend to, or in any other manner furnish a negro (bond or free) with any firearms, sword, bowie-knife, or any offensive weapon of any kind whatever, or any balls, shot, gunpowder or other ammunition, he shall be fined twenty dollars for each and every article so sold, given, lent, or otherwise furnished. And if any negro shall keep, or carry any such firearm, or other article or thing in this section before mentioned, he shall be punished by stripes, not exceeding thirty-nine at any one time.

22. If any person shall sell or furnish any medicine or drug to a slave, he shall be fined not exceeding ten dollars; but this section shall not prohibit any person from furnishing medicine to a slave, upon the written order or direction of the owner or employer of such slave, specifying the kind and quantity of the medicine or drug to be so furnished; nor to prevent the furnishing to a slave any medicine or drug upon the order or prescription of any doctor of medicine. And if any slave shall prepare or administer, or attempt to administer any medicine or drug to any person whomsoever—except a slave administering medicine by his master's order, in his family, or to some other person at his master's residence, by his master's consent—he shall be punished by stripes not exceeding thirty-nine. And no free negro shall prepare or administer any medicine or drug to any person other than a free negro; and any free negro offending against this provision shall be punished by stripes, not exceeding thirty-nine.

23. If any negro in this city engage or take part in any riot, rout, or affray; or commit any wilful trespass upon the person or property of any free person, or upon the person of any slave, he shall be punished by stripes, not exceeding thirty-nine at any one time.

24. Whenever five or more negroes shall assemble together on any foot-walk in front of, or immediately adjoining any church or other house dedicated to religious worship, or shall loiter upon the said sidewalk, or shall remain in or loiter about any such church or other house of religious worship, thirty minutes after divine service therein for the morning or afternoon of that day shall have concluded, the said negroes so assembled, and being together upon such sidewalk, or

loitering in or about the said church or house, shall constitute an unlawful assembly of negroes, and any negro found thereat may be punished by stripes, not exceeding fifteen.

25. Whenever any free person shall in this city permit to be at any one time on his lot or tenement more than five negroes, other than those belonging to or hired by him, such assembly—whether the negroes be free or not—shall be an unlawful assembly of negroes.

26. Any officer of police or night watchman may enter the place of such unlawful assembly, as is mentioned in the two preceding sections, and seize such negroes; and such negroes may, by order of a justice, be punished by stripes. There shall, moreover, be imposed a fine of not less than five, nor more than twenty dollars, upon the person permitting such unlawful assembly on his lot.

27. If any person shall unlawfully assault and beat a slave, he may —if a white person—be fined not less than one, nor more than twenty dollars; and if a free negro, he may be so fined or punished by stripes, at the discretion of the justice.

§ Slaves Hired in the City.
An Ordinance Providing for an Account of Slaves Hired in the City of Richmond, and of the Persons to Whom They Are Hired

1. Hirers of slaves to return list to the mayor, and to whom hired.
2. The list *prima facie* evidence of the hiring.
3. Lists delivered to the chamberlain at end of each year.

1. *Be it ordained by the council of the city of Richmond,* That every person or firm who or which has hired out, or shall hire out, slaves for the year, or any part thereof, to persons doing work in or dwelling in the city of Richmond, shall, on the 30th day of January of each year, deliver to the mayor of the city a list signed by himself or one member of the firm, containing the name of each slave hired out by him or them prior to that time, and the name of the person or firm hiring such slave. And such person or firm shall, on every fourteenth day, commencing from said 30th day of January, until the 15th day of March in each year, deliver to the said mayor a like list, signed as aforesaid, containing the names of all the slaves hired out by him or them, and to whom hired, not embraced in the preceding lists. And if any person or firm hiring out slaves as aforesaid, shall fail to deliver

such lists, so signed as aforesaid, he or they so failing shall be fined not less than ten nor more than twenty dollars. And each day (except Sunday) on which he or they shall fail to deliver the said lists to the mayor, shall constitute a distinct offence, and subject him or them to the fine aforesaid.

2. The lists so returned to the Mayor shall be *prima facie* evidence of the hiring of the slaves mentioned therein, and of the persons to whom they are hired, in all proceedings under the ordinance entitled an ordinance concerning negroes.

3. The lists delivered to the mayor shall be preserved by him; and at the end of the year, if no proceeding is then pending in which they may be necessary to be used, or as soon as such necessity shall cease, he shall deliver said lists to the chamberlain, who shall preserve the same.

[Richmond Black Code], *Charters and Ordinances* (1859),
pp. 193–201

"The City Was Thoroughly Jammed":
The Civil War Approaches (1861)

From a prominent South Carolina family, Thomas Cooper DeLeon (1839–1914) could claim a unique perspective on the Civil War era. At the outset of 1861, he was a government clerk in Washington, but his southern sympathies carried him to Montgomery, the first capital of the Confederacy, and then to Richmond. Well educated, "incredibly tireless and versatile," and armed with a facile and lively pen, DeLeon spent his postwar career largely in journalism and wrote two important books replete with firsthand impressions of the people and events of the period 1861–65. The selection below provides a vivid tour of the physical landmarks and environs of Richmond in the spring of 1861 and gives a sense of the problems confronting a city that suddenly found itself the capital of a new nation soon to be at war.

Passing out of the cut through the high bluff, just across the "Jeems" river bridge, Richmond burst beautifully into view; spreading panorama-like over her swelling hills, with the evening sun gilding simple houses and towering spires alike into a glory. The city follows the curve of the river, seated on amphitheatric hills, retreating from its banks; fringes of dense woods shading their slopes, or making blue background against the sky. No city of the South has grander or more picturesque approach; and now—as the slant rays of the sun kissed her a loving good-night—nothing in the view hinted of war to come, but all of holy peace.

Just here the James narrows its bed between high banks, and for some three miles—from Hollywood cemetery down to "Rockett's" landing—the shallow current dashes over its rocky bed with the force and chafe of a mountain torrent; now swirling, churned into foamy rapids, again gliding swiftly smooth around larger patches of islands that dot its surface. On the right-hand hills, behind us, rises the sub-urb village of Manchester, already of considerable importance as a milling town; and the whole *coup d'oeil*—from the shining heights of Chimborazo to the green slopes of the city of the silent, the grim, gray old capitol as a centerpiece—makes a Claud landscape that admits no thought of the bloody future!

The railroad bridge—then a frail, giddy structure, wide enough for a track and footway—spans near a mile across the boiling current. From the car-platform, the treetops far below and the rugged, foam-crowned rocks look inhospitably distant. I have whirled round the high trestles on the Baltimore & Ohio when the work swayed and rattled under the heavy train, threatening each moment to hurl us down the precipitous mountain into the black, rocky bed of the Cheat, hundreds of feet below; have dashed at speed round steep grades hewn in the solid rock, where the sharp, jagged peaks rose a thousand feet beneath us; and I have raced in pitchy nights on the western rivers in tinder-box boats, that seemed shaking to pieces away from their red-hot furnaces; but I do not recall any piece of travel that gave the same sense of the instability of railroad affairs as that James river bridge.

The city was thoroughly jammed—its ordinary population of forty thousand swelled to three times that number by the sudden pressure. Of course, all the Government, with its thousand employees, had come on; and in addition, all the loose population along the railroad over which it had passed seemed to have clung to and been rolled into Richmond with it. Not only did this mania seize the wealthier and well-to-do classes, but the queerest costumes of the inland corners of Georgia and Tennessee disported themselves with perfect composure at hotels and on the streets. Besides, from ten to fifteen thousand troops were always collected, as a general rendezvous, before assignment to one of the important points—Norfolk, the Peninsula, or the Potomac lines. Although these were in camp out of town, their officers and men thronged the streets from daylight to dark, on business or pleasure bent; and the variety of uniforms—from the butternut of the Georgia private to the three stars of the flash colonel—broke the monotony of the streets pleasingly to the eye.

Hotel accommodations in Richmond were always small and plain, and now they were all overflowing. The Spotswood, Exchange and American held beds at a high premium in the parlors, halls and even on the billiard-tables. All the lesser houses were equally packed, and crowds of guests stood hungrily round the dining-room doors at meal-times, watching and scrambling for vacated seats. It was a clear case of "devil take the hindmost," for their *cuisine* decreased in quantity and quality in exact ratio to augmentation of their custom. The Richmond hotels, always mediocre, were now wretched. Such a thing as a clean room, a hot steak, or an answered bell were not to be bought by fla-grant bribery. I would fain believe that all concerned did their best; but rapid influx absolutely overwhelmed them; and resources of the neighboring country—ample to support one-third the numbers now collected—were quickly exhausted under suddenly tripled demand. No transportation for private supplies was available in the overtaxed condition of the railroads; so the strangers, perforce, had to "grin and bear it," dry soever as the grin might be. Private boarding-houses sprang up like mushrooms on every block; bereaved relicts and ambi-tious spinsterhood equally clutching the chance to turn an honest penny. And naturally, ordinary trials of boarding-house life were ag-gravated by circumstance. Discomfort of the hotels was great enough; but, dessicated into the boarding-house can, it became simply un-endurable. In this strait many private families were induced to open their doors to the better class of strangers; and gradually the whole dense population settled down, wedged into comparative quiet. Hap-pily, my lines fell in these pleasanter places; and, whatever the un-avoidable trials, it were base ingratitude in an experimental pilgrim among the mail-bags to indite a new Jeremiad thereon.

Suites of rooms had been reserved at the Spotswood hotel for the President and some of his Cabinet; so that house naturally became headquarters. Mr. Davis' office, the "Cabinet-room" with the State and Treasury Departments were located in the custom-house; and the other bureaux of the Government were relegated to the "Mechanics' Institute," an ungainly pile of bricks, formerly used as library and lecture-rooms.

The State of Virginia, though not at all on pleasure bent in inviting the Government to her capital, had yet been of frugal enough mind not to commence preparations in advance of acceptance; and the hejira followed so swiftly upon it that we plumped down into their very midst. Miss Bremer—who declared Alexandria entirely finished because she never heard the sound of a hammer—would have been more than amused at Richmond. The great halls of the Institute were cutting up into offices, with deafening clatter, day and night; and one of the Cabinet secretaries—who did not exhibit, if indeed he possessed, that aspiration ascribed to the devil when ill—swore himself almost to a shadow.

Both these public offices faced upon Capitol Square; a large, iron-fenced space, beautifully undulating and with walks winding under grand old trees. On the central hill stood the old State Capitol, picturesque from the river, but grimly dirty on close inspection. It is a plain, quadrangular construction, with Grecian pediment and columns on its south front and broad flights of steps leading to its side porticoes. Below were the halls of the legislature, now turned over to the Confederate States Congress; and in the small rotunda connecting them stood Houdon's celebrated statue of Washington—a simple but majestic figure in marble, ordered by Dr. Franklin from the French sculptor in 1785—of which Virginians are justly proud. In the cool, vaulted basement were the State officials; and above the halls the offices of the governor and the State library. That collection, while lacking many modern works, held some rare and valuable editions. It was presided over by the gentlest and most courteous *Littèrateur* of the South. . . .

From the roof of the Capitol is had the finest view of Richmond, the surrounding country lying like a map for a radius of twenty miles. Only from this bird's-eye view can a perfect idea be gained of the elevation of the city, perched above a rolling country—its stretches of meadowland below cut by the valley of the James; the river stealing in sluggish, molten silver through it, or heaving up inland into bold, tree-bearded hills, high enough to take the light from the clouds on their tops, as a halo. Far northward alternate swells of light and depressions of shadow among the hills; the far-off horizon making a girdle of purple light, blended into the blue of undefined woods. On clear days, a splendid ozone fills the air at that high perch, the picture having, as far as the eye can travel, stereoscopic clearness.

Immediately beneath lies the Square; its winding walks, rare old trees and rich sweep of sod filled with children, so full of enjoyment that one is half-minded to drop down and roll over the grass with them. On the central walk, midway between the Capitol and St. Paul's church, stands Crawford's equestrian Washington in bronze, resting upon a circular-base and pedestal of plain granite, in which are bases for statues of the mighty Virginians of the past. Only the three southern ones were now occupied; but those figures—Jefferson, Mason and Henry—were accepted as surpassing in merit the central work. The Washington is imposing in size and position, but its art is open to criticism. The horse is exaggeration of pose and muscle; being equally strained, though not rampant, as that inopportune charger on which Clark Mills perched General Jackson, at the national Capital. Nor is this "first in peace" by any means "the first" on horseback; the figure being theatric rather than dignified, and the extended arm more gymnastic than statuesque.

An irate senator once told the august body he addressed that it was a warning to them—"pointing straight to the penitentiary!" So, as a whole, the group, if not thoroughly classic, may be admirably useful.

From Capitol Square, open, wide streets—neatly built up and meeting each other at right angles—stretch away on all sides; an occasional spire or dome, and frequent houses larger than the rest, breaking the monotony. Below, toward the river, lie the basins, docks and rows of warehouses; and further still is the landing, "Rockett's," the head of river navigation, above which no vessels of any size can come. Just under the Capitol—to the East—stands the governor's house, a plain, substantial mansion of the olden time, embosomed in trees and flower-beds. Further off, in the same line, rise the red and ragged slopes of Church Hill. It takes its name from the old church in which Patrick Henry made his celebrated speech—a structure still in pretty good preservation. And still further away—opposite the vanishing point of the water view—are seen the green tops of Chimborazo Heights and Howard's Grove—hospital sites, whose names have been graven upon the hearts of all southern people by the mordant of sorrow!

Just across the river, to the South, the white and scattered village of Manchester is prettily relieved against the green slopes on which it sits. There the bridge cuts the shining chafe of the river like a black wire; and just under it, the wind sighs softly in the treetops of Belle Isle, afterward to become so famous in the newspaper annals of the North, as a prison for the Union soldiers captured in the long struggle for the city.

Far to the west, higher shafts of Hollywood Cemetery gleam among the trees; and the rapids, dancing down in the sunlight, break away into a broader sheet of foam around its point. Except, perhaps, "Bonnie Venture" (*Buona Ventura*), at Savannah, there is no site for a cemetery in the South, naturally so picturesque and at the same time solemn, as this. Rising from comparatively level ground in the rear, it swells and undulates in a series of gentle hills to the river, that embraces it on three sides. Rows of magnificent old trees in many places arch quite across the walk—giving, even at midday, a half-twilight —and the sigh of the river breeze in their tops, mingling with the constant roar of the rapids, seems to sing a *Te Deum* for the dead. The graves are simple and unpretending—only an occasional column of any prominence rearing itself above the humbler surroundings.

On a hill—just behind the point where the river curves round the extreme point—rest the ashes of Monroe, enclosed in a large and ornate mausoleum, where they were laid when escorted south by the New York Seventh Regiment. That escort was treated with all the generous hospitality Virginia can so well use; and numerous and deep were the oaths of amity between the citizen-soldiers. Though the Seventh were not notoriously deadly, in the war that followed, only the shortest of memories—or, indeed, the most glowing of patriotism —could have erased the brother-love, then and there bumpered down!

Under the hills of the cemetery—the dirty, dull canal creeping between them—stand the buildings, dam and powerful pumps of the water service; ordinarily more than adequate for all uses. Usually, the water was pure and clear; but when heavy rains washed the river lands, the "noble Jeems" rushed by with an unsavory and dingy current, that might have shamed the yellow Tiber and rivaled the Nile itself. Sometimes the weary and worn patriot took his whisky and mud, thick enough to demand a fork; and for days

> The water is muddy and dank
> As ever a company pumped.

The outskirts of Richmond are belted by bold crests, near enough together to form a chain of natural forts. These were now fortifying; the son of wealth, the son of Erin and the son of Ham laboring in perspiration and in peace side by side. Later these forts did good turn, during cavalry raids, when the city was uncovered and the garrison but nominal.

Gamble's hill, a pretty but steep slope, cuts the river west of the bridge. Rising above its curves, from the Capitol view-point, are the slate-roofed Tredegar Works; their tall chimneys puffing endless black smoke against the sunshine, which reflects it, a livid green, upon the white foam of the rapids. So potent a factor in the aggressive power of the Confederacy was this foundry that it overtopped the regular government agencies. When the war began, this was the only rolling-mill of great capacity, of which the South could boast; the only one, indeed, capable of casting heavy guns. Almost the first decisive act of Virginia was to prevent, by seizure, the delivery to United States officers of some guns cast for them by the Tredegar Works; and, from that day, there were no more earnest and energetic workers for the cause of southern independence than the firm of Jos. R. Anderson & Co. It was said, at this time, that the firm was in financial straits. But it thrived so well on government patronage—spite of sundry boards to consider if army and navy work was not paid for at ruinously low rates —that it greatly increased in size; added to its utility by importations of costly machinery, through the blockade; stood loss of one-third of its buildings, by fire; used a ship of its own for importation; and, at the close of the struggle, was in better condition than at the commencement. The senior partner was, for a time, in the field at head of his brigade; but affairs were so well managed, in the interval, by the Messrs. Tanner—father and son, who were partners with General Anderson—that his absence was not appreciable in the work.

DeLeon, *Four Years in Rebel Capitals* (1890), pp. 85–91

"During the Night Began the Ghastly Procession of Wounded Brought in from the Field": The Ravages of War (1862–1865)

The "gala days" of early 1861 soon passed, and the grim realities came to the fore, as well described for the duration of the war by the lucid pen of Constance Cary Harrison (1843–1920). Forced to flee her home near Arlington in 1861, young Constance Cary took refuge in Richmond, where she became a stalwart Confederate—along with her famous cousins Hetty and Jennie—and soon gained a reputation "for her wit and beauty and for her performances in amateur theatricals." After the war she married Burton N. Harrison, a Yale graduate who had served as President Jefferson Davis's personal secretary. Both Harrisons in time prospered in New York City, he as a lawyer and she as a social and philanthropic leader and author. Southern women, like the Carys, have been called "the staunchest Rebels," but there are some conspicuous exceptions. For example, Richmond's Elizabeth Van Lew retained her earlier hostility to slavery and love of the Union and became a federal spy from her fine mansion on Church Hill during the war years.

We had come to the end of May [1862], when the eyes of the whole continent turned toward Richmond. On the 31st Johnston assaulted the Federals, who had advanced to Seven Pines! It was so near that the first guns sent our hearts into our mouths, like a sudden loud knocking at one's door at night. The women left in Richmond had, with few exceptions, husbands, fathers, sons, and brothers in the fight. I have never seen a finer exhibition of calm courage than they showed in this baptism of fire. No one wept or moaned aloud. All went about their task of preparing for the wounded, making bandages, scraping lint, improvising beds. Night brought a lull in the frightful cannonading. We threw ourselves dressed upon our beds to get a little rest before the morrow.

During the night began the ghastly procession of wounded brought in from the field. Every vehicle the city could produce supplemented the military ambulances. Many slightly wounded men, so black with gunpowder as to be unrecognizable, came limping in on foot. All next day, women with white faces flitted bareheaded through the street and hospitals, looking for their own. Churches and lecture-rooms were thrown open for volunteer ladies sewing and filling the rough beds called for by the surgeons. There was not enough of *anything* to meet the sudden appalling call of many strong men stricken unto death. Hearing that my cousin, Reginald Hyde, was reported wounded, two of us girls volunteered to help his mother to search for him through the lower hospitals. We tramped down Main Street through the hot sun over burning pavements, from one scene of horror to another, bringing up finally at the St. Charles Hotel, a large old building. What a sight met our eyes! Men in every stage of mutilation, lying waiting for the surgeons upon bare boards, with haversacks or army blankets, or nothing, beneath their heads. Some gave up the weary ghost as we passed them by. All were suffering keenly and needing ordinary attention. To be there empty-handed nearly broke our hearts. Bending down over bandaged faces stiff with blood and thick with flies, nothing did we see or hear of the object of our search, who, I am glad to say, arrived later at his mother's home, to be nursed by her to a speedy recovery.

The impression of that day was ineffaceable. It left me permanently convinced that nothing is worth war.

My mother was now in her element—expert, silent, incomparable as a nurse, she was soon on regular duty in an improvised hospital. I spent that night at the window of my room panting for fresh air, and longing to do something, anything, to help. The next day my friend, Emily Voss, and I had the pride and pleasure of having assigned to our care, under an older woman, two rooms containing fifteen wounded men lying on pallets around the floor. From that moment we were happier, although physically tried to the utmost. Gradually, some order came out of the chaos of overtasked hospital service. The churches gave their seat cushions to make beds; the famous old wine-cellars of private houses sent their priceless Madeira, port, sherry, and brandy; everybody's cook was set to turning out dainties, and for our own men we begged unblushingly until they were fairly well supplied. At night, carrying palm-leaf fans, we sauntered out into the streets scarcely less hot than in full sunshine. Once, literally panting for a fresh breath of air, a party of us went with an official of the Capitol up through the vapor bath of many steep stairs, to emerge on a little platform on the summit of the building. There—oh! joy—were actually breezes that brought relief. There we sat and looked down on the city that could not sleep, and talked, or listened to the voice of the river, that I seem to hear yet over the tramp of rusty battalions, the short, imperious stroke of the alarm bell, the clash of passing bands, the gallop of horsemen, the roar of battle, the moan of hospitals, the stifled note of sorrow—all the Richmond war sounds, sacred and unforgettable.

Day after day one heard the wailing dirge of military bands preceding a soldier's funeral. One could not number those sad pageants in our leafy streets: the coffin with its cap and sword and gloves, the riderless horse with empty boots in the stirrups of an army saddle! Such soldiers as could be spared from the front marching with arms reversed and crape-shrouded banners, passers-by standing with bare bent heads.

Funerals by night were common. A solemn scene was to be enacted in the July moonlight at Hollywood when they laid to rest my own uncle, Lieutenant Reginald Fairfax, of whom in the old service of the United States, as in that of the Confederate navy, it was said "he was a spotless knight." My uncle, who had commanded a battery on the James, was prostrated by malarial fever and taken to Richmond, where he died at the Clifton House, tenderly nursed by his sisters. He was to my brother and me a second father. His property, fortunately so invested in Northern securities as to be unavailable during the war, was left between his three sisters, thereby enabling us, after peace was declared, to resume a life of comfort, when many of our Confederate friends were in absolute want. My other uncle, Doctor Fairfax, of Alexandria, had, in the abundance of his belief in the Confederacy, put all of his fortune into Confederate bonds, and suffered a total loss of it.

A personal incident of the fight of Seven Pines was a visit during that morning from a young officer, sent into town from the battlefield with important despatches to the President. Whilst awaiting the reply, he came, with his orderly in attendance, to say a word to me, and as I stood with him at our garden gate the cannonading suddenly increased tremendously.

"*That's* my place, not this. If I don't come out of it, remember I tried to do my duty," he said with a hasty handshake, and springing into his saddle, the horse rearing fiercely, he waved his cap and spurred away, the orderly clattering after him. It was the last time I ever saw him. In one of the battles of July he fell, leading his men in a splendid charge, and in him many bright hopes and a noble future were extinguished. . . .

Dark days were in store for Richmond. An incipient bread riot occurred in her streets in April [1863] when a large number of women and children of the poorer class met and marched through Main and Cary streets, attacking and sacking several stores kept by known speculators. President Davis, Governor Letcher, General Elzey, and General Winder, with Mr. Seddon, Secretary of War, met the painful situation by prompt but kind measures and personal appeal. Rations of rice issued by the government aided to calm the disturbance, which left, however, a distressing impression upon all minds.

A thrilling day for us was the Sunday of Stoneman's raid, when, as usual, a large congregation met at St. Paul's Church, remaining for the communion service. We knew that a big and terrible fight was on at Chancellorsville, in which sons, husbands, brothers of many of the people present were engaged. Outside in the soft spring air, a tumult of war sounds continually distracted our thoughts and racked our nerves. The marching of armed men, the wheels of wagons containing shot and shell, the clash of iron gates in the Capitol Square opposite, went on without ceasing, while repeatedly messengers came up the aisle touching some kneeling or sitting worshipper on the shoulder, a summons responded to by an electric start, and then the hurried departure of shocked, pallid people from the church. These were the calls to come and receive some beloved one brought in dead or wounded from the field. To the rector of the church, Dr. Minnegerode, in the act of administering the sacrament with another clergyman, the sexton carried and delivered at the altar rails one of these dread messages, at once obeyed by the father whose son was reported dead and awaiting him at the railway station. A great weight was lifted from the congregation when the rector, looking dreadfully shaken but relieved, came back to resume his interrupted service. It was the corpse of another volunteer whom they had mistaken for his boy.

Nothing in the war, perhaps, excepting the surrender, ever struck Richmond with such stunning force as the announcement of Stonewall Jackson's fall, of the amputation of his arm, and finally of his death, following the battle of Chancellorsville. Even the brilliant victory of our arms was in total eclipse by this irreparable loss. From the first, when the shy Puritan professor of the Virginia Military Institute had startled the armies by his extraordinary daring and military skill, Jackson had taken hold of the popular mind as a supreme favorite. "Old Stonewall," "Old Jack," or "Old Blue Light" was by the soldiers held in the reverence bestowed by Napoleon's grenadiers upon the person of their sacred emperor. With Lee and Jackson to the fore, quiet people sitting in their homes felt themselves behind two massive towers of strength facing and meeting every adverse wind. . . .

And now, Stonewall Jackson, Lee's right arm, was dead of his wounds received, by the awful irony of Fate, at the hands of his own men. Dead? He, the stern Puritan leader, who, when he rose up from wrestling in prayer, launched himself like a destroying thunderbolt against the foe! He, whose sword never lay idle in its scabbard, whose iron frame had not once sought repose during all those months of fighting—who saved the day at Manassas, by standing like a stone wall and won himself a deathless sobriquet; who had fought and won so many desperate fights, independently, in the Valley; who had smitten McClellan's flank with fury at Seven Pines—Jackson, to follow whom the flower of our Southern youths were proud to suffer all things— this, indeed, was a blow under which his country staggered.

When they brought his body from the place of his death to Richmond, all citizens were in the streets, standing uncovered, silent or weeping bitterly, to see the funeral train pass to the Capitol.

We were admitted privately late at night into the hall, where the great leader lay in state. Two guards, pacing to and fro in the moonlight streaming through high windows, alone kept watch over the hero. A lamp burned dimly at one end of the hall, but we saw distinctly the regular white outline of the quiet face in its dreamless slumber.

How still he lay, the iron chieftain, the fierce, untiring rider of Valley raids! The Confederate flag that covered him was snowed under

by the masses of white blossoms left that day by all the fair hands of
Richmond, together with laurel wreaths and palms.

And then, Gettysburg! Morning fell like a pall of crape over the
entire South, even though beneath it hearts thrilled with deathless
pride in the charge of Pickett's Virginians. . . .

To return to my chronicle of Richmond gayeties. Now was instituted
the "Starvation Club," of which, as one of the original founders, I
can speak with authority. It was agreed between a number of young
women that a place for our soldier visitors to meet with us for dancing
and chat, once a week, would be a desirable variation upon evening
calls in private homes. The hostesses who successively offered their
drawing-rooms were among the leaders in society. It was also decided
that we should permit no one to infringe the rule of suppressing all
refreshment, save the amber-hued water from the classic James. We
began by having piano music for the dances, but the male members of
the club made up between them a subscription providing a small but
good orchestra. Before our first meeting, a committee of girls waited
on General Lee to ask his sanction, with this result to the spokes-
woman, who had ended with "If you say no, general, we won't dance
a single step!" "Why, of course, my dear child. My boys need to be
heartened up when they get their furloughs. Go on, look your pret-
tiest, and be just as nice to them as ever you can be!"

We even had cotillions, to which everybody contributed favors. The
gatherings were the jolliest imaginable. We had constant demands
to admit new members, and all foreigners and general officers who
visited Richmond were presented to our club, as a means of viewing
the best society of the South. . . .

Now came the winter's lull before the new fury of the storm should
break forth with the spring [of 1864]. It was evident to all older and
graver people that the iron belt surrounding the Southern country
was being gradually drawn closer and her vitality [was] in mortal peril
of exhaustion. Our armies were dwindling, those of the North increasing with every draft and the payment of liberal bounties. Starved,
nearly bankrupt, thousands of our best soldiers killed in battle, their
places filled by boys and old men, the Federal Government refusing
to exchange prisoners; our exports useless because of armed ships
closing in our ports all along the coast, our prospects were of the
gloomiest, even though Lee had won victory for our banners in the
East. We young ones, who knew nothing and refused to believe in
"croakers," kept on with our valiant boasting about our invincible
army and the like; but the end was beginning to be in sight.

Christmas in the Confederacy offered as a rule little suggestion of the festival known to plum-pudding and robin-red-breast stories in annuals. Every crumb of food better than the ordinary, every orange, apple, or banana, every drop of wine and cordial procurable, went straightway to the hospitals, public or private. Many of the residents had set aside at least one room of their stately old houses as a hospital, maintaining at their own expense as many sick or wounded soldiers as they could accommodate. On Christmas eve, all the girls and women turned out in the streets, carrying baskets with sprigs of holly, luckily plentiful, since the woods around Richmond still held its ruddy glow in spots where bullets had not despoiled the trees beyond recall. . . .

Things, as I recall them, seem to have rushed onward with the speed of lightning during the last winter of the war. We had again settled ourselves in quarters in town. I had recovered my full strength, and was almost always hungry. We had little money, little food. It was impossible to draw upon our funds in Washington, and my mother, with a number of ladies, took a situation to sign bank-notes in the Treasury Department. In what they called "Mr. Memminger's reception-room," she daily met gentlewomen, in whose veins ran the purest currents of cavalier and Huguenot blood. The names written upon those bank-notes might have served to illustrate the genesis of Southern aristocracy.

This time we had been able to secure only one room in a friend's house, with the use of her drawing-room and dining-room and service of her cook, the latter being a nominal one only; our breakfast, at 8 A.M., consisting of corn-bread with the drippings of fried bacon instead of butter, and coffee made of dried beans and peanuts, without milk or sugar. For luncheon we had, day in and day out, bacon, rice, and dried apples sweetened with sorghum. For our evening repast were served cakes made of corn-meal and water, eaten with sorghum molasses, and more of that unspeakable coffee. I cannot remember getting up from any meal that winter without wishing there were more of it. I went once to call upon a family antecedently wealthy, and found father, mother, and children making their dinner upon soup-plates filled with that cheerless compound known as "Benjamin" hard-tack, soaked in hot water, sprinkled with salt or brown sugar. It is to be said, however, there was in our community no discussion of diets, fads, or cures, and the health chase of modern society was an unknown quantity. People in better physical condition than the besieged dwellers of Richmond, when their cause was beginning to feel the death-clutch at its throat, were certainly not to be found. . . .

The engagement of my cousin Hetty Cary to Brigadier-General John Pegram having been announced, their decision to be married on

January 19 [1865] was a subject of active interest. My aunt, Mrs. Wilson Miles Cary, of Baltimore, had before Christmas obtained from Mr. Lincoln, through General Barnard (chief of the United States Engineer Corps, married to her adopted daughter), a pass to go to Richmond to visit her children. The presence of Mrs. Cary gave General Pegram opportunity to urge that his marriage should not be longer delayed, and such preparations as were possible were hurried on. My aunt was stopping at the house of her niece, Mrs. Peyton, whence the ceremony took place. On the evening of January 19 all our little world flocked to St. Paul's Church to see the nuptials of one called by many the most beautiful woman in the South, with a son of Richmond universally honored and beloved. Two days before, I being confined to my room with a cold, Hetty had come, bringing her bridal veil that I, with our mothers, might be the first to see it tried on her lovely crown of auburn hair. As she turned from the mirror to salute us with a charming blush and smile, the mirror fell and was broken to small fragments, an accident afterward spoken of by the superstitious as one of a strange series of ominous happenings.

While a congregation that crowded floor and galleries of the church waited an unusually long time for the arrival of bride and groom, my aunt and the other members of our family being already in their seats, I stood in the vestibule outside with Burton Harrison and Colonel L. Q. C. Lamar, speculating rather uneasily upon the cause of the delay. Mr. Harrison told us that Mrs. Davis (who tenderly loved and admired the bride) had begged to be allowed to send the President's carriage to drive her to the church, and he was sure it had been in prompt attendance at Colonel Peyton's door. Directly after, a shabby old Richmond hack drove up, halting before the church, and from it issued the bride and groom, looking a little perturbed, explaining that at the moment of setting out the President's horses had reared violently, refusing to go forward, and could not be controlled, so that they had been forced to get out of the carriage and send for another vehicle, at that date almost impossible to secure in Richmond.

When the noble-looking young couple crossed the threshold of the church, my cousin dropped her lace handkerchief and, nobody perceiving it, stooped forward to pick it up, tearing the tulle veil over her face to almost its full length, then, regaining herself, walked with a slow and stately step toward the altar. As she passed there was a murmur of delight at her beauty, never more striking. Her complexion of pearly white, the vivid roses on her cheeks and lips, the sheen of her radiant hair, and the happy gleam of her beautiful brown eyes seemed to defy all sorrow, change, or fear. John Pegram, handsome and erect, looked as he felt, triumphant, the prize-winner—so the men called him—of the invincible beauty of her day. Miss Cary's brother, Captain Wilson Miles Cary, representing her absent father, gave away the bride. After the ceremony we, her nearest, crowded around the couple, wishing them the best happiness our loving hearts could picture. General Pegram's mother, brothers, and sisters did the same; then, as they passed out, all eyes followed them with real kindness and unalloyed good feeling. There was but a small reception afterward, but one felt in the atmosphere a sense of sincere gladness in happy love, very rare on such occasions.

Three weeks later, to the day, General Pegram's coffin, crossed with a victor's palms besides his soldier's accoutrements, occupied the spot in the chancel where he had stood to be married. Beside it knelt his widow swathed in crape. Again Dr. Minnegerode conducted the ceremony, again the church was full. Behind the hearse, waiting outside, stood his war charger, with boots in stirrups. The wailing of the band that went with us on the slow pilgrimage to Hollywood will never die out of memory. Burton Harrison drove in the carriage with me and my mother, my poor cousin with her mother, brother, and General Custis Lee, her husband's intimate friend, who stood beside her, as, leaning on her brother's arm, she remained during the service close to the grave. General Pegram's family clustered beyond her. Snow lay white on the hill-sides, the bare trees stretched their arms above us, the river kept up its ceaseless rush and tumble, so much a part of daily life in our four years of ordeal that we had grown accustomed to interpret its voice according to our joy or grief. . . .

Harrison, *Recollections Grave and Gay* (1911), pp. 82–85,
137–38, 140–41, 150, 166, 190–91, 201–3

"We Heard the Very Welkin Ring with Cheers as the United States Forces Reached Capitol Square, and Then We Turned and Slowly Rode on Our Way": The City Falls (April 1865)

The twenty-four hours from Sunday morning, 2 April 1865, to that of Monday, 3 April, are the most horrifying and traumatic in all of

Richmond's history. President Jefferson Davis had been at his pew in St. Paul's Church when the fateful message arrived from Lee: the lines at Petersburg could no longer be held, the capital must be evacuated—thus setting in motion the mad scene described by Captain Sulivane below. The next morning, amid the unspeakable havoc of a civil populace abandoned to fire, devastation, and drunken mobs, the Federal Army arrived. Although instinctively hated as a conquering host and feared because of the burning of Columbia, South Carolina, and other cities, the Union troops acted with commendable restraint and saved Richmond from flames, disorder, and sudden impoverishment, as reported below by an aide to the commanding officer. Because Richmond had been the first city of the Confederacy in every way that is meaningful and measurable, it was ironically appropriate that precisely one week after her fall, General Lee surrendered at Appomattox.

§ The Fall of Richmond

The Evacuation.–By Clement Sulivane, Captain, C.S.A.

About 11:30 A.M. on Sunday, April 2d,* a strange agitation was perceptible on the streets of Richmond, and within half an hour it was known on all sides that Lee's lines had been broken below Petersburg; that he was in full retreat on Danville; that the troops covering the city at Chaffin's and Drewry's Bluffs were on the point of being withdrawn, and that the city was forthwith to be abandoned. A singular security had been felt by the citizens of Richmond, so the news fell like a bomb-shell in a peaceful camp, and dismay reigned supreme.

All that Sabbath day the trains came and went, wagons, vehicles, and horsemen rumbled and dashed to and fro, and, in the evening, ominous groups of ruffians—more or less in liquor—began to make their appearance on the principal thoroughfares of the city. As night came on pillage and rioting and robbing took place. The police and a few soldiers were at hand, and, after the arrest of a few ringleaders and the more riotous of their followers, a fair degree of order was restored. But Richmond saw few sleeping eyes during the pandemonium of that night.

The division of Major-General G. W. C. Lee, of Ewell's corps, at

---

*Mr. Davis attended morning service at St. Paul's Church, where he received a dispatch, on reading which he left the church to prepare for the departure of the Government.

that time rested in the trenches eight miles below Richmond, with its right on the James River, covering Chaffin's Bluff. I was at the time its assistant-general, and was in the city on some detached duty connected with the "Local Brigade" belonging to the division,—a force composed of the soldiers of the army, detailed on account of their mechanical skill to work in the arsenals, etc., and of clerks and other employees of the War, Treasury, Quartermaster, and other departments.

Upon receipt of the news from Petersburg I reported to General Ewell (then in Richmond) for instructions, and was ordered to assemble and command the Local Brigade, cause it to be well supplied with ammunition and provisions, and await further orders. All that day and night I was engaged in this duty, but with small result, as the battalions melted away as fast as they were formed, mainly under orders from the heads of departments who needed all their employees in the transportation and guarding of the archives, etc., but partly, no doubt, from desertions. When morning dawned fewer than 200 men remained, under command of Captain Edward Mayo.

Shortly before day General Ewell rode in person to my headquarters and informed me that General G. W. C. Lee was then crossing the pontoon at Drewry's; that he would destroy it and press on to join the main army; that all the bridges over the river had been destroyed, except Mayo's, between Richmond and Manchester, and that the wagon bridge over the canal in front of Mayo's had already been burned by Union emissaries. My command was to hasten to Mayo's bridge and protect it, and the one remaining foot-bridge over the canal leading to it, until General Gary, of South Carolina, should arrive. I hurried to my command, and fifteen minutes later occupied Mayo's bridge, at the foot of 14th street, and made military dispositions to protect it to the last extremity. This done, I had nothing to do but listen for sounds and gaze on the terrible splendor of the scene. And such a scene probably the world has seldom witnessed. Either incendiaries, or (more probably) fragments of bombs from the arsenals, had fired various buildings, and the two cities, Richmond and Manchester, were like a blaze of day amid the surrounding darkness. Three high arched bridges were in flames; beneath them the waters sparkled and dashed and rushed on by the burning city. Every now and then, as a magazine exploded, a column of white smoke rose up as high as the eye could reach, instantaneously followed by a deafening sound. The earth seemed to rock and tremble as with the shock of an earthquake, and immediately afterward hundreds of shells would explode in air and send their iron spray down far below the bridge. As the immense magazines of cartridges ignited, the rattle as of thousands of musketry would follow, and then all was still for the moment, except the dull roar and crackle of the fast-spreading fires. At dawn we heard terrific explosions about "The Rocketts," from the unfinished iron-clads down the river.

By daylight, on the 3d, a mob of men, women, and children, to the number of several thousands, had gathered at the corner of 14th and Cary streets and other outlets, in front of the bridge, attracted by the vast commissary depot at that point; for it must be remembered that in 1865 Richmond was a half-starved city, and the Confederate Government had that morning removed its guards and abandoned the removal of the provisions, which was impossible for the want of transportation. The depot doors were forced open and a demoniacal struggle for the countless barrels of hams, bacon, whisky, flour, sugar, coffee, etc., etc., raged about the buildings among the hungry mob. The gutters ran whisky, and it was lapped as it flowed down the streets, while all fought for a share of the plunder. The flames came nearer and nearer, and at last caught in the commissariat itself.

At daylight the approach of the Union forces could be plainly discerned. After a little came the clatter of horses' hoofs galloping up Main street. My infantry guard stood to arms, the picket across the canal was withdrawn, and the engineer officer lighted a torch of fat pine. By direction of the Engineer Department barrels of tar, surrounded by pine-knots, had been placed at intervals on the bridge, with kerosene at hand, and a lieutenant of engineers had reported for the duty of firing them at my order. The noisy train proved to be Gary's ambulances, sent forward preparatory to his final rush for the bridge. The muleteers galloped their animals about half-way down, when they were stopped by the dense mass of human beings. Rapidly communicating to Captain Mayo my instructions from General Ewell, I ordered that officer to stand firm at his post until Gary got up. I rode forward into the mob and cleared a lane. The ambulances were galloped down to the bridge, I retired to my post, and the mob closed in after me and resumed its wild struggle for plunder. A few minutes later a long line of cavalry in gray turned into 14th street, and sword in hand galloped straight down to the river; Gary had come. The mob scattered right and left before the armed horsemen, who reined up at the canal. Presently a single company of cavalry appeared in sight, and rode at headlong speed to the bridge. "My rear-guard," explained Gary. Touching his hat to me he called out, "All over, goodbye; blow her to h-ll," and trotted over the bridge. That was the first and last I ever saw of General Gary, of South Carolina.

In less than sixty seconds Captain Mayo was in column of march, and as he reached the little island about half-way across the bridge, the single piece of artillery, loaded with grape-shot, that had occupied that spot, arrived on the Manchester side of the river. The engineer officer, Dr. Lyons, and I walked leisurely to the island, setting fire to the provided combustible matter as we passed along, and leaving the north section of Mayo's bridge wrapped in flame and smoke. At the island we stopped to take a view of the situation north of the river, and saw a line of blue-coated horsemen galloping in furious haste up Main street. Across 14th street they stopped, and then dashed down 14th street to the flaming bridge. They fired a few random shots at us three on the island, and we retreated to Manchester. I ordered my command forward, the lieutenant of engineers saluted and went about his business, and myself and my companion sat on our horses for nearly a half-hour, watching the occupation of Richmond. We saw another string of horsemen in blue pass up Main street, then we saw a dense column of infantry march by, seemingly without end; we heard the very welkin ring with cheers as the United States forces reached Capitol Square, and then we turned and slowly rode on our way.

The Occupation. –By Thomas Thatcher Graves, Aide-de-Camp on the Staff of General Weitzel

In the spring of 1865 the total length of the lines of the Army of the James before Richmond (under General Godfrey Weitzel, commanding the Twenty-fifth Corps) was about eleven miles, not counting the cavalry front, and extended from the Appomattox River to the north side of the James. The Varina and New Market turnpikes passed directly through the lines into the city, which was the center of all our efforts.

About 2 o'clock on the morning of April 3d bright fires were seen in the direction of Richmond. Shortly after, while we were looking at these fires, we heard explosions, and soon a prisoner was sent in by General Kautz. The prisoner was a colored teamster, and he informed us that immediately after dark the enemy had begun making preparations to leave, and that they were sending all of the teams to the rear. A forward movement of our entire picket-line corroborated this report. As soon as it was light General Weitzel ordered Colonel E. E. Graves, senior aide-de-camp, and Major Atherton H. Stevens, Jr., provost-marshal, to take a detachment of forty men from the two companies (E and H) of the 4th Massachusetts Cavalry, and make a reconnaissance. Slowly this little band of scouts picked their way in. Soon after we moved up the New Market road at a slow pace.

As we approached the inner line of defenses we saw in the distance divisions of our troops, many of them upon the double-quick, aiming to be the first in the city; a white and a colored division were having a regular race, the white troops on the turnpike and the colored in the fields. As we neared the city the fires seemed to increase in number and size, and at intervals loud explosions were heard.

On entering we found Capitol Square covered with people who had fled there to escape the fire and were utterly worn out with fatigue and fright. Details were at once made to scour the city and press into service every able-bodied man, white or black, and make them assist in extinguishing the flames. General Devens's division marched into the city, stacked arms, and went to work. Parson's engineer company assisted by blowing up houses to check its advance, as about every engine was destroyed or rendered useless by the mob. In this manner the fire was extinguished and perfect order restored in an incredibly short time after we occupied the city.* There was absolutely no plundering upon the part of our soldiers; orders were issued forbidding anything to be taken without remuneration, and no complaints were made of infringement of these orders. General G. F. Shepley was placed on duty as military governor. He had occupied a similar position in New Orleans after its capture in 1862, and was eminently fitted for it by education and experience. As we entered the suburbs the general ordered me to take half a dozen cavalrymen and go to Libby Prison, for our thoughts were upon the wretched men whom we supposed were still confined within its walls. It was very early in the morning, and we were the first Union troops to arrive before Libby. Not a guard, not an inmate remained; the doors were wide open, and only a few negroes greeted us with, "Dey's all gone, massa!"

The next day after our entry into the city, on passing out from Clay street, from Jefferson Davis's house, I saw a crowd coming, headed

*As one of our aides was riding through the streets, engaged in gathering together the able-bodied men to assist in extinguishing the fire, he was hailed by a servant in front of a house, toward which the fire seemed to be moving. The servant told him that his mistress wished to speak to him. He dismounted and entered the house, and was met by a lady, who stated that her mother was an invalid, confined to her bed, and as the fire seemed to be approaching she asked for assistance. The subsequent conversation developed the fact that the invalid was no other than the wife of General R. E. Lee, and the lady who addressed the aide was her daughter, Miss Lee. An ambulance was furnished by Colonel E. H. Ripley, of the 8th Vermont, and a corporal and two men guarded them until all danger was past.—T.T.G.

by President Lincoln, who was walking with his usual long, careless
stride, and looking about with an interested air and taking in everything. Upon my saluting he said: "Is it far to President Davis's house?"
I accompanied him to the house, which was occupied by General
Weitzel as headquarters. The President had arrived about 9 o'clock,
at the landing called Rocketts, upon Admiral Porter's flag-ship, the
Malvern, and as soon as the boat was made fast, without ceremony, he
walked on shore, and started off uptown. As soon as Admiral Porter
was informed of it he ordered a guard of marines to follow as escort;
but in the walk of about two miles they never saw him, and he was
directed by negroes. At the Davis house, he was shown into the reception-room, with the remark that the housekeeper had said that
that room was President Davis's office. As he seated himself he remarked, "This must have been President Davis's chair," and, crossing
his legs, he looked far off with a serious, dreamy expression. At length
he asked me if the housekeeper was in the house. Upon learning that
she had left he jumped up and said, with a boyish manner, "Come,
let's look at the house!" We went pretty much over it; I retailed all that
the housekeeper had told me, and he seemed interested in everything.
As we came down the staircase General Weitzel came, in breathless
haste, and at once President Lincoln's face lost its boyish expression as
he realized that *duty* must be resumed. Soon afterward Judge Campbell, General Anderson (Confederates), and others called and asked
for an interview with the President. It was granted, and took place in
the parlor with closed doors.

I accompanied President Lincoln and General Weitzel to Libby
Prison and heard General Weitzel ask President Lincoln what he
(General Weitzel) should do in regard to the conquered people. President Lincoln replied that he did not wish to give any orders on that
subject, but, as he expressed it, "If I were in your place I'd let 'em up
easy, let 'em up easy."

A few days after our entry General R. E. Lee surrendered, and
early one morning we learned that he had just arrived at his house in
the city. General Weitzel called me into a private room, and, taking
out a large, well-filled pocket-book, said, "Go to General Lee's house,
find Fitzhugh Lee, and say that his old West Point chum Godfrey
Weitzel wishes to know if he needs anything, and urge him to take
what he may need from that pocket-book." Upon reaching General
Lee's house I knocked, and General Fitzhugh Lee came to the door.
He was dressed in a Confederate uniform. Upon introducing myself
he asked me in, showing me into a parlor with double or folding
doors, explaining that the servants had not returned. He was so over-

come by Weitzel's message that for a moment he was obliged to walk to the other end of the room. He excused himself, and passed into the inner room, where I noticed General R. E. Lee sitting, with a tired, worn expression upon his face. Fitzhugh Lee knelt beside his general, as he sat leaning over, and placed a hand upon his knee.

After a few moments he came back, and in a most dignified and courteous manner sent his love to Godfrey Weitzel, and assured him that he did not require any loan of money, but if it would be entirely proper for *Godfrey* Weitzel to issue a pass for some ladies of General Lee's household to return to the city it would be esteemed a favor; but he impressed me to state that if this would embarrass *General* Weitzel, on no account would they request the favor. It is needless to state that the ladies were back in the house as soon as possible.

"The Fall of Richmond," *Battles and Leaders* (1887–88),
4:725–28

"Slavery Chain Done Broke at Last": A Black Minister Returns (1865)

With the fall of Richmond in April 1865, most city blacks found themselves caught in a twilight world between slavery and freedom. This difficult transition could hardly have been consummated in the aftermath of war, but the process began in a halting fashion, as described below by Peter Randolph (1825?–93).

Formerly enslaved in Virginia, Randolph became a free man in 1847 and eventually settled in Boston where in time he established himself as a lawyer and a minister. Only "twenty-five days after the surrender," he arrived in Richmond, subsequently assisted in the difficult work of the Freedmen's Bureau, and accepted the pastorate of the Ebenezer Baptist Church. His narrative offers a firsthand perspective on racial practices and attitudes in a traumatic era of adjustment for the city's people, black and white.

The scene that opened before my eyes as I entered Richmond cannot be accurately described by word or pen. The city was in smoke and ashes, that is, a goodly part of it, for the Confederacy, on taking their departure, fired the city rather than let it fall into the hands of the Union forces.

The colored people from all parts of the state were crowding in at the capital, running, leaping, and praising God that freedom had come at last. It seems to me I can hear their songs now as they ring through the air: "Slavery chain done broke at last; slavery chain done broke at last—I's goin' to praise God till I die."

Many of the old people had prayed and looked forward to this day, but like Moses they were permitted to see it afar off, and not enter it.

The place was literally full of soldiers, "Yanks" and "Rebs."

The armies were breaking up and returning home. Richmond was the great centre of dispersions; all hours, day and night was the marching of regiments, going and coming. The sight of some of these would bring tears to the dryest eyes, as they beheld men wounded, maimed in every possible shape and form that could be mentioned. And many of these, like the poor colored people, were truly glad that the war was over.

The city of Richmond did not have accommodations enough for this great mass of colored people, so many were gathered on the suburbs and taken care of in the best way possible under the circumstances.

One of these principal camps, where the people were huddled in temporary structures, was called Chimborazo. Here I spent a part of my first Sunday in Richmond, and preached to a large congregation. Religious services were held in these camps all day, and several other preachers were present and readily lent their services. Among these was Rev. John Jasper, who has distinguished himself since, as the famous "Sun do move preacher." This was the first time I had the pleasure of meeting him. His preaching was much more excitable than mine, and seemed to effect the people in a way that I could not. This scene, and the day's work, was very impressive upon me, and made me feel and sympathize with these folks only as one who had been in slavery, could feel and sympathize.

It had been argued by some that, if the Negroes were set free they would murder and kill the white people. But instead of that, they were praising God and the Yankees for life and liberty. Of course, soldiers were stationed about these camps, and in all the streets of the city, to keep in check anything like an outbreak. I am sorry to say here, that the treatment of some of the soldiers toward the poor colored people was indeed shameful. For the slightest provocation, and sometimes for no cause whatever, the butts of their guns and bayonets were used unmercifully upon them.

The colored people held indignation meetings, resolutions were passed, and a delegation appointed to lay this whole matter before President Johnson. I was the instigator of the meeting being called. And not until these steps were taken did the colored people have rest from the ill-treatment of the soldiers.

This, also, must be said, relative to these soldiers: the most of them who committed these depredations were from the Middle States, and sympathizers with the South. They seemed to be mad because the "negger" was free, and took the authority given them by the wearing of the blue to express it.

The petition of the colored men was noticed by the President, and remedied by General Schofield. In addition to the Provost Marshal's, where soldiers were disciplined, bureaus were established for the freedmen, where they could be heard and assisted. The true condition of the colored people at this time will never be written. When I arrived at Richmond, I had letters of introduction from Governor Andrew to Governor Pierpont, and also to General Schofield. I was appointed by the General to issue tickets or passes, and distribute them to the people, in order that they might get what provisions and clothing there was for them through the agency of the bureau. It was a sight to behold to see these hungry souls crowding in at my office to obtain the slips of paper that was to give them the necessities of life. The Freedman's Bureau also took the place of the Court House, to protect and settle all difficulties that might arise among the people.

In this particular some of the incidents were heartrending, the most severe cases being where the former master and slave were concerned. Some of the masters were very reluctant in giving up their servants, and tried to defraud and rob them out of their freedom, and many of the slaves had to run away from their masters to be free. It is true that the proclamation had been accepted, and Lee had surrendered his sword to Grant, but some of the white people still contended that "these are my neggers."

When some of the white people found that they could no longer retain them as slaves they used them very cruelly. I was often called at the bureau to interest myself in and defend these poor people. One sad case I will here mention—a colored girl about eighteen years of age, who was brought before the bureau, with a charge against her former master. She had been shamefully whipped and her back burned with a hot iron. I well recall the words of General Merritt, who was at the time the president of the bureau.

As he beheld the condition of this girl, he exclaimed, "What is this!" The officer who had her in charge said, "It is the devil." An eye-

witness who was present photographed the back of this girl, and it can
be had if my readers would like to see it. Let me make another brief
mention about the South, especially during the dark days of slavery.
The colored man was expected to stop and let the white person pass
first, and often had to get off the sidewalk to let the white woman pass.
I was an eye-witness to this incident: A white woman was about to
cross the street, but the colored teamster, who had the right of way,
did not stop for her to cross. She had him arrested for attempting to
run over her. I went to the jail, and on my personal testimony, he was
released.

This simply illustrates the condition of things that I speak of, and
also the necessity and work of the Freedman's Bureau.

The Freedman's Bureau was only a temporary arrangement intended to help relieve the condition of the ex-slaves. While it had the
means to do so it was inestimable to the poor and needy. But soon the
sources of supply failed and the important work was abandoned. This
made the suffering and needs of the people more intense than ever.
Many had to go back to their former masters to work or starve, and
many of the whites tried to make the Negroes feel that freedom was
worse than slavery.

In slavery times the masters would see to it, that the slaves were fed
—that is, with such as they had to give them, but now, they would see
them starve. It is not hard to understand this state of affairs, when
one thinks of the situation; here the whites were smarting under their
defeat, the Negroes, who were their main support, were taken away
from them as slaves and goods of chattel, but still remained at their
doors. The unvented wrath they had for the Yankees, for meddling
with their pet institution, was poured out on the poor Negroes. . . .

§ Religious Condition

In the previous chapter I spoke more directly concerning the political
and social environments of the colored people in Richmond, as I
found them at the close of the war. In this chapter I wish to speak
more definitely concerning their religious condition. I arrived in
Richmond twenty-five days after the surrender, and was there only
two weeks when I was invited to assume the pastorate of the Ebenezer
Baptist Church. I accepted the same for three months' trial, and at
the expiration of that time was duly called as the regular pastor. This

was at the beginning of an important era in the religious history of the colored people.

This church, as well as others through the South, had never had a colored pastor. He who was considered the under-Shepherd and was expected to lead his flock into the green pastures, and beside the still waters, was always white. Why the colored people should now change their old pastors for new ones, may be more easily imagined than described. But this must be said, that the colored people as a whole, had but little confidence and faith in their white pastors as religious leaders. They rather looked upon them as parts of the machinery that belonged to slavery, and regarded them more as religious bosses, whose duty it was to keep them in their places by persuading them to be contented with their present lot and obey their masters in the flesh, for such was well pleasing to God. Now they were free and had a voice in selecting their pastor, it is not unreasonable to suppose, that they wanted a pastor who could sympathize with them in their afflictions, and remember the bondman as bound with him. They wanted one who could preach without fear, not only on obedience but on love, the Fatherhood of God, and the Brotherhood of man, and how Christ came to deliver the captive, and set the bondman free. On such topics as the foregoing the white pastor always had to touch lightly, for fear of losing his official head.

In this new state of affairs naturally new difficulties arose. There were no colored preachers educated and trained in the South for this important trust and responsibility. Whatever qualifications I had for the pastorate, and my ideas of the church polity, had all been received in the North and not from the South.

I was brought immediately face to face with strange customs and trying difficulties.

I found that the male and female members of the church were not allowed to sit together on the same side of the church. When the husband and wife entered the vestibule of the church, they separated, the husband going in at one door to his side of the house, and wife going in at another door to her side of the house. Likewise the mother and son, the bridal couple, the lover and the loved, all had to conform to this rule. I condemned and ridiculed such a custom as a relic of slavery, and soon had the families sitting together, and young men with the young ladies whom they accompanied to church.

This was a new state of things, and soon my church was named the "aristocratic church."

The women were allowed no part in the church meetings. I tried to show that the women bore the greater part of the burden and expenses of the church, and as members they were entitled to recognition. Before I left the church the women not only had a voice, but voted in the business meetings.

One of the most perplexing difficulties I met with at the beginning of my religious work in the South was the "Marriage Question." Not that phase of the question that is often debated—"Is marriage a failure?" but how to join in matrimony. During the days of slavery slaves were married according to the state law, but lived together more on the concubinage order. The husband and wife, after living together long enough to have children, were often separated and sold into different parts of the South, never to see each other again. And thus separated they were encouraged to marry again, and raise children for the slave-market. As I have intimated, Virginia, and Richmond especially, was the great slave-market that furnished the majority of the slaves for the rest of the South.

Now that freedom had been proclaimed throughout the land, hundreds of those who had been separated returned to their former home. But they found their former companions married again—they of course expecting never to see them again. Now here came the difficulty, as the marriage of the slaves consisted only in common consent among themselves and their masters, the state law had nothing to do with it. Therefore, special legislative enactment had to be made to meet the case; thereupon the legislature passed a law, recognizing all living together as man and wife. After this they had to be married according to the state law. Just before and after this enactment a large number came to me to be married, seven and eight couples a night.

Randolph, *From Slave Cabin to the Pulpit* (1893),
pp. 59–61, 87–90

"Strong Men Wept Like Women": The Capitol Floor Collapses (1870)

In what could be regarded as one of the last manifestations of military rule in the Reconstruction era, Richmond in early 1870 had two individuals who claimed to be its lawful mayor; one person represented the "Black Republicans," the other had been the candidate of the old-line whites. On 27 April 1870 the Virginia Supreme Court of

Appeals appeared ready to resolve the dispute. Not since the Burr trial (q.v.) had a judicial proceeding engendered so much local interest; the courtroom, then on an upper floor of the state capitol, was packed well beyond capacity. Thus the stage was set for a spectacular disaster, graphically described below by one of the presiding judges, Joseph Christian (1828–1905), in a letter written to his wife on the very evening of the great calamity. The crash injured 313 individuals, 62 of them fatally, including several notable citizens—and once again the city plunged into mourning.

Richmond   April 27th 1870
     Unite with me my precious wife in praise and thankfulness to God, for his marvelous mercy in saving me this day from a terrible death. The most shocking and appalling calamity that ever happened in this country occurred this morning at the Capitol. This day will long be remembered as a day of horror and death, and there is a wail of sorrow going up from this City tonight, such as never was heard before. *Seventy five* human beings (and it may be more) have been in a moment hurled into eternity—their forms crushed & mangled—and hundreds others wounded and maimed for life. Among them are some of the best and noblest men in the State, among them many of my dearest friends. Oh God what a day of horror, blood, and death it has been. I am hardly calm enough to write the sickening details. I send you the "Evening Journal" containing full particulars. I was saved by the merest accident or rather I will say by a special Providence growing out of a trivial circumstance. It was known that the Chahoon Ellyson Case was to be decided this morning which attracted a large crowd to the Capitol. The court room (which is in the upper story) and its gallery was crowded to its utmost capacity. The Court was to meet at 11 o'clock. Just before 11 the Judges had all assembled in the Conference room. We had on yesterday agreed upon the decision & heard the opinion written by Judge Moncure read. There was one passage or two which Judge Staples & myself insisted should be changed. This was not done yesterday and this morning a discussion ensued in conference which delayed us 15 minutes. But for *this delay* we should all have been victims of the terrible catastrophe. We had just re-written the passages referred to and started into the Court room, which adjoins the conference room, Judge Joynes & Judge Anderson had entered the room and the rest of us [were] about to enter, when the awful crash came. Suddenly the crowded gallery gave way precipitating its living weight into the centre of the court room

crushing those beneath. In a moment more the floor of the court
room began to sink and sway and then, horrors of horrors, it fell with
its struggling mass of 4 or 5 hundred human beings *forty feet* into the
Hall of the House of Delegates below. The floor of the Conference
Room did not go down, but left us (the Judges) on *the very brink* of that
awful abysm from which arose such a wail of agony as mortal ears
never heard before. To add to the horrors of the scene a midnight
darkness (caused by the dust of tons of plaster) settled over the dreadful chasm. The air was not only filled with the shrieks and groans of
the dying and wounded, but the dust was suffocating and we had to
rush out of the building for air to breathe. Then followed scenes
which cannot be described—heartrending, sickening, appalling. The
work of rescuing this living and dying and dead mass of human beings
from the awful grave in which they were buried, soon began. There
were comparatively few persons about the Capitol and outside, for
the great mass had gone down very few making their escape from the
court room when the floor sunk. A working force was organized at
once to remove the debris. The fire Bells were rung and soon all the
firemen & police were on the ground and the work of rescue began in
earnest. Men worked with the energy of despair and deeds of heroism
were performed such as no battlefield ever witnessed. Soon those who
fell on top began to be helped out. And as they came supported by
those who were engaged in the rescue, people began to realize the
terrible nature and extent of the calamity. Those who came out and
were brought out could not be recognized by their nearest friends.
That dreadful *lime dust* had covered them all and they all looked alike
in their horrible coating of lime and blood. They hardly look[ed] like
human being[s] but more like bloody ghosts from the regions of despair. Many were stripped of their clothing in their struggles for life.
All had (who could speak) to tell their names. This made it the more
terrible, for every now and then I would find that some poor mangled
& naked wretch was one of my dear friends. Oh my God what scenes
of anguish I passed through this dark and dreadful day. I will not
attempt them further. I cant dwell upon these awful scenes, they
were so heartrending so appalling that they unman me when I recall
them. The wail of sorrow that went up, as wives recognized husbands,
brothers & sisters, brothers, and mothers their mangled and bleeding
sons, filled the balmy air of spring, and the blood of the best men
in the City and State, crimsoned the green lawn around the illfated
building. Strong men wept like women and women who could not
weep were silent in the agony of despair. Men accustomed to restrain
their feelings, moaned and wept like children. Judge Moncure threw

his arms around my neck and wept aloud in outbursts of uncontrollable grief as friend after friend of ours was brought out, some mangled, some dying, some dead. Poor Joynes was almost frantic, for dear Tom was known to be in the centre of the room when it fell in, and then lay buried in its ruins, but God be praised he is alive and now in his mother's room on the same floor with me. He is out of all danger—no bones broken. He was saved as if by a miracle.

Eight or ten lawyers practicing in our Court were killed or dreadfully wounded. Patrick Henry Aylett, Nat[haniel P.] Howard and Powhatan Roberts killed outright. Poor Judge [John A.] Meredith whom you know, and my dear friend I fear will die. He is terribly crushed, his ribs broken and internal injuries, and H [M.] Bell of Staunton the friend of my Early youth who loves me and whom I love as a brother, was dreadfully mangled. But thank God he is alive and will recover. [James] Neeson too another dear friend, was terribly injured but I trust in God he will be spared to his poor motherless children. I went to see them this evening to weep with them. Oh God what an awful calamity has been visited upon this beautiful City, now weeping like Rachel for her children and will not be comforted because they are not.

Oh my dear wife and children—from what an awful fate have we been spared. I have often asked myself the question why was I saved. Oh God in the presence of this dread calamity, I would humble myself in thy presence and devote myself unreservedly to thy service. God help me a poor sinner to love and serve Him.

We shall be compelled to adjourn our Court. The Clerks office with all our records are destroyed and more than half the lawyers practicing in our Court are killed and wounded. We shall remain until the end of the week, to attend the public funerals & other sad ceremonies. You may expect me home on Monday or Tuesday next. May God bless you all.

Yours truly, Jos: Christian

[P.S.] None of the Judges were injured. *Tom Joynes* thank God is out of danger, but still suffering from *bruises, &c.*

Christian, "Capitol Disaster," *Virginia Magazine* 68
(April 1960): 193–97

"As Bloodthirsty as Human Ingenuity Could Make It": Of Duels and Dueling (1873)

Although the exact origin of the code duello is unknown, scholars think it began in Germany with the custom of "judicial combat," under which the accused party challenged his accuser to prove his allegations with weapons. Supposedly, so the theory went, the gods would vindicate the innocent man, against whom, or against whose family or friends, an insult had usually been directed.

Virginia men of the nineteenth century were involved in myriad duels, some of which took place in nearby states in order to avoid confrontation with the law. Among the duels fought and the challenges offered in Richmond four are of particular significance. They, along with more than one hundred other Virginia duels, are chronicled in a scrapbook compiled by Evan R. Chesterman and now deposited in the archives at the Virginia State Library in Richmond.

First, there was the meeting between newspapermen John Hampden Pleasants, editor of the *Whig*, and Thomas Ritchie, Jr., editor of the rival *Enquirer*, which occurred on the south side of the James River on 25 February 1846 and in which Pleasants was killed. Next was the confrontation between W. C. Elam, a later editor of the *Whig*, and Colonel Thomas Smith, which took place near Oakwood Cemetery on 6 June 1880 and in which Elam was shot in the face but recovered. Then there was the abortive meeting between John M. Daniel (q.v.), editor of the *Examiner*, and Edgar Allan Poe (q.v.) in the *Examiner* office in the summer of 1848, at which time Poe was talked out of the duel.

The most tragic encounter, by local account, however, took place in the early evening of 9 May 1873 near Oakwood Cemetery between John B. Mordecai and W. Page McCarty. This duel revolved around a Richmond belle named Mary Triplett. McCarty, who was then engaged in the tobacco business, was crippled for life, while young Mordecai, a lawyer, lingered for five days, only to die at the home of a relative at the corner of Belvidere and Franklin streets.

One might fancy that the baptism of fire and blood undergone by Virginia during the Civil War period, would have quite sufficed to allay the sentiment which countenanced duelling, but just the contrary appears to have been the case.

There were affairs of honor even among the Confederate troops and immediately succeeding the cessation of hostilities, but the period of greatest activity with revolver and pistol appears to have been between the years 1868 and 1885.

Politics, for the most part, was the cause of these troubles, and especially the politics attending the Mahone regime, though the most heartrendering of all the post-bellum duels was due to another cause —a quarrel which followed a supposed insult to a Virginia woman.

With this exception all the duels had their genesis in disputes touch-[ing political?] matters or in newspaper editorials, which, in some instances, were ferociously caustic and scathingly severe.

Verily it looked as if the editors and the political leaders could put no restraint on their speech or writings and that they fairly itched for a chance under the code duello.

The great majority of these meetings, however, resulted in little serious injury to the fighters, and in several instances the encounters bordered almost on the ridiculous. More than one had a Pickwickian aspect and instead of creating tears, left the whole State laughing in her sleeve.

But more of this anon.

The Most Tragic of Them All.

Most notable, as well as most tragic, of all the duels occurring in Virginia after the surrender at Appomattox, was that wherein John Mordecai, a young lawyer and a war member of the second company of the Richmond Howitzers, lost his life in an encounter with W. Page McCarty, at that time engaged in the tobacco business, but subsequently an editor of considerable note in Richmond.

This affair, which took place at 6 P.M. May 9, 1873, near Oakwood Cemetery, directly involved a famous society belle of unmistakable beauty and unimpeachable character, who, however, was in no way to blame for the trouble. She afterwards married and died some ten years or more ago.

Her name was never mentioned in contemporaneous newspaper accounts and, of course, will not be mentioned here, though it is known to hundreds who still hold her memory in the profoundest respect.

§ Was a Dashing Soldier

Mordecai, who was a son of Augustus Mordecai, of Henrico county, and a nephew of Samuel Mordecai, the author of the celebrated book,

"Richmond in Bygone Days," was born in 1840, and, therefore, was thirty-three years old when he met his end.

The breaking out of the war found him a student at the University of Virginia. When the Old Dominion seceded, he joined the University company and went with it to Harper's Ferry. From there he went to Yorktown and at that point joined the second company of the Howitzers. With that battle-scarred organization he remained, bearing a part in every engagement until Lee yielded to the superior strength of Grant.

After the hostilities, young Mordecai commenced the study of law with his uncle, Colonel John B. Young. He was popular in society and was noted for his quiet and unobtrusive demeanor. Although he fell mortally wounded on the field, his injury—the ball penetrated the abdomen—did not result fatally until Wednesday, May 14th. He died at the residence of his kinsman, Major E. T. D. Myers, on Belvidere and Franklin Streets.

Mr. McCarty, who was badly wounded in the right hip, between the hip bone and hip joint, was about thirty-three years old at the time of the duel. He was seriously disabled, but we shall hear more of him hereafter, as he figured later in other duels, though it is said that the death of Mordecai always lay heavily on his mind.

He died seven or eight years ago, a nervous wreck and a pathetic figure, who somehow suggested a man with biting, unforgettable sorrow.

McCarty was the son of Hon. William McCarty, of Fairfax, who for sometime was in the Senate of Virginia and several years in the Congress of the United States. His literary skill, both as a producer of poetry and prose, was unusual, though his prose style at times was far too aggressive.

To the last he retained a degree of physical courage which was his crowning characteristic. He never married and his manner of life suggested complete isolation from family ties, though he was neither austere nor unapproachable.

The direct cause of the duel was a poem which appeared February 5, 1873, in the Richmond Enquirer and which the editor, as well as pretty much everybody else, regarded as harmless. It was as follows:

The First Figure in "The German."

An Epigram.

When Mary's queenly form I press,
In Strauss' latest waltz.

I would as well her lips caress,
Although those lips be false.
For still with fire Love tips his dart,
And kindles up anew
The flames which once consumed my heart
When those dear lips were true.

Of form so fair, of faith so faint,
If truth were only in her;
Though she'd be then the sweetest saint,
I'd still feel like a sinner.

§ First Came A Fisticuff

Some incident, never explained, must have been back of the poem, for Mordecai demanded to know its author, and on being told that McCarty wrote it, he at once took personal affront and opened correspondence with the man whom Fate had destined to kill him.

At one time this interchange of letters promised to result in a duel, but by the intervention of friends the affair was amicably settled—at least for a time. Good feeling, however, was not restored, and a little later on the two men met one Monday night at the Richmond Club, at the southeast corner of Franklin and Third Streets.

McCarty was in the salon talking to a friend when Mordecai entered. The latter thought he heard some insulting allusion to himself fall from the lips of McCarty, and he immediately approached and demanded to know what had been said when his name was mentioned. The answer was far from satisfactory and a fight ensued.

In this fisticuff McCarty went down from a tremendous blow in the face, and when he arose it was only to get another pounding. In fact, he was badly beaten. This meant blood.

On Friday morning, as Mordecai was passing through the Capitol Square, he was met by Colonel W. B. Tabb, who informed him that, acting for McCarty, he had come to request Mordecai to name his friend.

Mordecai, as soon as he realized the import of the message, named William L. Royall, the well known, popular and big-hearted Richmond lawyer, who but recently had been in the political eye.

The name of Mr. Royall, like that of McCarty, will appear again in this series of articles, for he, too, was connected with other duels in one way or the other, but never as a principal.

It was agreed that the affair should take place at 6 o'clock in the evening near Oakwood, just east of the city, and that the weapons used should be Colts' revolvers, largest size, loaded with army balls, and to be fired at a distance of ten paces.

Mordecai's seconds were W. L. Royall and W. R. Trigg; McCarty's were Colonel W. B. Tabb and John S. Meredith. Dr. Hunter McGuire and Dr. J. Dorsey Cullen were the medical attendants.

§ A Contemporaneous Report

"The spot selected for the encounter," says a contemporaneous account of the duel, written by the father of this chronicler, "was on Harrison's farm, about half a mile beyond Oakwood Cemetery and in a little hollow where Gille's Creek makes a bend in the form of a horseshoe and is crossed by a county road. The ground was level and covered with broom sedge. A few scrubby pines and thick bushes screened the party from observation. Messrs. Mordecai and McCarty were both perfectly cool and collected; neither showed the least sign of agitation or slightest mark of excitement and when placed in position faced each other in a manner that indicated their determination to make a desperate fight. There was absolutely no advantage in position though the choice had fallen to McCarty. They stood on a line running north and south, and the sun, just sinking in the west, fell aslant each of them. The words were to be 'Are you ready? Fire—one, two, three,' and the parties were to fire 'not before "one" nor after "three."'

"The words, 'Are you ready?' were slowly and distinctly uttered by Mr. Tabb, and responses came promptly and clearly from Mordecai and McCarty. As the smoke cleared away both parties were observed standing quietly in place. It being apparent that his adversary was unhurt, Mr. McCarty demanded another fire. Mr. Mordecai readily acceded, and the same instructions as to firing as before were given the principals. They fired this time between 'two' and 'three,' and both fell simultaneously. Mordecai turned to the right as if about to raise his foot from the ground, then half fell and toppled over upon his side. McCarty fell forward like a statue pushed down from behind. His feet scarcely moved from their tracks, and he went to the earth face foremost.

"Surgeons were immediately sent for and Drs. Hunter McGuire and J. Dorsey Cullen in a few seconds appeared upon the scene. It was at first thought that Mordecai was dying, and the seconds without the exchange of any special formalities, came to the conclusion that the matter had gone far enough. Mordecai offered to give McCarty another shot, but, of course, the idea was not entertained."

§ Lay Long on the Ground

Major Poe, the Chief of Police, arrived shortly thereafter on the scene and took all present into custody, but it was 10 o'clock before carriages were procured, and the wounded men had therefore to lie upon the ground for four or five hours—a state of affairs which seems remarkable to people of this day. Not until midnight did the unhappy party reach the city.

As has been stated, Mordecai did not die until Wednesday, May 14th. The day following Coroner W. H. Taylor began an inquest which lasted two days.

The four seconds were promptly clapped into prison—McCarty was too badly hurt to justify such a course—and bail was refused them both by the Police Justice, and later, on June 12th, by Judge A. B. Guigon, of the Hustings Court.

On June 22nd the quartette were taken before Judge B. W. Lacy, of New Kent and Charles City county, at Turnstall's, on a writ of habeas corpus and procured bail in the sum of $5,000 each.

It is unnecessary to follow the legal proceedings further, as all of the prisoners later were acquitted.

> Chesterman, "M'Carty-Mordecai Affair," Richmond
> *Evening Journal*, 19 November 1908

"Smoking Was for Men Only": The 1880s and 1890s

The end of the nineteenth century found Richmond in different circumstances from what it had known in the past. Towering figures such as John Marshall, Thomas Jefferson, John Randolph, and Robert E. Lee, among others, were no longer to be found in the city, which had recovered substantially from the ravages of the fire that nearly destroyed it in 1865. But, as Michael Chesson argues in his award-winning monograph *Richmond After the War*, the city was still

captive to the conservative values of its heritage. In addition, its
ninety thousand citizens were also part of the fashionable Victorian
morality, which swept the nation.

   In this affectionate memoir, General John A. Cutchins (1881–
1976), a former city director of public safety and the author of other
works centering on Richmond, recalls Richmond as he remembered it
on the eve of the twentieth century.

As we look back, from a vantage point of more than three-quarters of
a century, it is probably not more difficult for the citizen of today to
visualize the Richmond of that day than it would have been for the
citizen of that period to visualize the Richmond of today. There is one
thing of which I am absolutely certain—the citizen of that day would
have found it utterly impossible to believe the things we now take for
granted and the changes in dress, habits, conduct, customs and the
everyday material things of life.

   Again, unlike today when a boy literally jumps from diapers into
long pants, the day a boy of the Gay Nineties wore his first pair of long
pants was one of the biggest milestones on the road to manhood. To
own and be permitted to wear long pants and to own and be allowed
to use a razor were the first great ambitions of every boy of that day.
Indeed the progression to long pants was a trying period in his life.
His first outfit was a dress with a skirt as much unlike a girl's as possible (something on the order of a Highlander's costume) but he rarely
could avoid lace cuffs on important occasions, particularly if he had to
have his picture taken. That, for some unknown reason, was always
with an elbow leaning on a piece of furniture and one hand stuck in
his shirt after the manner of Napoleon Bonaparte. Picture taking was
a painful, but required, ritual. Another awful thing was that most boys
were made to wear curls for quite a few years. The release from that
embarrassment was one of the greatest joys of boyhood days. Sometimes I wish that many older boys I see now on the streets could feel
the same embarrassment.

   After the little man's skirt, he graduated into short pants, a masculine prototype of the mini skirt of today. I have a photograph taken
with my mother, grandmother and great-grandmother, which shows
a wretched looking little sissy, hand in shirt front and with a mini-
mum of material in the tightest, shortest pants I have ever seen. The
photographer's studio was where the Mutual Building is today. It
was a terrible ordeal, sitting between my grandmother and great-
grandmother with my mother behind me, completely unhappy, as the

photographer emerged from the black cloth over the camera trying to make me smile. I didn't.

My own progression from short to long pants was not unaccompanied by real tragedy. The first time I wore them was to Henry Hotchkiss' party. A game, always suggested, we thought, by the girls and cordially disliked by the boys was "dropping the handkerchief." The present generation may not know that one. The boys formed a circle and the girls, in turn, galloped around behind the circle and dropped the handkerchief behind one of the boys, who, as soon as he became aware of it, had to chase the girl and kiss her. During the progress of the game one girl, who shall be nameless, in a careless moment dropped her handkerchief behind me, who in a most ungentlemanly fashion pretended not to have seen it. But no such subterfuge was allowed to work. The result was that I, who did not want to have to kiss a girl, gave chase to a lively damsel who didn't want to be kissed, and I overlooked a rug on the floor and fell rather violently on my knees. I arose with a slit in the knee of one leg of my pants three or four inches long. My parents concluded that apparently I was not old enough for long pants, so I reverted, for six months to the mini-pants!

The next thing a boy aspired to was a razor—the present safety razor was unknown. His razor was like those he saw Scott—in his barber shop on Ninth Street, opposite Reuger's Restaurant—use on the gentlemen who came in for tonsorial services. The row of shaving mugs each with the initials of its owner stacked up on one side of the shop, was the source of never ending interest. Incidentally the price of a hair cut was a quarter and a shave was ten cents.

Gentlemen in those days had whiskers or beards in infinite variety, but always well groomed. Some had full beards; others, sideburns and a mustache, and still others, a mustache only. Individuality was the order of the day.

At home deference was paid to the mustached gentlemen in the form of a coffee cup having over the top at one side a piece (of the same type glass) with an opening to drink through, the mustache being thereby kept out of the coffee. I have my father's coffee cup, which has survived, with its built-in mustache protector.

Realizing how completely incapable I am of relating accurately the parallel growth of the girl of that day I shall content myself with generalities. The little girl was a miniature woman, though with dresses to the knee rather than to the ground, as were those of the grown-ups. Dresses and hats took on all manner of shapes and forms as they do now. Perhaps it was the rigid corset that made one think of an hour-glass when noting the female dress. There was something—as I recall it—that went by the unattractive name rat, made of her own hair by a local artist in that field, which gave an elevated appearance to milady's hair. Hats changed from large to small and back again. Petticoats, without limit as to number, were worn, and when a charming lady got ready to go to the springs or to the country in the summer her trunks were not unlike a theatrical company on the move. One thing I remember most clearly, that to get sunburned was an unforgivable offense. She must at all times be "pale and interesting." Paint was not used and every care was taken to keep the sun away. The country women (and many city visitors to the country) wore home-made bonnets. All shoes were high button black leather, except of course, the dancing slippers which milady carried to the German or to parties, in a decorated cloth bag, and changed into after arriving at the party. Of course there were the usual toilet articles of the period, but never cigarettes or make-up. . . . Women wore long skirts and tried to hide as much of their bodies as possible. A natural complexion was the order of the day, now they go without hats to get sunburned. The high buttoned shoes of my boyhood days have given way to the flimsy product of some Italian designer. Men attended formal functions in morning coats, dress suits and tuxedos, now in sport coats, odd trousers and bermuda shorts. Cocktail parties were unknown as were cocktail dresses and cocktails themselves. College boys tried to see how many tickets they could make, not how many could get into a telephone booth, or who could collect the largest number of panties or eat the most gold fish or attempt to destroy the educational institutions for which their parents pay large sums in order that their descendants might have the opportunity to prepare for the future. Women washed their own hair with the help of a maid. Now a visit to the beauty parlor is a necessity before attending any function and is a weekly ritual. The white women pay large sums to have their hair curled, while the black women pay to have their hair straightened.

Smoking was for men only, as was voting, until many years later. Now the women smoke more than men and not only vote but occupy highest positions in government.

The boy upon graduation from college sought to enter some business or profession, expecting to start at the bottom, hoping to reach the top—all he wanted was a chance to rise.

Those really were the days in which to live. Seriously, it is hard to realize the changes that have come in my lifetime. It is very interesting to recall the student lamp of college days and the gaslight fixtures in our first home. The fireplace, with mantelpiece over it, left approximately a foot of wall space on each side. The gaslight fixture was affixed to that wall. It consisted of a long brass rod with an elbow midway on a movable socket. On the far end of the rod was a small burner which was lighted by a match, after turning on the little wing nut, at the base of the fixture, which controlled the flow of gas. Electric lights were yet to come and the telephone was still a novelty. In fact there had been great excitement when, with wires stretched across Main Street, Professor Winston of Richmond College on May 22, 1877, exhibited the use of the telephone and that night lectured on the wonderful invention.

Electric streetcars did not appear on the streets in regular service until February 2, 1888. The cars ran from Church Hill to the New Reservoir Park (now Byrd Park), at that time considerably beyond the city limits at approximately Lombardy Street. The tracks circled a large loop on Church Hill, then came down 21st to East Franklin Street, up Franklin to the Capitol Square, thence along the south side of the Square to 9th Street, then to Franklin and west on Franklin—past our home—up 7th Street to Clay and on Clay to Hancock, thence southwardly and westwardly past Richmond College, Hollywood Cemetery and the Old Reservoir up to the New Reservoir Park. One branch from East Franklin Street followed North 17th Street to the shops of the C & O Railroad. It has been claimed that Richmond was the first city to use the electric streetcar. That is not exactly correct: it was the first large city in which the streetcar was proven to be practicable. The story of the beginning of the car line in Richmond is an exciting one, too long to relate here.

At each curve in the system was a man with a brush and broom to keep the track clear. He also greased the track on the curves. Motive power flowed to the car from the trolley on top, the replacing of which by the conductor in bad weather when it slipped from the overhead wire sometimes presented a rather difficult task. I recall with what interest we youngsters watched the cars as they passed our house.

Perhaps no event in our earliest years was so important as the coming of the streetcar. Not only was this true in the business world but it brought about changes in social customs and daily living as striking as did the automobile a few years later. The open cars, in summer, afforded opportunities to take one's best girl on car rides to the Old Reservoir, Forest Hill Park and other outlying districts; and from a more material standpoint it brought about the development of suburbs, and practically all of the changes in every area of daily living. It was a great day for boys when the streetcar made possible the discovery of hitherto unknown lands on the outskirts of the city.

Many things that seemed very important in the quiet days of the late 80's have passed from memory, but, to this day I recall the set up of Christian & White's, afterwards R. L. Christian & Company's Grocery Store, on the north side of Main Street, between Eighth and Ninth. The aroma as we entered was indescribable—a marvelous mixture of coffee being ground, pickle in open barrels, spices, sweets in boxes and large glass containers, vinegar, flour, ham and every pleasant odor under the sun. Practically nothing was packaged, everything was measured and put in bags, boxes or bottles. Oysters in season were open for inspection in large containers with long handled dippers for the transfer into cans. Hams hung from the ceiling. Candy in huge bottled-shaped containers; crackers, pickle, flour and other things in barrels lined the aisles. Old Fulcher and Old Bumgardner whiskies could be purchased with one's groceries at one dollar per quart. A visit to Christian's was really a social event of considerable magnitude, as one always met many friends, not to mention the popular proprietors. The supermarket was far in the future and the wholesale grocer was the big man in the life of the city.

The Sixth Street Market was another place of great interest to us boys. As was the custom in those days the man—the head of the family —did the marketing. The Old Market on 17th Street was a place of never ending interest. The presence of so many farmers with their produce from surrounding counties gave the market a greater variety from which to choose than did the newer market. Marketing, as with most other activities of those days, was a very personal thing. The butchers, the fish mongers, the hucksters all maintained a cordial, friendly, personal relationship with their customers.

As a reward for good behavior we would be permitted to go to the market with our father on Saturday mornings and we got quite a thrill when we saw Judge Christian, who had lost a leg in the Confederate Army, come up in his buggy and direct his driver in the purchase of the family supplies for the coming week. In fact the market was an early meeting place for the city's finest citizens. I recall my amazement when I first heard one of the market men, replying to an inquiry as to the cost of an item, say the article in question cost "two shillings!"

Incidentally it was possible in those days to return home with plentiful supplies for the ensuing week and an impressive amount of change from a five dollar bill.

The high character and complete integrity of those men in the market, many of whom I came to know well in later years, was an accepted fact. The buyer did not have to beware—there was no *caveat emptor*! For that matter it may be said that honorable dealings almost without exception were the order of the day.

In our neighborhood, near Capitol Square, there were a number of boys of about the same age. Talbott and Wray Knight lived at the corner of Ninth and Franklin, in the home of their father, Mr. Wray T. Knight, who was the Republican postmaster of Richmond—a very high-toned, honorable gentleman. His home fronted on Ninth Street and extended to the alley in the rear (all now a part of the Federal Reserve Bank).

On Franklin, adjoining the alley on the rear of Mr. Knight's lot, was a small "office," which we used as our headquarters and in which our baseball and other equipment was stored. On Eighth Street, at the southeast corner of Grace Street, was the Macomber home, in which my boyhood friend, Robert Macomber, lived. The house fronted on Eighth Street and was located far back, with a beautiful yard, full of all kinds of lovely flowers, extending to the street line. The addition to St. Paul's Episcopal Church (from the original building to Eighth Street) so generously given recently by Elisabeth Scott Bocock and other members of the congregation, embraced the old Macomber property which, when acquired, was the site of a restaurant. Mr. Macomber was a partner in the firm of Lumsden & Company, Jewelers, on the south side of Main Street just west of Eighth.

There were other boys whose names I do not remember, but the two Knight boys, Robert Macomber, George L. Street, Jr., my brother Coleman and I provided a hard core ready for any adventure. On the east side of Eighth Street, in addition to the Macomber residence (far back from the street) was the Academy of Music. At the northeast corner of Eighth and Franklin was the Meredith home, all now a part of the Federal Reserve Bank.

As we grew up we were allowed to join a group of older boys and girls who played at night on Grace Street between Eighth and Seventh Streets. Among them was Stafford Parker and his sister Florence—one of the most attractive people I ever knew, who first married Marion Lambert, a founder of Listerine Company, and afterwards married into the Anheuser-Busch family—Andrew Pizzini and his sister Estelle, and many others. Dr. Parker, father of Stafford and Florence, lived on the south side of Grace, between Eighth and Seventh Streets. Captain Andrew Pizzini, a graduate of V.M.I., a former captain of the Richmond Light Infantry Blues and one of the organizers of the first electric streetcar company, lived at the southwest corner of Grace and Eighth Streets.

At nights, weather permitting, all of the boys and girls old enough to be allowed to stay up until 9:30 or 10 o'clock congregated and indulged in games, one of which might be the forerunner of the touch football of today. There was slight, if any, interference by traffic. Automobiles and movies were yet to come and only a doctor answering a night call in his buggy might once in a blue moon interfere with the games.

One of the sports I have touched upon but lightly was roller skating which our gang particularly enjoyed when Governor O'Ferrall occupied the Governor's Mansion. We were allowed to skate within the fence surrounding the Washington Monument with our friends, Frank and Helen O'Ferrall. The story of the governor's reply to a query of Mrs. O'Ferrall's as to the cause of a disturbance in the rear yard of the mansion was the source of much amusement at the time. Both the Governor and Mrs. O'Ferrall had been married before and both had children by their first marriages, and they also had children by their marriage. The governor's report was "It is nothing, my dear, only your children and our children fighting my children."

The coming of the automobile was destined to change our world to a greater extent than anything before or since had done or could do. Home life underwent a startling change. Personal habits and dress responded to the requirements and limitations of this form of transportation. The undesirable characters and the juvenile delinquent had been given great mobility; the criminal element was put on wheels; forms of dress were influenced by it; the high silk hat was "knocked into a cocked hat"; the development of the suburbs was greatly accelerated, country clubs were built, sea shore cottages were made possible and various forms of amusement and social activities developed; and later, churches joined the parade to the suburbs which the automobile made possible.

It became increasingly difficult to control this new mode of transportation and to fit it into the pattern of daily living. A problem was presented to the courts: What is this? How shall we fit it into our laws? The first decisions of the courts proceeded from the assumption that the laws applicable to wild beasts on the highway did not apply to automobiles. Then came the problem of regulating the few automobiles as they appeared on the streets, along with horse-drawn vehicles. One simple law was quickly enacted which required the operator of an automobile, if a horse became frightened at it, to stop and lead the frightened horse past.

At first the automobile was the plaything of the rich. The expense of even the best makes was astronomical. The chauffeur was called the mechanic. Any young man who owned an automobile in its earlier years was regarded as an impossible credit risk by the banks.

It was quite a while before the price and the mechanical development of the automobile made it practical for ownership by the average man. Before World War I it was still largely a plaything for the wealthy, but even then, the old "Tin Lizzie" was appearing in ever increasing numbers on the streets of the city; indeed, the transportation needs of the citizens of Richmond had become greater than the streetcars could meet, with the result that open five-passenger cars, with isinglass and leather curtains, were by law permitted to be operated on certain city routes for a five-cent fare. The nickel was often referred to as a jitney, hence the cars involved in rendering that service were called jitneys.

Incidentally the huge establishments of today were unthought of. The first dealers were usually businessmen who handled the sales and repair of bicycles and the display room for the automobile was the city street, usually Main Street, where the exhibition car would be parked with the salesmen in or near it.

Cutchins, *Memories of Old Richmond* (1973), pp. 22–24,
26–32

"Speaking of Kosher Milk":
Richmond's Jewry (1880s and 1890s)

Richmond's Jewish community began even before the American Revolution and had grown large enough by 1789 for the founding of Beth Shalome synagogue, forerunner of Beth Ahaba. Two years later the congregation established Virginia's first Jewish cemetery at the present-day location of Twenty-first and Franklin streets. From these pioneers, mainly of western European extraction, came many of the city's business and political leaders. The tradition of eastern Europe is represented by Joseph Joel (1882–1960), whose recollections below are of his experiences as a youth in Richmond and are useful for their ethnic flavor and social commentary. The Jewish community is but one of numerous cultural strains in the city's population. On the eve of the Civil War, for example, perhaps a quarter of the white inhabitants were foreign-born, most being of German and Irish origin.

§ My Recollections and Experiences of Richmond, Virginia, U.S.A., 1884–1892

My father [was] Salomon Czaczkes, who changed his name on arrival at Richmond, Va. to Salomon Joel. This changing of name was due to the fact that there were few foreigners here and the people just couldn't pronounce the "Cz" as "Ch" as in "Chicken," etc. He was an Austrian of Podwoloczyska, Galicia, a border town on the Austrian-Russian frontier. He married and resided (from time of his marriage to my mother who lived in a medium size town), [in] Proskurov, about 50 miles in Russia, until his expulsion and emigration to Richmond. He was, as we call now such emigrants, a Refugee.

My Father came to Richmond instead of going to Palestine, his preference, because he had here a sister—Mrs. Yetta Rashbaum (Jewish name Gitze), a widow with 4 daughters and 2 sons—all grown and capable of working & helping to support the family. He also had a single brother, a watchmaker, Herman Joel, who testified in the Cluverius Murder case.

My aunt had what was then known as a dry goods store on 17th Street near the old Slave Auction Market. Most of the Jewish Emigrants operated dry goods stores but they sold everything—notions —dry goods—men's suits—shoes—hats, etc. Ladys ready-to-wear clothes were not yet on the market then. Dresses were made, that is why the stores you called dry goods.

My uncle, Herman Joel, as stated was a watchmaker but he operated a jewelry store on West Broad just beyond Brook Ave. My aunt (Yetta Rashbaum) moved about 1886 to Baltimore and my Uncle down to E. Main, I think, somewheres between Eleventh and Twelfth Street where as I recalled—he also sold musical instruments. From there he returned to Europe—Tarnopol, Galicia. He had to leave because the public boycotted him because he testified in that famous Cluverius Case, that he repaired the *watchkey* which was found on the Iron fence at the Reservoir where the body of the girl was found. Due to his testimony, Cluverius was convicted and executed. I remember the case— the trial—the excitement. In those days, a murder case—a white one was a rarity and the whole town was excited especially as in this case —prominent people—conscience—a school teacher and pregnant were involved.

In Europe, my father was a merchant. He had a distillery. He dealt in grains because he needed rye for his distillery. He also manufactured yeast from the byproduct and shipped all over Russia as far as possible; also across the border into Austria. But after arriving here, he could not apply his knowledge of commerce and as he did not know a trade, he opened up a small jewelry store, corner 8th and Broad, a one window affair, with small glass panes. It was connected with the original Murphy's Hotel. I have a picture of the Hotel. It looked like a Western one built out of boards. As father didn't know anything of this jewelry line nor to repair watches, he hired old Mr. Harrison's son who was a watchmaker.

I remember now the wood and coal yard just across the street-corner 8th and Broad, north East corner. I remember the trains on Broad Street with a man flag[g]ing it who walked in front of the locomotive. I remember the passenger cars with the open platforms and though the cars are in comparison like palaces now, still the present riders do not get the pleasure when riding as in former days. Why just seeing a train coming into the station was a treat and an enjoyment. I also remember when the Electric lights first went on in the City and I think it was the first in the U.S. It was a large globe with a large carbon stick and this I think had to be changed and replaced often. One of these lights was right on the corner in front of our place.

I remember when we resided at Murphys, A[a]ron Gellman, the father of the late attorney, Sam Gellman, and Israel Weinstein, my father-in-law, arrived in Richmond. My father sent them tickets which he purchased for them on credit. Both of them left their homes to avoid military service. A[a]ron Gellman was a brother of a close friend of my father. He was from Kaminetz Podolsk in the Ukraine; Weinstein from Tarnopol in Galicia. Gellman knew no trade but Weinstein was a watchmaker. Weinstein began working for my father. What Gellman did, I can't recollect.

Weinstein married a daughter of my father's sister of Baltimore, Gellman a sister of Chane Leihe Spiegel, a widow, who operated also on 17th St. a drygoods store. Most of the so called Russian Jews had stores on 17th Street because it was a good shopping street. All the farmers, colored people and laborers traded there. Most people of that station bought second-hand shoes and clothing. They weren't as prosperous as these days. A person worked for one dollar a day. They did not go to work in automobiles but they never aspired to own a buggy or to live like people live now. Any table, any chair, any bed was good enough—even the Jews—the merchants. No women then in our class had the worries of matching furniture—carpets or curtains with the colors or flowers in the design. I tell you, people enjoyed their clothes, their food and whatever they acquired. Only the rich had carriages and sleighs. Bicycles were very, very few. I remember them with a real large front wheel and a small one in the rear.

All the kind[s] of cookies, fruits, vegetables were unknown then. We had in season—oranges were a treat but peaches, apples, pears and berries in season were cheap. We kids just had to go down to the canal when a ship was unloading bananas or pineapples and we got all we wanted. They were transferred in 2 wheel carts and draywagons and stored in cellars all along the Northside stores on Main Street up to 14th St.

Speaking of food, I'll tell you how things were sold—spring chickens by the *bunches*. I don't remember whether a bunch contained three or more chickens but they were sold by the bunch. I used to peddle them when a boy of 8–12, first on 17th Street market while we lived on Main Street—later on 6th St. Market when we lived on West Broad and I used to swap a pair of suspenders, matches or collarbuttons or something else for chickens, ducks, vegetables, or fruit with the farmers. Nothing was sold by the pound. They just started selling vegetables by the pound around World War I.

Food, rather living, was cheap but the people those days didn't earn enough to buy things—food, rent or others things though cheap. Children didn't know of the toys they get these days. One made his wagon or sleigh out of a wooden shipping box. Everything was boxed in wooden boxes and wooden barrels. Paper cartons were unknown. Kids got pennies and not too often either. A street car ride was a treat. One even didn't use it to fetch a doctor. I used to walk or hitchhike a ride on a slow-moving dray-wagon to fetch the doctor who lived on 6th St. near the Market, a doctor Graver, and we lived around 19th St. and East Main. My father believed in moving. He blamed the location for not making a living—not himself that is why we lived on 8th and Broad, 1503 E. Main, 1800 block, 1900 block E. Main. We resided in Manchester too but that was on doctor's recommendation.

Speaking of food in the early days was a problem for the so-called Polish Jews. One couldn't buy a regular salted herring here. The Christians used split mackerels. Father used to have things like a small wooden keg of herring—a large round cheese—*maslines*, these are black, oily bitter but delicious olives. What we get now are overripe olives or black ones soaked in salt water. We eat these and the grocer likes it for we pay him for a lot of saltpeter. The cheese then too was bitter ripe, dry and pungent. The American cheeses we are sold these days are wet—taste like rubber, flat and the ones that have a taste, it's bitter. Father also used to get from Baltimore, weather permitting, wurst of all types—hot dog kind, the ring kind, for cooking, bologna and salami. Also smoked meats and believe me all tasted better than what they sell us these days. None contained all that poison that they call preservatives. Just read what the labels read these days—chemicals and more chemicals. No the food isn't good as in former days. They taste good to you because you don't know of the taste of former days. Even the Christians ate better. I used to go to a Christian woman who had a cow to get our milk, for the milk to be kosher we couldn't use it of her utensils, so she milked it into my milkcan. I always went for the milk in the morning before going to school. It was always at breakfast time and what didn't they *fress* those days, the working people—hot bread, hot biscuits, fried mackerel, bacon, etc. Also so called ashcakes which was corn bread baked on cabbage leaves under the glow of the hot coals. They didn't buy and eat that tissue paper bacon. People always had a whole piece hanging on their wall, also saltpork, and they cut off what they wanted and the slices were finger thick. Their hot bread and biscuits were not store ones, pre-baked. Of course, to have breakfast ready so the men could be at work at 7 o'clock, the women used to get up early, I imagine at five. The men walked to work, not like now in the automobiles and on their way, they used to stop for a drink or two at their favorite saloon.

Speaking of kosher milk, I want to tell you so you will know more of your Grandfather. In Russia, he was a *Maskil*, one of the Enlightened ones. I heard that he and his friends used to drink a fresh made glass of tea and smoke a cigarette on *Shabbas*. He used to read besides his Hebrew paper that was just published, secular ones and secular books. He went to *schul* because that was the style just like we Jews now are members of some kind of congregation. Those days the *Schul* was the Club. There they *schmust* of everything before *davening*—politics— business—Jewish problems.

Although my father was a *yeshivenik* until his marriage, still he was a *Maskil* and spoke Polish and German. He was able to read Hebrew papers and books besides Torah but then he came to Richmond and found himself with a wife and three children. I had a sister who died in Richmond at Weinstein's home, 1703 East Main on the 2nd day of *Cholemoed Pesach* while we were visiting them. She is buried at Sir Moses Montefiore Cemetery which plot was sold to the Lovensteins in my father's absence from Richmond. She was 19 years old and the third one interred. The first one interred in that cemetery was a Jew (I can't remember who he was); the second one, Mr. Harrison, a store-keeper, a mason and a prominent Jew and my sister was the third one.

Well besides my sister I had a brother, Moses who was the second oldest and then I—the third child. Well here he (my father) was a refugee—poor—with wife and 3 children, couldn't speak English and didn't know a trade. This depressed him so much that he became "fanatical" religious. So much so that he found the present Reform congregation not pious enough—they were then orthodox but some members weren't. They all kept closed on *Shabbas*, ate kosher. He didn't find their *Schochet*, a Mr. Miller, kosher enough because he used to trim his beard so he organized a *Minyon*. This was the Sir Moses Montefiore *Schul* on the 3rd floor over a store, a farm implement store on the north side of Main Street bordering on the Canal. It was where the present RR station is.

I remember a Mr. Halperin became our *Schochet* and my Hebrew teacher. When I say Hebrew teacher, I mean that he taught us how to read the prayer book and the *Chumish*—not the Hebrew language. Whether this Mr. Halperin was a resident of Richmond or whether the orthodox Jews brought him to Richmond I don't know. I remember him as a tall—nice reverent looking man with a white beard. He always smoked a long cherry stem pipe which smelled so good. He lived on the west side of Mayo Street between Franklin and Grace. He had a wife and 2 daughters—her name was Fanny. I remember the place and the good times well. The *Rebitzen* used to cook fish every Friday and she used to use a lot of onions and fish bones as a bottom layer and she used to give us children, small pieces of her gefulte fish and the bones. You see fish were cheap. They used to catch plenty right here in the James, even sturgeons. So to give the fish a good flavor and to make the gravy, she used extra bone heads and fins of extra fish.

Well as father found the *schul*, whether it was the Polishe or the Beth Shalom[e], I don't know, not *frum* enough, he and the few other so called Russian Jews organized and formed the Sir Moses Montefiore. They didn't have a *Chazan*. Members led in prayer. My father mostly because he chanted nicely. He also was the president. He too was the one that arranged to have a *Mikvah* built. It was a one room affair right back of C. D. Kenny tea store, corner south east, 1701 East Main. We knew which *Yiddene* went to the Mikvah for my father used to go and fire the stove. Yes he was a *macher* of Yiddishkeit.

He used to walk around with every *shaliah*. This is a solicitor for some Jewish needed fund. He too saw that every newcomer was provided with a pack. That is a box fitted out with all kinds of notions for the poor devil to go out into the surrounding counties to sell to the farmers. Those days people didn't come to town in autos like they do now. That isolated-living farmer was glad to see that Jewish peddlar. He fed him and give him at nightfall a bed to sleep on some sofa or just a filled-in sack with straw. Most of those peddlars were *kosher-living* Jews so they ate eggs, hard boiled, milk, potatoes, a piece of herring, or cheese that they carried with them. They used to go out Sundays and come back Fridays for *Shabbes*. They all later on as they saved and prospered, opened small stores in towns or in some villages and brought their families to the U.S.

Whenever a *shaliah* or an emigrant came to Richmond, my father was the man to care for him. He went around with him soliciting. He fed him and they slept at our place during their stay, and as it wasn't polite to leave a person just sitting around, so he kept him company and helped him emptying the *samovar*. My mother brought along her *samovar*. I still have it and of course, they talked and talked. Of course this running around with these people and attending with *schul* politics—firing the *Mikvah* made him neglect his business and that is why he never made a living and caused him to move around.

Later on I remember they had a *Shamas*, a Mr. Passamaneck, the father of the late Dentist. He too had a tea store on 17th St.

The Polish Jews were few. I recollect Chane Leihe Spiegel who married later a Mr. Barrow or Barove. She had 3 boys—Bennie, Joe and Moische. A[a]ron Gellman married her sister. I remember the wedding. It was at home. Not like now at a hotel. I helped putting up the bed. Boy did they have wedding gifts! Many sets of water pitchers and glasses and wash basins, pitchers and nightpots. Thats what the Jews gave for presents so he had a set from each friend. Those days they didn't have bathrooms, at least not the 17th Street and Main Street residents so in each bedroom there was a washstand with a por-celain water pitcher, basin and night pot. I recollect 2 weddings in our crowd. These were Gellmans and Weinsteins. There were no young men or girls of marriageable age.

There was also a family, Moshe Brown—Spiegels, Weinberg. Later on a baker whose name I don't remember. I recollect he used to bake large round rye bread and it was rye bread, not what the bakers sell us now a mixture of anything that is dark. And it was *sour* dough natural soured. He also made Pumpernickel bread out of stale bread, white and rye. His *chales* too were nice, crusty and so tasty. Everything was well baked out, slowly and not in pans but in brick ovens, fired by wood not gas or electricity.

There was a Shloime London, Mr. Harrison and a few others whose names I can't remember. All of them had stores. The only one with a trade was that baker and he came after we did.

From that Main St. flat, that *Minyon* moved to Mayo Street. They still didn't have a *chazen* but they had a Mr. Gerson, the father of the present sons and daughters. Him my father brought down from Bal-timore after Halperin left town. He too taught us 6 boys Hebrew. He stayed with us and sometimes, I accompanied him to the slaughter house in the country, which is now Brook Road. It couldn't have been far for we used to walk but the walk of 5 miles was nothing. I used to walk to Mayo Street *schul* from the 14th street block of Hull Street every *Shabbas* and from *schul*, father, my brother Moses and I and we weren't tired either. Later on we had also a Jewish butcher, a Jewish hawker of delicatessen so we didn't have to have things shipped in from Baltimore.

Life was serene in those days. We children and the grown ups had a good time now as then when a child, a boy was born. They celebrated a month. *Simchas Torah, Purim* or *Succos*, we had a real *Yomtov*. The people were closer to one another, real friends. They shared their happiness and their troubles. A friend wasn't just a person you met twice and when we nowadays call by his first name and whom we wouldn't even lend a dollar but a friend whom we loved and shared his homeliness, his troubles. When one visited, they didn't play cards, but they sat around, drank tea or a glass of beer and talked and talked.

When people had a gathering of friends, it was not like now when a bunch of people mill around with a glass of diluted whiskey which they call a cocktail in their hands and are bored. Those days, they didn't have a name for a gathering like a cocktail party but they had a vessel of beer—some herring—cheeses or wurst, smoked meat. Or the hostess cooked a supper like borscht or cabbage soup—pirogen or knisches and everybody was really happy.

Those so called cocktail parties weren't often but when one had one it was a party. It was had only on some holiday and they drank and ate. None of your fancy junk—a cracker with some liver paste or such. Their liver was *gehackte leber* with goose fat—*grivene* chopped in onions. Their liver wasn't broiled in a pan but under a glowing coal fire which made the liver dry, crumbly and had that toasted taste. Often the supper existed of *gebratene* such as goose and it wasn't baked or fried like they do now but *gebratene*. You women folks don't know how to cook these days. You are lucky you don't remember good tasty food. Otherwise you would be miserable like I am. You too wouldn't enjoy eating.

Well this is all I remember of Richmond. It is snowy today, December 12, 1957, which reminds me of the winters here as a child. There was a store keeper, I think on the 18th—19th or 20th St. Block E. Main. He was a *balegale*—we call him a dray man. When the snow was thick and frozen, he used to take a barn door hitched on his pair of mules and used to treat the kids of the neighborhood to a sleigh ride. His name was Nachman.

Speaking of weather reminds me of the floods we used to have those days. We kids used to watch the water rising in the cellars—then it came up to the street. Those days, a lot of freighters, sail boats used to be in the canal so the sailors used to have a good time with the life-boats. People appreciated those boats. If I think of something else, I'll add to it. In 1892, father moved to Chicago to try his luck at the then existing exposition. He went there because Uncle Herman came back to Chicago from Europe, but there too father never attended to his business but to *schul* matters and poor people's troubles. So in 1894, we all returned to Podwoloczyska, Galicia. I returned to Richmond in 1914.

Joel, "Recollections and Experiences," ed. Berman, *Virginia Magazine* 87 (July 1979): 344–56

"The Confederate Flag Was Everywhere Conspicuously Displayed": The Lee Monument (1890)

Although Robert E. Lee was a citizen of the South at large, he had particularly strong ties to Richmond. Following the secession of Virginia from the Union, he accepted command of the Virginia state forces in the capitol and throughout the latter part of the war maintained his official residence in the city, at 707 East Franklin Street, the home to which he returned following the surrender at Appomattox. After the defeat of the Confederacy, Lee passed into the popular mythology of the South in general and that of Richmond in particular. One of the great events surrounding the leader occurred in 1890 when his equestrian statue arrived at the city by ship. Virginius Dabney (q.v.) has noted that Richmond's black community, led by John Mitchell, Jr. (q.v.), argued vehemently against the city's appropriating money for the statue; nevertheless $10,000 was allotted for the purpose. Sculpted in France by Jean Antoine Mercié, the statue was pulled by Richmond's citizens to a location at the end of Franklin Street, the extension of which became Monument Avenue. Fifty former Confederate generals, along with fifteen thousand veterans from every state in the South, were in attendance. Some local families still keep as souvenirs fragments of the ropes used to move the statue to what was then Richmond's suburbs.

The occasion of the unveiling of the Lee statue at Richmond, Virginia, on the 29th of May, possessed features that render it a unique event in history. It was a mighty tribute to the central figure of a lost cause, attended by an undercurrent of satisfaction even that the cause was lost. The man commemorated was the chief General in a four years' war waged to rend in pieces this union of States, and perhaps no better proof of the willing relinquishment of that object could be furnished than by what was said, as well as written between the lines, in the celebration in question. There certainly, if anywhere, was to be found the residuum of the feeling that existed in the South but little more than a quarter of a century ago, and in the accounts given of this vast assembling there is no evidence whatever of any lingering intelligent repugnance to the Union or of a desire for the re-enslavement of the blacks.

The confederate flag was everywhere conspicuously displayed. The military companies affectionately bore it in the line of march, but with it they bore the Stars and Stripes, and bore them loyally. The paradox is explainable only by the fact that the former no longer meant disunion. It stood, rather, for past trials and heroism in adversity looked back upon from the standpoint of changed views and unforeseen prosperity. The very spot on which the monument stands, now laid off in avenues and streets to supply the wants of the city's growth in population and wealth, was farmland at the time of the war. How far the cause of the cleared vision is indicated by this evidence of progress need not be dwelt upon. It is enough that though the memory of the struggle must remain, its bitterness is gone to an extent that once was deemed impossible. The national flag was not exhibited at Richmond, prominently as it appeared, as a matter either of policy or of courtesy, but with the honest feeling that it was owned and belonged there. During the ceremonies this sentiment was constantly cropping out, and in no case was it more felicitously expressed than in the address of Miss Fanny Dickinson at a presentation of a stand of colors, peculiar in design, to the New York Camp Confederate Veterans. "Take it," she said, "and wreathe it in graceful folds with the flag of your country, as I do now, and love the one as the sentiment that awakened in your souls the grandest deeds of daring performed by mortal man, and revere the other because you are Americans—patriots—and it is your flag."

All sections of the South were represented in the great throng that took part in and witnessed the proceedings. It is estimated that more than twenty thousand men were in line of march, and four times that number of people in the streets. The resources of the city were taxed to the utmost to entertain the host of visitors, and if the accommodations in some respects fell short, the situation was accepted in good spirit. The procession formed about noon, with General Fitzhugh Lee at its head. Every Southern State supplied its quota of veterans and militia. There were many thousands of the former, and they greeted their old commanders who were present with hearty cheers. Among those thus hailed were Generals Joseph E. Johnston, Jubal Early, James Longstreet, and Gordon. The fact that General Longstreet's Republican affiliations since the war did not in the least diminish the ardor of his reception by the ex-Confederate soldiers strengthened the abundant evidence that it was the influence of old associations, and not political feeling, that dominated the scene. In the line were Misses Mary and Mildred, the two daughters of General Robert E. Lee, who were repeatedly cheered. The sons, General W. H. F. Lee and Captain Robert E. Lee, Jun., were also present.

The site of the memorial is at the western end of Franklin Avenue, one of the finest residence thoroughfares of Richmond, and here the great crowd gathered and the dedicatory speeches were made. About four o'clock Governor McKinney, chairman of the association under whose auspices the monument was erected, opened the exercises with a short speech. He was followed by General Early, and he in turn by the Rev. Dr. Charles Minnegerode with a prayer. Then the orator of the day, Colonel Archer Anderson, was introduced, and made an appropriate address, giving a record of Lee's life, his conscientiousness, devotion to duty, sacrifices, and the salient excellencies of his character in general. When the orator had concluded, General Joseph E. Johnston pulled the cord which held the covering of the statue, and the figure was quickly exposed to the multitude who greeted it with enthusiastic shouts. A picture of the monument is printed in the present issue of the *Weekly*. The height of the whole structure is 61 feet 2 inches, the pedestal being 39 feet, and the equestrial figure itself 22 feet and 2 inches. The latter is of bronze, by the sculptor Murius Jean Antoine Mercié of Paris, and has been represented and described in detail in a previous number of this periodical. The effect of the whole is, in a high degree, satisfying from an artistic point of view, and is an important addition to the adornments of Richmond.

The opinion has with much reason been expressed that an occasion of such magnitude as the one described, with reference to the late Confederacy, is not likely ever to be repeated. General Lee personified what was best in a bad cause. His individual virtues gave the Southern people, who craved a demonstration commemorative of an indelible epoch in their lives, something substantial and unquestionably creditable to rally around. The honor to the hero of their vain struggle has been paid, and the full conditions for another such gathering are wanting. It may therefore be surmised that in the great outpouring of the ex-Confederates at Richmond the final obsequies of the war of secession have taken place, and the circumstances attending it show how completely the wounds of the conflict have been healed, and a most important chapter of American history closed.

Harper's Weekly, June 1890, p. 470

"My Boyhood Overlapped a Few of the Warriors": The Mythology Is Strengthened (Early 1900s)

Following the defeat of the Confederacy, there arose across the South a renewed sense of regional identity and pride that rivaled any seen previously in the country. In Richmond, the former capital, a new city was built phoenix-like on the ashes of the old. Monument Avenue was laid out and quickly came to accommodate the statues of great Confederate heroes, chief among them being that of Robert E. Lee (q.v.). In addition, a successful campaign to save the White House of the Confederacy was launched by the Confederate Memorial Literary Society; the Robert E. Lee Camp of the Confederate Veterans, locally known as the Old Soldiers' Home, was founded; its counterpart, the Confederate Ladies' Home, also came into being; and the United Daughters of the Confederacy continued to grow in popularity. Veterans' parades and reunions were common, and the libraries began to fill with proud southerners bent on learning their genealogies. Leading all other projects in scope and intent was the emerging plan to build the Battle Abbey, envisioned as a permanent memorial to the Confederacy.

One social organization of particular interest that arose during the time in question was the Westmoreland Club. The forerunner of the present-day Commonwealth Club, it was founded by Confederate veterans and was named for the county of General Lee's birth.

In the following selection, J. Bryan III describes the Westmoreland Club as he knew it as a boy. Bryan is a former editorial writer for the Richmond *News Leader* and served in the U.S. Navy during World War II. A former associate editor of the *Saturday Evening Post,* he has written articles that have appeared in the leading journals of the day, and he is also the author of several books, among them *The Windsor Story.*

I can't remember, now, how old I was before I realized that there had been different wars—many, many of them. My first, childish assumption was there had been only one: *The* War, like *The* Flood. I didn't know where it had been fought, or when. But all the Heroes were there: Sir Lancelot, in shining armor; and General Washington, with a Hatchet in one hand and a Silver Dollar in the other; and Robin Hood and William Tell, with bows and arrows. General Lee, noble and silent, rode Traveller; Robert Bruce and Arnold Winkelried were afoot. Vaguely in the background, the Boy Stood on the Burning Deck, and Horatius on the Bridge. And one night, they buried Sir John Moore, with the Lanterns Dimly Burning and the Yser Rolling Rapidly. The roster of heroes lengthened as Grandmother read more to me, but the enemy was always the same: Pharaoh's army, wearing blue coats and forage caps.

. . . Richmond used to have a proud old club called the Westmoreland. Its house had been the home of Poe's "Helen," the beautiful Mrs. Stanard; and in its garden, like a green fountain, was a weeping willow grown from one at Mount Vernon, in turn grown from one over Napoleon's grave. Many of the senior Westmorelanders, veterans of The War, liked to sit around the bar and talk about "battles long ago," to the boredom of the younger members, including Father and my uncles. I assume this from what Uncle Bob did to me. I was entering my teens at the time, and, apropos the news of Verdun in the headlines just then, I mentioned my regret at never having seen a real battlefield.

"Nothing simpler," Uncle Bob said. "How'd you like to see the bloodiest battlefield in the whole War? . . . Fine! I'll pick you up at noon tomorrow."

Naturally, I expected a jaunt to Cold Harbor, Seven Pines, the Crater, Yellow Tavern, or some other nearby field where (as I quoted to myself with tingling scalp) "superstition nightly hears the neighing of chargers, and still sees with heated fancy the rushing squadrons of spectral war." But where Uncle Bob took me was to the Westmoreland, downstairs, to the door of the bar.

"Here it is, son," he said. "Gaze your fill! Right here, in this very room, more Yankees have been slaughtered than at Bull Run, Fredericksburg and Gettysburg put together!"

Considering that the Westmoreland had been founded by Confederate officers and named for General Lee's native county, that it had held its first meeting in his former Richmond home, and that its first nonresident member was Capt. Robert E. Lee, I felt that the elders were well within their rights when they reminisced about The War—that, indeed, any other topic would have been inappropriate, unbecoming, and even downright indecent.

Still, the younger members weren't always alone in their impatience. Judge Hunter Marshall, himself a veteran, was sipping away in the bar one afternoon when he was cornered by the club bore, Major W.

"Judge," the major asked, "did I ever tell you how I was nearly given a colonelcy on the field of battle?"

"Yes, by God!" cried the judge in anguish. "Ten *thousand* times!"

The judge and the major are also celebrated for another similar passage. The judge told one of the club servants, "Nathan, open that window, please."

The major hitched up his chair. "That reminds me of a story, Judge. It seems—"

The judge didn't waste a moment. "Nathan!" he called. "Nathan, close that window!"

And again: the judge came into the club one morning with a new anecdote trembling to be told, but found the rooms empty except for the major. He weighed the beauty of the anecdote against the penalty for opening the conversation, and this is how he handled it: "Major, I'll tell you an extraordinary story, if you'll promise you won't tell me one right back."

When I became old enough to make the acquaintance of the Westmoreland, as a very junior and very occasional guest, the club was already past its prime. Its original personality had changed. The years had thinned the ranks of its warrior-founders—those wits and scholars, epicures and raconteurs, who were as easily able to identify an unlabeled Madeira as to pun in Greek and Latin. Worse, the picturesque old "characters"—in the Southern sense of the word—were being supplanted by mere eccentrics. These, too, were picturesque in their way, but it was a wilder, coarser, more self-conscious way. In place of the older member who was known to trudge nineteen blocks uptown from the club every day, and back again, just to salute General Lee's statue, there suddenly appeared a younger member who was known to sleep in leather pajamas. Another always carried a game cock in his pocket, until he rashly matched it against a vulgar owl which had never heard of the Queensberry rules; the owl clutched the cock by the neck and pulled its head off. Another member, who dined exclusively on wild duck and chocolate ice cream, used to drive around Richmond in a Pierce-Arrow with a built-in bed, toilet and cookstove. The car was easy for us to recognize; he had it painted in blue and white stripes, to match a favorite shirt.

Still, my boyhood overlapped a few of the warriors. Some of them I myself knew; others I knew through Father's accounts. Mr. Frank Nalle, for example, I remember well. I remember his Prince Albert coat of rainbow-colored tweed, the only one I ever saw in my life; I remember his reciting Virgil by the hour; and I remember how hard it was for me to realize that this mild, soft-spoken old gentleman had been a rebel-yelling V.M.I. cadet at the battle of New Market, in May '64. Dampness had swelled and stuck the wooden ramrods, so the antiquated Austrian rifles couldn't be fired but once, yet the cadets charged and carried the Federal guns—these *boys*, some of them only fourteen, *my* age!

And I remember Capt. Thomas Pinckney, my great-uncle. He had starved as a Yankee prisoner at Morris Island, and once told me off-handedly, "You get used to them after a while, son. Rats don't taste all *that* bad."

And I remember Mr. Egbert Leigh, who had known the excitement of being a youngster in Petersburg in the '60s, and awakening to the guns rumbling over the cobblestones, and seeing General Beauregard slap laggards with the flat of his saber. Mr. Leigh maintained that by far the ablest of the Yankee generals was George H. Thomas, also of Petersburg. He said that when the city fell, in January '65, General Thomas rode up to the house where his sisters still lived, and sent word to them that their brother was downstairs, and the terrible word came back, "We have no brother."

And I remember Major Robert W. Hunter, the Confederate archivist. Thirsty, and barred from refreshment by a lady's ignorant, adoring and interminable disquisition on General Washington, he broke it off with a desperate "I must decline to discuss him further, madam, because of his personal morals!"

Whenever Major Hunter was invited to "take something" and was asked what it would be, he invariably replied, "Whatever *you* are taking, sir." This courtesy of his inspired Father and my uncles to a typical piece of their mischief, one afternoon at the club. Father led off. He challenged the major to a game of checkers, purposely lost it, and remarked, "Drinks on me, Major! What's your pleasure, sir?"

As expected, the major bowed and replied, "I'll have what you have, sir."

"Splendid!" said Father, tapping the bell. "Boy, two sas'p'rillas, please."

This was the signal for Uncle Jonathan to appear and demand the privilege of challenging the winner. Uncle Jonathan, too, lost on purpose, asked the major's pleasure, and ordered two sarsaparillas. Then came Uncle Bob. When *he* ordered sarsaparillas, the major's courtesy wore through. "No!" he cried. "No, no, *no*! Damme if I'll fill my belly with the east wind! Boy, bring me whisky!"

(If there seems to have been a surfeit of colonels, majors and captains in the Westmoreland, it should be remembered that a diarist visiting Richmond nearly 200 years ago noted that it was apparently "a haven for heroes"—that every man had a military title, by courtesy if not by desert. The custom has died out now, but even today the stranger who accosts a Richmonder with "Excuse me, Colonel—" runs only a negligible risk of being slapped with a gauntlet and haled to the Field of Honor. However, it should also be remembered that there was a period in the '80s when all five Justices of Virginia's Supreme Court were former privates in The War.)

Yet another colonel, *primus inter pares* (he loved Latin tags), was W. Gordon McCabe, Grandfather's friend and eulogist, and formerly adjutant of Pegram's Artillery Battalion. I have been told that he was famous throughout Virginia for his scholarship as well as his heroism, but I remember him as drinking his champagne from a celery vase, and as knowing Lord Tennyson intimately enough to write him, "Dear Alf—"

"Champagne" reminds me of the famous champagne breakfast that Cousin Jim Tucker gave at the Westmoreland—famous both for its duration and for the occasion. It lasted three days, by which time Cousin Jim and his guests felt that they had fittingly celebrated his brother Bev's ordination as Bishop of Southern Virginia.

Cousin Jim Tucker was a "catbird," as Negroes say in admiration: a catbird and a he-coon. At sixteen, he had been regimental color bearer for Fitz-Hugh Lee, who protested that "He went at the enemy so fast, the troops couldn't keep up with the colors." He was wounded three times (two bullets, one saber), had five horses killed, and was twice cited for "reckless bravery." Before that, he had swum ashore from a sinking blockade runner, with a parcel of dispatches for Jefferson Davis. And after that—well, he narrowly escaped being shot with Emperor Maximilian, in Mexico; he locked himself in the office with James Gordon Bennett, of *The New York Herald*, and brandished

a Cuban cattle whip until Bennett promised to retract his false statement that Cousin Jim's father had been a confederate of John Wilkes
Booth's; working as a waiter, he spilled soup on a French princess, but
persuaded her to accept his apologies a week later, when he waltzed
with her at a court ball; he—but this is no place to start talking about
Cousin Jim Tucker. He'd run away with the story.

Incidentally, Cousin Bev (who later became the Bishop) figured in
one of the oddest coincidences in The War. A very young private, he
was detailed as a guard on a prison train bound for Salisbury, North
Carolina. Most of the prisoners were foreigners, of a nation uniden-
tified; the language they whispered was strange. They were therefore
doubly astonished when they broke for freedom at a way station and
found themselves ringed by the bayonets of the entire guard. Bev
Tucker, who had overheard their conspiracy, was probably the only
man in the whole Army of Northern Virginia who could speak the
patois of the Swiss canton from which the prisoners hailed. He had
been to school there.

My mentions of champagne are misleading. The Westmoreland's
standard drink was not champagne but "mountain" (i.e., bourbon),
taken neat, by the "dram," and reverently. Venerable Westmorelanders
have not forgotten the vehemence, becoming violence, with which
Major S. protested that his dram "reeked" of turpentine. The house
committee traced the dram to a bottle on the bar, and the bottle to a
barrel in the cellar, and the barrel to a vat in the distillery. One of its
oaken staves had split, they found, and had been ignorantly replaced
with a stave of pine.

The house committee also had trouble with little Mr. G., who filed a
regular complaint that they were watering the whisky. It would have
been better for him if they had taken his complaint as a suggestion,
for he met his early end with a full retinue of the horrors. When word
reached the bar, trade fell away steeply, until Mr. M. suggested that at
least the lankily built men were unduly apprehensive. Mr. G.'s demise,
he said, should be properly blamed not on the volume of his consumption, but on the fact that he was "close-coupled and chunky."

"People with short necks got no business drinking neat whisky,"
Mr. M. went on. "It don't have time to cool on the way down. It hits
their stomach red-hot and burns it right out."

Then there was Major A., whose experiences in The War, hideous
as many of them were, seemed pinpricks and fleabites compared with
one that befell him years later, in Atlantic City, when he incautiously
ordered a mint julep. I won't attempt to repeat his story; only the
major himself could do it justice, and he, alas, has long been roaming

the Elysian mint fields. But as he related how the bartender piled Ossa on Pelion, orange on pineapple, and crowned the monstrosity with a maraschino cherry, his face deepened in purple, his veins swelled, his temples throbbed. And finally, pointing a disgusted forefinger at the imaginary glass before him, "Gentlemen," he would say, "I pledge you my sacred word that what he had served me—this Yankee dog, this charlatan, this disgrace to his noble calling—was nothing but a Goddam—*whisky*—*SMASH!*"

. . . Old Colonel——. I'm ashamed to admit that I've forgotten his name, and yet I see him quite clearly, sitting in the front window, looking out on Grace Street. I see his gray moustaches and sporty waistcoat, and I see that, as always, he is wearing something yellow—a yellow silk handkerchief, a cravat with a yellow stripe, or a jonquil in his buttonhole. Yellow is the cavalry's color, and the colonel didn't want anyone to forget that he—then a dashing young trooper—had taken part in Stuart's Ride 'Round McClellan. Before that he had been a boy telegrapher, but he would consent to be reminded of it only for the purposes of a standard club prank.

The victim had to be a stranger, preferably a Northerner. The host would point out the colonel—there, in the big black chair—as one of the few members left who had actually talked with General Lee on the battlefield.

The Northerner: "In-*deed*! And what did General Lee say?"

"You may well ask! It was something you won't find in the history books, I can promise you that! He said—but maybe the colonel will tell you himself."

The colonel would demur at first, but eventually a toddy or two would persuade him: "Well, sir, it was in the early days of The War, when I operated a field telegraph. One morning—we were near Staunton—a message for General Lee came over my wire. I could tell it was urgent, so as soon as I had written it down, I hurried to his tent.

" 'General,' I said, saluting, 'here's a message for you, sir.'

"He read it slowly and carefully, then read it a second time. And what do you think he said?"

"Tell me!" the visitor would implore. "Tell me!"

"The general said, 'Thank you!' "

Here the colonel would look from one to the other, nodding his head gravely, as if to agree, "I know it's hard to believe, but—" and then he would close his eyes dismissively, exhausted by the strain of telling so complicated a story in such minute detail.

Well, the Westmoreland disbanded in 1936; its library, silver and portraits were dispersed; and the building was torn down. Where it stood, a parking garage stands now. The old warriors are gone. Their place is empty forever. But I will be forever grateful for the privilege of having known them and listened to them.

Bryan, *The Sword over the Mantel* (1960), pp. 32, 62–71, 78–79

"The Product of Negro Hands and Negro Brains": The Exposition in Richmond (1915)

In addition to exalting commercial progress, the "New South" movement preached the gospel of racial tranquillity—partly as a prerequisite for a stable business climate—and argued that this might be best accomplished by the ideal of "separate but equal" and by paternalistic white support of black self-help projects in largely vocational fields. These themes characterized numerous "expositions" of the era, the most notable being in Atlanta in 1895 when Booker T. Washington pleased Southern whites by endorsing the concept of black industrial education within a segregated society. Giles B. Jackson (ca. 1852–1924)—a prominent black lawyer, business publicist, and leader in Richmond—played a central role in the Negro Exhibit at the Jamestown Tricentennial Exhibition (1907) and in the Negro Exposition at Richmond (1915), the latter of which is described below.

The Negro Historical and Industrial Exposition which was held in the city of Richmond, Virginia, from July 5 to July 27, inclusive, was in a number of ways interesting and encouraging, but in two respects was altogether preeminent. The first of these was the proof which was exhibited by the Exposition of the cordial relations and complete understanding which exist at the present time between the two races in the South; and the other the indisputable evidence of the natural ability of the negro to achieve things worth while when living and working under the proper environment.

As an index of the relations existing between the races, the Exposition must have proved astounding to those visitors and students of social economy who have not lived or traveled during recent years in the South, and who have not had an opportunity to observe the understanding and cooperation which has grown up, particularly within the past one or two decades, in all parts of the country where the negro is in evidence. As distinct proof of this, nothing could have surpassed the manner in which the Exposition, both in its beginnings and its progress, was supported by the white people of Virginia and the South. It was largely through the efforts of the leading white citizens of the South that the Exposition was made possible. Then again, the newspapers of Richmond were indefatigable in their efforts to create interest in the Exposition, and devoted columns of space to bring the value of the enterprise prominently before the people, urging the support of white people in strong articles on their editorial pages.

It is interesting, in this connection, to note the manner in which the Exposition had its inception. A year or more ago the Negro Historical and Industrial Association was formed in Richmond, and was incorporated under the laws of the State for the purpose, among other things, of holding an industrial exposition which should show the progress of the negro during the past fifty years. Giles B. Jackson, a well-known negro lawyer of Richmond, was made president, and he immediately began a campaign for the raising of funds. United States Senator Thomas S. Martin began the fight for an appropriation by Congress, and with the aid of other Senators and Representatives, succeeded in getting the sum of $55,000 from the Government. Later the city of Richmond appropriated $5000, and the State of New York appropriated the sum of $7500 for purposes of showing the progress of the negro in that State. These sums, together with private contributions, were used for the purpose of collecting exhibits from all parts of the country. Shortly after the announcements were made exhibits began to flow in from all parts of the South and North,—from industrial schools, county school systems, industrial associations, business organizations, firms, and private individuals.

In June of this year Governor Henry Stuart, a kinsman of General Jeb Stuart, who was killed at Yellow Tavern, a few miles from the Exposition grounds, about fifty-two years ago, issued a proclamation calling earnestly upon the people of the State to support the Exposition in every possible way. Said he in part: "The friendly relations between the white people and the negroes of Virginia is a source of gratification to both races, and should be recognized as an important asset in our civil, political, and industrial life."

On July 1 President Wilson, a Virginian, who fifty years ago was a lad in the old Presbyterian manse at Staunton, Virginia, issued a proclamation saying among other things that "the action of Congress in this matter [the appropriation] indicates very happily the desire of the nation, as well as of the people of Virginia, to encourage the negro in his efforts to solve his industrial problem." And he urges the entire nation to lend every facility to the leaders in the enterprise.

On July 5 the Exposition was opened in the State Fair Grounds just outside the city, the buildings of the Fair Association being used for the exhibits. At the opening Mayor Ainslie, of Richmond, delivered an address and President Giles Jackson made a powerful and characteristic speech, reviewing the work which had been done and emphasizing the importance of the Exposition.

§ The Exhibits

The exhibits, the product of negro hands and negro brains, comprised by far the most important feature of the Exposition. These exhibits, shown in the main buildings, were hardly less than marvellous in their wide range and their simplicity and usefulness. The exhibitors were private individuals, negro firms, negro manufacturers, negro mechanics, negro associations, negro poets, negro painters, and all kinds and grades of negro schools.

The exhibits consisted of a varied line of useful things, from uplift poems on picture post-cards and oil paintings to plows, and lines of manufactured goods and sets of harness, and beautiful fancy work, and every kind and grade of household furniture.

As might be expected, the exhibit from students of the Hampton Normal and Industrial Institute was one of the most complete and noteworthy. Here was to be found almost every conceivable kind of furniture and tool, fancy work, and the product of women. In the midst of this exhibit was a handsome brass locomotive, all parts complete, in running order, built entirely by Joseph Hall, a negro of Portsmouth, Virginia.

The great industrial school on James River, known as Rock Castle, exhibited very fine specimens of wagons, buggies, carts, farming tools, and furniture of all kinds, as well as much woman's work, including all kinds of sewing and canning. All the work was done by young colored men and women under their own instructors.

Other schools which exhibited articles of marked interest were the Virginia Normal School, of Petersburg; the Colored Deaf, Dumb, and Blind Institute, of Raleigh, N.C.; Shaw University, Raleigh; Vorhees College, South Carolina; the Virginia Deaf and Dumb School, Newport News; the St. Paul School, of Lawrenceville; and the colored high school of Richmond.

A markedly fine exhibit came from Washington County and Hagerstown in Maryland; and Henrico County, Virginia, whose Superintendent of Schools, Jackson Davis, was the originator of the "Henrico Method," had a full exhibit at the Exposition. The "Henrico Method" provides a skilled and highly educated colored instructor who travels from rural school to rural school, teaching teachers and children alike all kinds of industrial work, and in summer provides for neighborhood teachers of canning, gardening, and sewing.

The New York exhibit was a noteworthy one, and occupied a prominent position. This comprised an infinite variety of manufactured goods, all from factories owned by colored men. There were also many exhibits from colored schools in New York and from individuals.

Among other displays was a booth occupied by a negro poet from Charleston, South Carolina. He was surrounded by thousands of postcards, each bearing some poem, epigram, or motto of his composition. These, being largely of the "uplift" variety, sold readily to the crowds. The walls of one of the rest rooms were hung with portraits and paintings of a negro Indianapolis painter twenty-three years of age.

At first an entrance fee of fifty cents was exacted at the Exposition gates, but later this fee was dispensed with, all visitors being allowed to come in free. Only a dime admission was charged at the doors of the principal exhibit building.

On Thursday, July 8, "White Folks" day was observed, many white citizens of Richmond and vicinity inspecting the Exposition.

In every way except financially the Negro Exposition will rank as a great success. Some one has aptly said that in its simplicity, practicableness, and unique interest the Negro Exposition at Richmond was the most truly "American" exposition ever held in this country since the Centennial at Philadelphia in 1876. A prominent speaker at the Exposition thus summed it up:

> This exposition, first of its kind in the history of the world,
> is a most splendid tribute to the courage, the strength, the perseverance, the indomitability, and the versatility of the negro race.
> It signifies the achievements of marvellous things by a once
> downtrodden race within a short span of fifty years. It typifies the
> industry, the development, the advancement, and the indefatigability of the negro race, whose era seems just dawning. Another
> fifty years of such accomplishment as has characterized the negro
> race during the past fifty years, and the colored man will stand

in his place in the sun, mentally, morally, industrially, socially, and financially, as well as physically, emancipated.

Jones, "The Negro Exposition at Richmond," *American Review of Reviews* 52 (August 1915): 185–88

"Richmond Is Not Expressed Tangibly": The 1920s

Emily Tapscott Clark [Balch] (1892–1953) was the founder and editor of *The Reviewer*, an important "little" magazine published in Richmond from 1921 to 1924. In her position as editor, she met, and brought to Richmond, many of the nationally prominent literary figures of the day. Although uncomely, she possessed a sharp wit coupled with the kind of ironic prose style that was much in vogue in the 1920s. Her *Stuffed Peacocks*, the introduction to which forms the following selection, contained in large part thinly veiled satirical portraits of a number of her Richmond contemporaries. Her second book, *Innocence Abroad* (1931), recounts the story of the founding and editing of *The Reviewer*, which was produced by the joint labors of Emily Clark, Margaret Waller Freeman, Hunter T. Stagg, and Mary Dallas Street. After four years of operation in Richmond, it was bought by North Carolina playwright Paul Green, the four young editors having gone their separate ways. Emily Clark married Edwin Swift Balch, many years her senior, and spent the remainder of her life in Philadelphia, where her spacious house, left her at the death of her husband, became a gathering place for artists and intellectuals.

With a piquantly inexplicable reputation for the quality conveniently known as old-world this most contradictory of towns is in most of its physical aspects so floridly new-world as to be nearly indistinguishable from a Middle Western city. Except for the small section formerly known as "the court end of town" Richmond is not expressed tangibly. No more definite tribute to what must, in the face of all contrary evidence, be the psychic aura of the place, or perhaps an intelligence so instinctive as to be feminine, is possible than the triumphant preservation of this legend in an atmosphere which created the most celebrated of the heroes of Mr. Sinclair Lewis long before Mr. Lewis was old enough to recreate him. The capital of the Confederacy has achieved an attitude of serene social and aesthetic superiority to Norfolk, to Raleigh, to Atlanta, to Birmingham, to all of the larger Southern cities except only Charleston. And those other cities have, measurably, been defeated by this attitude. If Richmond had done nothing more than maintain an untenable position, a position which even the North half irritably grants her, her performance would not be negligible. What other community indeed, however efficient, has accomplished the impossible? If the Virginia city, like Charleston, possessed physical beauty—that most glorious and incontrovertible form of superiority—had she, like Charleston, allowed herself exquisitely to crystallize in the essence of a past at least as historically important as any American past, her position today would be less distinctive because more meritorious.

But, like a woman without beauty whose personal attitude creates the semblance of beauty, this quite ordinary town has, through the very commonplaceness of its materials, constructed a more impressive fabrication than that other. Aside from the green glory of trees which reflects a seductively transient illusion of youth on the drab middle years of Richmond in May, and the golden glory of trees which lends an equally beguiling illusion of real, ripe age to the homely middle years of Richmond in October, the charm that is the property of the Virginia counties and estates departs from Richmond several miles away from the houses of those who make the Richmond of this moment. It is here that the knowledge that a few miles down the James are Shirley, Brandon, Westover and Tuckahoe, like Sleeping Beauty palaces in a lost wood, must be held close. Far below what is now Richmond, in shabbiness, dirt and a rooming-house mustiness penetrating even into the streets outside, lives loveliness, and a peace so long ago established that it reached maturity before its permanence was threatened. In Leigh and Clay and Marshall Streets are still houses of rose and cream-coloured brick, of faded-flower shaded stucco, whose iron gates open on walks ascending under crape myrtles and magnolias to urbane porticoes, decorated in summer by shirt-sleeved men and damp, exhausted women. Close beside the dreary whites appears Africa, picturesquely blasphemous here. For this belonged to the men and women who made Richmond one of the few places west of England where soft and charming, if sometimes erratic, English was spoken, and people lived leisurely, though not in the more spacious manner of the plantations. That early population of

Richmond called its plantations home, and knew the town for only a small part of the year.

While in New York and Boston and Philadelphia there was a dignified society, it could never be irresponsible, was never an end in itself, nor purely decorative, for the great fortunes which preserve those cities to-day from many of the evils which have overtaken Richmond were then in the making. They were being made by men who were attempting at the same time to make a social system, and an entirely successful social system cannot be utilitarian. Here, it was quite otherwise. There was no visible industrial life, as the means of living was furnished by a system of labour self-evidently impractical and impermanent, which created a social surface impossible of attainment in any other way, which will not be again, a surface unrivalled. A hint of this can be caught sometimes on spring mornings, or, better still, on hot September afternoons, when the sunlight at "the court end of town" lies over the worn brick sidewalks so thick and yellow that it seems ready to be scooped up, and the blue haze beyond the pillars of the White House of the Confederacy—now the Confederate Museum—leads straight to Lotus Land, or, it might better be called in Virginia, the Land of Lost Leisure.

Then it is that the figures who were familiar to these streets in different periods, the old Chief Justice in the austere doorway of the Marshall House, Constance Cary, before whom all austerity melted even in the grimness of Civil War days, or the great General himself, are not only possible but real. Except for the Marshall House, the Confederate Museum, the house which was first Wickham, then Valentine, and now the Valentine Museum, and Mr. Edward Valentine's studio, few of these dwellings have been preserved for ends even approximating their original uses. Away to the south-west, however, defiantly facing down both business and slums, several delightful old houses stand, protected by their high grey garden walls, continuing to shelter the authentic descendants of their builders. Among these is Miss Ellen Glasgow's. But surrounding the scene of the Confederate administration there is neither business nor slums, only apathy and decay. Because of this, on blue and yellow afternoons, when the householders are too much occupied within to sit in the porticoes, and the stillness is broken only by an occasional cart, for motors are infrequent here, it is transiently imaginable that people are again unaffectedly careless and useless and that there is literally nothing to do, anywhere.

I never leave this part of town without wanting to stay, and wishing that the social surge backward of New York and New Orleans were possible here. That movement must begin quickly, or it will be too late, for the stucco is crumbling and the white marble mantels with the fat-cheeked cherubs and thick clusters of grapes are being transported to glistening, hopefully Colonial houses uptown. And all the time are mellowed houses that cannot be again, with magnolias requiring generations to grow, waiting to be taken. Everything of importance did not occur in these special streets, but nearly everything of social importance did, and that has been always the primary importance here. Uptown, there are not only innumerable reminders of the War, which is always that of '61 to '65, but of Revolutionary times and of Bacon's Rebellion, long before the Revolution was conceived. These spots are marked only by sleek stone tablets set in raw new walls, asserting that certain things happened here and certain people stood here. There is probably no city in the United States so wasteful of inherited beauty and dignity as Richmond, partly for the reason that Virginia was so rich in possessions of this sort that they were taken easily for granted, and partly from an ingrained aversion to what is troublesome. Colonial landmarks disappeared at one time with alarming rapidity, although the wholesale annihilation is now being checked. Lesser landmarks, too, associated with such picturesque people as Poe and Aaron Burr, have become infrequent.

The political rulers of Richmond had almost to be mobbed in order to save the square old grey bell tower in the grey and green Capitol Square, where the alarm was sounded in the Civil War when the Federal troops—better known then as Yankee—were about to enter Richmond after the Seven Days' Fight. These same political rulers were restrained by force from painting the statues of the great Virginians on the Washington Monument in the Square, whose dim greenness makes the surrounding trees appear a bit garish, a nice, new, shiny black, to prove how truly progressive this new South has become. In fact they had already begun their work when the horrid news got abroad, and the mild-mannered, long-suffering population arose in mutiny. But the Governor's House in the same Square remains unmolested and unafraid, the oldest and the most nearly perfect in the United States. The Westmoreland Club has lately been snatched from the jaws of death in the form of a new building uptown, and Richmond is gradually recovering from the nightmare picture of the brilliant Mrs. Stanard's former home, where generals, statesmen, Dickens, Thackeray, and an earlier and portlier Prince of Wales, were made comfortable if not happy, diverted into civic rather than social channels. General Lee's war-time house has stood without threat of change. And the bricks from Poe's *Literary Messenger* building, destroyed by the inscrutable guardians of public safety, now form a pergola in the garden of the old stone house of King James's time—once arbitrarily called Washington's Headquarters, for the reason, it appears, that it was the only house in the Thirteen Colonies where he failed to stop—which has been transformed into a Poe memorial. It is also the only house in Virginia that carries the initials of Jacobus Rex carved in one of its stones. But all this, and more, forms a fragile basis for the successful assumption of superiority which is the city's basic title to fame.

Another radical change in the life of Richmond is the complete extinction of its line of beauties and belles, now fabulous as the gods and heroes. These did not vanish with the War, for several traditions, including the tradition of beauty, lasted through and long after the Reconstruction. They were, of course, all a part of the same aesthetic ideal, literature, leisure, and good horses and drinks. Concerning the authenticity of a literary habit I have been always assailed by the gravest doubts, but it is mentioned usually as a part of the defeated ideal. And, since the entire ideal is admittedly departed, a detail such as letters are, and must always have been in the South, need detain nor embarrass no one. I can remember, as a small child, running quite around a block to see Miss May Handy, now Mrs. James Brown Potter, pass. No one would walk around a block now to see anyone pass. Whether it is beauty or the worship of beauty which has died would be difficult to say. But it is certain that if Miss Mary Triplett could once more drive down Franklin Street on a sunny afternoon, graciously on view in her victoria, with her hair as dazzlingly blond as ever it was, the passing crowd would not properly appreciate its luck in the lady's choice of a victoria instead of a limousine. Nor would the historic after-dinner announcement at the Old White Sulphur that "beauty, grace, and wit make a Triplett" bring the reputed multitude of men to their feet with glasses ringing. There were, from time to time, women with international as well as local reputations for beauty and charm, such as Amélie Rives, now the Princess Pierre Troubetzkoy, and the Langhornes, notably Mrs. Charles Dana Gibson, whose face and figure became familiar to the world as the first Gibson Girl, and Lady Astor, M.P., more lately turned to utilitarian ends. At present there are numbers of women who are pretty enough, smart enough, and charming enough to be satisfactory, but not sufficiently pretty, sufficiently smart, or sufficiently charming to change the course of human events, or to be able to afford any exceptionally eccentric habits and caprices. This may mean that beauty is more plentiful and less concentrated, by grace of those most useful and celebrated of all women of our time who are making a degree of beauty possible to practically everyone who can afford it; and that startling speech and eccentric habits are too frequent to remain either startling or eccentric. Or it may mean that men grow more phlegmatic and less imaginative as they grow more preoccupied. Certainly there are legends of old Richmond which make the current gossip of young Richmond since 1918 less breath-taking than young Richmond likes to realize. Perhaps only beauties, wits, and belles were granted those indulgences once that are now the property of everyone. The beauty cult lasted late, because it was nourished by survivors of ante-bellum Richmond as the special part of their tradition with which it was hardest to part. But the rest, the tradition of culture, separate from the nebulous tradition of letters, died long before. There rages, of course, education in its most frightful meaning, that of preparation for some special sort of work, but preparation to enjoy life to the full with every aesthetic sense, has been rare since 1861. The followers of the early ideal were forced to ignore it while they raked the ashes from their devastated country and used their hands for unaccustomed purposes. And the job, with its consequences, was less disastrous for the dashing figures who passed through the flames than for the drab ones who were born in the ashes. They and their sons attended to it with such unprecedented spirit that physically their inheritance has been saved, for there is much money now in this tobacco-scented city, and there will be much more. . . .

Moreover, I can think of no other place where frequent parties composed of people with exactly the same amount of intellect, information, and experience would be endurable. Those who can do nothing and say nothing worth doing or saying usually manage it with a reasonable amount of grace and plausibility. They manage it too, in some cases, since 1919, without the same quality of liquid aid available elsewhere, partly, no doubt, because Richmond is not a seaport town. And a really spontaneous indulgence in the South's own vodka of the deceptively soothing name is more friendly to delirium than to mellowness. Therefore strangers are impressed with the fact that people here can sometimes regard each other with perfectly clear eyes and unclouded minds and find each other not unendurable—sometimes. As for aesthetic Richmond, or anaesthetic Richmond, there is noticeable, within the last few years among a minority of people, a ripple that may possibly swell to a wave, of interest in ideas, and the life of ideas. Ideas are at times even admitted socially into conversation. Whether this is a temporary fad or the beginning of a gradual change, no one can say yet. But this much is certain: if ideas should ever become vital here, they will be made more presentable for drawing-room use than they are at the moment in other cities. Ideas, it is probable, will be dealt with in a mildly deprecating manner, with no appearance of haste and not too much excitement or earnestness. Business and bridge, golf and law, horses and Africans, are not taken as hard here as in the North. They are all treated with gentle, even humorous indulgence. All, except the single bit of realism locally recognized as reality, the unflagging necessity to be personally pleasing. That this small city contains an internationally discussed figure in letters, a novelist whose long-established importance is yearly increasing, and one of the most celebrated of American composers, has not noticeably affected the atmosphere of the town. Those distinguished facts are merely taken for granted. And the significance of this, too, need not be commented upon here. Why visiting literary celebrities enjoy Richmond remains always a mystery, since the indifference of these persons to public attention is not notable, and the city, for the most part, remains suavely unaware of their presence.

When the Middle West has grown accustomed to its discovery of itself, and to New York's discovery of it, and the elder city's turn comes, it will treat its own brand-new ideas, always supposing these should be evolved, in the same manner that it treats those of others. The town which had discovered itself and had been discovered while New York was still a Dutch traders' post and the Middle West had not yet begun to be could not possibly be swept off its feet in the event of rediscovery by its great-grandchildren. It will, however, smile graciously, for the old invariably appreciate attention from the young, however seldom they make an effort to get it. If it produces ideas worth discovering, there will be nothing like it this side of Europe, for a gently humorous attitude to ideas is foreign to the American cities where the American product known as the Young Intellectuals flourishes like the green bay-tree. It will not become excited about itself or its complexes or its ideas.

Clark, Stuffed Peacocks (1927), pp. 3–16, 24–27

"The Train That's Never Been Found": The Tunnel Collapse of 1925

When William Byrd II of Westover (q.v.) founded Richmond in the 1730s, he envisioned it as a trading center because of its proximity to the James River and its easy access to planters in the central Virginia area.

What Byrd could not have envisioned, however, was that ocean-going ships would grow larger and have deeper draughts and that rock lying in the river channel below Richmond would soon prove to be an obstacle to further dredging, thus limiting plans to use the James River and the Kanawha Canal to link Richmond by water to the area beyond the mountains.

The coming of the railroad solved the problem, however, and kept Richmond competitive with other cities. As a matter of fact, in the nineteenth century the city once had five separate railroads terminating there—the Richmond and Petersburg; the Richmond and Danville; the York River Railroad; the Richmond, Fredericksburg and Potomac; and the Virginia Central, which later became part of the Chesapeake and Ohio.

Of all activities centering on the railroads in Richmond, none has captured the residents' imaginations as did the collapse of the Chesapeake and Ohio tunnel on 2 October 1925, which killed four men. Local legend still insists that others were trapped, although such allegations have never been substantiated. The locomotive remains to this day entombed in the tunnel, its mouth sealed and the veracity of its legends still a mystery.

The following newspaper story by Richmonder Louis D. Rubin, Jr., although written twenty-four years after the accident, is based on contemporary accounts. A nationally recognized authority on Southern literature and culture, Rubin is professor of English at the University of North Carolina at Chapel Hill and the author of the introduction to the present volume.

It is shortly after 3 o'clock on the rainy Friday afternoon of Oct. 2, 1925.

A Negro laborer, Lemy Campbell, is working near the entrance to the Chesapeake and Ohio Railway tunnel at Nineteenth and Marshall Streets in Richmond. He is one of a force of several hundred men engaged in rehabilitating the old tunnel for further use.

Campbell works in silence and listens to the wheeze of the little passenger locomotive being used to switch flat cars in the tunnel. It is resting some 100 feet inside the tunnel near where Campbell is working.

Suddenly he hears the sound of a brick falling from the roof of the tunnel. He looks upward.

Several more bricks fall. Then there is a crackling sound from along the tunnel roof.

That is enough for Campbell. He drops his tools, bolts for the tunnel entrance. Behind him the roof comes crashing down. The screams of frightened, trapped men, the roar of earth, bricks and timber smashing to the tunnel floor, and the hiss of escaping steam from the locomotive tear the air.

There is a frenzied dash for safety on the part of the gangs of laborers and the train crews. A few bolt for the western exit a few hundred yards away, and make it. Most of the others flee in the other and safer direction, toward the eastern opening to the tunnel nearly a mile away at Thirty-first and Grace.

Lights Go Out

The electric lights which illuminate the tunnel go out at the beginning of the avalanche. The interior of the tunnel is pitch black as the men paw madly along the damp clay walls of the tunnel, feeling their way toward daylight 4,000 feet away.

Not so fortunate is the crew of the work train. Burly, affable engineer Tom Mason, of 107 Orleans St., is pinned to his seat by the reverse lever. Fireman B. F. Mosby, of 516 North Thirty-second St., is wiry and slender, and he slips out of the cab underneath the tender, where he begins to work his way to the other end, screaming in agony from the scalding steam. He crawls underneath the 10 flatcars, starts down the tunnel, is helped along. Finally he reaches daylight, and is loaded into an ambulance and rushed to the hospital.

He turns to someone, and in his panic manages to say that he is all right, and would like to have his wife and baby girl told that he is not badly hurt. But courage is not enough. He is too badly burned to live, and he dies that night in the hospital.

Another member of the train crew, Conductor C. G. McFadden, of 3105 Fifth Ave., fares better. When the roof comes tumbling, he is standing between two flat cars near the engine. The mass of earth and masonry knocks him down, and his arm catches on the flat car and is broken at the shoulder.

§ Groping Toward Safety

He crawls under the flatcars. When he reaches the last one he is helped to his feet by Brakeman C. S. Kelso, who is himself cut about the head. McFadden and Kelso join the men feeling their way through the black tunnel toward daylight and safety a mile away.

One other train-crew member, Brakeman A. G. Adams, is standing very close to the engine and tender when the roof caves in. He is knocked to the ground, stunned. But he gets up and gropes along the side to the flatcars, crawls under them toward safety. Eventually, he makes it.

The earth continues to give way periodically. The way to the locomotive is blocked. As night falls, it is evident that Mason, whether dead or alive, is a prisoner in his cab underneath tons of slippery blue marl and yellow clay soil.

Is he alone? Were other men trapped with him? Did all the laborers make their way to safety before the falling roof trapped them?

Digging parties are hastily set up. A steam shovel begins work from a spot on Jefferson Park Hill directly atop where the locomotive is estimated to have been located at the time of the fall. Other digging parties start work from either end, after the tunnel roof is reinforced to prevent further tragedy.

Huge crowds gather about the scene, blocking traffic. Richmond police, under the direction of Lieutenants Ryan and Campodonica, throw up emergency lines around the western end.

How Many Missing?

The C&O calls its rolls of laborers, announces that only two men are still missing. They are R. Lewis and H. Smith. But those who escaped from the tunnel scoff at the low figure. From 10 to 15 men are still in there, they insist.

The rescue squad works steadily. Hours become days. New slides of earth delay progress. The operations at either end of the tunnel are constantly impeded. Overhead the steam shovel digs on. Sunday it is 20 feet down in the earth. Monday the middle shaft is 33 feet deep. Tuesday it reaches 42 feet. But new cave-ins imperil the operation, force new starts.

Meanwhile, rumors continue spreading, kindled by hope and wishful thinking. One workman tells police that he heard calls for help behind him when he fled from the tunnel. Maybe the men who called are still alive. On Sunday a rumor spreads that a Negro laborer has crawled to safety and has said that others are alive under the engine. But the story is denied by police, who insist that no one has come from out of the tunnel since the frantic exodus right after the roof caved in.

Finally, on Sunday night October 11, nine days after the disaster, a worker cuts his way through the floor of a flatcar, and works up to the engine. A shaft of light from his lantern shines on a ghastly spectacle. It is the decomposed body of Engineer Mason sitting bolt upright in the cab where he was pinned into position trapped without a chance of escape. He could have died from suffocation, fatal scalds, or the blow of the reverse lever. Whichever it was, he died almost instantly after the cave-in.

Missing Bodies

Further search fails to reveal any trace of the bodies of the missing Negro laborers. Whether they were at the scene when the roof fell is unknown. Between the engine and the western entrance is several hundred tons of earth. If they were caught under it, their bodies will never be located.

Railroad and municipal engineers survey the scene, and decide that nothing more can be done. The locomotive is wedged fast. They decide to leave it there and to fill up the rest of the mile-long tunnel with sand, to prevent further cave-ins. So the tunnel is plugged and its entrances sealed. The locomotive is entombed under Jefferson Park Hill.

Today, 24 years after the cave-in railroad men still talk about it. Are the crushed bones of the two Negro laborers still under there too? Were others caught, as the survivors insisted? The construction gangs were said to have taken on some new laborers that morning, whose names had not yet been added to the rolls. Several Negroes were said to have gone into the mouth of the tunnel to seek employment just before the cave-in.

Nobody knows.

Today all three of the engine crew members who survived the cave-in are still alive. Kelso, one of the two brakemen, operates a farm in Fluvanna County. Adams, the other brakeman, is still with the C&O and has risen to the post of yardmaster for Fulton Yard. McFadden, the conductor, retired from service in 1943, after 48 years of service with the C&O. He and his wife still live at 3105 Fifth Avenue in Highland Park. Grey-haired and 72 years old, McFadden still gets about, and sometimes tells us about that day in 1925 when he just missed death.

Among Survivors

R. C. Gary, foreman of a crew working at the eastern end of the tunnel that day, and who braved death to make his way into the tunnel to help the train crew to safety, is also alive and still with the C&O.

The entombed locomotive became railroad legend, and Llewellyn Lewis, a Southern Railroad brakeman who died in 1935, wrote a song about it. Billy Pierce, of Richmond, set it to music and published it. Its words went as follows:

> Remember the Church Hill tunnel,
>   Near a mile under Richmond
> There's a story I want to tell you
>   Of a train that'll never be found.
> On a bleak afternoon in the Autumn
>   When the skies were overcast
> A train and its crew were working
>   In the tunnel performing their tasks.
>
> Chorus:
> Brothers keep shovelin',
>   Pickin' in the ground.
> Brothers, keep listening
>   For the train that's never been found.
>
> No one ever dreamed of danger:
>   Of a death that was hoverin' near—
> They were happy while they were working
>   For the loved ones home so dear,
> When all of a sudden a tremble,
>   A large gap in the slimy clay—
> Then the earth claimed a few in its clutches,
>   In the darkness the rest groped their way. So:
>
> Chorus: Brothers, keep, etc.
>
> Many shovels and picks were diggin'
>   For their pals in the buried train—
> But the cold slimy clay held its victims
>   Soon their hopes were found in vain.

Many hours did they search for their comrades
Who might live in this cold, cold cave,
But they never found one who was living
Way down in this untimely grave. So:

Chorus:
Brothers, keep shovelin',
Pickin' in the ground.
Brothers, keep listening
For the train that's never been found.

The old locomotive is still there, imprisoned under the marl and clay of Jefferson Park Hill. And there, too, are the remains of any laborers who were caught in the cave-in.

On Eighteenth Street just north of Marshall a pair of rusty railroad tracks still lead past a building through high weeds to the walled-up entrance to the old tunnel, now sealed forever.

Rubin, "Railway Tunnel's Collapse," Richmond *Times-Dispatch*, 8 May 1949

"That Was in 1932. Jobs Were Scarce and Getting Scarcer": Self-Help during the Depression (1932)

The Great Depression of the 1930s brought unparalleled economic hardship to the United States, but Richmond fared better than most cities. The explanation, according to Virginius Dabney (q.v.), was the "stability of tobacco manufacture, more than anything else," but also a "well balanced economy," and federal assistance. The latter, among other contributions, left a legacy of such new public buildings as the Maggie L. Walker High School and the Virginia State Library. Dabney also gives credit to the initiative and enterprise of individual Richmonders, many of whom helped to organize and sustain a nationally praised self-help project, the Citizens' Service Exchange. This unique program is described below in an article by Stanley High (1895–1961), a contemporary journalist and later editor of *Reader's Digest*. The Exchange, incidentally, lasted until 1945 "when it was transformed into a Richmond branch of the Goodwill Industries."

The Citizens' Service Exchange in Richmond, Virginia, is a self-help project through which, at present, nearly 800 families are lifting themselves out of relief to self-support. What is happening in Richmond may be a wholly unorthodox chapter in the history of relief. But it is an exceedingly significant revelation of what takes place when the unemployed are given, instead of relief, an opportunity.

The Citizens' Service Exchange grew out of an improvised reading room for the unemployed where men foregathered "to kill time" and, incidentally, to make it plain to those in charge that what they wanted —more than amusement—was work. When, one day, the able men present were asked what they needed most, the unexpected answer was razor blades: "We can't get a job unless we look halfway decent." An appeal thereupon was made for razor blades and Richmond donated them by the thousands—with sharpeners. But the Richmond Council of Social Agencies began, at once, to look for a better answer.

That was in 1932. Jobs were scarce and getting scarcer. The Community Fund—hard pressed by a mounting relief load—had set $50 a month as the minimum relief income for a family of five, and even that minimum, in many instances, was not available. It was therefore suggested that the unemployed work for each other. Inquiry was made as to the success and methods of self-help projects in other communities—notably in Ohio and California. The reports received were encouraging, and the Council of Social Agencies presented the plan to a group of the unemployed. It was heartily endorsed. Thereupon a Board of Sponsors and a Board of Directors—representing businesses and welfare interests and organized labor—were organized, a small initial cash outlay for equipment was secured from the Community Fund, and the experiment, with some misgivings, was undertaken.

An abandoned warehouse was loaned, rent free, for headquarters and, with the approval and support of Richmond's labor leaders, 50 unemployed carpenters, bricklayers, plumbers and paperhangers went to work to recondition it.

At that point, of course, the question of pay arose, and the simple economic procedure that is still followed was worked out. There are no dollars and cents transactions among the members of the Exchange. But there is an initial "investment," which the unemployed themselves suggested. At one of the earliest meetings between the representatives of the Community Fund and the spokesmen for the unemployed, a painter arose and proposed that "since you people are putting up your money we will put up our work—that's all we've got to put up." Since that time every new member "invests" as an initiation fee 40 hours—a week's work—when he enters the organization. He can withdraw this investment, in commodities, if he leaves.

Thereafter, for every hour of work, the member, male or female, receives Exchange Currency—a little blue work certificate valued at approximately 25 cents "redeemable for such merchandise or services as may be available in the Citizens' Service Exchange to the value of One Hour's Labor." The Exchange store sells exclusively to members and these work certificates are the only currency that is honored. Prices are calculated in terms of work-hours. Thus, a broom costs from two to five work certificates; a haircut, one certificate; a lunch, one certificate; a permanent wave, 20 certificates; a quarter of a cord of wood, nine certificates.

At the near-by Methodist Church, which many members attend, work certificates are put in the collection plate. Every week the minister appears at the Exchange with the previous Sunday's offering and redeems it, for church bulletins at the print shop, or in terms of janitor work, upholstering and furniture repair.

When the Exchange was organized it was determined that the three things most desperately needed by Richmond's unemployed were fuel, shelter and clothing. Those three things, therefore, were accepted as the immediate objective.

Clothing was first on the list. The Red Cross of Richmond issued a call "to share what you have with those who have nothing." The city responded with 60 truckloads of salvageable clothes and shoes. Another call went out—this time for sewing machines. Twenty-three were quickly delivered. And almost overnight the Exchange was a going concern. Today, after five years, the salvaging and reconditioning of clothes is still one of its major industries.

Fuel and shelter, however, were less easily procurable. In regard to shelter, the aid of the Police Department was enlisted and a survey made of the city's unoccupied property. It was found that there were 3050 flats and houses not in use—many of them in a bad state of repair. Thereupon, the Real Estate Board came forward with a plan that resulted in an agreement between the owners of many of these properties and the Exchange. The owners agreed to provide the materials for repairs. The Exchange—up to 200 hours on any one house or flat—agreed to provide the labor. In return, the owners turned their property over to the Exchange, rent free for six months, to "sublet" to its members for 40 work certificates a month.

On the problem of fuel, the newspapers lent their aid to a campaign for donations of standing timber. As a result a good many hundreds of acres of timberland were made available without charge, and old trucks were patched up for hauling. Ever since, the production of fuel has been a major Exchange activity. In 1937, 464 cords of wood were delivered to the homes of Exchange members.

After so auspicious a beginning, it was clear that the work of the organization could not be limited to its three initial objectives. Among other things, something had to be done about food for the midday meal served at the Exchange to the workers. Toward the end of 1933, therefore, a request was made through the newspapers for 200 acres of unused land. More than 3000 acres were offered. With equipment provided by the federal government and with a seed loan from the Reconstruction Finance Corporation, the farm and truck-gardening projects got under way.

Today the Exchange runs a farm for transients, in cooperation with the Travelers Aid Society, where some 350 men are given board and lodging every month. These men are not listed as Exchange members and they pay their way by work on the farm. The food production, from all sources, in 1937 included not only a vast amount of food stuffs for immediate consumption and for canning, but also some 50,000 loaves of bread from the Exchange bakery and an average of 2600 midday meals per month from its dining room. In the last five years a total of 120,000 scrip-hours of food has been sold to members.

This enlargement of the work of the Exchange has continued until it has become almost a self-sustaining community. Surplus products from the United States Government—hides from cattle slaughtered in the drought, wool, etc.—came to the Exchange as donated raw material. The unused schoolhouse which now serves as headquarters contains barber shops and beauty parlors (a presentable appearance means much in building up morale); a chemical department which tans donated hides into good leather for the shoe shop and which turned out last year 2091 bags of soap; a laundry which is serving 180 families per month; weaving, sewing, quilting and shoe departments, and an exceedingly busy machine shop whose chief product is an inexpensive but exceedingly practical "drum" stove made from empty steel barrels donated by a Richmond manufacturer.

But even with the Exchange a going concern, the major interest of most of the men and women at work there was still re-employment in private industry. As a result and in addition to its other activities the Exchange has assumed a responsibility for training and reconditioning its members for jobs. In this, teachers furnished by the Richmond school board aided. During the last 18 months, 280 young people have gone from its daytime vocational classes into employment.

For older men and women—many of whom had lost their skills—

the problem was largely one of reconditioning. The industries at the Exchange itself provided the best answer to that problem. The bakery, for example, is also a school where a number of men—guided by a veteran—are being trained to be bakers. The two beauty shops have had little difficulty finding jobs for the "graduates" of their courses. When I visited the Exchange, classes were being organized in hat-making because a recent survey of Richmond's industries had revealed a shortage of experienced milliners. Within three months 11 people—products of these classes—had found jobs in hat factories in the city.

The records show that more than 700 people have been trained out of the Exchange into private employment—as printers, cobblers, painters, auto mechanics, truck drivers, barbers, beauty-shop operators, domestics, telephone operators, filing clerks, broom- and brush-makers, and gardeners. The annual turnover from the members to private employment is about 40 percent. The annual turnover from the WPA has been shown in some surveys to be no higher than two and a half percent.

Back of this achievement is the Board of Sponsors and the Board of Directors. But more important than either, perhaps, is Mrs. Amy A. Guy, the Executive Secretary. Mrs. Guy has not only believed in this project for the unemployed—she has believed in the unemployed. With few precedents to guide her and a considerable amount of skepticism to combat, she has developed an enterprise, which began as a "dubious experiment," into an institution which is likely to endure in Richmond as long as unemployment continues to be a problem.

I think it is quite likely that Mrs. Guy would say that the most significant contribution of the Exchange has been in the maintenance and the building of morale: "the discipline and habit of work, self-respect, and the desire to get ahead." "Relief" is a taboo word at the Exchange and the relief attitude is altogether missing. Members know that the things they make are needed. And the goods they carry home each night from the store are purchased with earned certificates.

The members have their own Participants' Assembly. There—with the Exchange Directors excluded save on special invitation—they discuss the problems of organization, settle matters of internal discipline, carry on a welfare work for those of their number who are ill or otherwise in trouble, and when they have suggestions or complaints, present them, formally, to Mrs. Guy. In the entire five years of her direction of this enterprise it has not been necessary to discharge more than three or four people from the membership.

The several thousand people who have been members of the

Exchange during those five years have turned in a total of nearly 1,000,000 work-hours. The goods and services produced by that work-investment have been socially useful. The relatively small sums invested by the federal government and the Richmond Community Fund for equipment and personnel have paid human dividends out of all proportion to the amounts involved. And these sums have not been a dole for men and women who believe that the world owes them a living. They are, rather, a modest stake for men and women who believe that what the world owes them is a chance.

That is why the self-help agency, as it exists in Richmond, appears to be the least costly answer to the problem of the unemployed, and the one that is the most authentically American.

High, "By Their Bootstraps," *Reader's Digest*, March 1938,
pp. 73–77

"Small Boys Ran Around Shouting the Bad News": World War II (1941–1945)

At the close of the war, the Richmond World War II History Committee commissioned Francis Earle Lutz (1890–1958), who had served in three wars and in addition had lost his only son in World War II, to write the city's history from 1939 to 1946, from which the following is taken. "The history," Lutz wrote in the introduction of the book, "was not designed simply to record the things directly tied in with the war effort, but was to show the political leanings, editorial opinions, social life, economic and financial problems, municipal growth, industrial and business developments, cultural activities and last, but not least, the unpleasant side of life." Accordingly, Lutz took for two of his major sources the daily newspapers, the Richmond *News Leader* and the *Times-Dispatch*, in whose pages the day-to-day story of the city can be found. To read Lutz's account is to be an observer of a cross section of Richmond's routine, when the nation was at war and when residents huddled by their radios at night in an attempt to learn what had happened that day and to speculate about what might happen the next.

. . . December 7, 1941 dawned clear and moderately cold on Richmond. Church services were well attended that morning. There was no inconvenience such as food rationing to curtail the traditional heavy mid-day meal and there was gasoline in plenty for an afternoon drive. For the sports lovers the pleasant weather was an invitation to ride or golf. It was ideal, too, for window shopping in the downtown retail district on whose broad sidewalks the Salvation Army's Yule kettles had been installed two days before.

Some Richmonders had slept late that morning, after seeing *Life With Father* at the Lyric Theater the night before. Others had watched the tense matches in the National Bridge Tournament at the Jefferson Hotel. More than 1,500 girls and as many service men had attended the weekly dance at the Mosque where 250 of the girls had received the Richmond Defense Service Unit's pin for faithful attendance at these functions. Hundreds of Shriners were resting up from the high jinks in connection with Acca Temple's "victory" ceremonial at which the largest class in years had crossed the hot sands.

Those who scanned the front page of the morning newspaper were interested, somewhat remotely, perhaps, in reading that President Roosevelt had sent a personal appeal to Emperor Hirohito for a peaceful settlement of the menacing differences between the two nations. Turning to the editorial page, they read that "the issue of peace or war with Japan hangs by a thread" but were reassured by the further observation that "there may be no hostilities for weeks or months." They felt even more assured to read the opinion of James R. Young, noted foreign correspondent, that "actually the Japanese are no threat to any country of fighting consequence."

Mr. Young held that "we can stop the Japanese now if we get a strong grip on our diplomatic big stick." The editor of *The Times-Dispatch* showed no fear for our prowess, saying, "It is to be hoped that the British-American-Dutch forces will act instantly if Thailand is invaded and will prevent the Japanese from getting the initial advantage which might be gained through Allied hesitation." The editor added that "the time has come for action by the Allies rather than words, and that goes for America as well as the other powers now girding for the defense of the Far East . . . war may yet be avoided but, if not, the United States must strike hard and quickly."

It was more pleasant to keep turning the pages and to read the plans for the first Richmond German of the year set for December 15 and to scan the pictorial page of lovely girls to be presented to society. Many of the younger set turned directly to the sports page, there to read that Bill Dudley, of Virginia, had been named to Collier's All-

American by Grantland Rice and that Richmond's own Bill Chewning, of the Navy, had been named on the All-Eastern team. Duke's chances for victory in the Rose Bowl were as gravely discussed as were the more sedate foreign affairs on the editorial pages. Baseball followers were happy to learn that Ben Chapman had signed to manage the Richmond Colts. Members of the Deep Run Hunt had had a fine drag the afternoon before and a jolly dance that night. Supporters of V.M.I. were reading glumly how Miami's last-minute field goal had defeated the Cadets 10 to 7 on Friday night. It was said the deciding score was made after the clock had stopped in the waning seconds of the contest.

Movie fans were debating whether Greta Garbo's flat flanks and gleaming torso really made *Two Faced Woman* as torrid as some censors elsewhere had claimed. If they decided to heed the League of Decency's ban on Garbo, then they could see Fredric March and Martha Scott in *One Foot In Heaven* or Abbott and Costello in a piece of nonsense called *Keep 'Em Flying*. Other titles inspired by the conflict in Europe on the current screens were *Flying Cadets, A Yank in the R.A.A.F.* and *Underground*. The perennial favorite *Smilin' Through* was playing at several neighborhood houses.

Before the last peace time meal for five years, there had been overflow congregations in several churches. At First Evangelical Lutheran Church tribute was paid to Dr. J. J. Scherer, Jr. on his thirty-fifth anniversary. First Baptist Church launched its every-member canvass. The annual woman's day service drew a big crowd at Colonial Place Christian Church and Harvest Home Day was observed at Fulton Baptist Church. Second Baptist Church members were distressed that the Rev. C. W. Cranford had accepted a call to Washington. All denominations were building up to the annual observance of the birth of the Prince of Peace while, on the other side of the globe, a treacherous enemy already was striking a shattering blow at American bases and American bodies in the far-off Pacific outposts.

First word of the incredible sneak attack on Pearl Harbor came from semi-hysterical radio announcements in mid-afternoon. The first "flash" interrupted a National Broadcasting Company program at 2:26 P.M. Soon the raucous yells of "Extra!" shattered the Sunday calm as newsboys raced along the streets with the ink still wet on the shocking headlines. Nobody thought to turn down the blaring radios as they repeated or elaborated on the meager details of what had happened. All commercial programs were suspended to make way for the grim news. Strollers, many of them service men, could not grasp what the shouting was all about. One puzzled woman motorist stopped at the curb to ask, "What football game is being played today?" Wherever people gathered, the verdict was, "Now is the time to shoot." As early as 5 P.M., applicants were lining up at the door of the Navy Recruiting Office.

Before the sun was down the radio flashed word for all service personnel to return to their stations. Small boys ran around shouting the bad news to the men in uniform. Around 6 P.M. motion picture theaters interrupted their programs to pass on the order to the uniformed men in the audience. Men in olive drab, forest green and navy blue crowded the rail and bus stations. Trains were jammed; the Greyhound Bus Company ran sixty special trips to accommodate the uniformed men and the Richmond Service Unit's motor corps worked all night carrying them to nearby military posts. One applicant who wanted quick transportation by motor to Texas was turned down. The Chesapeake and Potomac Telephone Company, by 7:30 P.M., had 325 long distance operators manning the board here.

Even while service men were hurrying campward, police were being rushed to strategic municipal installations to prevent possible sabotage. Before dark, soldiers from Camp Lee had bivouacked at the south end of the R. E. Lee Bridge and were augmenting the civilian guards on the bridges, the water works, gas and electric plants and some public buildings. Volunteer airplane spotters, before dark, were casting an anxious eye in the skies. Police, on the alert for enemy aliens, reported no Japanese in the city.

Meanwhile, only ninety miles away, at South Hill, the 29th Infantry Division, 14,000 strong, was on the alert. The Blue and Gray, which included Richmond's historic commands, the Blues, the Grays and the Howitzers, was en route from the Carolina maneuvers, where for thirteen weeks the division had been participating in realistic war games.

Along with the rest of the country, Richmond awoke on December 8 feeling that "it can't be true." But the newspaper headlines and the still hysterical radio announcements dispelled this. As Richmonders started for office, shop or school, they got a preview of Uncle Sam's might and, incidentally, the first and only chance to wave a good-bye to any considerable body of Virginia troops during the entire war period. It was the 29th hurrying north to its home station at Fort George G. Meade. Traveling in 2,400 dirt and mud covered vehicles, the men of the Blue and Gray sped through the city. Businesslike 75's and 155's were towed behind the artillery trucks, but it was depressing to note that many of the anti-aircraft weapons were of wood or tin, while it must have made many persons uneasy to see the heavily scrawled word "tank" on many of the vehicles used in the maneuvers in lieu of the real things and to observe stove pipes posing as mortars.

The weather overnight had turned from pleasant to a nipping cold. Four hours it took for the martial display to clear the city. The division came in two columns, one over Mayo Bridge and the other over Lee Bridge. Stationed in Capitol Square were five regimental bands which kept up an uninterrupted musical salute to the east column. In Monroe Park four more regimental bands carried out a similar welcome to the west column. Governor Price, in spite of the biting wind, alternated between the two points to wave to the chilled men in their canvas-topped vehicles. The war news momentarily whipped up unprecedented enthusiasm as Richmonders crowded the streets by tens of thousands to see the stirring pageant. Apples, candy, cigarettes, and sandwiches were tossed into the speeding trucks. That night the division bivouacked at A. P. Hill Military Reservation and the following day was at Fort Meade to continue training for the brilliant exploits it was to perform later on the beaches of Normandy and the bloody fields of France and Germany.

Just what to do puzzled most Richmonders that day. Some saw their duty clearly and the Army, Navy and Marine recruiting offices were jammed with applicants—some grimly patriotic and others jovial over the coming adventure. Solemnly, *The News-Leader* warned that "wild rumors which have mounted higher and higher must not be credited." It was no rumor, however, that the Philippines were under enemy aerial bombardment, although no further attacks were being made on Hawaii.

The realization that there were scores, perhaps hundreds, of Virginians, in the danger zone of the Pacific was a sobering influence. That some Richmond youths, at that very moment, were dead or maimed was a grim possibility. These bitter forebodings proved too true in the succeeding days and weeks. In time, Richmond was to be proud of the exploits of some and saddened by the sacrifice of others. . . .

Richmond's plans for defense were under way before the clamor of the frantic radio announcements had died on December 7, 1941. Two days later, local architects were ready to consult with civilians on plans for private air raid shelters. Blackout arrangements were made and instructions published on what to do in case of air raids. Public raid shelters, casualty centers and other emergency matters were soon past the planning stage. Plane-spotting groups were formed and spotter posts opened. Drives for rubber, aluminum, tin cans, scrap metal, paper, and old clothes were early popular outlets for energies.

Many of the local yachtsmen, with their yachts, volunteered for service in the Coast Guard Auxiliary. Some 15,000 other Richmond volunteers were in the State Guard, Reserve Militia, or serving as air-raid wardens, fire guards, auxiliary firemen, auxiliary police and various other activities during the 1941–46 period; yet, Richmond newspapers felt it necessary to chide the citizenry at regular intervals with the reminder that a war was being fought abroad. Many of these rebukes were administered when black, screaming headlines were telling a bitter story of losses and reverses.

Activities for servicemen, which had a pre-war start, were expanded daily. Information centers were organized and every conceivable comfort was offered uniformed visitors. By popular demand, the City Council excluded homes taking only service men as overnight guests from paying a license as rooming establishments and established a low rental ceiling price. Early in 1942, the Richmond Defense Service Unit spread out its activities and organized a "stock" company to supply more diversified entertainment at home and in adjacent camps. By 1943, visiting service men reached a peak of 34,000 a week.

Each Sunday, under the guidance of Miss Caroline Rivers Harrison, tours of the historic sections of the city were made available for service personnel. These tours inspired the preparation of two booklets by Miss Harrison, *Footpaths In Historic Richmond* and *Walking Guide To Richmond*, which were sponsored and distributed by private business firms.

On July 30, 1944, the first casualties from the Normandy beachhead reached McGuire Hospital here. This was one of the heart-rending events that brought the war closer home and gave cause for serious thoughts toward the goal of helping the service men through civilian efforts. The Richmond *News-Leader* raised a $20,000 fund out of which to pay for a long-distance telephone call to his home immediately upon the arrival of a wounded man at the hospital.

Among the more apparent changes in the local set-up was the transition of women to men's jobs. The realm of taxi-drivers, trolley operators, elevator operators, draftsmen and even mechanics and barbers, suddenly began to be invaded by the ladies. In 1943, the masculine defense position of Air Raid Warden turned feminine. The Virginia Mechanics Institute reflected the trend by admitting women in its welding courses. Domestics found the lure of war production more glamorous and profitable than enduring the possible sharp tongues of Lady Simon Legrees; hence, departed from household duties, leaving housewives to fend for themselves. It finally reached the point where women could be found "most anywhere except at home."

Travel habits were changed considerably. By 1942, anything going anywhere was loaded to capacity. Share-the-ride centers were set up in the city to offset the overloaded trolley cars and buses. To conserve gasoline, tires and automobiles in general, a 35-mile State speed law was passed. A long train trip was a regretful incident in anyone's life. In 1943, the Southern Railroad advertisements in Richmond newspapers read: "Please don't ride on a Southern Railroad train this summer."

Travel by air, for the civilian, was almost out of the question, due to the priorities for the uniformed services. The Eastern Air Lines, by 1946, had recovered somewhat and was operating eighteen daily flights, compared with seven in 1944, but a prospective passenger still was subject to being a victim of priorities—being "bumped" was the name for this unpleasant experience.

When pleasure driving was banned in January, 1943, agents of the Office of Price Administration went to work to enforce the regulations. Of course, tourist trade promptly vanished, but military personnel from nearby bases more than made up for this loss.

An unusually large number of bicycles quite early made their appearance on the local scene, frequently putt-putting along on the power of rebuilt washing machine motors. Almost instantly after the Japanese capitulation all major restrictions on rail passenger travel were lifted, the skip-stop system eliminated by the Virginia Transit Company and the highway speed limit raised to 50 miles an hour.

Another shadow on the old Richmond way of life was the scarcity of new automobiles. By 1943, new cars became a rarity and didn't appear again in any appreciable numbers until 1946, but even then strikes cut the number expected from the assembly lines. The price ceiling which had been placed on new automobiles was kept in effect, but the price restrictions were taken off used cars in 1946. This inconsistency caused such devious subterfuges as driving new automobiles around the block and selling them for used cars at considerable profit. The designation "gray market" was given to questionable automobile dealings.

Most of the holidays found people pretty close to home, not from choice, but due to the shortage of automobiles, rationing of gasoline and tires, and various other restrictions on travel. Of course, this stay-at-home situation among motorists cut into the operation of service stations. The number did not vary greatly, although some station operators took on new lines of merchandise, such as fruits, baskets, and novelties. Tire re-treading and repair work saved many service stations from going to the wall.

In 1943, the hunting season opened with plenty of game but a shortage of hunters. Those who could find transportation had a further problem finding ammunition. In 1944, a rumor spread that a local sporting goods store had shells and .22 rifles. Fifteen hundred hunters suddenly converged on the establishment, much to the amazement of the store personnel. The shooting situation did not improve in Richmond until it was over abroad.

The war years had a bad effect on distribution of commodities. Generally, Richmonders had more money than ever before and they were ever ready to take the elastic band off the bank roll. However, there was less to buy. In January, 1942, rationing boards were set up under government regulations to get fairer distribution of scarce foods. Richmond found itself in the national dilemma—the seller's market—and discovered that its citizens had to be particularly polite to the man handling the butter and other scarce items in grocery, hardware, building supply or, for that matter, almost any other store. Delivery of merchandise became a thing of the past and self-service grocery stores became firmly rooted. Families, hoping to save precious ration points, began eating out frequently; at the restaurants, they found signs asking them to be considerate of the waitresses.

Jewelers were jubilant as weddings and a double ring fad boosted business, and in 1944 extra crews of clerks struggled to accommodate crowds of women shoppers stocking up on jewelry, to beat the 20 per cent Federal luxury tax which went into effect in April of that year. Shoppers kept salespeople busy in the fur, cosmetic, luggage and purse departments, trying to get in under the same deadline. The most encouraging news the buying public had in a long time was dispensed in September 1945 when a survey disclosed that customers again were being treated with more courtesy and given more personalized service than during the previous war years.

The war brought many changes to women's clothes. Women hitherto would not have dared go out in public without hose, but finally got used to doing just that. Once having exposed well-turned legs, they were willing to keep them on display. Silk hose practically became extinct. The chance to buy a pair of nylons was worth all sorts of elbowing. Hat styles were as silly as usual and, as it affected other items of apparel, war suggested the design for women's headgear. Decorative buttons, costume jewelry and the lines of women's coats took on a military air. Rationing caused many of the fair sex to choose what might be termed "sensible" shoes. Sandals and toeless shoes became standard footwear and, later, flat heels became a fad.

Slacks were found safer for women than skirts in many industrial plants and soon workers were wearing them between home and factory. The popularity of this sort of garment spread and a dressier type for street wear developed. Meanwhile, teen-age girls went into blue denim overall trousers rolled to the knee and added Dad's shirt with the tail out as part of this weird outfit. Neatness and femininity were tossed out of the window in this youthful revolt.

Important changes came in women's hair styles. The military motif demanded simplicity. Many women other than those in the services were in uniform so they naturally followed the fashion set by the WACS or WAVES, depending a great deal on the type of hat to be worn.

With so many men in service and the cost of hair cuts so high, the short GI style prevailed for the males. Another fad among teen-agers of both sexes was to peroxide one lock of hair and to comb it back to create a light streak in the center of the head. Some Richmond high school boys were detected using cosmetics.

Men's dress habits became less formal. Possibly the informality and the obvious comfort of service men had its effect upon the civilian populace. Men were seen on the street and in public places without coats, hats and neckties in this period of liberation from convention. By government decree, suits made during the war appeared without cuffs on the trousers. Two-pair-of-pants suits were forbidden, and vests were not allowed with double-breasted suits. Finally, in 1944, it became increasingly difficult to find a suit with one pair of pants. The next two years found veterans wearing mixed clothing of civilian and Army issue. Shirts, shorts and pajamas doubled in price, a fact that bothered few people because there were none to buy. Even cheaply made shirts sold like the proverbial "hotcakes," and local firms began having shirts made up from bed sheets—when they could find bed sheets. One of Richmond's extra stout public officers unblushingly admitted wearing women's bloomers when it was no longer possible to purchase shorts to fit him.

There were "eggless days" and as far as the markets were concerned most days were "meatless days." Women learned to count two kinds of currency to pay for their groceries—the money and the ration points. Whenever a storekeeper condescended to place such wares as hose, candy, gum, cigarettes, decent cuts of meat, bacon and other scarcities on the counter for legitimate sale, lines formed immediately. In fact, if two women stopped to chat, a line was apt to form behind them in the belief that something scarce was on sale. The anticipation of a pair of nylons at the counter was alone worth standing in line a half day.

Another of the rigors civilians suffered was a shortage of Coca-Cola, which had come to be an American institution. Confections were practically extinct and ice-cream almost became a memory. Children were hard hit in the bubble-gum market and some strange and tasteless brands of chewing-gum were found on the counters. The well-known makes of gum were being purchased by the government exclusively for its uniformed men and women.

At one point a cigarette shortage became the hardest civilian inconvenience, and acute suffering was reported among smokers. Later, hoarders here begged stores to take back stale cartons of cigarettes.

The merest suggestion of an impending shortage sent greedy buyers hurrying, thus to cause an actual shortage by buying up all of that commodity they could lay their hands upon. But the novelty of peace soon wove its way back into the habits of Richmonders who again became indifferent to the many blessings of our plentiful country.

The war caused people to become food conscious. Rationing sent many bridge addicts out in the sun to start victory gardens. Some flower gardens and lawns were plowed up to make way for vegetables, and civic associations started "harvest classes" to tell the people how to do it. Victory gardens doubled from 1942 to 1943, making a total of 11,729 gardens from six tomato plants to twelve acres within the corporate limits in the latter year. Garden clubs added canned goods and vegetable exhibits to their fall flower shows.

Santa Claus had his troubles, too! He found it difficult to supply the kiddies with toys of good quality. Metal and rubber items were scarce even in 1942 and were replaced by wooden substitutes. Santa's department did not get back to anything resembling normalcy until the 1946 Yule season.

Another Richmond custom that practically faded into oblivion was the annual September 1 moving day. Rent controls, a housing shortage and other government regulations automatically erased this old habit.

Church membership made a gain of substantial proportions between 1941 and 1946 but, for various reasons, due to war time restrictions, there was a decrease in Sunday school attendance. Even in the period of automobile travel restrictions, the church attendance did not decline, though that of Sunday schools did because the family simply didn't have sufficient gasoline to permit use of the car for both

Sunday school and church. Therefore, the first trip was sacrificed. Visiting military personnel kept church attendance high by filling the pews vacated by Richmonders in service.

The number of churches in Richmond increased from 267 to 286 during the war years. However, this increase was due to some new congregations taking over stores or other vacant buildings for their services.

War vitally affected schools. Pupils and staffs withdrew to enter the armed services and courses were inaugurated to provide direct training for military service. Attendance was poorer during the 1942–43 period than in 1941–42, which may be explained by the fact that employment opportunities for young people increased. The restlessness that war brings to young people also caused irregular attendance. The war inspired Thomas Jefferson High School to organize a cadet corps in the 1942–43 season, with a membership of approximately 400 boys.

Lutz, *Richmond in World War II* (1951), pp. 38–43, 89–93

"That Bewitching Vegetable": In Celebration of Tobacco (1949)

Although the subject of tobacco has been mentioned many times in this book, no volume on Richmond that omitted its individual discussion could claim to be complete. Indeed, since the inception of the city, it has been one of the area's most important industries.

The social use of tobacco has taken many forms since it was introduced by Indians to the early European settlers. At first the colonists followed the native Americans' practice of smoking shredded tobacco in clay pipes. Later, however, the tobacco leaves were rolled, thus fashioning them into cigars. Chewing tobacco, for which the city was nationally famous in the nineteenth century, and snuff were other well-known forms of tobacco before the introduction of the cigarette, whose widespread consumption has eclipsed all other forms of tobacco use during the twentieth century.

Although Virginia lost its preeminence in the tobacco industry to North Carolina during the cigarette era, tobacco manufacturing and preparation is still a major industry in the city. The Universal Leaf Tobacco Company, Inc., as a matter of fact, is the largest leaf tobacco

company in the world, while Philip Morris, Inc., advertises its operations as "the world's largest and most modern cigarette manufacturing center."

So important have the city fathers considered tobacco to be that
they inaugurated in 1949 a formal event to commemorate its place in
Richmond. Called the Tobacco Bowl Festival and highlighted by
a gala parade, the crowning of an annual Tobacco Bowl queen, and
an annual football game, the event remains a distinctive part of
the Richmond fall season.

The following newspaper stories, all centering on the first Tobacco
Bowl Festival, tell the tale of what "that bewitching vegetable," as
William Byrd (q.v.) called it, has meant to the city.

§ Local Business, Clubs Endorse Tobacco Bowl Opening Here Oct. 15

Civic clubs and merchants of Richmond are quickly falling into line to
assure the success of the first annual Tobacco Bowl football game
between VMI and the University of Richmond at City Stadium on
October 15.

After four months of work on the project, General Chairman
E. Tucker Carlton formally announced the game last night during a
dinner at the Commonwealth Club.

The Optimist Club will sponsor the game, with the Police-Fire Boys'
Club and the American Legion helping as cosponsors.

Since the sponsors are vitally interested in boys' work around the
city, all profits from the games will be used in juvenile work.

"This project has the 100 per cent backing of the Optimist Club,"
Carlton told representatives of various civic clubs, radio and newspapers. "The motto of our club is 'Friend of the Boy,' and we will use
all money made from these football games in boys' work."

Teams Will Differ

Although VMI and the University of Richmond were chosen to participate in the first game, Carlton explained that teams will differ each
year, but that at least one Old Dominion "Big Six" team will appear in
each game.

Harry Simkins, president of the Police-Fire Boys' Club, and M. S.
Robinson, chairman of the American Legion's central committee,
heartily endorsed the game at last night's meeting.

Athletic Director Frank L. Summers, of VMI, and Mac Pitt, of Richmond, attended and said their schools considered it a high honor to be selected to play in the first game.

Richmond's large tobacco industry also likes the idea of a "Tobacco Bowl Festival" in conjunction with the game on October 15.

A large number of floats will be entered in a gigantic parade while crack formation flyers of the Virginia Air National Guard have promised VMI and UR formations all during the day of the game.

Cherry Watkins is serving as Carlton's assistant in working up the inaugural game.

Richmond *Times-Dispatch*, 9 April 1949

§ With Gold Cups For Two: It's Frankie!

By William Bien

The scene in Frank Sinatra's hotel room was reasonably quiet and sane this afternoon.

There were no women present, except for Tobacco Bowl Queen Dorothy Kirsten and a woman news reporter, and the thin, blue-eyed singing star could relax after his airplane trip to Richmond from New York City.

"We were almost an hour late arriving at Byrd Field," he said, "because they held us up in Baltimore. No trouble—just the weather."

Standing among a crowd of press and radio representatives in a fifth floor room at the Hotel John Marshall, Sinatra agreed with Miss Kirsten that "We are ready for a busy week end."

First public appearance of the singer will be at the "Presentation of Celebrities Show" tonight at the Cavalier Arena—one of the major attractions on the list of events of Richmond's first annual Tobacco Festival.

Gold Cup Awards

Sinatra didn't want to talk about music or singing this afternoon. He was more interested in what the festival stands for.

"When I heard that the proceeds from this show are to help underprivileged children, I was really enthusiastic," he said.

"As my contribution to the event, I am awarding a set of gold cups to be kept in Richmond permanently.

"One is to go to the Boy of the Year and the other to the Girl of the Year annually. Your city Board of Education will make the selections. Each winner will have his or her name engraved on the trophies."

Sinatra was very enthusiastic about the Tobacco Festival. He wondered why Richmond hadn't started the idea before.

Cameramen All Set

"This is the natural center for such a celebration," he said. "Here you are, right in the heart of the tobacco country, with the largest sun-cured tobacco markets in the world."

Sinatra and Miss Kirsten chatted a few moments about their busy schedule for the next two days.

"I think they're going to allow us about two minutes between appearances," Sinatra laughed.

When he arrived at Byrd Field shortly after noon today, a group of cameramen were all set for pictures. Perhaps he thought Richmond's young feminine element was more reserved than in some cities.

If he did, his attitude changed as he entered the lobby of the Hotel John Marshall. Lining the stairs were groups of youthful business girls on their lunch hour, just waiting for a glimpse of "Frankie."

They Gasp

As he hurried up the steps toward a waiting elevator, the usual gasps accompanied his progress.

"Oh, isn't he cute!" exclaimed many of the admirers.

Later today the guest stars were to attend a party at the Hotel Jefferson. Other celebrities invited include Governor W. Preston Lane, Jr., chief executive of Maryland, and Virginia's Governor Tuck.

Tomorrow morning Sinatra will make the official announcement of the Boy and Girl of the Year awards at a "brunch" breakfast for the benefit of underprivileged children in Richmond. The event will be held at the Hotel John Marshall, and will be attended by Sinatra and Miss Kirsten.

Richmond *News Leader*, 14 October 1949

§ Mardi Gras Air Sweeps Over City; Crowds Off To Tobacco Bowl Game

By Martin Millspaugh

The festival spirit swept over downtown Richmond today—the day of the Tobacco Bowl.

The streets, from the Capitol west, normally quiet on Saturday morning, were thronged with crowds out for the huge festival parade.

The parade, when fully under way, stretched 38 blocks. Police estimated that roughly 55,000 spectators lined the parade route, many of them watching from the center of Broad Street as the marchers moved west along the north lanes of the thoroughfare.

All available policemen were assigned to the parade route, and traffic authorities described the crowd as "tremendous." They said they were having difficulty keeping the line of march open.

The skies threatened alternately with rain and wind, but Fall and football were in the air.

Streets Choked

Tinsel-spangled floats and brightly uniformed marching units converged on the corner of Broad and Ninth early in the day, choking up the streets as far east as Fourteenth.

They moved out almost exactly on schedule—at 10:07—with mounted policemen gently opening a way through the throngs. Behind them came open cars with festival and military dignitaries and the United States Marine Band.

The floats, built by local tobacco and other companies and by the sponsors of the festival, were adorned with beautiful girls clad in tobacco leaves. Each float had its own theme, and all were bright with tinfoil and colored bunting.

It was the kids' show, primarily, but there were enough adults to line Broad Street four or five deep all the way along the two-mile route. Thousands more watched from windows and rooftops, from ledges three stories above the street, from telephone poles and from the tops of cars.

Spirits Not Dampened

One disappointment was noted: Frank Sinatra and Dorothy Kirsten, the stars of the Tobacco Bowl Festival, did not appear on their floats. The festival headquarters said the drizzle that fell during the parade would have endangered their singing voices.

The rain didn't dampen the spirits of many others, though; cars were parked bumper-to-bumper on adjacent streets, from downtown to the Boulevard, and traffic slowed to a snail's pace all over town. Through traffic was rerouted.

Festivity centered earlier in Capitol Square, where the Fiftieth Army Band gave a concert under the towering columns of the south portico.

Square Is Gay

The square was gay with bright fall fashions, uniforms and gleaming band instruments. Drum majorettes pranced up and down, awaiting the signal to start down Broad toward Broad Street Station.

The parade was headed for the Tobacco Bowl football game at City Stadium at 2:30 P.M. That was the day's main event but later the Mardi Gras spirit was to carry on for two big Tobacco Bowl dances at the Rural Exposition Grounds and Tantilla Gardens.

Tickets for the two free "Hit Parade" broadcasts at the Cavalier Arena were long since gone—snapped up by first comers who stood in line for as long as two hours at the Hotel John Marshall. A second performance had to be added by the show's sponsors to handle the crush of applicants to see Sinatra and Miss Kirsten.

The corps of cadets from VMI was on hand last night, and 16 bands were assembled for the march.

Full Schedule

The two stars of the festival, Miss Kirsten as queen and Sinatra as master of ceremonies, had a full schedule today, starting with the breakfast for 10 boys and 10 girls from Richmond orphanages.

They were to go from there to their posts in the parade, then to lunch, and out to City Stadium, where a second pregame parade went on at 1:20 P.M.

The football game, which started all the rumpus, pits the University of Richmond against VMI. The cadet corps was on hand to provide a military air. Patrons were advised to get to their seats early, for the performance of the cadets and of the corps of Richmond high schools, with the United States Marine Band.

Proceeds from the game are to go to the boys' work of the three sponsors of the Tobacco Bowl Festival: the Optimist Club of Richmond, the American Legion, and the Police-Fire Boys' Club.

The festival is theirs primarily but the companies that own Richmond's huge cigarette industry brought their radio stars here for the big day, and the three-day show had grown by game time to proportions advertised as the biggest in Richmond's history.

Tonight, the two Hit Parade shows were on tap at 6:30 and 8:30 P.M. at the Cavalier Arena. The festivities are to wind up with two big dances—one for barn dance fans, at the Atlantic Rural Exposition Grounds, and the other a Tobacco Bowl Ball at Tantilla Gardens.

Sinatra and Miss Kirsten are scheduled to make appearances at both, to wind up two days of whirlwind activity.

Yesterday, they arrived amid police sirens and fanfare at the Hotel John Marshall. They had a swift press conference with local reporters and writers from New York and then hurried off for personal appearances at local department stores.

Miss Kirsten was featured in a fashion show, before a crowd of well-dressed women who packed the auditorium. Sinatra came on stage on the roof at another establishment. Fences were set up and aides on hand for any eventuality, but the crowd was quiet and appeared merely curious.

It was a different set than that which met Miss Kirsten, however; ages ranged from babes in arms to elderly women, and some men were noted, in the tow of their female companions.

There was a reception yesterday afternoon by the tobacco company that sponsors the stars' radio program, and then the presentation show at the Cavalier Arena.

The arena was less than a third filled—this one was not free—and the Tobacco Bowl princesses from market towns in Virginia and from five neighboring states were seated on stage opposite Dean Hudson's orchestra.

Sinatra and Miss Kirsten appeared, briefly, and then were whisked away for what the press program described as a private dinner with officials of the tobacco company.

E. Tucker Carleton, chairman of the festival committee, appeared for a speech, and provided the biggest surprise of the event to date when he charged mysterious "other interests" with attempting to kill the festival idea.

Those who were there were not sure when he was through what those interests were, and some left during his short talk. Another committee official, Joseph Eanes, spoke after Carleton, and also expressed disappointment at the poor turnout for the second night's most-advertised event.

Then the affair ended on a note of "be-bop" from Dean Hudson's band, and the crowd filed out.

It was all over at 9:45 P.M., and Hudson invited the princesses and their escorts to a hastily assembled party at the Hotel King Carter.

Richmond *Times-Dispatch*, 15 October 1949

"Honky-tonk Vice and Rusted-out Mufflers": The 1950s and 1960s

Tom Robbins (1936–) is a native North Carolinian who attended Washington and Lee University and, after a stint in the Air Force in Japan, graduated from the Richmond Professional Institute, now a part of Virginia Commonwealth University, with a degree in journalism. Robbins, who was active in Richmond's bohemian life in the late 1950s and early 1960s while working for the Richmond *Times-Dispatch*, moved to Seattle where he continued his newspaper work and also became an art critic. His first novel, *Another Roadside Attraction* (1971), was immediately successful and was followed by *Even Cowgirls Get the Blues* (1976), which moved him to the front ranks of current popular writers.

The first part of *Even Cowgirls Get the Blues* is set in South Richmond, part of which was formerly the city of Manchester before it was incorporated into Richmond in 1910.

In South Richmond, smelling as it did of tobacco, honky-tonk vice and rusted-out mufflers, social niceties sometimes failed to make the six o'clock news, but one thing the citizens of South Richmond agreed upon was that it was not fit, proper or safe for a little girl to go around hitchhiking. . . .

So Sissy lived in Richmond, Virginia, in the Eisenhower Years, so called as if the passing seasons, with their eggs hatching and rivers rising, their cakes baking and stars turning, their legs dancing and hearts melting, their lamas levitating and poets doing likewise, their cheerleaders getting laid at drive-in picture shows and old men dying in rooms over furniture stores, as if they, the passing seasons, could

be branded by a mere President; as if time itself could toddle out of
Kansas and West Point, popularize a military jacket and seek election
to Eternity on the Republican ticket.

In the croaked air of the Eisenhower Years in Richmond, Virginia,
she must have been a familiar sight. In clothes that were either too big
for her or too small—floppy coats whose hems rubbed the cement,
summer slacks that disclosed everything anyone might wish to know
about her socks—she moved through the city (the city of which it has
been said, "It is not a city at all but the world's largest Confederate
museum").

At all hours and in every weather the girl could be seen, if not
admired.

Her soon-to-be-lovely features were still getting their sea legs and at
that unsteady stage of their development must have clung clumsily to
the bleached deck of her face (which, due to unusually high cheek-
bones, appeared as if it were pitched aslant in rough waters). . . .

South Richmond was a neighborhood of mouse holes, lace curtains,
Sears catalogs, measles epidemics, baloney sandwiches—and men who
knew more about the carburetor than they knew about the clitoris.

The song "Love Is a Many Splendored Thing" was not composed in
South Richmond.

There have been cans of dog food more splendiferous than South
Richmond. Land mines more tender.

South Richmond was settled by a race of thin, bony-faced psycho-
paths. They would sell you anything they had, which was nothing, and
kill you over anything they didn't understand, which was everything.

They had come, mostly by Ford from North Carolina, to work in
the tobacco warehouses and cigarette factories. In South Richmond,
the mouse holes, lace curtains and Sears catalogs, even the baloney
sandwiches and measles epidemics, always wore a faint odor of cured
tobacco. The word *tobacco* was acquired by our culture (with neither
the knowledge nor consent of South Richmonders) from a tribe of
Caribbean Indians, the same tribe that gave us the words *hammock*,
canoe and *barbecue*. It was a peaceful tribe whose members spent their
days lying in hammocks puffing tobacco or canoeing back and forth
between barbecues, thus offering little resistance when the land de-
velopers arrived from Europe in the sixteenth century. The tribe was
disposed of swiftly and without a trace, except for its hammocks,
barbecues and canoes, and, of course, its tobacco, whose golden
crumbs still perfume the summer clouds and winter ices of South
Richmond. . . .

Richmond, Virginia, has been called a "depression-proof" city. That is because its economy has one leg in life insurance and the other in tobacco.

During times of economic bellyache, tobacco sales climb even as other sales tumble. Perhaps the uncertainty of finances makes people nervous: the nervousness causes them to smoke more. Perhaps a cigarette gives an unemployed man something to do with his hands. Maybe a pipe in his mouth helps a man forget that he hasn't lately chewed steak.

In times of depression, policy-holders somehow manage to keep up their life insurance premiums. Life insurance could be the only investment they can afford to maintain. Perhaps they insist on dignity in death since they never had it in life. Or is it that the demise of one of its insured members is the only chance a family has of getting flush?

Each autumn for many years Richmond has celebrated its depression-proof economy. The celebration is called the Tobacco Festival. (Somehow "Life Insurance Festival" didn't set any leather to tapping.)

Sissy Hankshaw liked to watch the Tobacco Festival parades. From a Broad Street curb, where she would secure an early position, it was her habit, once her courage climbed, to try to hitch the open convertibles in which the various Tobacco Princesses rode. The drivers, Jaycees one and all, never noticed her; they kept their gaze straight ahead for the safety that was in it—tobacco gods would cough lightning should a Jaycee drive up the hindquarters of a Marlboro Filters float—but the waving Princesses, projecting eyebeam and toothlight into the multitudes, ever on the alert for kinfolk, boy friends, photographers and talent scouts, the Princesses sometimes would catch sight of a pleading pod, and for a crowd-puzzling second—Oh the perils of innocence in the service of nicotine!—lose their carefully coached composure. We may wonder what thumbtales—thumbfacts evolving into thumbmyths—those beauties carried home to Danville, Petersburg, South Hill or Winston-Salem when that year's Tobacco Festival had burned down to a butt.

In 1960, the Tobacco Festival parade took place on the night of September 23. The *Times-Dispatch* reported that there were fewer floats than the previous year ("but they were fancier, and wider by six feet"); even so, it took ninety minutes for the procession to pass a given point. There were twenty-seven Princesses, from whose company Lynne Marie Fuss—Miss Pennsylvania—was the next day named Queen of Tobaccoland. The parade grand marshal was Nick Adams, star of a TV series called "The Rebel." Adams was a perfect choice since "The Rebel" had a Civil War theme and was sponsored by a leading brand of cigarettes. The actor became piqued at one point in the parade when he discovered, rather abruptly, that his horse's flank was the target of a gang of boys armed with peashooters. There were marching bands, clowns, military formations, drum majorettes, dignitaries, animals, "Indians," a few temporary cowgirls, even, their reptile-shiny shirts loaded down with embroidery and udders; there were hawkers of souvenirs and the aforementioned gang of evil peashooters. City Manager Edwards estimated attendance at the "noisily lavish extravaganza" at close to two hundred thousand, by far the largest crowd in festival history. Sissy Hankshaw was not among the throng.

Miles across town from the thousands (who, according to the newspaper, "yelled, giggled and clapped"); across the James in South Richmond, where, economic theories to the contrary, it was always depression time; in a dim, dinky house, frescoed with soot and some termites' low relief; before a full-length mirror merciless in its reflection of thumbs—Sissy stood naked. (Never say "stark naked." "Naked" is a sweet word, but nobody in his right mind likes "stark.")

Sissy was making a decision. It was a point in life that could not hold still for ninety minutes' worth of bright-leaf boosterism to pass it by.

Her long, svelte body, as eloquently as it might assert itself, could not have been heard above the funky din of the clothing she wore.

Certainly her mind didn't count for much: in the sotweed suburb of South Richmond, no mind did. Few were the schoolmates to notice the headlight shine of her eyes and wonder who was driving around inside there. . . .

One June, Richmond, Virginia, woke up with its brakes on and kept them on all summer. That was okay; it was the Eisenhower Years and nobody was going anywhere. Not even Sissy. That is to say, she wasn't going far. Up and down Monument Avenue, perhaps; hitching up and down that broad boulevard so dotted with enshrined cannons and heroic statuary that it is known throughout the geography of the dead as a banana belt for snuffed generals.

The old Capital of the Confederacy marked time in the heat. Its boots kicked up a little tobacco dust, a little wisteria pollen, and that was it. Each morning, including Sundays, the sun rose with a golf tee in its mouth. Its rays were reflected, separately but equally, by West End bird baths, South Side beer cans, ghetto razors. (In those days Richmond was convoluted like the folds of the brain, as if, like the brain, it was attempting to prevent itself from knowing itself.)

In the evenings, light from an ever-increasing number of television

sets inflicted a misleading frostiness on the air. It has been said that
true albinos produce light of a similar luminescence when they move
their bowels.

Middays, the city felt like the inside of a napalmed watermelon.

Whenever possible, men, women, children and pets kept to the
shade, talked little, stirred less, watched the blades of fans go 'round
as is the nature of fan business.

Robbins, *Even Cowgirls Get the Blues* (1976),
pp. 16–17, 30, 36–40

"She Ripped a Broad Path of Destruction": Hurricane Agnes, 22 June 1972

Richmond is located in a temperate zone and only rarely suffers
the ravages of nature common to many other parts of the country.
Situated at 37.30 degrees latitude and 77.20 degrees longitude, it has
an average mean temperature of 57.8 degrees Farenheit and an
average rainfall of 42.59 inches. Owing to the mild climate, the city,
which ranges in altitude from zero to 300 feet above sea level, is not
subject to heavy snows; and although an occasional tornado makes
its appearance, rarely if ever does it do the kind of damage routinely
experienced by residents of the midsection of the country.

Richmond has not been totally without its share of unusual weather
and natural disasters, however. Severe floods occurred on the James
River in 1771, 1842, and 1870. Frost appeared every month in Richmond in 1816, and a severe drought, which caused a shortage of
drinking water, occurred in 1880. The river froze from bank to bank
in 1884 and again in 1893. Additionally, a severe earthquake did
extensive damage in 1886. In 1951 a tornado destroyed houses and
businesses, and in 1954 Hurricane Hazel, one of the worst storms
of this century, took its toll.

The summer of 1972, however, brought to Richmond one of its
most devastating natural disasters ever, when the James River, swollen by rains from Hurricane Agnes, rampaged through the streets,
destroying houses, businesses, and industrial property alike. In the
following selection, *Times-Dispatch* Lifestyles Editor James Berry
(1931–) tells what the James River was like in one of its angriest
moods since the eighteenth century. Berry, a native of Columbus,

Ohio, worked as a reporter on the Farmville, Virginia, *Herald* for two years before joining the *Times-Dispatch* in 1956.

It was summer officially at 3:06 A.M., June 21. In the capital of the Old Dominion, Richmonders peeked out at the summer solstice from under their umbrellas.

By late afternoon the summery shower turned vicious. High winds buffeted the historic old city on the banks of the James River and just before the rush hour downtown Richmond was blacked out by a power failure.

It was anything but ominous despite the fact that 80 trees had been uprooted, many persons were stranded in elevators and a lot of firms simply shut down and sent the help home. For those who stood in the shelter of doorways looking at everyone else standing in the shelter of doorways the blackout seemed hardly an omen. Besides it was over in little more than an hour and the bustling city began to settle in for a soggy evening.

Still, the weather didn't look good especially for the first round of the Richmond Golf Association's city amateur tournament scheduled the next day.

Five days earlier the National Weather Service had begun plotting the movement of a tropical storm named Agnes which had formed off the Yucatan Peninsula. The Associated Press bulletin that clacked over teletypes in newsrooms across the country slugged the message "Agnew." As the bulletin was flawed, so was Agnes. She was supposed to strike the Florida Panhandle, thrash about for a day or so and die.

Instead of growing old gracefully, Agnes grew more powerful, more unpredictable and then . . . deadly. She ripped a broad path of destruction across the deep South and churned awkwardly toward the Atlantic. As she moved ponderously over the Virginia Capes, Agnes collided with another storm and turned inland . . .

Half a state away, the National Weather Service escalated its flash flood watch to the more critical warning level. As much as three inches of rain had fallen by early evening in the mountainous areas of Virginia and by 9 P.M. minor flooding was reported across the Blue Ridge. At the little town of Massies Mill about a dozen families were evacuated as a precautionary measure. The devastation wreaked on the hamlet three years ago by Hurricane Camille was a horror too easily recalled there in Nelson County where more than 100 people died.

"It's raining pretty hard now," said a sheriff's deputy in neighboring Amherst County, "and we had right much rain over the last few days."

Still, Nelson is a long way from Richmond and the weather service said the main body of the James was not in danger of overflowing. "We're not taking any chances," said the deputy, "I lived through one of those."

Camille was what the experts called a 100-year rain. Nothing like it in recorded history. Nothing like it probably ever again. At least not for 100 years . . .

A stunned populace woke up to dramatic news on the morning of June 22. The mighty James was beginning to rise, stained by swollen mountain rivers that were dumping billions of gallons of floodwaters into the western reaches of the James River Valley.

Roanoke had been hard hit, . . . little Scottsville which was almost wiped out in 1969 was under water again, . . . an 800 foot bridge at Cartersville had been swept away, . . . and Agnes had started killing Virginians.

To the north, Virginia was already cut off from the nation's capital. Interstate 95 was closed because State Police feared a dam less than a mile from the superhighway was about to burst. To the west, sections of some 40 primary routes were blocked because of high water or mud slides and hundreds of secondary roads were closed.

Northwest of Richmond, a man, his wife and two children drove around a roadblock on U.S. 60, a main artery to the capital city, and were swept away into the raging James.

Richmond began to prepare for the worst . . . It came Thursday, June 22 . . . or so everyone thought . . .

The night before, a couple driving in a small foreign car was swept off a bridge in neighboring Hanover County. They were rescued. In adjacent Henrico, one man refused to be evacuated along with about 100 families who were warned of impending high water. "He said he has a canoe and he would decide when he had to leave," said a disgruntled policeman. When the area was checked again, water had surrounded the house.

Richmond's city government moved to a command post set up at Parker Field, home of the Richmond Braves of the International League. The Braves wouldn't be playing any home games for awhile.

Ironically, just 10 days before Agnes struck, the State Civil Defense command had distributed its battle plan for disaster to its network of key people and agencies around the state.

The Red Cross and the Salvation Army set up evacuation centers at four locations in the East End.

Richmond was ready . . . or so everyone thought.

The James was boiling toward a record flood crest within a matter of hours, the highest water in recorded history—36.5 feet—far beyond the 28.6 feet in 1969 when Camille swept through. Camille had been the ultimate storm. Nothing could approach the havoc dealt by that treacherous lady. There were many who refused to believe that the James could possibly rise beyond the 1969 level. Until Agnes . . .

Putting into practice the lessons learned from Camille, three of the city's main bridges—Boulevard, 14th Street and the old 9th Street spans—were closed.

Hundreds of city workmen and volunteers sandbagged the dikes along Dock and Cary Streets. It was a futile effort. The James continued its inexorable rise and by mid-evening the vital Shockoe Valley pumping station at 17th and Byrd Streets was put out of action. "There goes the whole ball game," shouted one man as the work crew scrambled for safety. Without the pumping station, nothing stood in the way of the James as it pushed its way through the sewer system and behind the dike.

Around 2 A.M. the flood waters flowed into lower Main Street and on to Broad Street at 17th. "Now, in '69 it wasn't nothing like this," said a man helping evacuate the area. "The water didn't even get up to 18th Street."

Businessmen, some still paying off notes for damages suffered three years ago, looked on helplessly as the water rose relentlessly, flooding some buildings to the second story. Many stood and wept.

During the night 11 Vepco workmen were trapped on the roof of the power substation at First and Decatur. A temporary sandbag dike burst under the swelling James and the crew scrambled to the roof. Eight feet of water rolled into the building. Rescuers got six men into a boat. Then it capsized. All got back safely by some miracle.

As the James pushed toward its peak crest, the 17th and Main area was inundated on the north bank. On the South Side the floodwaters rolled over the sprawling commercial and industrial complex between Commerce Road and the river.

At daylight, Governor Linwood Holton stood at 14th and Cary. "This is going to be bad," he said sadly. It not only got bad as the Governor predicted. It got worse . . .

Friday, June 23, disaster turned into calamity. At 7 A.M. the city ordered the downtown area sealed off. Floodwaters had covered the approaches of key bridges serving the city and a major power failure occurred. Barricades went up, manned by police and National Guardsmen. The capital of Virginia took on the look of an occupied city. Only armed troops, some of the 1,800 called out, were in sight.

Downtown Richmond stood almost deserted on a bleak, drizzly Friday that got progressively bleaker.

In the West End, in the suburbs, anywhere on the high ground it was business as usual. Then the Agnes-spawned floodwaters that seemed so far away brought the full impact of the disaster home to the entire city. About 6 A.M. Friday, Richmond's 66-million gallon per day water purification plant was knocked out.

Within 36 hours the faucets in the homes of nearly 200,000 persons began to go dry . . .

"Conserve water but don't panic," said Gov. Holton in an early morning appeal. And conserve they did. Some didn't shave. Some didn't bathe. Dirty clothes piled up in hampers. Said one Richmond mother of five. "It was impossible to wash diapers; . . . if it had gone on any longer I think the governor would have declared my house a disaster area."

The Shockoe Valley corridor was under several feet of water and impassable. Hundreds of vehicles were backed up on either side of the Lee Bridge which was carrying the bulk of all north-south traffic. Interstate 95 was blocked just south of the river. Thousands were temporarily jobless. Many couldn't have gotten to work if they wanted to. Propane gas began leaking from a storage tank area in Fulton forcing police to evacuate the area. Some 500 people were housed in the evacuation centers.

One 80-year-old man refused to leave his second story apartment on flooded E. Main Street. He told would-be rescuers, "I knew the water wouldn't get that high." If it did, he quipped, "I had another floor to go. I didn't move when the last came through, so I didn't see any need to move this time."

The Army flew in 10,000-gallon collapsible tanks from as far away as Ohio in a massive effort to provide water for the city's residents. Neighboring communities sent in water by truck and thousands of Richmonders lined up at fire stations for their rations. Restaurants shut down and air conditioners were turned off. Washing cars and watering lawns was prohibited.

At the most critical stage there were twenty 5,000-gallon tankers stationed throughout the city, all furnished by the Army. Before the Army arrived, local dairymen furnished 13 tankers of water and other trucks came from as far away as Philadelphia.

Everywhere there were lines of Richmonders carrying all manner of containers waiting for their allotted five gallons of pure water. They carried glass jars, ice chests, plastic trash cans. A preacher brought two one-gallon wine bottles. One resident, worried that he hadn't stored any water, suddenly remembered the 260 gallons in his water bed.

It would be the water shortage that Richmonders will remember most when they tell the story of Agnes to their grandchildren.

Within 28 hours city crews got the filtration plant going again. Water went back into the lines. There was no cheering. Everyone was too tired. What came out of the taps was only good for fighting fires or flushing toilets. "Maybe you could mix it with bourbon or scotch," one man cracked, "but who wants to waste good whiskey." It was Thursday before pure water flowed through the taps. Meanwhile, people went to work with a jug of water in one hand and a lunch pail in the other.

Bridges were reopened and traffic began to flow smoothly again. Downtown Richmond began to stir but without water nothing was the same. With many restaurants shut down shoppers went hungry. With the air conditioning off sales clerks were as miserable as their few customers. Most worked in their shirtsleeves. The few restaurants that were operating served meals on paper plates. Diners ate with plastic forks and drank soda pop.

Commuters looked unbelieving at the troops guarding the bridges with M16s cradled under their arms. Helicopters fluttered over the stricken area, their olive drab military colors delivering the message that Richmond was still under tight control.

In Shockoe Valley, the presence of troops virtually eliminated looting. Crime, surprisingly, practically declared a holiday during the emergency. Businessmen were allowed back into the flooded area to begin the task of cleaning up but Safety Director Jack Fulton ordered them out of the district by nightfall so police "could tell the good guys from the bad guys." The lack of water made cleaning up difficult at best.

For city officials who hadn't slept in days there was a chance for a few hours rest. City Manager William Leidinger checked into a nearby motel and left strict orders to be awakened shortly before an evening session of the disaster staff. Leidinger is a notoriously heavy sleeper. That evening a clerk roused the city manager with news that he had somehow been allowed to doze well past time for the meeting. Leidinger hopped out of bed in a rage. Then the smiling clerk told him he had plenty of time to make the session. The ruse had worked.

City employees were worn to a frazzle. Essential government employees, including police and fire departments, worked 12-hour shifts for more than a week. Some guardsmen were on duty 36 hours without sleep. The Army dispatched 300 soldiers from nearby Ft. Lee who manned water purification units round the clock to ease the shortage.

By week's end the cleanup was getting organized and the city began to function near normal. Highly chlorinated water was flowing through the taps once more. It tasted awful, but it was pure enough to drink. Garden hoses were dragged out to help wash away the ooze in stricken Shockoe Valley. Store employees were told to come back to work with shovels and boots.

On East Main, Richard Motley, owner of a furniture store, looked glum. "The water only came across the street last time. So I moved things higher this time. I didn't expect it to come this high." Motley had put a lot of furniture on the highest first floor room in his building. The room looked like the aftermath of a Pier Six brawl. One piece of furniture washed out a broken window and was last seen on Broad Street.

Businessmen were hard hit and bitter. Some threatened suits against the city. But it was bad for residents of Fulton as well. Some 50 families were homeless. About half of them could never return.

On Thursday Vice President Agnew flew into Richmond for a two-hour stay to survey the damage and make certain that state officials were getting cooperation from the federal government. More than one newsman accompanying the vice president remembered that flawed bulletin that came in over the teletypes.

Agnew wanted to talk to some of the flood victims. A policeman was dispatched to find some. He brought back two mud-spattered businessmen in work clothes: Irving Koslow and Lewis Cowardin. "I still owe the government for the last time," Cowardin told newsmen before he talked with Agnew. Both men were angry because Richmond had never qualified for flood insurance after Camille. They talked with the vice president for five minutes. "All right gentlemen. Sorry to hear about this," Agnew said. He gave both men ball-point pens bearing his signature and the policeman drove the pair back to Shockoe Valley and the waiting muck.

Agnes was the most destructive storm ever to hit Virginia. Final damage totals may not be available for months. Some officials predict the figure will reach as high as $330,000,000. That's three times the damage done by Camille. The misery can't be measured in dollars.

In many ways Agnes somehow lacked the dramatic, deadly image of Camille. Camille touched the lives of fewer Richmonders. Agnes affected almost everyone in the city. Agnes was the more efficient rainmaker. Camille was the more efficient killer.

Yet through it all not a single life was lost in Richmond. Perhaps that is what people will remember most of all.

Berry, *Richmond Flood* (1972), pp. 2–13

"It's Like Living in a Foreign Country": Desegregation in the 1970s

Following the far-reaching and controversial Supreme Court decision in *Brown* v. *Board of Education of Topeka* in 1954, there was first a retrenchment, then a gradual moving forward, in the Richmond public school system. Not until the implementation of court-ordered busing to achieve racial balance, which began in 1970, did the realities of the task come to the citizens of the city, however. Although equitable in concept, integrating Richmond's educational institutions proved to be easier to legislate than to implement. The following selection by J. Harvie Wilkinson III, a member of the law school faculty at the University of Virginia, former clerk to Supreme Court Justice Lewis F. Powell, Jr. (q.v.), and former editor of the Norfolk *Virginian Pilot*, recounts the pangs accompanying the legal desegregation of the city's schools. Wilkinson is currently deputy assistant attorney general for civil rights in the U.S. Department of Justice.

Richmond, Virginia exhibited those circumstances under which court-ordered busing was least likely to succeed. The city had a 65 percent black school population when busing began; two overwhelmingly white suburban school systems—Henrico and Chesterfield—lay just outside the city limits; many white Richmonders could afford private schools or to leave the city altogether; and the area's attitudes, set by the two daily newspapers, were unabashedly conservative. In upper crust precincts of west end Richmond, busing provoked gestures of earnest futility: petitioning, landslide votes for antibusing candidates, formation of parent associations for neighborhood schools. In August 1970, the editor of the Richmond *News Leader*, Ross Mackenzie, delivered to the Supreme Court 29,122 letters with 37,438 signatures decrying the abolition of freedom of choice. For others, petitioning was altogether too polite. "It's getting to the point," one attorney told a huge crowd in Chesterfield, "where federal courts and the federal government will only listen to the mob—so if we have to get a mob, let's get a mob."

From the first, the white suburban schools of Henrico and Chesterfield feared their forced merger with Richmond in the desegregation decree. The district court so joined them, but the Fourth Circuit reversed, holding that a district judge may not "compel one of the States of the Union to restructure its internal government for the purpose of achieving racial balance in the assignment of pupils to the public schools." At the Supreme Court, the suburbs escaped consolidation by a narrow stroke of luck. As a former chairman of the Richmond School Board, Justice Lewis Powell declined to sit in the case. The remaining eight justices split four to four and thus left standing the Fourth Circuit's opinion. The release of the suburbs deflated the most strident resistance. It also left Richmond's school system, almost two-thirds black, to desegregate alone.

That proved a failure. To suppose Richmond whites would attend black schools with white suburban and private ones close at hand was fatuous. Integration through busing left precious few whites around with which to integrate. In 1970, Richmond's first year of busing, the city's school population was 35 percent white; by 1976, the seventh year of busing, it was less than 20 percent and heading downward. Unless trends were reversed, white enrollment by 1982 was projected to sink to 10 percent. Not only had whites fled the system, but many middle-class blacks as well. So severe was the drain that by 1977 Richmond's black school superintendent, Richard Hunter, recommended greater parental free choice for a few elementary schools. The affected schools promptly registered a slight white enrollment again.

Academic standards plummeted badly after busing in Richmond, in part because administrators concluded that white middle-class standards should not be "yoked on black children from poor families overnight." But in 1978 Superintendent Hunter concluded that eighth-grade performance was so poor that his system flunked 34 percent, three times as many as the previous year. Deserted by the middle class of both races, Richmond schools were fighting uphill. College preparatory courses were barely holding on; the outlook for them, in the face of further middle-class flight and natural enrollment declines, was not good. A middle-class presence, so it seemed, helped preserve opportunities for the gifted poor.

"Between the races now, there is a truce," wrote Richmond *Times-Dispatch* education reporter Charles Cox in the summer of 1978. "In some schools, some days, it is a fragile truce. Small wars are fought on occasion. . . . When the last bell of the day rings, whites and blacks, students and staff, tend to go separate ways to homes in different parts of town." Everyone agreed, Cox continued, "that Richmond has a 'black' system to which whites are asked to adjust if they wish to attend." Now whites, not blacks, had to learn what being in a small minority was like. "It's like living in a foreign country," said one white at Richmond's Maggie Walker High, a school of 50 whites and 850 blacks. "I go to school, I go home, that's it."

White Richmond's headstrong reaction to busing in 1970 had caused some to opine that "the tone of the late 1950s is back." But that was too simple a reading of the South in the 1970s. The region had experienced remarkable change. As Professor William Havard put it: "Cotton has moved west, cattle has moved east, the farmer has moved to town, the city resident has moved to the suburbs, the Negro has moved north, and the Yankee has moved south." Political change, noted Havard, had been "slower to develop than the conditions would seem to warrant," but it too came. Men of moderation occupied many southern statehouses in the early 1970s: Askew of Florida, Bumpers of Arkansas, Holton of Virginia, West of South Carolina, and Carter of Georgia. Books appeared, heralding *The Changing Politics of the South* and *The Transformation of Southern Politics*.

It was, of course, easy to exaggerate true change in the South, as prophets have been doing since the days of Henry Grady. The South in 1970 remained the nation's most conservative region: racial changes may have owed less to a new spirit of brotherhood than to the rapid increase in the black vote. Yet surely there were deeper currents. The immediate effect of *Brown* v. *Board of Education* had been to give the South's demagogues their day: Eastland, Talmadge, Thurmond, Barnett, Faubus, and Wallace, that long, oppressive verbal heatwave of racial hatred *sans* end. But in the long run, *Brown* helped to convince southerners that segregation was neither the most moral nor the most practical way to live. "Southern senators like Mr. Eastland were themselves unexpected beneficiaries of the battle they lost in Congress and the courts," noted the Washington *Post*. "They were freed up to think about something other than how every act or proposal that came into their line of vision could be used to bolster the doomed racial dispensation of the South." Whether because of urbanization, black votes, or the moral message of *Brown* (or, indeed, the interaction among them), the early 1970s produced some southerners committed, as Virginia's Linwood Holton put it, "to an aristocracy of ability, regardless of race, color or creed."

Holton himself performed the single most courageous act in the politics of busing. A moderate Republican from Virginia's southwest hills, Holton determined to erase the racial legacy of the Byrd organization. On the opening day of classes, he personally escorted his thirteen-year-old daughter Tayloe to predominantly black John F. Kennedy High School in Richmond, the school to which she was assigned under the court's busing plan. After shaking hands with teachers and students, the governor was greeted by a Negro honor guard, which led the two of them to Tayloe's ninth-grade homeroom. "It's always hard for a child to change schools," explained Holton. "They don't want to leave old friends. But my children go where they are assigned." The governor's wife, meanwhile, was taking two younger Holtons, Ann, 12, and Woody, 11, to Mosby Middle School, where they were the only whites in their respective classrooms. "They're going to be all right," the governor commented. "They're going to give this as much leadership as you can expect from 11 to 13-year-olds, which is right much." Holton did not mention that he might have sent the children elsewhere. The governor's mansion was on state, not city, property, and thus technically exempt from any busing decree.

Some Virginians were exultant. Editor Raymond Boone of the Richmond *Afro-American*, confessedly "supercautious about praising most Virginia politicians," felt that "for once the government stood for justice. For once, we felt we were being counted in, not out. For once, we felt we were a part of the whole." And former Governor Colgate Darden called Holton's act "the most significant happening in this commonwealth during my lifetime."

The voters were less rapturous. Holton-backed candidates were clobbered in the next two statewide elections. "Make no mistake," the Richmond *Times-Dispatch* editorialized. "If Mr. Shafran is elected lieutenant-governor of Virginia, the voice that speaks from the Capitol about busing will be the voice of Governor Holton. And what will the voice say? 'Busing is working in Virginia.' Incredible!" The Richmond dailies, countered Holton, "wanted me to stand up on the Capitol, face toward Washington, and shake my fist." His only concern, Holton stated, "was to keep schools open and make sure they survived." Only then could the school-closing heritage of massive resistance truly be overcome. The governor's solitary act of leadership helped do that, but did little to stem Richmond's white enrollment decline.

Wilkinson, *From Brown to Bakke* (1979), pp. 151–54

"What's Ahead for Our City?": Richmond in the 1980s

Richmond's place in the history of the nation is unique; its essence derives from the events that have taken place there. Moreover, Richmond of the future promises to be as exciting as Richmond of the past. Currently underway are such renewal plans as Project One, which when complete will have revitalized a major portion of the downtown business district; Shockoe Slip renovations, which is restoring for commercial use one of the oldest parts of the city; and Historic Richmond and Jackson Ward renewal, which is returning both black and white residential areas of the past to new domestic use. In addition, plans are being made to return Main Street Station and the Jefferson Hotel to their former splendor, while the old Broad Street Station has been modified to accommodate the Science Museum of Virginia. Finally, the James River Park has been constructed and is in use, while such projects as Richmond on the James and the reclaiming of Belle Isle will return to a part of Richmond's waterfront its former beauty. Richmond Renaissance, begun in 1982, has as its goal the overall revitalization of the city.

In the following selection, John V. Moeser comments on the city as it moves toward the twenty-first century. Moeser is associate professor of urban studies at Virginia Commonwealth University and the editor of *A Virginia Profile, 1960–2000*. His most recent work, coauthored with Rutledge M. Dennis, is *The Politics of Annexation: Oligarchic Power in a Southern City*.

The future, in my estimation, is not a matter of pure chance. Nor is it a matter solely predetermined. Instead, the future will bear some relation to the moves we make today just as the present reflects those made by our predecessors. I also believe it is far better to knowingly participate in shaping our future than face whatever consequences stem from our unconscious choices. But choices presuppose alternatives, and how we go about selecting among alternatives should involve some process other than random selection. The act of choosing should flow out of some idea of what kind of future we want for our city. Assuming that years from now we want our children to speak with pride about their city, our choices today must incorporate our willingness to accept three responsibilities: (1) we must shed our illusions of the past; (2) we must accept the realities of the present; and (3) we must develop a vision for the future.

To suggest that citizens of Richmond should eliminate their illusions of the past is not to suggest they should deny the past. Quite the contrary. Richmond has a long history and one which, I believe, is the very factor which can insure us a future. We are all familiar with the revitalization currently underway in some of the oldest areas of the city such as Church Hill and Shockoe Slip, and the renovation started or planned for such landmarks as the Monumental Church; Main Street Station; the Tredegar Iron Works; the Hotel Jefferson; and Loew's Theater. Slowly the word is spreading that Richmond no longer is simply the place to be *from*, but the place to *be*. No longer is it the bathroom stop on the way to Washington, D.C., and points north, but it is a *destination*, and the charm which is associated with places like Savannah, Charleston, and New Orleans may soon be appropriately applied to this city.

What, then, is meant by shedding our illusions of the past? Simply put, it means being *honest about the past* and accepting the bad along with the good. It means recognizing that the glory days for some Richmonders represent painful memories for others. It also means acknowledging that the continuity of leadership provided by the Richmond gentry kept the city on a safe, steady course, though such was easy when the ship, built for the sea, seldom ventured beyond the dock.

In the past, power was not divided along racial lines as it is today with blacks having a modicum of political power and whites dominating the economic resources. Rather, political and economic powers were fused; however, the union was not one involving blacks and whites. It was what Robert Dahl has called "cumulative inequalities" in which a few wealthy, well-bred whites controlled both political and economic resources. The illusion is that this power served public ends and those who exercised it were objective and evenhanded. Without question, Richmond produced an impressive number of gifted leaders, but the fact remains that they were human and, while perhaps more courtly and polite than the average American, they were prone to error. Moreover, their use of power may well have served the public good, though it was often difficult to determine where private goals ended and public interests began. Usually, it was easier, since it was less abstract, to assume that their own perceptions of what was best constituted the public interest.

This fairly cohesive structure of power was characteristic of Richmond's politics for decades. It began to deteriorate, however, with drastic shifts in the population. It disintegrated when the city, under mandate from the U.S. Supreme Court, reverted to ward representation. It was only recently, in 1977, that power became bifurcated. Blacks acquired a majority on City Council.

The tensions between blacks and whites, most noticeable between the respective leadership, are not new. They have become more evident since blacks have acquired some leverage. Unfortunately, some whites still refuse to accept this fact and their illusions exacerbate the conflict. Unfortunately, too, some blacks live with their own illusions and assume any criticism directed against the Council is racially motivated and the critic is bent on discrediting black legislators. Our mistrust of each other, especially that of blacks toward whites, is not without cause. It springs from events of the past which cannot be denied. Acknowledging such events is painful, but our future as a community hinges, in part, on one's capacity to be honest about the past and the other's capacity to forgive.

No quick fix produces reconciliation. To overcome a history of racial division requires long, consistent, often agonizing efforts to construct substantive interracial dialogue. But those efforts alone are not enough. Leaders of each community must take their role as opinion-makers seriously and aggressively use their influence to consciously shape attitudes conducive to justice and mutual respect. Obviously, some leaders themselves may constitute a problem. Their nostalgia for quieter times or, for still others, their political naiveté, ill-equip them to work effectively in a pluralistic, politically charged environment.

The clergy, in particular, given the regular forum available to them, have a unique opportunity to affect values. Unfortunately, as the Rev. Dr. Albert C. Winn of Second Presbyterian Church recently noted in a biracial gathering sponsored by the Richmond Human Relations Commission, "The churches are not producing people who, no matter how much they disagree with another person, accord them their dignity as human beings." Moreover, he said, "I don't know any churches that actively preach racism, but they are not actively combatting it."

Richmond is not without hope. Richmonders, black and white alike, feel strongly about their city and, though this common affection stems from divergent experiences and histories, it nevertheless constitutes the soul of the city. One tangible reflection of this soul was the creation last year of the Richmond Urban Institute. A biracial, socially diverse organization comprised of Richmonders sharing a common attachment to the city, the Institute provides a forum for identifying the forces dividing the city and an effective coalition for countering those forces. Such a group, like other organizations and individuals equally honest about the past and equally devoted to reconciliation, provides one basis for the growing confidence among many citizens, that a city which rose from the ruins of the 1860s, can surmount as well the racial tensions of the 1980s.

To secure a good city for future generations also requires our acceptance of current realities. Richmond is clearly a Southern city, culturally, but when one examines its demography and economy, it is much more like the cities of the North.

First, Richmond has lost population and has lost it at an alarming rate. The population today, 220,000, stands roughly where it did in 1960. Only 10 years ago, the population was 250,000, and when one considers that between 1970 and 1980 there were over 4,000 more people born in Richmond than died, the actual out-migration exceeded 43,400, representing more than a 13 percent decline in the total population over just 10 years. That rate of decline is comparable to that of some of the nation's largest and most depressed cities.

The most significant population loss is occurring in the 20–44-year-old age bracket, the major revenue-producing group. True, many middle-class singles and childless couples are moving back to the city, as they are in places like Washington, Baltimore, and Philadelphia. But for Richmond and larger cities to the north, this in-migration does not balance the out-migration and the result is a net loss.

Moreover, while the "back-to-the-city" trend, prompted partly by the energy factor, is highly visible and of considerable significance in some neighborhoods like Church Hill, it is creating a serious problem of displacement. Poor people are being uprooted as their neighborhoods begin to attract middle-class people hunting for a bargain. Precious little attention is given to the poor who either don't want to move or, when forced to move, can't find affordable housing. In that regard, our housing policy today hasn't changed radically from that of the past.

Richmond's family size is also dropping, down by one person per household since 1950. Had the family size remained the same, the city's population, according to city planners, would now stand at 302,000. The declining size of the family is a reflection of many factors, not the least of which are deferred child bearing; birth control; divorce; abortion; more working men and women; and the expense of raising children.

The result of these demographic shifts is that a large number of persons remaining in the city are those who require extensive public services such as health care, welfare assistance, and public transportation. Yet, those needing these services are least able to pay for them.

The fiscal strain, therefore, is felt most severely by city homeowners who already pay higher property taxes than their suburban counterparts.

To make matters worse, those who commute to the city for jobs rely on streets, police, and fire services supported financially by city residents. That which results is the city resident subsidizing the suburbanite.

Second, Richmond's economy is beginning to look a bit peaked. By no means is it in intensive care as is the economy of Cleveland, but it's temperature is rising and remedial measures are necessary. The city has traditionally been the center of economic growth within the Richmond region. From 1950 to 1960, about 75 percent of total employment gain took place in the city. However, things changed during the 1960s. The city's share of the total regional employment gain dropped below 50 percent while Chesterfield and Henrico Counties' share of the gain increased to about 50 percent. Between now and the end of the century, it is anticipated that, given current trends, the city will acquire only about one-third of the new jobs expected and that the two counties will acquire the other two-thirds of the jobs.

Though Richmond's unemployment rate is not excessively high compared to the nation's, it does obscure one problem. Job opportunities are growing in clerical, semiprofessional, and professional categories, but jobs for unskilled, semiskilled, and skilled workers are drying up in the city and are becoming more readily available in the counties. The problem is that the city's low-income areas, where unemployment is higher than that for the city as a whole, have a larger number of unskilled and semiskilled workers who are unable to take advantage of jobs in the counties due to lack of public transportation and lack of standard low-income housing in the counties.

Manufacturers, retailers, wholesalers, and warehousers have left the city to acquire cheaper land and single-level floor space. This, too, has damaged the tax base which already was strained by the heavy loss of middle-class, middle-aged population.

The consequence is that the revenue necessary for running the city is not keeping pace with the city's needs. The city will be further handicapped by its inability to meet its obligations by tapping federal and state money. National and state demographic change, coupled with the reapportionment of congressional and state legislative seats, will lead to less emphasis in the Congress on the problems of older cities in the Frost Belt and to more emphasis in the Virginia General Assembly on suburban and rural areas.

To accept the realities of the present means that Richmond must plan its future based on the certainty that internal resources will not be abundant, that the city cannot look externally for additional resources, and that the city must rely on its own creative powers and look to its citizens at the neighborhood level to engage in self-help programs.

Again, hopeful signs abound. The forward movement now evident in Project I; the recent decision of the new CSX Corporation, the nation's largest rail system, to locate its corporate headquarters in Richmond; the announcement of Ethyl Corporation to initiate a building program at its Tredegar site and to expand its Richmond operations; the multiple neighborhood development programs, particularly such new creations as the Neighborhood Housing Service and the Richmond Revitalization Program, are examples of significant undertakings involving business, citizens, and government. The future depends on such action, especially action linking the three actors in imaginative, locally based, cooperative ventures.

Thus far, I have dealt primarily with problems. But how can one pose solutions in the absence of some overall objective, some idea of what form the city could take, some vision of what it is that constitutes the good life? Otherwise, to use philosopher Lawrence Haworth's words, "finding a solution to the various urban problems would not mean so much that the city had become good as that it had overcome many of the respects in which it was bad."

Clearly, we need to determine what is meant by a *good city*. Haworth has identified two criteria that, in my estimation, are worthy of examination. One criterion is self-realization. Any concept of the good city must include an idea of *individual good*. A city should enable one to *develop as a person*, to enable the person to fulfill dreams and to realize potentialities. The second criterion is *community*. Put differently, a concept of the good city must also contain notions of obligation, responsibility, and service. For a person to pursue only his or her own thing, to seek only that which leads to self-gratification may enable one to fulfill dreams and to realize potentialities, but such pursuits *may* not lead to fulfillment in the larger sense of the term. Fulfillment occurs when a person melds personal goals and ambitions with the obligation and responsibility to society.

Currently, one of the major obstacles encountered in cities today is that, instead of a sense of overall community, there is a plurality of communities, one for the race, one for the class, one for the elderly, one for transients, and so on. Also, as urban societies become more complex, urban institutions become more differentiated. Loyalties are directed to particular institutions or groups, seldom to the larger

community. Often, these subloyalties are shaped by economic necessity or by prejudice and discrimination.

Sociologist Noel Gist, in an interesting article on urbanism in India,
notes how people who move from a particular village to the large
Indian cities remain villagers, living among those of the same village
background largely because of the difficulty of acquiring a stable
source of income. Persons live among those of the same religion. Some
city districts are occupied by Moslems, others by Hindus, others by
Christians. People are also separated out on the basis of caste and
economic status so that poor Moslems live together, poor Hindus live
together, poor Jews live together, and poor Christians live together.
"In a real sense," to quote Gist, "many of these people are *in* the city
but not an integral part *of* it." Of course, the same phenomenon
occurs in other cities of the world, including those of the West. Richmond is no exception. *Exclusion* rather than *inclusion* is the rule. Less
by choice than by lack of choice, people of the "wrong" color or economic standing may live in the middle of the city, but may not participate in the mainstream of city life.

The ethical response to our problems today involves merging the
goals of self-fulfillment with public consciousness. Nothing less than a
basic alteration of attitudes is required, but such an attitudinal change
is difficult, given the rampant materialism of our time—materialism
which evaluates personal worth in terms of buying power, which measures personal fulfillment in terms of economic gain, which diverts
attention from human suffering to self-sufficiency, and which sustains
the subloyalties in a city to the benefit of the rich and the detriment of
the poor.

I do not believe that people acquire a new perspective or develop a
vision for the future simply by mustering up sufficient willpower. It
requires a change of personal values that, in turn, are reflected in a
rethinking of social structures and institutions. Yet, regardless of how
such change occurs, the fact remains that the conflicts we know so well
in Richmond, the conflict between rich and poor, black and white,
land owner and tenant, are resolvable *only when we become willing to
assume the risks of living for others.*

What's ahead for our city? William Byrd II probably raised that
question, not knowing, of course, that food riots and fire would be-
fall Richmond over 100 years later during a civil war. And that same
question was surely asked by those who witnessed those events, not
knowing that the city would rise like a phoenix from the flames. And,
in all likelihood, that question was raised by our grandparents, never
predicting their grandchildren would witness, on one hand, racially

based power struggles, population losses, and a weakened tax base, and, on the other hand, a neighborhood renaissance, a preservationist trend, an economic awakening, and an emergent sense of community. For us, the question remains: What's ahead for our city? No one knows for sure, but it is certain the kind of future we face will stem largely from *choices we make now* and our capacity to drop illusions, face reality, and develop vision.

Moeser, "What's Ahead for Our City?" *Richmond Lifestyle Magazine*, March 1981, pp. 56–59

*By 1856, Richmond's economy was thriving. Large sailing vessels could be found
at the city docks, the downtown business area featured the Gallego Mills (left center),
and the smokestacks of Tredegar Ironworks (far left center) gave visible proof of
economic well-being. Several bridges now spanned the James, including Mayo's
(directly below the capitol).*

In 1810, as this engraving by Peter Maverick shows, Richmond was a placid little village architecturally dominated by the new capitol building designed by Thomas Jefferson. Mayo's Bridge is visible in the foreground of this illustration, which looks north from the Manchester side of the James River.

The viewer who stood on the edge of Gamble's Hill in 1857 and looked south toward the old city of Manchester saw several reasons for the prosperous nature of Richmond's antebellum economy. At the base of the hill is the James and Kanawha Canal, just beyond to the left is the Virginia State Armory, to the right is the Tredegar Ironworks, while the river itself is crossed by several bridges, including that of the Richmond and Petersburg Railroad in the center.

In the era before the American Civil War, Gallego Mills helped to make Richmond one of the world's greatest flour centers. Its huge brick building burned several times and was located on the east end of the turning basin of the James and Kanawha Canal. In modern times the basin has been hard-surfaced to create a multiblock parking area near the river in downtown Richmond.

This is how Richmond looked from a west window in Libby Prison, at the corner of Cary and Twentieth streets, as based on a sketch by a Federal officer-inmate and published in Harper's Weekly in October 1863. The Confederate capitol is visible in the upper right-hand corner, while part of the city's dock area is in the left foreground. Several buildings near Libby were also used as prisons, as Richmond had the distinction of incarcerating at one time or another far more Union soldiers than any other place in the South.

Pictured above is the Union enlisted men's prison on Belle Isle as it looked just prior to the city's fall in April 1865. Captured Federals lived in field tents and shared the island with the Old Dominion Iron and Nail Works. Belle Isle, Libby, and a dozen or so other places of incarceration made Richmond the prison capital of the Confederate states. The prominent bridge to the right center served the Richmond and Petersburg Railroad.

More than twenty city blocks fell victim to the evacuation fire of 2–3 April 1865. Started by the withdrawing Confederates to deny supplies to the enemy, extinguished by the incoming Federals, the conflagration consumed virtually all the business district and left in its wake gutted buildings and mounds of rubble. The above view, looking east from the vicinity of Gamble's Hill, graphically depicts the catastrophe. The photograph was taken by an associate of the famed photographer Mathew Brady, who himself arrived in Richmond shortly after the fire.

By the fall of 1865 transportation services had resumed in Richmond, as indicated in this view of a Richmond, Fredericksburg, and Potomac train proceeding up the middle of Broad Street. The neoclassical building with a heroic American flag is the Marshall Theater at Seventh and Broad streets.

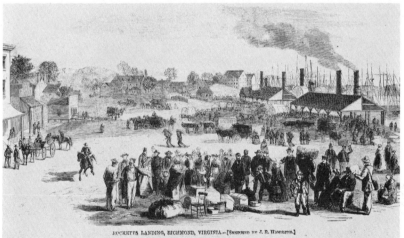

ROCKETTS LANDING, RICHMOND, VIRGINIA.—[SKETCHED BY J. R. HAMILTON.]

Rocketts or Rocketts Landing, shown here in the 1860s, was a waterfront extension of Richmond east along the James River. A depot area for steamboats and other substantial vessels, Rocketts shared many characteristics of a New England maritime village and was the point of arrival or departure for many travelers to and from the Virginia and Confederate capital.

President Abraham Lincoln, who had been waiting near City Point (now Hopewell) so that he might enter Richmond after it fell to Union forces, is depicted here on his arrival by the famous illustrator Thomas Nast. Lincoln made his way from Rocketts Landing to Jefferson Davis's White House of the Confederacy. Along the way he enjoyed the adulation of many freed slaves, as the woman kissing his hand in the above scene would suggest.

*Few disasters in Richmond's history could match the one that occurred on 27 April
1870 when a floor of the state capitol suddenly collapsed. This illustration from*
Harper's Weekly *depicts rescue teams at work in an attempt to remove the dead and
wounded from the chamber of the House of Delegates.*

This is an architect's sketch depicting Richmond College as it looked when located in the area bounded by Broad and Franklin and by Lombardy and Ryland streets. Following a fire in the building on Christmas eve, 1910, the institution was moved to its present location, later becoming the University of Richmond.

At the present-day intersection of Broad and College streets once stood the First African Baptist Church. Evolving from a racially mixed congregation, it became black with a white minister in the early 1840s and entirely black after the Civil War. The wood engraving above is from Harper's Weekly *(1874) as rendered by Richmond artist-sculptor William L. Sheppard.*

From 1874 to 1901 Davenport and Morris, wholesale grocers and commission merchants, operated from an impressive building at the corner of Seventeenth and Dock streets, itself a hub of commercial activity accommodating both canal and river vessels.

This is Main Street looking west from Seventeenth during the great flood of 1886. The Old Market building can be seen on the right, just east of where the Main Street Station now stands. (The mottled effect in the sky is caused by water damage to the negative, which was made by the famous Cook studio of Richmond.)

This is the Tredegar Ironworks as it looked ca. 1890. Gamble's Hill is out of view to the right, but Hollywood Cemetery is visible in the background. Tredegar remained active at the same location until the 1950s and is presently undergoing a partial restoration underwritten by the Ethyl Corporation, current owners of the property.

Main Street has always been the center of business activity in Richmond, but over the decades its face has markedly changed. The above photograph, looking east from Seventh Street, was taken in the mid-1890s, just prior to the advent of the automobile.

Timeless in its simplicity, St. John's Church, from whose presence Church Hill takes its name, has played host to countless photographers, one of whom caught these three children posed in anonymity about a century ago.

The simple classical lines of the Virginia state capitol are evident in this front-view photograph. Taken in the nineteenth century or long before the wings and front steps were added in 1906, the picture also shows portions of the First Presbyterian (left) and Broad Street Methodist churches.

Emancipation Day was celebrated with a Lincoln banner on the front of this store at East Main and Twenty-first streets, as captured in an undated photograph by Huestis Cook.

Beginning in the late-colonial period, tobacco was often rolled into Richmond in hogsheads, such as the one depicted above which belonged to E. K. Vieter. The driver may have been on the road for days, camping along the way. Note at right center the man with a horn, a blast from which would announce the start of a new sale of Virginia's golden leaf.

Among the many black-owned-and-operated enterprises in Jackson Ward was the Reformer Mercantile and Industrial Association Grocery and Feed Store at the corner of Sixth and Clay streets. Taken in the early 1900s, this photograph was found inside the wall of a hotel in Omaha, Nebraska, in 1962.

When General J. E. B. Stuart's monument was unveiled just a short distance away in 1907, Richmonders took the occasion to decorate the Lee Monument, then seventeen years old, with a huge Confederate flag. The design was formed by city residents seated in a temporary grandstand. On 6 February 1983, Richmonders commemorated the 150th birthday of Stuart with ceremonies at Hollywood Cemetery and at St. James's Episcopal Church.

Hull Street, in the old city of Manchester, became the center of an advertising campaign when city residents there were asked to vote for annexation with Richmond in 1910.

This Richmond view of 1911, taken in the 1700 block of East Franklin Street, might be mistaken for one of more modern times were it not for the rows of horse carts visibly lined up on either side of the street. The "Old First Market" of Shockoe Valley originated in the same general location in the era before the American Revolution.

Much of the Broad Street of 1914 bears a striking resemblance to that of today, except for the streetcars, vintage automobiles, and an occasional horse-drawn vehicle. This view, looking east from Jefferson Street, depicts an era before the myriad shopping malls took shoppers to the counties.

The Richmond Equal Suffrage League had the active support of many prominent women. This photograph, taken at the Virginia State Fair shortly before World War I, depicts efforts to gain public support.

"United We Stand Behind the War" was the motto this float bore as it made its way over cobblestone streets at the 2000 block of West Broad Street, ca. 1918. In the background is a long-familiar Richmond landmark, the building of C. F. Sauer Company.

The downtown theater district, in the 800 block of East Broad Street, is depicted in this panoramic view made at the beginning of the 1920s. The Bijou and the Isis (above center) occupied the spot of the famous Swan Tavern, which was razed in 1903.

Visible at the far left is the Crozet house, a city landmark that stands at the northeast corner of First and Main streets. The remainder of these houses occupied the northern side of Main Street between First and Second streets, the site of part of the present-day Richmond Public Library.

Although the Ku Klux Klan was not so popular in Richmond as in other Southern cities, this photograph, taken at the intersection of Fifth and Grace streets in the 1920s(?) would suggest otherwise.

At a reunion held in Richmond in the early 1930s, Confederate veterans gather around one of the surviving cannons from Fort Sumter. The photograph was taken at what was then the Confederate Old Soldiers' Home, now the area occupied by the Virginia Museum of Fine Arts, at the corner of Grove Avenue and the Boulevard.

Bell-bottom trousers were the order of the day when this photograph at Richmond's U.S.O. was taken during World War II. As the billboard indicates, area churches provided services and the city's women provided escorts for the many servicemen whom the war brought to town.

Sir Winston Churchill, accompanied by General Dwight D. Eisenhower, arrives at the state capitol at the end of their trip by open car from Broad Street Station. Churchill visited the city in March of 1946. Following a ceremony on the capitol portico, he addressed the Virginia General Assembly, praising "Richmond, the historic capital of world-famous Virginia."

The decade of the 1970s brought social and racial strife following court-ordered busing, which was imposed on Richmond by a federal judge. Here citizens against the plan demonstrate in favor of the neighborhood-school concept.

The end of the 1970s was also the end of the intense athletic rivalry that had existed between Maggie L. Walker and Armstrong high schools. The message on this person's shirt graphically depicts the event, which marked the end of a sports era for these two famous schools.

II § The People and Their Cultural Tradition

"No Man, Perhaps, Ever Lived Who Was Freer from Pretension and Ostentation": The Home Life of John Marshall

First citizen of Richmond in Jeffersonian times was, ironically but unquestionably, the title due John Marshall (1755–1835), Jefferson's kinsman but bitter enemy. After coming to the city as a young lawyer in the 1780s, Marshall married well and built a fine house, where he resided for the rest of a long and eventful life. In the process, he established at least three claims to the distinction of the town's premier citizen. First, few men had enjoyed a more noteworthy public career than had the Fauquier County native even before his appointment as chief justice of the Supreme Court in 1801 and his unequaled tenure, in both length and impact, in that lofty post. Second, the gregarious Marshall also was an active member—and usually the founder and leader—of numerous civic and social organizations, including a volunteer fire department, a lending library, a dance assembly, and the Virginia Historical Society. Indeed, no public function was complete without his participation. Finally, and simply put, he was an exemplary individual in his private life, a man of character and quality, admired and esteemed by all who knew him, as indicated in this essay by an unknown author.

§ The Home Life of Chief Justice Marshall

By C. M. S.

Richmond, March 22, 1879.—Chief-Justice Marshall was as noted for his simplicity of character, modesty, and suavity of manners as for his ability and legal learning. It is not designed here to sketch his public career; that is a part of the history of the country. The purpose of this paper is less ambitious, being to present some reminiscences of him as a man, and to glance at his home life and his private habits and tastes.

He was a devoted husband, and exhibited toward his wife, Mary Willis Ambler, the most chivalrous tenderness and delicacy throughout their married life. They were married January 3, 1783. She was in her seventeenth year and he in his twenty-eighth. Their union lasted forty-eight years. During that whole period their home was in Richmond. For many years Mrs. Marshall led the life of a recluse. Her health was extremely delicate, and she suffered from excessive nervousness. Noises of all kinds affected her so painfully that she endeavored as far as possible to protect herself against them. The house was kept perfectly still. All the inmates walked as softly as possible. She was so gentle and thoughtful of the comfort of others that all near her endeavored to promote her own comfort and to avoid doing anything that would cause her annoyance. It was her good husband's habit to slip off his shoes as soon as he entered the door of his house and to walk as lightly as possible. His voice, naturally soft, grew even gentler when in her presence. The house in which he lived, on the corner of Marshall and Ninth streets, is still standing. His office was near the house and within the same enclosure. It was taken down some years ago, and no vestige of it remains. In that office the Chief Justice, or "Judge Marshall," as he was universally called, spent much of his time, day and night, when not in attendance on the Supreme Court. There was his library, and there his studies were pursued. His wife's health was such that she received no visitors except her most intimate friends and relations. Her love of quiet was so well known that she was rarely intruded upon. At a certain hour every good day, and when well enough, she rode out for fresh air and exercise. When the carriage drove up to the front of the house the Chief-Justice's office door was sure to open and his tall form issue from it. He proceeded to the house, where he joined her and escorted her to the carriage. Handing her tenderly in, he closed the door and stood until the carriage moved off. When she returned he was promptly on hand to help her from the carriage and to escort her to the house. He endeavored to shield her from all annoyances. He was frequently known to go among the neighbors and request them, in his gentle manner, to keep an eye upon a barking dog or a bleating calf. A gentleman, then a boy and a near neighbor, had a barking dog, and he well remembers being called on more than once by the Chief Justice, who so politely requested him to try and keep his pet quiet that he took unusual trouble to do so.

It is said that during the early years of Judge Marshall's married life he was a frequent attendant at card parties, then much in vogue, and that Mrs. Marshall was in the habit of sitting up until his return. He is believed to have attributed her nervous trouble to this cause, and to have endeavored to atone for former inconsiderateness by the utmost tenderness and watchfulness.

The writer, then a boy, well remembers Chief-Justice Marshall's appearance in his latter years. There was no object more familiar to the people of Richmond than the tall, spare, straight figure of that universally-revered man. His sparkling dark eyes were full of good humor and benevolence, and his smile was like sunshine. He was by no means a careful dresser. It must, indeed, be confessed that he was something of a sloven. He generally appeared in a rusty black coat and shorts. The latter came down to the knees, where they were met by long, black stockings. His shoes were large and loose. He wore a black hat, which was not kept in very nice trim. His head and face were small. Every motion was free and natural. His whole bearing was characterized by an easy, unaffected dignity. No man, perhaps, ever lived who was freer from pretension and ostentation. He was a striking figure, somewhat quaint and old-fashioned, and suggestive of the old school of gentlemen. Richmond was much smaller then than it is now, and there were few persons of any age, class or condition, who were not familiar with Judge Marshall's appearance. He was reverenced by young and old, and all who passed him on the street either touched or took off their hats to him. He never allowed himself to be outdone in politeness, but returned the salutations of old and young, high and low, in the most respectful and courteous manner.

What the Chief Justice lacked in style was fully made up by his head servant, old Robin Spurlock, who dressed after the same fashion as his master, but in a much more elegant manner. Robin regarded his master as the greatest man in the world, and himself as the next. He stood at the head of the colored aristocracy of Richmond. So extremely indifferent was Judge Marshall to appearances that he did not hesitate to carry home any article, no matter what it might be, that he chanced to purchase on the streets or at the stores. A friend, who was then a boy, assures the writer that he once saw the simple-hearted old Chief Justice carrying in his hand an article of domestic crockery which cannot be named to "ear polite." It was his habit to go to market every morning with his basket on his arm, and to return home with the marketing.

He was very fond of theatrical entertainments, and used to go to the theatre whenever the opportunity offered. An excellent company, known as Hillson's Company, played for some time in the Richmond Theatre, to the delight of the citizens of that day. The Chief Justice, who was a great admirer of Mrs. Hillson's acting, was an habitual attendant at the performances. He was much fascinated by Mrs. Hillson's dramatic talents, and was heard to express his regret that her beauty was not equal to her talents. The Chief Justice had a decided convivial turn, and no one enjoyed more than himself the Saturday meetings of a famous club of which he was for many years, and to the time of his death, a member. This club was composed of the most eminent citizens—such men as Judge Marshall, John Wickham, Benjamin Watkins Leigh, Chapman Johnson, Daniel Call, Judge Nicholas, etc. There were skilful caterers among them, and their cooks were thorough masters of their art. The very pick of the market and the choicest liquors were provided for those occasions. When a small boy the writer was present more than once at these meetings—as a looker-on and intruder. They were held at Buchanan's Spring, then a nicely-shaded place at the head of Clay street (as now known). The long table stood under a frame structure, which sheltered it from sun and rain. It was there that those rare and dignified old gentry assembled once a week to drink, to eat, to pitch quoits, and to roll ten-pins. They threw off all ceremony and enjoyed themselves thoroughly—none more heartily than the good Chief Justice. It is hinted in a good-natured and sort of confidential way, by some old citizens whose memories are still unclouded, that on some of these occasions that good man and great lawyer returned home in spirits more exhilarated than was his wont. The city has since extended beyond Buchanan's Spring, and buildings have sprung up all around it. A few only of the old trees now remain. The city owns the Spring lot, which will doubtless at some future period be converted into a park.

It has been said that Judge Marshall was regarded by old and young with affectionate reverence. But there was one boy who was noted for his mischievous disposition and his total want of reverence. That boy was once going through "Fisher's old field," as a vacant lot near Judge Marshall's residence was called. He had in his hand a gun loaded with bird-shot, and seeing the Judge some distance in advance of him, what should he do but raise the gun and fire at the venerable figure before him. As good luck had it, no harm was done. The mischievous urchin ran off, and afterwards told some of his companions about the affair, saying that the old Judge's back presented so fair a mark he could not resist the temptation to fire at it.

A young kinsman or connection with whom the Judge frequently talked, and whose quaint sayings amused him, met him on an anniversary of his birth, and offering his congratulations, said: "May you live a hundred years, Judge." The Judge responded quickly: "God forbid, God forbid that I should."—*C. M. S., in Louisville Aye.*

William and Mary College Quarterly Historical Magazine,
2d ser. 12 (January 1932): 67–69

"The Celebrated Barbeque Club": Parsons Blair and Buchanan, and Their Fellow Notables

A luminary of the first magnitude himself, John Marshall (q.v.) enjoyed the company of a host of outstanding Richmonders in the Jeffersonian era. The city's bench and bar from 1789 to 1826, for example, is perhaps the foremost of any one locale at any one time in all of American history, and it boasted two Supreme Court justices, two United States attorneys general, and two secretaries of state. Thomas Ritchie, of the Richmond *Enquirer*, ranks among the most influential newspaper editors of his day, and few men have ever enjoyed more local popularity than the famous "Two Parsons"— Presbyterian John D. Blair (1759–1823) and his close friend Episcopalian John Buchanan (1743–1822). Many of these worthy citizens belonged to a unique institution of social edification and pleasure— "the Barbeque Club," the activities and attractions of which are delightfully captured in the following sketch.

We have endeavored to show, from the materials in our possession, how our worthy Parsons acted on various occasions when they were accidentally thrown amid worldly amusements, and if our readers will bear with us, we shall proceed on our journey.

Of all the good citizens of Richmond at this period, there were but few, we imagine, who had not heard of the celebrated Barbecue Club, which held its weekly meetings on Saturday, during the summer months, at Buchanan's Spring. This was the delightful retreat on Parson Buchanan's farm to which the volunteer companies resorted for recreation on festive occasions.

The Barbecue Club was composed, at that time, of thirty members, all of high standing, of literary and scientific tastes, of genial dispositions and rare social qualities. Their humor, wit and knowledge of the world rendered their society most attractive. It was indeed delightful to them and their friends to pass an hour or two together when they wished to beguile cares with innocent amusements. It was a pleasure to all to lay aside their several occupations, and with them the pomp and circumstance of official position, to throw off the weight and burden of public affairs, to get rid of the bustle, confusion and strife of the bar, the anxieties and troubles of frail humanity with which physicians are familiar, the quotations of the stock exchange, the deep-laid schemes for speculation, and the paraphernalia attendant on the routine of mercantile life.

It was considered a great honor to be elected a member of this Club, as it was known that selections were made with great care. Two members objecting would prevent an election.

It was not often that a vacancy occurred. The number was limited, to avoid the danger of coteries and small circles, and to bring all around the social board within the range of hearing, allowing each to mingle in jests and repartees, and partake of the genial warmth that such spirits must elicit.

Each member was allowed the privilege of inviting one guest, but with the restriction that the invitations were to be confined to distinguished strangers who might be in the city on the day of meeting. This afforded to each one the opportunity of becoming personally acquainted with them.

It was considered a special privilege to be elected an honorary member of this Club. The governor, during his official term, had a standing invitation; but as far as our information extends, there were no other honorary members except Parsons Blair and Buchanan.

To show the class of men who at that day were members of this Club, we will name: John Marshall, the eminent jurist, ambassador, Secretary of State, and subsequently Chief Justice of the United States, with his plain, simple, unassuming manners and great intellect; Dr. John Brockenbrough, the President of the Bank of Virginia, who subsequently managed its affairs with such ability and skill; the great barrister, John Wickham, a most courtly and genial gentleman, who pursued his profession for more than thirty years with distinguished reputation; Dr. William Foushee, the head and front of the medical profession of this city; Thomas Ritchie, his son-in-law, who had then but lately established his celebrated *Richmond Enquirer*, and who was afterwards known as the Napoleon of the press; William Wirt, the author, scholar, lawyer, Clerk of the House of Delegates, Judge and Attorney General of the United States; Philip N. Nicholas, the Attorney General and Judge of the Circuit Court of the State, and subsequently President of the Farmer's Bank of Virginia; Daniel Call, a leading member of the bar, practising in the Court of Appeals, and the peer of the best lawyers of that day; Thomas Rutherfoord and Charles Ellis, both prominent, upright, conscientious, influential merchants of the city; Major James Gibbon, the hero of Stony Point; William Munford, a member of the Executive Council, subsequently Clerk of the House of Delegates, author of legal reports, and translator in blank verse of Homer's Iliad; Dr. Peter Lyons, an eminent physician, a gentleman of fine acquirements and moral worth; Col. John Ambler and Col. John Harvie, the Mayor of Richmond and the

Register of the Land Office, both worthy progenitors of illustrious families, each of exemplary character, of wealth and great popularity; James Brown, Jr., then a most worthy merchant and subsequently Second Auditor of the State; besides others, equally meritorious, full of life, joyous and grave, in every way qualified to add to the merriment and sober pleasantries of such a party.

The meetings of the club were from May to October annually. The expenses were met by a regular contribution, assessed at the commencement of the season, and paid in advance to the treasurer. This officer had the power to select two members as caterers, who presided at the board on the following Saturday.

At this time Major Gibbon was the treasurer, and he had appointed Mr. Marshall and Mr. Wickham the caterers; and as they were *bon vivants*, and had with them old Robin and Jasper Crouch, the colored caterers, we are certain they obtained for the dinner the best the market afforded. Being connoisseurs in drinks too, they would have nothing but the best. The rules of the Club prohibited wines except upon the special occasions. Julep, punch or toddy, and porter or ale, were the ordinary drinks. . . .

Mr. Marshall sat at the head and Mr. Wickham at the foot of the table. A better dinner of the substantials of life was rarely seen. The only dessert they indulged in was a steaming, juicy mutton chop, cooked to a turn, and "devilled ham," highly seasoned with mustard, cayenne pepper, and a slight flavoring of Worcester sauce, and these were passed along the board.

After these condiments had been discussed and disposed of, Mr. Marshall said, "The treasurer had, according to the request of the club at its last meeting, reminded our honorary members, the Rev. John Buchanan and the Rev. John D. Blair, that it would be exceedingly agreeable to the club if they would meet us on this occasion, and he was happy to see them both present. He was also pleased to have received the written answer of Mr. Blair, which he would read to the club." This was received with marked approbation, each member taking the cue from Mr. Wickham and striking the table with the handle of his knife in three successive rounds.

Mr. Marshall then added, "It was known to the club that two of the members at the last meeting had, contrary to the constitution, introduced the subject of politics, which ought to be tabooed here, and though warned to desist, had continued the discussion. The consequence was that, by unanimous vote, they had been fined a basket of champagne for the benefit of the Club. They had submitted to the imposition like worthy members, and the champagne was now produced as a warning to evil doers. It was so seldom the Club indulged in such beverages, they had no champagne glasses, and must therefore drink it in tumblers." Mr. Wickham begged leave to add, "as nobody objects to the tumblers, we will drink to the health and happiness of our two honorary members, who have gratified us with their presence to-day." Parson Buchanan immediately said, "that for himself he had no objection to a *little* wine for his many infirmities," and he emphasized the word little; "but he hoped that those who indulged in tumblers at the table would not prove to be tumblers under the table." Parson Blair promptly said, "In looking around he saw so many gentlemen distinguished for their oratorical powers and eloquence, that he had no fears they would ever sink into bathos, which he would define to be the art of tumbling from the sublime to the ridiculous, and this he considered would be the case with tumblers under the table."

These brief remarks were received with great pleasure, and, as Parson Blair had said, "the table was set in a roar," and all formality was at an end.

In a little while those who played quoits quitted the table, and, taking their coats off, were full of the game. Many of the members did not play, and remained at the table in pleasant converse, when jest and story and song were the order of the day.

Parson Blair joined the quoit players, while Parson Buchanan remained with the jesters, saying he did not see much fun in pitching a quoit.

Mr. Marshall challenged Parson Blair to make up the game, and each selected four partners. Most of those who were in the habit of playing had procured for themselves handsome, smooth, highly polished brass quoits, which were kept in order by Jasper Crouch. Mr. Marshall, on the contrary, had a set of the largest, most uncouth, rough iron quoits, which very few of the Club could throw with any accuracy from hub to hub; but he threw them with great ease, and frequently rung the peg. It was exceedingly pleasant to witness the eagerness with which such men engaged in this sport, and to see with what earnestness they would measure the distance of each quoit from the hub. We have seen Mr. Marshall, in later times, when he was Chief Justice of the United States, on his hands and knees, with a straw and a penknife, the blade of the knife stuck through the straw, holding it between the edge of the quoit and the hub, and, when it was a very doubtful question, pinching or biting off the ends of the straw until it would fit to a hair. His extreme accuracy and justice were so well known that his decision was invariably submitted to without a murmur.

Munford, *The Two Parsons* (1884), pp. 326–29, 331–33

"He Undoubtedly Thought of Richmond as Home": Edgar Allan Poe

Of all the figures in the panoply of American letters, few had so unhappy a personal life as Edgar Allan Poe (1809–49). Orphaned in Richmond when his mother died in the winter of 1811 while on an acting tour, he was taken into the home of the Scot merchant John Allan, who never legally adopted him.

Poe and Allan were temperamentally incompatible from the beginning, but nevertheless the young Edgar, who had large hazel eyes and long brown curls, won the heart of Allan's wife, Frances Valentine Allan. Poe lived with the Allans until he was nineteen, including a stay abroad with the family. As a youngster in Richmond, he spent his time like the other boys, swimming in the James River and playing in the nearby woods, which were then not far from the Allans' home at Fifth and Main streets. Following a brief period in 1826 as a student at the University of Virginia and a particularly acrimonious confrontation with Allan in 1827, Poe made his way north.

After a stint in the Army Poe became one of the major literary critics and short story writers of his day. He lived briefly in Richmond again from 1835 to 1837 with his child bride and cousin, Virginia, and his aunt, Maria Clemm, when he edited the *Southern Literary Messenger*. In 1849, his young wife Virginia now dead, he returned to the city for the final time in the summer before his death, lecturing and rekindling a love, begun years before, with Sara Elmira Royster Shelton, whose house, directly behind St. John's Church, can be visited today. Poe died mysteriously in Baltimore before he could return to Richmond for his marriage to Elmira.

The following excerpt, chronicling the poet's life in Richmond, is taken from Agnes Bondurant's *Poe's Richmond*. Now retired, Agnes Bondurant Marcuson was for many years an English teacher in Richmond's public schools.

§ Poe in Richmond

Edgar Allan Poe, who was born in Boston on January 19, 1809, was brought to Richmond in August, 1811, by his mother, Elizabeth Arnold Poe, an actress in Mr. Placide's company of players. This was not Poe's first visit to Richmond, but it marks the beginning of a period of twenty-six years in his life during which he was associated with that city. The following outline shows the intervals from 1811 to 1837 when Poe was in Richmond, and gives the main facts known of his life during his actual presence in the city as well as other events which contributed to his Richmond association:

I: *August, 1811–June 17, 1815*

On August 13, 1811, there appeared in the Richmond *Enquirer* an announcement of the opening of the Richmond Theatre on the next evening. This would indicate that Mrs. Poe and her two children, Edgar and Rosalie, with the company of actors, were in town before the middle of August. Mrs. Poe, whose ill health made her appearances at the theatre fewer and fewer during the fall of 1811, died December 8th. On December 9th Mrs. John Allan took Edgar to her home while Mrs. William MacKenzie took Rosalie.

Little is known of the four years which Poe spent in John Allan's home before that family's departure for England on June 17, 1815. Where he first went to school or who were his earliest teachers is a matter of conjecture. It is fairly certain, however, that before leaving Richmond Poe went to school to William Ewing. The master evidently found the six-year-old pupil precocious, for he wrote to John Allan in England two years later and inquired what Edgar was reading. Poe was then in England, having accompanied his foster father on a business and social trip which was to last about five years. In the party were also Frances Valentine Allan, wife of John Allan, and Anne Moore Valentine, sister of Mrs. Allan.

II: *August 2, 1820–February 14, 1826*

When Poe returned to Richmond on August 2, 1820, he had seen more of the world than the ordinary boy in his twelfth year. He had visited the Scottish cities of Irvine, Kilmarnock, Greenock, Glasgow, and Edinburgh, as well as Newcastle, Sheffield, and London in England. Much of the region through which the Allan family had traveled was famous for its association with Burns and Scott. Besides,

Edgar had spent some time in several foreign schools: he had attended the grammar school at Irvine, Scotland, the boarding school of the Misses Dubourg in Chelsea, London, and the Manor House School of the Reverend John Bransby at Stoke Newington, then a suburb of London.

Once back in Richmond, he continued his studies at Joseph H. Clarke's English and Classical School. By the fall of 1823, when Clarke resigned his school to the charge of William Burke, Poe, it is said, had made several trials at verse writing. He was reading the English quarterlies that he found on the second floor of the Ellis and Allan business house. Not all of his time, however, was spent in reading and writing. He fished and swam in the James. He roamed about the Richmond waterfront and explored the woods, like any normal boy of thirteen or fourteen years. While making friends with boys of his own age, he formed a lasting attachment to Mrs. Robert Stanard, who died in April, 1824. When still a student at Master Burke's academy, Poe showed an interest in military drill and display. In fact, he served as lieutenant in the Richmond Junior Volunteers, an organization which welcomed Lafayette to Richmond and honored him during his visit in October, 1824. In March of the next year, Poe left Master Burke's academy and "spent the remainder of the year in preparing himself for the University of Virginia, then in its first session." On February 14, 1826, he was no longer in Richmond, for on that day he registered in the Schools of Ancient and Modern Languages at the University of Virginia, in Charlottesville.

III: December 24, 1826–March or April, 1827

Poe returned to Richmond on December 24, 1826, conscious of John Allan's displeasure at the large number of gambling debts he had made at the University. But Allan could not complain of his scholastic record, for he had stood among the first in both his Latin and French classes. During the fall and winter of 1826–1827 Poe's creditors wrote letters to Allan, and some of them issued warrants against the debtor, but Allan refused to assume the debts. It was, therefore, impossible for Poe to return to the University of Virginia. The two men could not agree, moreover, as to Poe's future career. For these reasons Poe left John Allan's house on March 19, 1827. How or where the young man maintained himself during the weeks before he left Richmond for Boston is not exactly known. He wrote Allan several letters asking for money to pay his fare to Boston and requesting that his trunk be sent to the Court House Tavern. There is no evidence that Allan complied with either request. At any rate Poe reached Boston certainly by the middle of April, 1827. There he enlisted in the United States Army on May 26, 1827.

IV: ca. March 1, 1829–March 9, 1829

On March 1, 1829, Poe went from Fortress Monroe, Virginia, to Richmond, hoping to be present at his foster mother's funeral. He arrived too late but nevertheless stayed out his ten days' furlough at the home of John Allan. Since his last sight of Richmond in the spring of 1827, Poe had published his first volume of poems, and on May 26, 1827, had enlisted in the United States Army, in Boston, under the name of Edgar A. Perry. As Poe had not found army life conducive to literary work, he now wished to obtain a release. This matter he discussed with John Allan, and, by way of compromise, considered seeking an appointment to West Point. No definite decision, however, was reached until later, after Poe had returned to his post of duty. He wrote to Allan from Old Point Comfort on March 10, 1829.

V: April, 1829–ca. May 7, 1829

Approximately a month had passed before Poe was able to obtain his release from the Army. When he had secured this, he went to Richmond to stay until he could persuade Allan and others to recommend him for the West Point appointment. Here he stayed another month and then set out for Washington and Baltimore. He had obtained letters of recommendation to the Secretary of War from James P. Preston, John Allan, Colonel Worth, the Representative in Congress from the district, and from Major Andrew Stevenson, the Speaker of the House. In addition Poe had testimonials from his former superiors in the Army.

VI: ca. January 1, 1830–ca. May 12, 1830

Poe's visit to Richmond beginning either late in December, 1829, or early in January, 1830, marked the close of his waiting for the actual appointment to West Point. Since May, 1829, he had been in Baltimore, staying with relatives or subsisting on the money sent him at various intervals by John Allan. In the meantime, to advance his literary reputation, he had consulted William Wirt, formerly of Richmond, and had made the acquaintance of Robert Walsh, editor of the *American Quarterly Review*. Some of his poems had come to the attention of John Neal, who had given him slight notice in the *Yankee and Boston Literary Gazette*, published in Portland, Maine. Furthermore, in December, 1829, Hatch and Dunning had published his second volume, *Al Aaraaf, Tamerlane, and Minor Poems*.

How Poe spent his time in Richmond during the winter and spring of 1830 is a matter of conjecture. That he was not always on good terms with Allan is evident from a letter to Sergeant Graves at Fortress Monroe. Certainly he did not again leave Richmond until his appointment as cadet was sure. It was secured, perhaps, by a letter from Powhatan Ellis, United States Senator from Mississippi, to the Secretary of War. Though examinations at West Point were not held till June, Poe probably left Richmond around May 12th for "on that date John Allan is charged on the books of his firm with a pair of blankets for Poe's outfit."

VII: ca. June, 1832

That Poe visited Richmond in June, 1832, is not based upon any known documentary evidence. The traditions of the Allan, the Mac-Kenzie, and the Ellis families affirm, however, that Poe entered John Allan's house while the latter was away and made himself disagreeable to the second Mrs. Allan. At this time Poe was undoubtedly interested in the contents of the will which Allan was then making in consequence of his ill health.

In June, 1832, Poe had been out of West Point more than a year, having been dismissed on January 28, 1831. Through the aid of subscriptions from his fellow cadets he had published in New York about this time a third edition of his poems, which, however, he had marked "second edition." Most of the time since the "West Point interlude" Poe had spent in Baltimore, it is generally thought. There he came to know better his Aunt Maria Clemm and her young daughter, Virginia. It was from Baltimore that he went to Richmond in June, 1832.

VIII: Latter Part of Winter, 1833–1834

Evidence of Poe's visit to Richmond "sometime during the latter part of the winter of 1833–1834, probably in February," rests also on tradition rather than fact. It is said that Poe and John Allan quarreled and that the younger man was ordered from the house. Just when Poe returned to Baltimore, where he was living—probably with Mrs. Clemm and her daughter—is not known. It is certain, however, that he had been in Baltimore during the summer and autumn of 1833, for he had competed in July for a prize of fifty dollars offered by the *Baltimore Saturday Visiter* for the best short-story contributed to that weekly. The committee of judges, composed of John Pendleton Kennedy, Dr. James H. Miller, and J. H. B. Latrobe, awarded Poe the prize in October for the story, "MS Found in a Bottle." When Poe visited Richmond in the winter of 1833–1834, he had already made the acquaintance of John Pendleton Kennedy, who was destined to help him some months later. He had not yet, however, unburdened his troubles to this new acquaintance.

IX: August, 1835–ca. September 11, 1835

Poe's going to Richmond in August, 1835, was the result of the kind efforts of John Pendleton Kennedy. Following Kennedy's advice to try to publish all the *Tales of the Folio Club*, Poe had asked Carey and Lea in Philadelphia to undertake the project. To further his cause with the publishers, Poe wrote to Kennedy explaining his destitute condition since Allan's death and asking that Kennedy speak to Carey and Lea for him. This was in November, 1834. By March, 1835, Kennedy had helped Poe arrange with Thomas W. White, in Richmond, to make contributions to the *Southern Literary Messenger*, a publication just begun in August, 1834, in Poe's former city. Consequently, the young writer had been contributing regularly to the *Messenger* in the months preceding August, 1835. In the early part of that month he went to Richmond upon the invitation of White, to help with the editorial and other work of the magazine. It was now necessary for Poe, who was alone, to stay at a boarding house, since the Allan home was no longer open to him. He went to Mrs. Poore's on Bank Street, Capitol Square. Though Poe had friends in Richmond and though he was doing the kind of work he preferred, he did not find his social and literary life altogether satisfying. On September 11, 1835, he wrote John P. Kennedy a most depressing letter, in which he begged him for consolation. Before Kennedy's reply, dated September 19, 1835, could reach him in Richmond, he had returned to Baltimore, where he found the semblance of a home with Mrs. Clemm and her daughter. Evidently there had been a break with White.

X: October, 1835–January, 1837

Poe returned to Richmond in October, 1835, after having received a letter from White in which the writer stated that if Poe should come back and help with the *Messenger*, all engagements on his part would be dissolved the moment Poe got drunk. With the young editor were Mrs. Clemm and Virginia. They went to live at Mrs. James Yarrington's boarding house in the neighborhood of Mrs. Poore's. On May 16, 1836, Poe and his cousin, Virginia Clemm, were married at Mrs. Yarrington's.

For the most part Poe was very busy with the editorial duties of the *Messenger*. He published during the period from March, 1835, to January, 1837, no less than fourteen tales and the first serial of a long adventure story, "The Narrative of Arthur Gordon Pym." Thirteen of his poems, four of his essays, and two serials on "Autography" appeared in the *Messenger*. He printed two serials of "Scenes from an Unpublished Drama" [*Politian*] and some of the notes and comments on his reading. These comments he called "Pinakidia." To every issue he contributed critical reviews of the latest English and American books. It was in Richmond that Poe, for the first time, attracted nationwide attention. His fearless reviews received notice from newspapers and magazines in both the North and the South.

In January, 1837, Poe's Richmond career came to an end. He had greater ambitions than he could realize in his home town of the South. Furthermore, he and White did not always agree as to editorial policy. Neither did White approve of his drinking. By the middle of January Poe had gone to New York, and a notice appeared in the *Messenger* stating that Mr. Poe's attention had been called in another direction and that he would "decline with the present number, the Editorial duties on the Messenger." With this change Poe left the city which he had considered his home and to which he had turned again and again for help from his foster parents. It was, moreover, the city where he had held his first successful editorial position.

As long as Poe lived, he undoubtedly thought of Richmond as home. "I am a Virginian, at least I call myself one," he wrote in 1841, "for I have resided all my life, until within the last few years in Richmond."

Bondurant, *Poe's Richmond* (1942), pp. 17–27

"All o' My Folks B'longed to De Same Master": Slave Narratives

One useful trend in the current writing of history is the attempt to view the past in part "from the bottom up"—meaning, to search out and incorporate evidence from often-forgotten rank-and-file Americans, as opposed to the presidents, generals, and famous individuals to whom scholars so readily turn for their raw material. An example of this new approach is the use of interviews with ex-slaves from the Old Dominion, as compiled by an "all-Negro unit of the Virginia Writer's Project" of the Federal Works Progress (later Projects) Administration in the 1930s. Of several hundred interviews originally conducted, those extant were published in a remarkable volume, *Weevils in the Wheat* (1976). The interviews must be subjected to the same critical analysis given other historical evidence, but they clearly provide "insights into Afro-American culture that are not obtainable from other sources." Some Richmond selections follow.

§ Mrs. Patience M. Avery (b. 1863)

215 Kentucky Ave., Petersburg, Va.
Interviewer: Susie R. C. Byrd
Date of interview: March 19, 1937
Source: Va. State Lib.

I was born on a Easter Monday. I can reckon my age from some'n dat happen when I was a little girl. One morning my mother come down from her cookin' place an' gave me three cents an' said, "I'm goin' where de Capitol Building fell in Richmond." De Capitol, you know honey, sets on de brow o' de hill in Capitol Square. Dat very yeah I was 7 yeahs ole (1870).

Now let me tell you what I did wid de money. Can you guess? Well, I used dem few pennies for a party, an' a party I had, too. I had three cents for a party on a cheer [chair?]; a two cent piece an' a big one cent piece. You see, money in dem days was made a little different. We had gra' big pennies an' half cents. Fer dis party I bought one horse cake, one long stick o' pepermint candy, an' a apple. No chile, I can never fergit dat. You see my mother gimme dem pennies to mek me hush cryin'. Yes, yes, I can 'member dis as good as ef 'twas yestidy; how mother stole out an' lef' me.

Mother b'long to Thomas Hatcher, in Chesterfield County, Virginia, an' my daddy was de young master. He was name directly after his daddy, Thomas Hatcher Junior. Some o' de descendants is still in Richmond. Rev. Hatcher who was connected wid de first Church is a descendant. He may be daid now.

I seen my father one night at a restaurant where gra'ma an' mommer wuk. I was 'sleep. Lord! Lord! I can 'member jes' as good how dey woke me up to see him. Sussie, dey had me 'sleep on a ole bench wid gra'ma's ole yarn dress an' coat spread fer me to lay on. I was covered wid mothers shawl, an' dis little bed o' mine was push under de counter so I could sleep 'till dey close de restaurant fer de night. I kin 'member dat very night. I woke up jes' cryin' an' a-rubbin' my eyes an' a-ketchin' my breath between sobs. Dis is what I hear 'em say now to him (my father). "Dis is your little Patience." Lak little chillun will do, I put one han' up to my face an' was rubbin' my eyes, an' a-cryin', an' a-snifflin', an' a-sayin', "I ain' got no father; I ain' got no father. No, I ain' got no father 'cause my mother told me dat de buzzards laid me an' de sun hatch me; an' she came 'long an' pick me up. He no father o' mine! He white!" Den he took my han' an' patted it; an' Sussie, do you know I thought twas pizen. Yes, I did. Jes' think! Um! Um! God is wonderful to some us to spare us dis long, honey, to tell de tale. How kin we help from praisin' him.

All o' my folks b'longed to de same master—mommer, gra'ma, an' Uncle Robert Richardson. Uncle Robert was heid [head] man an' hired hisself to Smelling, de proprietor o' dis sportin' house. Dis house was on Franklin Street near de Ballad House in Richmond. Dis was de las' place dat I, Patience Martin Avery, saw my gra'ma an' mommer.

Yes, Tom Hatcher was very kind to his slaves an' didn't 'low dem to be too severely punished. Yes, sometimes slaves would run away an' take refuge on Tom Hatcher's place an' he was very kin' to 'em an' didn't return 'em to dey masters. Yes, he protect dem 'til he foun' out where dey came f'om an' de circumstances o' de leavin'. Well, yes his 'state was said to be a refuge fer slaves when dey ran away f'om dey cruel masters.

Yes, 'tis plenty o' places dey use to sell slaves. Well, de way dey did was to bring slaves in groups, tied an' chained together. Den dey would put 'em in pens lak cattle. You seen horses an' cows in a pen havencha? Well, dat's de way humans was treated. Chile, it gives you de creeps up yo' spine to think 'bout it. Sometimes dese po' slaves has walk miles an' miles. De ole masters didn't keer. Dere was a block dey would stan' you on. Firs' dey 'xamine you a bit, den dey start off sellin' lak a auction sale o' property. You know how dey do. Say, "$50.00, $50.00, $50.00, etc., $100.00, $100.00, $100.00. Fine young wench! Who will buy? Who will buy? She got little niggers, good an' healthy." De higes' bidder would get de slave. Um! Um! Um! All de time de sale is goin' on you hear de mos' pitiful cries o' mothers bein' part from dey chillun. Sometimes de same master would buy de mother an' her chillun. Seldom you'd find dat, 'cause dey say de chillun was too much trouble. Richmond was a great slave market. . . .

§ Uncle Moble Hopson (b. 1852)

Poquoson, Va.
Interviewer: Unknown
Date of interview: November 28, 1936
Source: Rare Book Room, Lib. of Cong.

. . . Oncle Shep Brown lived down aways on de ribber. 'Long 'fore de Yankees come he jined up wid de 'federates. He fit in dat battle at Big Bethel but he ain't get uh scratch. He tell me all 'bout de war when he come back home. He tell me all 'bout de fall uh Richmond, he did.

Was one day down en de lower woods in de shade he tell me 'bout Richmond, Oncle Shep did. Why, I remember et jes' lak it was yestiddy. Was whittlin' uh stick, he was, settin' on uh stump wid his game laig bunched up ontuh uh bent saplin'. He was whittlin' away fo' uh long time 'thout sayin' much, an' all at once he jump up in de air an' de saplin' sprang up and he start in tuh cussin.

"Gawdammit, gawdammit, gawdammit," he kept sayin' tuh hisse'f an' limpin' round on dat laig game wid de roumatissum. Ah know he gonna tell me somepin den cause when Oncle Shep git excited he always got uh lot tuh say.

"Gawdammit," he say, "twas de nigguhs tuk Richmond." "How dey do dat Oncle Shep?" ah ast, though ah knowed he was gonna tell me anyway. "De nigguhs done tuk Richmond," he keep on sayin' an' finally he tell me how cum dey tuk Richmond.

"Ah seed et muhse'f," he say, "my comp'ny was stationed on de turnpike close tuh Richmond. We was in uh ole warehouse," he tole me, "wid de winders an' de doors all barred up an' packed wid terbaccy bales awaitin' fo' dem Yanks tuh come. An' we was a-listenin' an' peepin' out an' we been waitin' dere most all de ev'nin'. An' den we heer uh whistlin' an' uh roarin' like uh big blow an' it kep' gittin' closer. But we couldn't see nothin' uh comin' de night was so dark.

Dat roarin' kep' a-gittin' louder an' louder an' 'long 'bout day break there cum fum down de pike sech uh shoutin' an uh yellin' as nevuh in muh born days ah'd heerd.

"An' de men in dat warehouse kept aslinkin' away in de darkness widdout sayin' nothin', cause dey didn't know what debbils de Yankees was alettin' loose. But ah stayed right there wid dem dat had de courage tuh face et, cause ah know big noise mean uh little storm.

"Dar was 'bout forty of us left in dat ole warehouse ahidin' back of dem bales uh cotton an terbaccy, an' peepin out thew de cracks.

"An' den dey come. Down de street dey come—a shoutin' an' a-prancin' an' a yellin' an' asingin' an' makin' such uh noise like as ef all hell done been turn't loose. Uh mob uh nigguhs—ah ain't nevuh knowed nigguhs—even all uh dem nigguhs—could mek sech uh ruckus. One huge sea uh black faces filt de streets fum wall tuh wall, an' dey wan't nothin' but nigguhs in sight.

"Well, suh, dey warn't no usen us firin' on dem cause dey ain't no way we gonna kill all uh dem nigguhs. An pretty soon dey bus' in de do' uh dat warehouse, an' we stood dere whilt dey pranced 'rounst us hoopin' an' holl'rin' an' not techin' us at all tell de Yankees soljers cum up, an' tek away our guns, an' mek us prisoners an' perty soon dey march us intuh town an' lock us up in ole Libby Prison.

"Thousings of 'em—dem nigguhs," he say, "Yassir—was de nigguhs dat tuk Richmond. Time de Yankees get dere de nigguhs done had got de city tuk. . . ."

§ Mrs. Hannah Johnson (b. ca. 1850)

819 St. John St., Richmond, Va.
Interviewer: Faith Morris
Date of interview: Unknown
Source: Va. State Lib.

Well my folks belong to de Joe Crews of Richmond. Dey were Quakers before dey were married, but afterwards dey had slaves. Dey was kind people. Always set de slaves free after twenty-one an' would let dem go out to work an' would only take some of dey money which dey earn. My mother was de cook; her name was Hannah too. Dey was crazy 'bout her. I come up as one of de white chillun—didn' know no difference. We et together at de same table. I slept in de same bed wid de white folks and I played wid de chillun. I didn' go to school wid dem, but went ev'y place else most, 'cept to church and parties. Dey would always tell me what dey learned in school so I knowed as much as dey did, near 'bout. When I got 'round ten, I was a nurse an' den I had to stop playin' so much. I always call de ole misses "grandma," like de other chillun.

No, I won't in Richmond durin' de war; I was in Hanover wid Mrs. Crews' daughter, 'bout three miles this side of Ashland. I 'member Sheridan and his army. Dey stopped at our house and demanded our keys to de smoke house. Dey walked in an' took what dey wanted an' left a guard to keep watch over it. He stayed there 'bout a week. He wouldn' let us go in fer anything.

'Bout six months later, early one mornin' we thought we heard some one at de door. Miss Margaret came to my room an' asked me if I heard anything. Den Mr. Ellis (Miss Margaret's husband) came an' tol' me to go to de do'. Miss Margaret said, "Go yourself! I don't want Hannah to go." He went an' there was some of de Yankee men. Dey asked Mr. Ellis de way to Fredericksburg to see if he would tell dem de truth. He tol' dem de right way so den dey said, "Have you heard de latest news? Richmond is on fire an' whiskey an' wine is running th'ough de streets like water, an' we did it. Dere won't be no mo' slaves."

Another time Sheridan's army was goin' by an' dey asked a nigger de way to Richmond. He tol' dem de wrong way an' dey came back an' foun' him an' took a rope an' tied it to his two thumbs an' tied him up on a tree. He stayed there 'til he died. His fingers just dropped off. Dey did dis 'cause he tol' dem a lie.

Ef dey knew of any masters dat was mean to dey slaves, dey would do something mean to him. I know Mr. Walker Luck was a mean master an' de Yankees went in his house an' broke it up inside an' out. Dey took him an' beat him up. He tol' dem on bended knees dat he would never treat another wrong. But dey beat him jes' de same.

After freedom I came back to Richmond an' married James Johnson. He is daid now, has been most twelve years. I'se got only one chile; I live here wid her.

I never went to school. De fus' Sunday School I went to was where de City Hall is now. It was called Dr. Hold's church; I went dere to Sunday School fer two yeahs. Den I went to Fus' Baptist Church. You see dey give it over to cullud people. Dr. Ryland was preachin' den. Dr. James Holmes was de fus' cullud preacher.

I been livin' in St. John Street fer nigh thirty years an' I don' know nothin' 'bout it being called "Apostletown"; ef it is, I reckon it is 'cause its streets is named after de Bible people. . . .

§ William I. Johnson, Jr. (b. 1840)

516 Harrison St., Richmond, Va.
Interviewer: Milton L. Randolph
Date of interview: May 28, 1937
Source: Va. State Lib.

... After the surrender in Appomattox our regiment was sent to Washington and we were mustered out in October, 1865. I stayed in Washington until Christmas Eve.

Christmas is always a get together time for all slave families on the plantation, so I left Washington for Goochland to visit my mother, sisters and brothers. Master Johnson and his brothers were there for their family get-together. We talked things over 'bout the war and the outcome. He laughed when I told him how we escaped from the camp; he didn't show no anger at all but instead said, "Johnson, it was what the Lord intended to happen—we of the South thought we were right and the folks of the North thought they were right and God settled it all like he wanted it, so I suppose everything has happened for the best."

In January of 1866 I came to Richmond and got a job as "hod carrier" for Maynard Brick Contractors and followed brick work for ten to twelve years during which time I learned to be a bricklayer. I helped to build Fort Harrison. Later I worked for the firm of Crumm and Powell for six to seven years; then Ellis Redform as foreman of his brick construction work for 17 years, until 1907.

In 1907 I started contracting for myself and ran an active business until 1932 when I lost my leg, through an infection in my left foot. Although at 97 I am still active in my Fraternal connection I gave up my business and decided to take it easy. (Mr. Johnson enjoyed the reputation of being one of the leading contractors in Richmond during the days of his active work 1907 to 1932.)

Now with all I have done in my life I have my first day to go to school. I can read a little, but when it comes to figures I don't ask nobody any question.

I've been an active member of the First Baptist Church of 67 years —since May, 1870, and am an active member in the Good Samaritans, Odd Fellows, Masons, St. Luke, and Ideals. I joined the Good Samaritans March 18, 1872 and today at 97 years of age I am their elected delegate to the Grand Lodge Session to be held in Petersburg, Virginia this year. I am the only living person in Virginia who was a member when the Grand Lodge was organized in 1872.

My membership in the Odd Fellows started in December, 1879. Last December 8th I had been active with them for 57 years. I am the oldest man in the "Past Grand Masters Council," and am the oldest man in the Richmond Patriarch #6.

Joined Masons, December 1879; St. Lukes, October, 1874; the Forrester's Council #9, first male council made in City of Richmond; and joined National Ideals in May, 1921.

I contribute my good fortune of health, long life and prosperity to my love and kindness to my mother, sisters, brothers and kinfolks. My mother died in Philadelphia about six years ago at the age of 105. I had promised her that when she died I would see that she got a good burial and I had her fixed up good, brought her to Richmond and buried. I have raised all of my children, educated them, then college, those who wanted it. I've helped grandchildren and now I help to educate great grandchildren. The Lord is just blessing me that's all.

Note: Mr. Johnson died in his 98th year. . . .

§ George Lewis (b. ca. 1859)

611 N. Fifth St., Richmond, Va.
Interviewer: Faith Morris
Date of interview: April 9, 1937
Source: Va. State Lib.

I was born in the city of Richmond just before the Civil War.

My mother was set free by her young mistress two years before I was born. She came to Richmond along with her sister; here they met two young men and married. My father was a business man (free), hiring boats on the James River.

I know little of the War, but I will tell of that I do know. We lived on Grace Street near First. On the morning of April 3rd, there was so much noise and so much excitement that my mother took me out of bed—changed my night clothes, dressed me for my day ones—and started with me out of the house. Just as we left the porch three or four Yankee soldiers with guns on their shoulders stopped us, and told my mother that they wanted her to cook breakfast for them. I never shall forget the look that came across my mother's face, but she turned around, took me in her arms and returned to our house. I was frightened and hid behind the kitchen door. After they had finished eating the cakes and fish, they got up from the table and took money out of their pockets and paid my mother for her food and for the trouble. These were Negro troops! They asked her the way to some place; she told them, and they were gone. Later the city was on fire and for a time it rocked. This was all I remembered of the War.

Immediately after the War the Yankees from the New England states sent teachers down to the South to teach the children of exslaves. Such schools were opened in the different colored churches of the city; namely, First Baptist, 3rd Street, Second Baptist, and Ebenezer Baptist.

The first school I entered during this era was Second Baptist Church between First and Second Streets on Byrd Street. I remained there for about four years. Then I entered Dills' Bakery; this was also a school conducted by Yankees. The next school I attended was Navy Hill and then to the Old High and Normal. I graduated in 1877 from this school.

During this time I was in school I had several jobs to help myself. I worked along with my lifelong friend, Mr. Eddie R. Carter, selling newspapers. We also had a contract to fold papers and put them up for mailing.

In 1878 I became a teacher in Henrico County; this county in which Richmond is listed—some folks say that Richmond isn't in a county, but it is. I taught in the county for eight years. The school ran for eight months, and my salary was thirty dollars a month. I came to Richmond once or twice a month. During the time that I was teaching, I also did private study. I took up very nearly all the studies taught in the leading universities of the day.

In 1886 I entered Howard University Law School. While there I had as my fellow students, Judge Robert H. Terrell, Prof. W. H. H. Heart, and others. I graduated from the law department in the class of May 30, 1888.

I started the practice of law in the city of Richmond in October, 1888 immediately after I passed the bar, and I have continued up to the present time. No, I cannot tell you about any of my cases. I never talk of them.

I was married September 9, 1891 to Miss Lucy Brooks. Her father was a business man in the city, having bought his freedom long before the War. Her brother, Robert Peel Brooks, was the first Negro lawyer admitted to the bar in Richmond; another brother, Rev. Walter H. Brooks, is a hospital minister in Washington, D.C. We have two daughters, Leah and Lucille. One teaches at Virginia Union University, and the other at Virginia State College.

I think you have all the important things in my life, and if you will excuse me, I shall get to work. . . .

§ Mrs. Martha Harper Robinson (b. 1856)

1300 Westwood Ave., Richmond, Va.
Interviewer: Milton L. Randolph
Date of interview: Unknown
Source: *Negro in Virginia*, MS version, draft no. 1, chap. 13, p. 17

The night was just right for our escape. The overseer's daughter was getting married, and most of the folk around the Ryland farm were getting ready for a big time. A friendly slave they called Bill crept up to the window and beckoned for me. I ran out of the door, and he handed me over the fence to my uncle, who had another man with him. He grabbed me up on his shoulder and away through the woods, with uncle carrying me on the first lap of the journey.

It was about eight o'clock when we started. Along about 12 we heard the yelping of blood-hounds. My poor heart started jumping as the sound neared and neared. I just knew every minute that we would be caught and carried back, but Uncle Jack kept saying, "Dem's Ryland's hounds: I've outdistanced them before and I'll outdistance them this time." They started running faster and faster, soon reaching the Pamunkey River. Then Uncle shoved me high up on his shoulders and waded out into the stream. We ploughed through to the other side, and we stretched out for a brief rest under the brush on the opposite shore where we could see the pack of hounds and their drivers on the edge of the river. Finally they started downstream. As soon as we had made a safe getaway and the men had rested, they started on.

I guess I was 'bout six years old, but I remember every detail of that trip as if it was yesterday. We hid in the woods all day and travelled only at night. I would get hungry and cry, and one night I remember my uncle held my mouth until I got quiet. One night we arrived at a cabin deep in the woods which was tended by an old colored man and his wife. The cabin was built half in the ground and half out. We got food and something hot to drink and rested there until the next night. After dark we started out again, and I recall how I cried at starting out on my uncle's back again. But before morning we reached a farm in Hanover County where my father had left his wagon for us. They placed me under a pile of vegetables and proceeded toward Richmond. When they got to the Yankee lines, Uncle showed father's pass, and they let us pass through the lines. Outside of Richmond he had to show it to the Confederates, and they let him pass into the city because he was bringing provisions. He went down old Brook Road, then down St. James Street. When my mother saw us coming, she screamed so loud that they must have heard her all over Richmond.

Perdue et al., eds., *Weevils in the Wheat* (1976), pp. 14–16, 145–46, 158–59, 169–70, 196–97, 239–40

"He Was Born an Editor": John M. Daniel

Small though it may seem by contemporary standards, nineteenth-century Richmond was the site of a tremendous amount of printing and reading activity. Great newspapers such as the *Dispatch*, the *Enquirer*, the *Examiner*, and the *Whig* tell only part of the story. Other smaller publications, catering to special-interest groups, made their appearance, lived only a short life, and then disappeared. As a matter of fact, the city saw the birth of some 150 new publications during the century. In addition, many small circulating libraries were in existence, as were a number of bookstores.

On the surface it may seem puzzling that so many and varied publications came to life in Richmond. Their births were due in large part to the city's eclectic population, but they were due to a greater extent to the inordinate number of printing shops in operation there. Lured by the tobacco (q.v.) industry, which needed labels, advertisement fliers, and other such materials, many printers set up shop in the city during the nineteenth century. It was obviously easy for any interested party to find a printer who was anxious to do his work.

Of the newspapers printed in Richmond, the *Examiner* was among the most influential. Begun in 1847, it lasted until 1867, and during most of the years of the Confederacy, it was a thorn in the side of the government, taking to task as it often did the policies of President Davis.

John M. Daniel was without doubt the most colorful editor of the *Examiner* during its controversial life. Irascible, exacting, caustic, and a taskmaster of the first order, he also served briefly in the Confederate army and engaged, when he thought it necessary, in dueling (q.v.) to protect his and his paper's integrity.

The following excerpts were written by Dr. George William Bagby, himself a highly respected local editor, writer, and raconteur.

Some days ago, I found in an old drawer the latch-key, which the editor of the Richmond *Examiner* gave me in 1863. It fitted the door of the house on Broad street, opposite the African church—the house in which he died. A bit of brass, differing in nothing from others of its kind, this key, nevertheless, has its charm. It is the only souvenir I have of one of the most remarkable men Virginia ever produced. Coming upon it unexpectedly, after I had given it up as lost, the bare sight of it crowded my mind, in an instant, with pictures of its former owner. I saw him in Washington, just after his return from Europe, conversing with Seddon and Garnett; in his own room over the *Examiner* office, as he sat lord-like, in a high arm-chair, in August, 1861, questioning me about the battle of Manassas and exhibiting the major's uniform, which he intended to wear as Aid to Gen. Floyd; in the editorial room, cutting and slashing leaders, which had been written for him, or denouncing fiercely the Administration; at his dinner-table, pledging Wigfall and Hughes in a glass of old Madeira; in the bed, where he lay wounded, after the duel with Elmore; and last of all, I saw his marble face—how changed! as he lay in his metallic coffin, March the 31st, 1865. . . .

My acquaintance with him began in Washington, after his return from Turin. He registered his name at Brown's Hotel in a small hand, simply as "Mr. Daniel, Liverpool." Although I had never seen a scrap of his writing, I knew the moment I saw his name on the register, that the man for whom so many were anxiously looking, had arrived. The next evening, I was introduced to him. I had long been curious to see "the great editor," and availing myself of his animated conversation with other visitors, eyed him intently, seeking in the outward man some indication of the extraordinary being within. My search was not in vain. The poorest physiognomist could not have seen Daniel's face, even for a moment, without being attracted—I am tempted to say fascinated by it. True, we always find what we are taught to expect in a face, and often discover what does not exist; but here was a countenance singularly marked—a dark, refined, decidedly *Jewish* face. The nose was not very large, and but slightly aquiline; the mouth thin-lipped, wide, unpleasing, and overhung by a heavy black moustache; the chin square, but not prominent; the cheeks thin; and both cheeks and chin covered by a dense, coarse, jet-black, closely-trimmed beard; eye-brows very thick and black, shading deep-set, rather small hazel eyes; head as small as Byron's or Brougham's, beautifully shaped and surmounted by masses of hair, which in youth, hung long and lank and black to his coat collar; but in later life, was worn close cut. Such was John M. Daniel as he sat before me in a room at Brown's Hotel in the memorable winter of 1861.

... I made many visits to him at his house on Broad street; and had many talks with him on all sorts of subjects. He was not a secretive man; on the contrary, he conversed with the utmost freedom about himself, his early life, his residence abroad, his relations and friends, his political associates and opponents, indeed almost everything. Unless he happened to be out of humor (which was not often the case at his private residence), he loved to talk; and though a recluse, he was delighted with the visits of gentlemen, who came without solicitation on his part and who called in a friendly and social way. He urged me to visit him at night, and in order to tempt me to repeat my visits, would give me, each time, what was then a great and costly treat, a bottle of English ale. This he repeated several times, but finding that I did not play chess and was a much better listener than talker, in fact, that I could not talk well enough to provoke him to talk, he soon became tired of my visits—a fact of which he gave me convincing proof by yawning in my face! ...

Such was John M. Daniel at home. What he was at his office, I will now proceed to tell. Whilst I was contributing to his paper, my habit was to hand my article to the manager in the morning, and at night I would go around to read the proof. Daniel himself always read the proofs, though not with as much pains as I liked. He reached the office generally between 8 and 9 o'clock, and I was almost always there before him. In those days, garroters were abundant, and the first thing he did, after entering the room, was to lay a Derringer pistol, which he carried in his hand ready for any emergency, on the large table which sat in the middle of the floor. This done, he would offer me a cigar—he could never be persuaded to smoke a pipe, and his cigars were of the weakest—and then begin the work of examining proofs. First, the proofs of the news columns, then of Legislative or Congressional proceedings, next the local news, and lastly the editorials. All these, he examined with care, altering, erasing, abridging and adding as he thought fit. Even the advertisements were submitted to him, and I have known him to become furious over an advertisement which he thought ought not to have been admitted.

He was the only newspaper proprietor I ever heard of who would throw out, without hesitation, paying advertisements, sometimes of much importance to advertisers, in order to make room for editorials, or for contributions which particularly pleased him. Oftentimes his news-column was reduced to the last point of compression to make room for editorial matter. The make-up of his paper engaged his serious attention, and I have known him to devote nearly half an hour to the discussion of the question where such and such an article should go, and whether it should be printed in "bourgeois," "brevier," or "leaded minion." He loved to have two or three really good editorials in each issue of his paper. Short, pointed articles, he had little faith in, believing that the length of a column, or a column and a half, was essential to the effect of an article. The London *Times* was his model, and he promised himself, in case the Confederate cause succeeded, to make the *Examiner* fully equal to its English model. A pungent paragraph was relished by him as much as by any human being—indeed, he was quick to detect excellence in anything, long or short—but the sub-editorial, or "leaded minion," column was left apart for just such paragraphs, and the dignity of the editorial column was but once, within my recollection, trenched upon. Even then, the article was a short editorial rather than a paragraph. It was near the close of the war, when, despairing of the cause, he urged, in a few strong sentences, the duty of Virginia to hold herself in readiness to resume her sovereignty and to act for herself alone in the great emergency, which he felt was approaching. I am inclined to think that this was the last article he ever penned.

Laying so much stress upon editorials, it was but natural that he should pay particular attention to correcting them. This, in fact, was his main business in coming to his office at night. At times he preferred to do his own writing, but in general, and certainly in the last year or two of his life, he much preferred to have his ideas put into words by others. Then he would alter and amend to suit his fastidious taste. Any fault of grammar or construction, any inelegance, he detected immediately. He improved by erasure as much, or more, than by addition; but when a thought in the contributed article was at all suggestive, he seldom failed to add two or three, and sometimes ten, or even twenty, lines to it. This was a labor of love to him, and did not fatigue him as it does most people. On the other hand, he disliked extremely to read manuscript. This sometimes brought trouble upon him. Coming in one night, he found on the table the proof of an article on finance, which I had written. He read it over carefully, and, to my surprise, did not put his pencil through a single line of it. Whilst I was pluming myself on this unusual circumstance, he looked up at me and laughed.

"Very well written," said he, "but diametrically opposed to the views of the *Examiner*."

Too old a hand at the bellows to be disgruntled by this, I replied
quietly:

"Pitch it in the fire."

"What! and fill two columns myself between this and midnight?
This is every line of editorial on hand."

"I am really very sorry. But what is to be done? It is impossible for
me to write any more. I never can write after dinner; besides I am
broken down."

"Let me see. Let me see."

He took up the unlucky editorial, read it over more carefully than
before, and then said, in a tone of great satisfaction:

"I can fix it!"

And so he did. Sitting down at the table, he went to work, and
within twenty minutes, transformed it completely. It appeared the
next morning. There were certain awkwardnesses, which we two who
were in the secret could detect, but to the bulk of the readers of the
paper were doubtless quite imperceptible.

When he had to write an article himself, his first question, after the
usual salutation was not "What is the news?" but "What are people
talking about?" and he upbraided me continually for not doing what
he himself never did, "circulating among the people." He aimed always to make his paper interesting by the discussion of subjects which
were uppermost in the popular mind; nor did it concern him much
what the subject might be. His only concern was that it should be
treated in the *Examiner* with dignity and ability, if it admitted of such
treatment; if not, to dispose of it humorously or wittily. But the
humor or wit must be done cleverly and with due attention to style.
He began to write about ten o'clock, wrote rapidly, in a crumpled,
ugly hand, and completed his work, revision of proofs and everything,
by midnight, or a little thereafter. He then returned to his house, and
either sat up or laid awake in bed, reading until two or three o'clock in
the morning. . . .

If at his house, Daniel was affable and almost genial; in his office
he was too frequently on the other extreme. He loved to show his
authority, and, as the saying is, "to make things stand around." His
scowl at being interrupted while in the act of composing, or when
otherwise busily engaged, will never be forgotten by any one who ever
encountered it. Holding drunken men in special detestation, he was,
as by a fatality, subjected continually to their visits, both at his office
and at his house. More than once, I have been sufficiently diverted by
intoxicated officers just from the army, who called in to pay in person,

their maudlin tribute of admiration to the editor of the *Examiner.*
Sometimes he bore these visitations with a patience that surprised me;
but he never failed to remunerate himself by awful imprecations
upon the intruder as soon as he was out of hearing. While his tone to
his employes was, as a general rule, cold and often intolerably dicta-
torial, I have seen him very frequently as affable and familiar as heart
could wish; indeed, I have known him to go so far as to come out of
his *sanctum* into the small room occupied by his sub-editors with the
proof of a contribution in his hand, in order that they might enjoy it
with him. Occurrences of this sort, however, were rare. . . .

Long as this article is, I cannot close it without some allusion to
John M. Daniel as an editor and as a man. He was born an editor.
Whatever may have been his abilities as a diplomatist and a politician,
whatever distinction he might have attained in the forum or in the
field, his forte lay decidedly in the department of letters and more
especially in the conduct of a newspaper. He was not a poet, not a historian, a novelist, an essayist or even, if I may coin the word, a maga-
zinist. He had talent enough to have excelled in any or all of these, but
his taste led him in another direction. It was hoped by everybody that
he would on his return home write a volume about his residence in
Europe. Such a book would have been exceedingly interesting and
valuable. But he was not a book-maker. Moreover, it is not improbable
that he expected to return to diplomatic life, and did not wish to embarrass himself by reflections upon the manners and customs of the
people among whom he expected to reside. He could not have written
about the Italians or any other people without dipping his pen in
vitriol. The publication of a part of one of his letters to his friend,
Dr. Peticolas, had brought him into trouble with the Italians and made
him furious with his associate, Hughes, who took charge of the *Examiner* in his absence. This occurred early in his career as a *diplomat,*
and made him cautious. He preserved his dispatches with utmost
care, in large handsomely bound volumes; but whether with a view to
publication or for his own use in after years, I am unable to say. . . .

John M. Daniel was emphatically an editor—not a newspaper contributor, but an editor and a politician. He was enough of the latter to
have made a name in the Cabinet. He was no orator, although he had
an orator's mouth. I never heard of him making a public speech. He
must have had a great natural repugnance to speaking. Could he have
overcome this repugnance, he had command enough of language to
have ensured him considerable distinction in forensic display; but his
temper was far too hot and quick to admit of success in debate. He
knew men, in the light in which a politician views them, thoroughly

well. His natural faculty of weighing measures and of foreseeing their effects, was much above the common. He had in him the elements of a statesman. His historical studies and his knowledge of mankind were not in vain. Before the first blow was struck and when both Mr. Benjamin and Mr. Seward, speaking the sentiments of their respective peoples, were issuing their "ninety days notes," he prophesied not only the magnitude, but the inhuman and unchristian ferocity of the late war. And who, in this sad hour, can forget how, as the struggle drew near its close, he strove day after day and week after week, to revive the flagging spirits and to kindle anew the energy and courage of the Southern people by terrible pictures of the fate which has ever attended "oppressed nationalities?"

Bagby, *John M. Daniel's Latch-Key* (1868), pp. 7–28

"Hunger Makes Riffraff of Us All": The Bread Riot of 1863

The summer of 1863 was one of the hardest for Richmonders, who were by then enduring the worst that war has to visit upon a people. Hospitals were jammed, amputations and deaths were numerous, and morale was low. The preceding summer there had been a flicker of hope, when General Lee had routed McClellan's forces from the environs of the city, but the cruel winter, followed by the effectiveness of the blockade, had taken its toll by the spring of 1863. On 2 April there occurred an event still referred to as the "Bread Riot." Because speculators had made the situation worse by greatly inflating prices, city residents were running out of food. Accordingly, a group of desperate women met at the Belvidere Baptist Church on Oregon Hill and began a march to the capitol, a distance of over a mile. On the way they looted numerous shops, finally raiding the Confederate commissary. Both the governor and the mayor were called out to quell the disturbance, but it was not until President Davis himself arrived and made ready to have troops fire into the crowd that its members dispersed. Because he wanted to avoid news of Richmond's plight reaching the North, Davis requested that the city's newspapers not print stories about the event. The *Dispatch* complied, but the *Examiner* did not. However, the latter did say that the mob was composed of riffraff. In the next selection, Clifford Dowdey (q.v.) has dramatized the Bread Riot, enabling the modern-day reader to share directly in the misfortunes of those who actually lived them.

Elizabeth had loved, since she could remember, to walk among the homes around Fourth and Fifth Streets. There lived the great tobacco men: Harris and Ginter and Bransford, Walthall and Scott, Childrey and Taylor, and Enders and Scott. In the springtime her favorites were those on Main and Cary, where the rear gardens were built on elevations above the sloping streets and she could see the flowers. She liked best the big, square, red-brick house on the corner of Fifth and Main, with magnolias in the front lawn and high-pitched, double balconies overlooking the rear garden. Next she liked the Barrett house on Fifth and Cary, square and gray with the narrow white porch and two columns in front, and in the back the highest balconies of all and the tallest garden wall, for there Cary Street was a steep hill. Then, set deep in its lawn of tall oaks, was the Allan house where the poet Edgar Poe had lived, and down on Main the Caskie and the Boucher.

It was the life they evoked that moved her. She lived in the core of Richmond, the genesis of its mood, when she breathed in the atmosphere of sweet-smelling flowers and the cooling shade of tall trees, of rambler roses climbing the old bricks of garden walls and ivy reaching toward the dormer windows of sloping roofs, of ladies and gentlemen on the upper balconies cooling in the river breeze. There lived the long memories that weaved and reweaved into the present: of the first fort by the Falls, the first cluster of farmhouses by the riverbank, the first tobacco warehouses and bright-painted taverns, the liquid voices of negroes singing at their work, and the cursing voices of barge drivers at the wharves; of the first checker-board lots on Church Hill's red-clay streets, the frame story-and-a-half Queen Anne houses, the negroes drying clothes on the grassy banks of Shockoe Creek, the soft foreign voices of South American sailors whose ships brought coffee for flour, and the Tidewater voices yelling at the Fairfield races; of the cobblestoned streets climbing west beyond Shockoe Creek, the three-story brick houses forming the new Court End of town, the coon-skinned mountaineers with mule packs and the silk-ruffled dandies from the English ships, and the country voice of Patrick Henry ringing over the churchyard graves from St. John's white-frame Episcopal Church; of the hollow voice of drums marching the First Virginia Regiment off to meet the British redcoats and the singing voice of bugles marching the First Virginia off to meet the Yankee bluecoats, and of the golden voices of forgotten ladies who transmitted all the memories, from huddling in the old fort during Indian raids to cheering the president of their third country at the Spotswood Hotel. *In Dixieland I'll take my stand* . . .

Today the ghostly voices were silent. No memories wove into this April morning. Where Main Street dipped downhill many of the houses were shuttered, with death inside, and others were open to strangers, foreign faces with unfamiliar names. Within herself, Elizabeth felt their broken mood. Her own life, like theirs, seemed suspended between a lost past and an uncertain future. Chester had belonged to the old world. What was he now? What was she?

When she reached the stores across the street from the Spotswood Hotel, where the business section began, she felt that the life suggested by those houses symbolized the life of Richmond. All other lives had somehow been built around that centre, which was an ideal and a base. Now there was nothing to look up to. Everything was changed. The old English-Virginia names, associated in her memory with Richmond as her home, were gone from most of the stores. Gone too were the familiar gentlemen, in their beavers and frock coats, who linked the past with the present through the long memories of her kinspeople. *So you're Charles Kirby's little girl. . . . What's your name? . . . Well, Elizabeth, I've danced with your mother many's the time at Corinthian Hall. . . .* None of these hurrying strangers had danced with her mother or laughed with her father in the yard of Masonic Hall. None of these slowly moving men, hairy and dirty and dusty gray, with slings and bandages and crutches and sticks, would care anything about the little girl of Judy and Charles Kirby. She was a stranger on this bustling street, splattered with red auction flags fluttering in the April breeze.

She hated to enter the unfamiliar stores just as she shrank from entering a room full of strangers. At Ninth Street, Robinson and Adams were auctioneering off a secondhand dinner set, painted blue and gilt-edged, and behind the bellowing man in a wilted collar and brocaded waistcoat some kegs of butter stood on a second-hand Brussels carpet. They would have no tallow here. The auctioneer of Dunlop, Moncure, stood among tins of bicarbonate of soda and bottles of Hennessey brandy and yelled for attention to their blockade goods. They would have no tallow for her candles. Gaudily dressed women strolled out of the Linwood House, arrogance on their painted faces and shrewdness in their eyes. They didn't have to make candles. She watched them, awed, almost envious. They were more at home in this Richmond than she. The next windows displayed candles, homemade too, she saw. She was frightened to think of many other people selling candles. Another window was bright with bonnets, stuck on top of cavalry boots. She stopped and stared at them. Inside, the auctioneer held up pastel-colored organdies out of a big case.

"Fresh from Europe! Just up from Wilmington! These beautiful organdies that came through the blockade—"

She hurried down the street. The windows swam before her eyes, piled with prayer books and playing cards, umbrellas and rifles, cartridges and groceries. On the sidewalk, near a doorway, a barrel of flour had a sign of $100 and a canteen on top. A harsh voice croaked from a store, punctuated by thumps. A fat man in a frock coat and striped trousers pounded four feather beds to exhibit their softness.

"From one of the best families in Richmond . . . little used. . . ."

She moved around barrels of molasses with "$15 per gal" scrawled on the wood.

"Smell of it, gentlemen, smell of the ineffable fragrance of this fine soap, made by the delicate hands of one of Richmond's fairest ladies, perfumed as she would perfume herself for her gallant Southern knight. Step up and convince yourself by a sniff, right from a lady's bood-wah."

Elizabeth stared at the lavender cakes, neatly moulded, and thought of the misshapen lumps Marie made by boiling lime and salt with the kitchen scrapings of grease and ashes. They would laugh if she asked for tallow.

"Right from the Valley of Virginia, the first crop of real, native, home-grown apples. Only twenty-five dollars a bushel. Stock up now, ladies and gentlemen, before the speculators raise the prices."

Behind the auctioneer an odd assortment of boxes were stacked. They might have tallow. She tried to screw up her courage to enter. She must get some to-day. The auctioneer suddenly broke off and cocked his curly head to one side. Elizabeth heard shouting in the distance. The other voices along the street grew quiet and the swelling shout was the only sound. The customers plunged through the door. Before she could retreat, she was caught in the midst of sweating men. They looked anxiously up and down the street. The tocsin hadn't rung to call out the local defense troops. The raging voices seemed to roll up from Cary Street. Then she heard glass smashed. Someone screamed. She was hurried along with the crowd.

Across the street government clerks ran out on the steps of the Customshouse. At the corner a man yelled down from his perch on the iron-grille rail of the American Hotel balcony, where he was polishing the big globes. No one answered him. Elizabeth was pushed into Eleventh Street. Down the hill, where Cary Street crossed, the intersection was choked with women. They crept along in a solid mass. They were the shouters and their voices echoed and reëchoed in the narrow street canyon. Elizabeth was carried down the street by the surge of men. The familiar trembling of fear weakened her and her breath came in short gasps.

Then she was at Cary Street, jostled and bumped in the milling mob. She glimpsed the pack of women. Their clothes were tattered and torn, their hair hung disheveled above bestial faces. Her panic shook her as she stared at them, and their animal cries beat at her. Glass was strewn all over the flagstone crossing. Drays and carts swayed in the midst of the women and they shoved and fought over the piles in them. She glimpsed hams and flour barrels and molasses kegs and slabs of pork. The last of the women passed in front of her.

Beyond them she saw an aproned man across the street trying to close a store door in their faces. They screamed and snarled and a small boy waved a hatchet at the shopkeeper. He fell back and the women swarmed over him into the store.

The main mob ebbed down Cary Street, leaving solitary women, drooping, like waste left by a tide. The street was littered around them. The stores were wrecked. In a broken doorway a gray-bearded shopkeeper moaned. Women started to come out of the store Elizabeth had seen them enter. They came singly, stood a moment, looking around with wild expressions. Some followed the mob. A bent, grayed old woman staggered toward Elizabeth. The men in front of her gave way and stared at the woman. She clutched loaves of bread and a handful of salt herring, and glared out of wide eyes, fever-bright and glassy. She panted like a dog. Dank gray hair tumbled from under her bonnet, half off her head. She came through the lane straight toward Elizabeth, and Elizabeth recognized her family's former dressmaker. "Mrs. Fitchett," she said weakly. "Mrs. Fitchett!"

The woman stopped and slowly her gaze focused. She shifted as though she might be ashamed. Then she lowered her eyes.

"What are those women after, Mrs. Fitchett?"

"*Bread!*"

Elizabeth recoiled. "But surely you're not breaking into stores?"

"We broke in the commissary store," she muttered.

A big-boned woman, thin and sallow, her lips drawn back over her teeth, plunged through the men, facing them defiantly. A pair of boots were tied around her neck. Something shone in her hand.

"But they're breaking open stores and that woman has stolen something."

"I cain't he'p what they're doin'. They're so hongry I reckon they've gone crazy." She faced Elizabeth doggedly.

"But what started them? How could—"

"I reckon 'twas that explosion at Brown's Island. A lot was killed and hurt theah and they're desp'rit. Oh, Lord Jesus, look! Heah comes the City Battalion."

Elizabeth turned. Bayonets gleamed in the morning sun.

"Foh Gawd," Mrs. Fitchett moaned, "whut'd my boy Joe say if he knew the militia had to be called out agin his own mother?" She raised the hand holding the fish to set her bonnet on straight. Her torn sleeve fell from her arm. The grayed skin was drawn tight over the bone. "You won' tell Mistuh Brose, will you? Joe'd think hard of me if'n he knew and he's all I got. You won't tell, will you?"

Elizabeth shook her head. The exposed arm had made her sick.

The old woman started to speak again. Then she closed tight her lips and defiance replaced the shame. She whirled and went scuttling up Eleventh Street. Elizabeth half turned. Men ran toward her. From behind and around her men and women of the mob scattered up the hill. Their shouts shook her. *Riot, riot . . . close the stores . . . riot . . . going into Main . . .* She just stood there, weak and terrified, while the crowd eddied about her.

She turned back when the City Battalion marched past. She wanted to appeal to them. Not one grim face moved. They were advancing on their first enemy. When the guide sergeant at the end of the column walked stiffly by, she saw that she stood alone in the débris. Then she started up Eleventh Street, almost stumbling in her weakness. Her legs would not steady. Main Street looked like Sunday. The stores were tightly barred, but glass was sprinkled on the sidewalk and some windows were broken. The mob had passed on. She hurried on toward Bank Street. She heard their shouting up the hill.

Government clerks talked quietly in the Bank Street entrance of the Customshouse and there was one white-haired old gentleman who belonged in one of her favorite houses. A trim cavalry colonel halted his horse in front of him. The colonel was one of President Davis's aides.

"It's all over, Mr. Paxton," he called cheerfully. "The President tried talking with them, but one of them threw a loaf of bread at him. Then Governor Letcher threatened to have the City Battalion fire into them and they went off, sullen as animals. I didn't know we had such riffraff in the city."

"What you don't know, apparently," the old aristocrat said coldly, "is that hunger makes riffraff of us all."

The officer flushed. He spun his horse around and galloped up Bank Street. Elizabeth looked closely at the old gentleman as she passed him. Mr. Paxton . . . that must be Uncle Virginius' friend. If Uncle Virginius could be a friend of such a fine gentleman of that world suggested by the houses, and Brose could be Mildred Wade's sweetheart, why should she think that Chester's life kept them apart? She climbed the steps into Capitol Square. Negro nurses talked while the children they watched played near them. The nurses were glancing at a pale young woman who leaned back on a bench, as though she might be sick. Elizabeth glanced at her. Her poor dress was torn and her cheek was bruised. She wasn't sick; she was weak to the point of fainting. In her lap she held a man's shoe.

The shock of the bread riot, which had gripped her in a paralysis, broke into its horrible details and she saw again each hunger-crazed woman. They flashed before her vision like colored slides. Their bestial screams rang again through her brain. She forgot her morning errand, forgot their need of tallow, forgot Chester, everything, in a sudden frenzy to be home, where she could shut out the visions, where she felt safe, where things were familiar.

Dowdey, *Bugles Blow No More* (1937), pp. 263–70

"Walk under a Gracious Linden Tree": Mid-Victorian Richmond

Helena Lefroy Caperton (1878–1962) was the author of both fiction and nonfiction. Born of an Irish father and a Virginia mother, she spent much of her youth at her grandfather's home in Ireland. Although generally forgotten today, Mrs. Caperton enjoyed considerable success as a short story writer earlier in this century. For a number of years she was a regular book reviewer for the Richmond *Times-Dispatch*. By today's standards, "Mellow Days: A Sketch of Mid-Victorian Richmond" is laden with overt racism, in that the black characters are stereotypes of the white consciousness. This is doubtless true. It is also equally true, however, that the story accurately reflects a part of our collective past.

Walk under a gracious Linden tree, up a brick path, mount the white
steps and stand under swaying clusters of wistaria, pause a moment
beneath the Corinthian columns to enjoy the coolness cast by their
deep shadows, then lift the brass knocker—Simultaneously with its
cheerful sound the heavy door will swing wide, not as who should say,
"Why are you here and what do you want?" but open to the fullest
extent of welcome in its truest sense; and there stands Uncle Juba with
his silver card-tray extended, a wealth of welcome on his fine old face.

"Are the ladies at home, Juba?"

A look of infinite sympathy and disappointment invades the old
butler.

"Naw, Miss Delia, dey's out. I suttenly sorry; dey'll be mo den dis-
comoded not to see you ladies!"

"We're sorry, too; good-bye, Juba, be sure and give them our cards."

"I sholy tell dem you called"—

Cards being very well in their way, but lifeless things compared with
communicating the news in person. The visitors unfurl their sun-
shades, and with fluttering organdies enter their victoria and are
driven away.

From my cool corner of the drawing-room I see Juba place twelve
silver goblets upon a tray, and go pantry-wards, whence come the
sounds of heavy pounding. This ceases and he again appears.

"I'se done crack de ice, honey, and I'se gwine out in de yard and
pick de mint; don't you sqush hit, whatever you do."

Every afternoon I make grandfather's juleps, and likewise every
afternoon Juba says in prayerful tones: "Don't sqush de mint." Do not
be alarmed. Grandfather does not consume one dozen juleps, the
other eleven are for certain gentlemen who, sooner or later, will "drop
in" for a game of cards during what we call in Virginia, "the cool of
the evening," which means that it will be somewhat less sweltering
than it was at noon, and always has, to my mind a Biblical sound—
didn't Adam walk somewhere in the cool of the day?

Perhaps it may seem a useless thing to instruct the younger generation in the making of a mint julep, except that then it was a sacred
rite, performed to slow music and mayhap some of its gracious pun-
gency will envelope these reminiscences and, without evil effect, give
them a more vivid aroma of the past. The twelve chased silver goblets
stood upon their tray, first came two leaves of mint, then the sugar,
then the goblets were piled high with finely shaved ice until on their
monogrammed and crested exterior a thick coating of frost appeared.
Juba would elevate the heavy decanter and pour in that which is now
no more. Placing fresh sprigs of mint at one side, together with a ripe

strawberry, the ceremony was accomplished. There would be many gentlemen on the veranda and as one stepped from the French window they would rise in greeting with courtly dignity though curls were flying and skirts short. Juba followed with the tray. After I had kissed my grandfather and heard the many pretty speeches that now seem a lost art, he would say: "This way, Major; this way, Judge; your good health, Colonel," then all together, "and your good health, my dear," upon which I would spread my flounces, make a curtsy and vanish.

Out of sight, but not out of hearing, for no young girl was ever so privileged in listening to those rich in memories. No Arabian Knights could equal the stories of wars and gallantry, loves and hates reaching as far back as my grandfather's boyhood (and he remembered his Grandfather), making a wealth of historic color learned at first hand and stored away never to be forgotten. As Mrs. Ewing says, "Jackanapes was great friends with the postman, for the postman's grandfather could remember a man who carried arrows at the battle of Flodden Field."

One of these stories concerned John Randolph, of Roanoke. At my request, it was written down, and I give it here:

"I was taken when a small boy into the Virginia Convention of 1829, and was kindly lifted and seated on the shoulders of a friend of my father's, that I might see and hear Mr. Randolph, who was delivering one of his fiery Philippics.

"Too young to appreciate the subject debated, I well remember its force, fierceness and effect on the vast audience which hung spellbound on his lips until the close. As Heinie says of Napoleon: 'I saw him once again.' It was in the early thirties. I was in Lynch's Coffee House, which stood on the site of the State Bank and was a reading-room to which the subscribers resorted to see the files of the *National Intelligencer* and other papers of the day. The room was filled with the most prominent citizens. I recall John Wickham, George Fisher, Daniel Call, Norborne Nicholas, General Harvie and many others, all well known to Mr. Randolph.

"Taken to the front door I was told to note carefully the gentleman who was in the act of dismounting from a thoroughbred, his servant holding his stirrup. My interest was aroused by being told that I 'would hear much of him in the future.' The intentness of my gaze so fixed him in my memory that if I had any artistic ability I could picture him accurately. He was then in declining health, his face about the color of a new saddle, illuminated by the most piercingly brilliant eyes I ever saw. He dismounted and strode through the throng without saluting any one, scanned the files of the Washington papers for a while, the cynosure of all eyes, and returned as he had come, remounting and galloping up Main Street. Dr. Robert Archer, who about that time was the Army Surgeon at Old Point Comfort, told me that standing on the wharf one day with a great crowd, Mr. Randolph was observed on the upper deck, and was saluted from the shore by many friends and acquaintances. He cried out: 'Mr. Blank, can you tell me why your brother and you are like a pair of shears?'

"'No,' said the gentleman accosted, 'Why?'

"'Because you do not hurt each other, but woe to the fellow who gets between you!' at which the whole company laughed heartily, for the two brothers were notable for their aptitude in their use of money."

Looking back upon the Richmond of that day one is invaded by a sense of ample leisure which seems now utterly lost, even to those possessing wealth which would have been unbelievable then. Now we have everything except time, then no one seemed to have very much money, but a broad tranquillity to enjoy life. To-day we are like the Red Queen in Alice. After a frantic race they stop, and Alice says: "We have been running as hard as we can and we are still in the same place." "Of course, my dear," replies the Red Queen, "you have to run as hard as you can to keep in the same place." This being true it is well that certain of our luxuriously inclined ex-slaves have passed over. Behind the old house on Franklin Street there is a lovely garden with box hedges and a sun dial. At the end of this garden were the "Offices" where the colored servants lived, pensioners upon their Masters and Mistresses.

On a certain morning before breakfast while cutting roses I came upon "Uncle" Winston at ease upon a bench in the sun. He had only two duties—to sweep the garden paths, and to shine the family shoes. On this occasion he seemed to be suffering from extreme prostration.

"Good morning, Uncle Winston, how are you?"

"Poly, thank Gawd, honey, you have to tell Marse John I can't shine de shoes no mo, hit jars me." Pax, Uncle Winston, how severely jarred you would be to-day!

At this time no party was a success unless John Dabney served the refreshments. He was a negro gentleman (the word is used advisedly) of remarkable and stately dignity and as a chef unequalled.

His terrapin and canvass-back were immortal foods. Surely he must have been the man for whom Diogenes searched, for when the slaves were freed Dabney bought himself from his Mistress. Could anything be more touchingly humorous or more splendidly honest? Setting a high value on himself he paid his former Mistress, bit by bit, till he felt himself free; for the war had left her penniless.

It was Dabney who gave Edward the Seventh his first julep, when as Prince of Wales he visited Richmond. His Royal Highness was so well pleased that he presented Dabney with a huge silver loving cup inscribed with the Royal coat of arms, and words of appreciation. This cup is still in the possession of Dabney's descendants.

There came a time when the ranks of our good and faithful servants became thinner. "Mammy" was the first to go, after nearly half a century of unwavering devotion, first as Empress of the nursery, then, when the young people no longer needed her, as my grandmother's personal attendant. So long had she been identified with the family that her own name was lost in the mazes of antiquity, and every one called her Mary Montague. Even when we had outgrown her ministrations as to the adequate washing of ears, the curling of hair, and the approved friskiness of skirt that should obtain in the case of little girls of "delicate filigree"—meaning a high standard of refinement —"Mammy" never gave over the responsibility of our spiritual welfare. The morning after a ball she would come sailing in before the breakfast trays, and picking up satin and tulle, and creating some sort of order, she would quote blood-curdling passages with a scriptural resonance. Sooner or later a sleepy voice would say: "Oh, do hush, Mammy, and let me sleep, you know that's not in the Bible."

"Well, honey, ef taint dar, hit orter be!"

Together with a childish simplicity there is in the Darkey an inherent love of form and ritual, mingled with a rapt admiration and wish to emulate their "white folks."

In the days of the old Holland House a high-living bachelor uncle would take his body servant with him to New York. He always attended Divine Service at St. Thomas's, and Rastus would sit in the gallery and drink in the beauty of its pomp and ceremony.

On a day the old Darkey appeared before one of the curates in the parish house and announced that he wished to join St. Thomas's. Now, this young priest had been preaching with white heat on the subject of the white man's burden being regarded as a brother, his fervor equalled only by his innocence of his subject. Rastus, standing respectfully before him, was a breathing, living admonition to practise what he preached out, but . . . our young brother in God at once saw the beauty of compromise.

"You know, Rastus," said he, "there are no other . . . ah . . . colored gentlemen in our church, and I fear you will find it lonely . . . however, I suggest that you think it over a day or two; in fact, Rastus, I

would suggest that you pray over it and take such an important matter to the font of all Wisdom and ask for guidance on the subject."

Promptly the next day Rastus appeared.

"And did you earnestly ask for guidance, my good man?" inquired
the young clergyman.

"Yas, Sir, I sho did, I ben wrastlin' in prayer wid de Lord all night
and I done got my answer."

"And what is that answer, Rastus?" asked the curate, glowing with
admiration of the old Darkey's childlike faith.

"I done sputed wid de Lord bout hit and de Lord said to me, 'Yas,
Rastus, Son, ef you kin git into St. Thomas's, you do hit, becase effen
yo does hit will be more den I've ever been able to do.'"

Caperton, "Mellow Days," *Reviewer*, May 1921, pp. 206–11

"It Is Doubtful Whether an Abler Business Man . . . Ever Lived in This State": Joseph Reid Anderson

What John Marshall (q.v.) was to his generation in Richmond,
Joseph Reid Anderson (1813–93) was to the next. He is best remembered for his spectacular leadership at the Tredegar Ironworks,
which without question ranks as the greatest industrial complex of
the antebellum and Civil War South and rightfully earned the appel-
lation, "Mother Arsenal of the Confederacy." But Anderson was a
man of many roles, all creditable. He held public office on several
occasions and helped to launch and later headed the city's Chamber
of Commerce and other organizations. He was a pioneer in race relations (and much admired in the black community), and he took the
lead in a variety of charitable enterprises. Finally, like Marshall,
he was widely esteemed and beloved for the warmth of his personality
and the depth of his character.

§ Career of General Anderson

Joseph R. Anderson was born on the 6th of February, 1813, at Walnut
Hill, the seat of his father, William Anderson, near Fincastle, in Bote-

tourt county. He was one of six children, his brothers being the late Dr. William Anderson, the late Judge Frank Anderson, of the court of appeals, and the late John T. Anderson, all men of the highest standing for character and usefulness. The mother of General Anderson was a Miss Thomas, a member of the family to which the late brilliant Governor Francis Thomas, of Maryland, belonged. The early life of the General was passed in Botetourt county, where he received his education previous to his appointment as a cadet at West Point. His career as a student in the Military Academy was one of the highest distinction. He graduated as second in a class of sixty-eight. He was at once appointed to the engineer corps, and was stationed for a short time at Fortress Monroe. From this point, he was sent to Charleston, but returned in the same year, 1837, to Fortress Monroe. While stationed there before, he had met Miss Sallie Archer, daughter of Dr. Robert Archer, surgeon of the Post, and one of the most distinguished members of his profession in the United States Army. Miss Archer was as lovely in character as she was beautiful in person. In 1837, Lieutenant Anderson and herself were married. In the succeeding year he was detailed to assist Colonel Crozet in important internal improvements, in which that well-known engineer was engaged by the direction of the State of Virginia. It was at this time that General Anderson surveyed and superintended the general construction of the great turnpike, which was long the only highway between Staunton and the lower valley, and which remains to-day a monument of engineering skill. About 1838, he resigned from the army, and took up his residence in this city. For a short time he was engaged in the commission business, and it was while in this business that he first formed the connection, which was to open up to him his distinguished career in the branches of iron manufacture, which he followed.

§ Tredegar Works

At this time, the Tredegar Works was owned by the firm of Dean & Cunningham, and were run on a small scale, there being only one bar mill, a guide mill, a foundry and a puddle mill. General Anderson became the commercial agent of this firm. Recognizing the great possibilities which lay in the business, he leased the works for five years, beginning in 1843. In this step he was associated with several members of his wife's family. His next step was to buy out the whole interest of the old firm, the company then formed being known as Anderson, Morris & Co. This was subsequently changed to Joseph R. Anderson

& Company, headed by the General himself, Dr. Robert S. Archer, Major Robert S. Archer, and the father of Colonel William E. Tanner. This firm entered into the manufacture of general foundry products and various forms of rolled iron. A large proportion of the machinery for the sugar mills of Louisiana was manufactured by the firm, and a vast quantity of Government ordnance, projectiles and cable iron for Government ships. The Tredegar Works had now grown to be one of the most important of its kind in the United States, and under the direction of General Anderson was constantly assuming larger proportions. The Armory Iron Company, which had been started by Dr. Robert S. Archer, was consolidated with the Tredegar before the war came on, enlarging its capacity and increasing the variety of its work. When the war began General Anderson was commissioned a brigadier-general by the Confederate authorities, but with the distinct understanding on the part of Congress that he should be recalled from the field whenever the interests of the Confederacy required that he should give a personal supervision to the Government material in the process of manufacture at the Tredegar. Under this commission he took part in the terrible battle at Gaines' Mill.

§ General Anderson's Gallantry

About a year ago there appeared in these columns a letter from a valued correspondent of The Times, who now resides in Essex county, giving a graphic account of the impressions which the writer had formed of the splendid gallantry of General Anderson in one of the most bloody episodes of that awful conflict. The Government's dependence upon the Tredegar Works for supplies of ordnance becoming greater as the war went on, General Anderson, in opposition to his own wishes, was ordered to take personal charge of the works again. As its executive head his services to the Confederacy were of the very highest value, and no man in the South contributed more in the sphere in which he operated to the success of the Confederate arms. During the great contest he enjoyed the entire confidence of the members of the Government, and his judgment was very much relied on. His intimacy with Mr. Davis, begun during the war, was continued until the death of that great man. It was only in the course of the last twelve months that General Anderson entertained Mrs. and Miss Davis as guests for several weeks at his home. When the war closed the Federal authorities took possession of the Tredegar Works as Government property on account of its connection with the old armory, but this appropriation lasted only for a short while.

§ Tredegar Reorganized

In 1867 the Tredegar Company, capitalized at a million dollars, was formed with General Anderson as president, and with a corps of unusually able and experienced assistants. The Works was placed on a more efficient basis than ever, and its scope of operation was further enlarged. It had manufactured spikes before the war, but now the capacity for turning out all kinds of railroad product was very much increased. After a period of great prosperity, the works in 1873, owing to the general collapse in business, which followed that year, and which crippled many of the most important of the railroad corporations dealing with the Tredegar, it became involved, and three years later passed into the hands of a receiver, General Anderson being appointed to that position. In 1878, the original company was restored, and from that time to the present day has enjoyed a steady prosperity. It ranks to-day as one of the three most important works of its kind in the United States. It is no reflection on those who have been associated with General Anderson in the management of this great establishment for so many years to say that he has always been the leading and controlling spirit, and that it is chiefly due to his extraordinary business capacity that the Tredegar has attained its present proportions. It is doubtful whether an abler business man than General Anderson ever lived in this State. With an astonishing capacity for details, he joined a power of combination, a clearness of foresight, a readiness of comprehension, a quickness to adapt himself to new business conditions that would have made him a distinguished man in the greatest business communities of the world.

§ His Character as a Business Man

No man was more conservative in forming his conclusions in a business transaction, but when once formed he never looked back, but acted with a vigor and a pertinacity that forced success where it could not otherwise have been won. The Tredegar Works will always be a monument to his sagacity and enterprise. In expanding these works he justly entitled himself to the grateful remembrance of the people of this city. General Anderson was not so much absorbed by his own private business as to feel only a passing interest in the general affairs of the community. No man was more public spirited than he was; no man more ready to devote his time, abilities and fortune to purposes which were calculated to promote the general welfare of the city. He had always taken a warm interest in the prosperity of the Chamber of Commerce, and in 1874 he was unanimously elected president of that body, to which office he was re-elected October 19, 1875. He resigned the presidency of the Chamber March 9, 1876, in consequence of his election to the presidency of the City Council.

During the whole course of his connection with the Chamber of Commerce he was one of the most active and indefatigable members, and for a number of years served as one of its directors, in which capacity his experience and ability were invaluable. In recognition of his great usefulness a meeting of the Chamber will be held this evening at 6 o'clock to take suitable action upon his death.

§ Warm Interest In Political Affairs

General Anderson was always distinguished for the warm interest which he took in political affairs. In 1857 he was elected to the House of Delegates. He again represented the city in the House 1873–74 and 74–75. The South had then just commenced to recover from the disastrous effects of the war and the reconstruction measures, scarcely less disastrous than the war itself. We were living under a reconstruction constitution recently imposed upon us by the Federal Government. Novel and grave questions, perhaps the most important which had arisen since the revolution which made us independent of Great Britain, were constantly presenting themselves for consideration and action. Although a man of large and varied business affairs, General Anderson devoted himself strictly to the duties of his representative office. He was consistent in attendance at committee meetings and the sessions of the House.

When an important question concerning the interests of the Commonwealth, or when any question affecting the welfare of Richmond was under consideration his seat was never vacant, his voice was never silent. His views were delivered with an energy that forced attention and evident honesty of purpose that went straight to the hearts of his hearers and a logical clearness that carried conviction. His fine presence, his personal magnetism, his broad liberality, his well-known honesty of purpose, acquired for him an influence and a following amongst his fellow-members which greatly redounded to his own credit and to the advantage of his constituents.

Happy the people who could always have such men for legislators and representatives.

§ His Political Capacity

General Anderson was never a candidate for the highest political offices, but there is little reason to doubt that if he had permitted himself to be drawn into the more conspicuous political sphere of national politics he would have attained to a position of national influence and distinction. His extensive political information, his remarkable knowledge of men, his tact and skill in managing them, his ripe experience, his great natural sagacity, all associated with a power of expressing his opinions forcibly and convincingly when on his feet, would have given him a strong hold upon the attention of any legislative body, however large or however able, of which he might have been a member.

Few men who have ever resided in the city have been more earnest in promoting the interests of the church than General Anderson. From the foundation of St. Paul's he was an active member of its vestry, and at the time of his death the senior warden. While devoted to his own denomination, he did not allow that fact to restrict his religious sympathies and feelings. He was as liberal and generous here as he was in all the relations of life. . . .

§ Influence of Such a Man

The influence of such a man upon society is invaluable for good. His public spirit which led him to take an active part in all that concerned the Commonwealth, his firm conservative tendencies and the practical wisdom which gave weight to his opinions, made him a leader in every public question; while his earnest support of all that was just and right, and his immediate perception of whatever was unsound or untrue, made him a tower of strength in any doubtful issue.

An account of General Anderson's life would be incomplete which omitted the cordial and all-abounding hospitality which formed so large a part of his life and made his home a social centre. His roof has been graced by the presence of every stranger of note who has visited the city during his residence in it.

A visitor's book of that beautiful mansion would be a most interesting record of our social life. But it was not alone distinguished guests to whom this welcome was extended. He never asked whether the visitor had been or might possibly be useful or agreeable to him. It was sufficient that he was a stranger in the city and required attention. And what a welcome it was! How free and warm, and with what grace it was tendered. . . .

The delicacy and tenderness that marked his family life is sacred ground, on which we forbear to tread, nor may we invade the yet more sacred relation which binds the soul to its Maker. We may but offer our heartfelt sympathy to the bereaved who miss the strong hand and sheltering love that have guided them so long, while from heaven's pure heights comes the assurance: Well done, thou good and faithful servant! Enter thou into the joy of thy Lord!

> The graceful tact, the Christian art that joined
> Each office of the social hour
> To noble manners, as the flower
> And native growth of noble mind.

It is not yet known when the body of General Anderson will arrive in the city. The active pall-bearers have already been selected, and will be eight of his grandsons. No additional arrangements have yet been made for the funeral. The interment, however, will be in the family section in Hollywood.

Richmond *Times*, 8 September 1892

"It Seemed That Everything He Touched Turned to Gold": Lewis Ginter

Like Joseph Reid Anderson (q.v.), Lewis Ginter (1824–97) personifies a Richmond tradition of the businessman–public benefactor. Unlike Anderson, however, Ginter was born outside Virginia (in New York) and made and lost fortunes in various enterprises before striking gold in the 1870s with the mass production and merchandising of a new form of tobacco consumption—the cigarette. A lifelong bachelor and inveterate world traveler, the charitable Ginter greatly enriched his adopted city, and his vision and philanthropic spirit—along with that of his niece Grace Arents—can be seen in many quarters of Richmond even today. His career is conveniently

summarized below by local attorney and author, Samuel J. T.
Moore, Jr. (1913–).

During the last century there lived in Richmond a veritable Midas. It
seemed that everything he touched turned to gold, and so great was
his fortune that during his lifetime he was called the richest man in
not only Virginia but in the entire Southland. Though he was handsome, kind, and courteous, he never married, but through the three
score and thirteen years of his life he harbored a love in his heart that
was undying, even unto the end.

His name was Lewis Ginter and his one great love was for his
adopted city and home, Richmond. So great was his affection for this
enchanting Virginia city that his fortune, estimated at twelve million
dollars during his lifetime, had dwindled to only two million dollars at
the time of his death, wholly because his generous heart and hands
were always open to his fellow Richmonder. A beggar never left his
home hungry, nor was a friend ever refused aid of some kind, while
the most distinguished visitor would leave his presence awed at the
genial hospitality that seems to have been born in this nineteenth-
century multimillionaire.

From poverty and obscurity Lewis Ginter rose to wealth and prominence and at various times during his life he was a merchant prince, a
financier, and a manufacturer. During the metamorphosis of his life,
he never forgot his courteous smile or his kind manner and, least of
all, the affection that he held for Richmond. In his travels through this
country and abroad he would often become impatient and anxious to
keep moving, but when Richmond was his goal he was content, and
even more content when this goal was reached. Illustrative of his
fidelity to Richmond was his reaction to the burning of the Rotunda of
the University of Virginia in 1895. When the loyal alumni of that institution sought financial aid from Major Ginter to restore the building,
he flatly refused their suggestion to donate $10,000.00, saying that his
interests were in Richmond, "first, last, and always." At another time
when he learned that a movement had been started to move the Union
Theological Seminary from Prince Edward County, near Farmville,
to Richmond, he unhesitantly gave to the cause twenty-five thousand dollars' worth of his most desirable property, deeded to it in
fee simple, whereas the movement had asked only for a lease on the
property.

In retribution, Richmond admired and honored this philanthropist
who was so loyal to her, and though his life ended almost a half cen-

tury ago his name is still synonymous with "Richmond." He is the only "Ginter" ever to have lived in this city, yet immortal monuments to that name are: Ginter Park, Ginter Gardens, Lewis Ginter Land and Improvement Company, Ginter Park School, Ginter Park Woman's Club, and the Lewis Ginter Community Building.

How Lewis Ginter spent his boyhood no one seems to know; we do know, however, that he was born in New York City on April 4, 1824, of that staid Knickerbocker stock and descended from a Dutch lineage that he proudly referred to on more than one occasion. Originally, his name had been spelled "Guenter," but that spelling was later contracted to "Gunter"; then his parents changed the name to "Ginter" so that its spelling and pronunciation would conform to the exactness that growing New York of the early eighteen hundred's demanded. We know also that Ginter had visited Richmond once or twice in his early boyhood, previous to his settling here in the spring of 1842, since he would often accompany his favorite uncle on business trips through the South, and Richmond was one of the largest cities in their itinerary. What induced the lad to seek his fortune here was never explained.

Nineteen years before the outbreak of the War between the States, however, a small linen store was opened on Main Street, opposite the old St. Charles Hotel and in the vicinity of the present Chesapeake and Ohio Railway Station. On the outside of the store and across the plate glass window were printed these words: "Lewis Ginter—Fine Linens." On the inside, a handsome lad of eighteen politely received the customers and, equally politely, sold them his wares. It is said that young Ginter would buy the finest linens that were obtainable and then wrap them in such attractive packages that they caught the eye of the most casual customer and likewise sold themselves. He himself admitted that he would often spend many hours in his store, sometimes far into the night, figuring new wrapping designs and new ideas that would catch the buyer's attention and entice him to come in and inspect the linen stock.

The proprietor of this small store watched his business carefully and it was not long before he was forced to seek larger quarters on the south side of Main Street, between Twelfth and Thirteenth Streets. The site selected was later occupied by the Western Union Telegraph Company.

During this period Ginter roomed with a Mr. Alvery, a successful business man who was not reluctant about noticing the keen business ability of his boarder, and consequently approached him with two propositions; first, that he change his business from a retail concern to a wholesale concern; and second, that he take him, Mr. Alvery, into the new venture as a partner. After a careful study of all the points involved young Ginter accepted both of Mr. Alvery's propositions, and with the admittance of Mr. George Arents, a nephew of Ginter's, the wholesale house of "Ginter, Alvery, and Arents" was established.

With the characteristic "Ginter" touch the firm prospered enormously and soon reached the peak of a $40,000.00 a year business. Ginter, being the senior partner, traveled throughout America and Europe to replenish the firm's supply, and often brought to Richmond the finest linens that Ireland could offer, as well as the finest wools that were produced in Scotland. At all times his firm carried the finest dry goods obtainable and it is said that there was not a retail store in the eastern section of the state at that time that did not carry goods furnished by this famous Virginia concern.

Through Ginter's keen business appreciation he foresaw the panic of 1857 and only by his acting upon such foresight was he able to save his firm from failure during that period. Previous to the panic he expressed to his partners that he was certain of a financial crisis to follow in the wake of the success that the country as a whole was enjoying. The partners dismissed the prophecy with a laugh but Ginter did not stop with the laugh. Instead he purchased additional horses and buggies and sent collectors to all of the firm's clients; for six months these collectors called on the debtors of their employer and forwarded to him all the cash that they could secure, and when the crash came, as he had predicted, Ginter's firm had on hand sufficient funds to meet the emergency. Surrounding concerns failed by the score, but the wholesale dry-goods house of "Ginter, Alvery, and Arents" continued on the crest of prosperity.

The company was located originally on, what was then Pearl Street, now, South Fourteenth, between Main and Cary, but was later moved to the southeast corner of Thirteenth and Main Streets. This later building was burned during the evacuation of Richmond in 1865 but was later rebuilt and occupied by Stephen Putney and Company.

At the outbreak of the Civil War, the firm was dissolved and Lewis Ginter joined the Confederate cause by enlisting under General Joseph R. Anderson. There was over a quarter of a million dollars due the firm in outstanding accounts at that time but not one debtor was forced to pay or liquidate his debt. Richmond was too busy with "Yankees" just then.

From a Quartermaster, Ginter was soon promoted to the rank of a Commissary and, because of his eagerness to fight at any time, he was appropriately called "the Fighting Commissary." It was not until the second day of the Second Battle of Manassas that Ginter was given an opportunity to fight, but the maneuver that he undertook that day saved his company from a heavy loss and stamped his character deep into the memory of every man who witnessed the act. Captain William Norwood had been wounded and was unable to command his company of Georgia troops and the Union forces, aware of their opponent's vulnerableness, planned to thrust themselves through the Confederate line and cut General A. P. Hill's division from that of General Stonewall Jackson's. If this feat could have been accomplished the Confederate regiment would have been thrown into a panic and defeat was sure to follow.

It was at this point that "the Fighting Commissary" volunteered his services to replace the wounded Captain Norwood and lead his company into, what seemed to be, imminent defeat. Reluctantly, he was accepted, but what happened within the next few hours of fighting was a far different story. When the order came from the Union forces to charge, Ginter was ready; he gallantly rallied his men and immediately counter-charged into the thick of the battle with such ferocity that the enemy was repulsed almost to defeat, and all further attempts to divide the Confederate line were abandoned. The courage and foresight of "the Fighting Commissary" had saved the day.

The superior officers who witnessed that act of bravery sought to make Ginter a Brigadier-General but all of their undertakings were discouraged by the retiring Commissary. Later, when Dr. Hunter McGuire wished to use this incident in an address on the occasion of the dedication of the Jackson Memorial Hall at the Virginia Military Institute, the reserved Ginter asked him as a personal favor not to use it. Before the end of the war, however, Ginter was made a major, a title that characterized his name for the remainder of his life.

After Appomattox, Ginter turned homeward to Richmond, but it was not the same Richmond that he had left in 1861. Instead of gaiety and splendor he saw only poverty and desolation, and the city that had seemed so promising to him once lay smouldering now in ruins. Desperately he tried to borrow money to open another wholesale drygoods house but the money that Richmond had to offer was worthless. Then he went to New York and there, in partnership with a stock broker who had been in his employ as a clerk prior to the war, he opened a banking house on Wall Street. Here he found that the North had prospered during those eventful years of the Civil War; here also did he discover that the country was not without some stable currency; and here, "in old New York," his birthplace, he found success again.

But the success that Ginter found was doomed to an early failure.

On that memorable "Black Friday" of 1873, his bank too was caught in that undercurrent of crafty Jay Gould's schemes, and like scores of similar concerns, it was swept by the flood downstream to oblivion.

Thus, at fifty years of age, the debonair Major Lewis Ginter was penniless and a failure. He was without a home or means of a livelihood, and with a realization that life meant little to him and his advancing age now, he returned once more to his beloved Richmond. Here among the scenes of his first success his future took on a different aspect, yet little aware was he of the fact that the next enterprise he would enter would elevate him from poverty to that of the richest man in the Southland.

So in 1874, with a willingness to accept work of any kind Major Ginter entered the tobacco firm of John F. Allen and Company, a concern that had been established two years previously for the manufacture of smoking and chewing tobacco. His job was to travel and introduce the company's products to the surrounding retail markets, and it is not doubtful that some of the territory that he visited was the same that *his* salesmen had visited some 20 years prior.

During the course of his travels Major Ginter noticed the use of tobacco in the new form called the "cigarette" which had been introduced by Kinny Brothers of New York and, with the alertness characteristic of his mind, he approached Mr. Allen with the idea of manufacturing them also. Mr. Allen finally consented and in the year of 1875 the "Richmond Gems" were formally placed on their tobacco market. Success was not immediate, for it was not until the following year that Major Ginter made the greatest investment of his career. The occasion for this was the Centennial Exposition at Philadelphia and the Major was right there with an exhibit of his "Richmond Gems" packed in small but attractive packages by his own hands.

Visitors at the Exposition came, saw, and smoked Ginter's "Richmond Gems" and from their reaction the Major could foresee the success of his new enterprise. Before the end of 1876 orders began pouring in from all sections of this country and Europe, and in the years that followed branch distributing offices were set up in London, Paris, and Berlin. It was said that the Sultan of Turkey pushed aside his native product for one of Major Ginter's blends, namely, "Richmond Straight Cut No. 1." Some other brands that were manufactured by Allen and Ginter were: "Perfection," "Napoleon," "Virginia Pets," "Danties," "Duebec," "Virginia Brights," and "Old Dominion."

To his cigarettes Ginter applied not a little of the merchandising that he had learned in his dry-goods business, and the mode of advertising that he adopted to sell his products later became the standard in the American advertising field. Perhaps few today can remember the "Flags of All Nations," or "American Birds," or "Kings and Rulers," or "Actors and Actresses," but each and every package of Ginter's products carried a picture from one of these series inclosed in the package as a premium for the purchaser.

In 1884 Mr. Allen, desirous of retiring from the tobacco business, sold his interest in the company to Major Ginter, who changed the name of the now highly successful firm to "Allen and Ginter." Mr. John Pope, a former messenger boy whom Ginter had befriended when he lived in New York and who was later adopted by the Major, was taken into the new organization to replace Mr. Allen and, with only a few other minor changes, the firm continued to grow by leaps and bounds. In 1888 the company was incorporated and in 1890, upon the formation of the American Tobacco Company, "Allen and Ginter" was made a subsidiary of that corporation. Major Ginter was offered the first presidency of this latter company but declined such an honor because of his advanced age. He remained a director of the American Tobacco Company, however, until his resignation a few months before his death.

From 1890 until his death Major Ginter lived the quiet unassuming life that his heart most desired. He gave up his home that was located next to the corner of Fourth and Cary Streets and built a magnificent brown-stone house at 901 West Franklin Street, which typified the dainty French ideals that dominated his whole life. The house, which is used today as a part of the Richmond Professional Institute of the College of William and Mary, cost Major Ginter $250,000.00, and during his lifetime was the social center of Richmond.

He was a man possessed of delicate refinements and of varied and intricate accomplishments. He always delighted in having his friends near him and even in the fifties, when he maintained an apartment at Eleventh and Bank Streets, he entertained liberally. Whist was his favorite game, but when Major Fred Scott, Captain Frank Chamberlayne, Major Thomas Peyton, Mr. Alexander Cameron, Mr. John Dunlop, and Major Robert Archer were his guests, it was draw poker, and although the limit was twenty-five cents, each player watched his cards as though thousands were at stake.

Perhaps Major Ginter's greatest role as a host was displayed on the occasion of the Fiftieth Anniversary of Rev. Moses D. Hoge's pastorate at the Second Presbyterian Church, which was celebrated at Major Ginter's Franklin Street home on Tuesday evening, February 19, 1895. Among the guests present at that elaborate affair were: Rev. R. P. Kerr, Rev. Hartly Carmichael, Rt. Rev. A. Van De Vyver, Rev.

J. J. Gravatt, Governor Charles T. O'Ferrall, Dr. Hunter McGuire, Mr. James Pleasants, Major F. R. Scott, Mr. John Dunlop, Mr. Joseph Bryan, Dr. W. P. Palmer, Mr. Robert T. Brooke, Mr. William Wirt Henry, Mr. Alexander Cameron, Colonel A. S. Buford, Rev. Moses D. Hoge, and Mr. John Pope. These men were the most prominent in Richmond during the gay nineties, yet each was an intimate friend of the host, Major Ginter.

The genial Major shrank in horror from notoriety and chose, instead, the placid life of an average citizen. He was a model of neatness in both business and pleasure, and though he dressed immaculately at all times, it is said that he purchased his clothes from Richmond concerns only; even though he might be in New York or London he would send to his beloved city for his outfits, accepting without hesitation the wares that her haberdasheries would offer. He was devoted to art and music, and though he possessed some of the finest paintings of his day, only a few of his friends were aware of the fact that he was an accomplished pianist and could speak French and German fluently. Always a constant reader, he admired the works of Edgar Allan Poe most, and was an intimate friend of John R. Thompson, the poet.

Once while visiting in Australia Major Ginter noticed that the business men of Melbourne maintained their residences outside of the city where the home life was quieter and more reserved. On returning to Richmond the Major immediately made plans for a country estate of his own which later took form in the present "Westbrook," located just north of the city limit . This was his favorite abode and it was here that he spent the last years of his life under the watchful eyes of his sister, Mrs. Arents, and her two daughters, Misses Josie and Grace Arents. He spent months in planning the estate, added hundreds of acres to its original plot and spent a fortune in erecting the magnificent house and landscaping the fertile land that surrounded it. Through the entire countryside he built winding roadways and, in order that no harsh object might strike his visitors' eye, he inclosed the adjacent property with beautiful hedges and shrubs. So beautiful was the arrangement of his country home that one distinguished visitor, on beholding the sight for the first time, exclaimed, "This man works like a Pharaoh."

Major Ginter was a Democrat, a Jeffersonian Democrat, to the core. In the middle eighties, when all of his friends in Richmond were joining the ranks of the Whig party, he remained loyal to the Democratic cause. His Jeffersonian attitude can be illustrated better by his connection with the *Times* newspaper which was later (1903) consolidated with the *Dispatch* to form the present Richmond *Times-Dispatch*.

The *Times* was first issued on October 22, 1886, with Captain Page McCarty as Editor-in-Chief. It was a six-column folio and sold for only one cent, but Major Ginter became interested in it at the beginning, and when Captain McCarty suffered financial reverses, he came to his aid and bought the paper. McCarty was retained as president of the paper but a Mr. Robert T. Brooke, a friend of the financiers, was appointed as secretary. On learning of his appointment Mr. Brooke turned to the new owner and said: "But I don't know anything about running a newspaper," to which Major Ginter replied: "Never mind about that; all you've got to do is to come down once a week and pay off."

Major Ginter felt a lively interest in the paper, though he never wrote for it, and occasionally would drop in at the offices on Main Street, between Eighth and Ninth, just to look matters over. Later he sold the paper to Mr. Joseph Bryan, who subsequently consolidated it with the *Whig*.

Characteristic of his Jeffersonian attitude was Major Ginter's reaction to any correction of his use of the double negative. In his public speeches or in his private conversations he persistently used that blemishing combination of words, and on more than one occasion public comment followed his use of it. He would humorously dispose of the matter, however, without the least bit of embarrassment, by saying that more emphasis was derived from the practice of using it.

Thus it is not a wonder that we find a monument of Jefferson guarding the entrance to the hotel that Major Ginter had erected, for Jefferson was the one human he admired most, yet peculiarly enough, the one human he resembled most. Today Valentine's statue of Thomas Jefferson still stands in the lobby of the hotel, the likeness of a statesman, yet a memorial to the man who had put it there, he being too modest and retiring to want a likeness of himself. On the occasion of the opening of the hotel, when he heard that some friends were planning to donate a loving cup to him for his outstanding work, he promptly had the idea dismissed, declaring that he would not accept it if it were offered to him. At another time, when he learned that a movement was on foot to erect a likeness of him as a monument in one of the clubs, he immediately had the movement stopped, which was typical of the "Modest Major Ginter."

Perhaps no other person in the South, during his lifetime, traveled as much as Major Ginter. He circled the globe three times and crossed the Atlantic not less than 30 times, and maintained personal friends in England, France, Germany, Spain, Turkey, Australia, and other parts of the world. It was during his travels that his keen foresight awoke to the realization that Richmond was without a first-class hotel, so, single-handed, he undertook to build one that Richmond would justly be proud to call her own. Today, the Jefferson Hotel stands as a solemn tribute to the memory of Lewis Ginter, the man that conceived the idea and made such an idea a realization.

Moore, *Jefferson Hotel* (1940), pp. 5–18.

"If I Do Not Prove by Bible Authority that the Sun Do Move, I Will Never Preach Again": The Reverend John Jasper

The Reverend John Jasper (1812–1901) was born a slave in Fluvanna County. Spending much of his life in agricultural and industrial slavery, Jasper early came to the ministry. During his years in bondage his preaching was limited because of his social condition coupled with his lack of education. Finally, however, a fellow slave taught him the rudiments of the alphabet, and he delighted in the stories of the Bible, "skipping the long words," he purportedly once said.

Following the Civil War, Jasper soon became a major force in the religious life of Richmond. His most famous sermon, "The Sun Do Move," always guaranteed a full house on the numerous occasions when it was preached. In the body of the sermon, Jasper based his observations on the premise that the Bible was the bed-rock authority for moral as well as scientific truth. So grounded, few could argue against his web of logic.

The gavel with which Richmond's mayor today calls the City Council to order came from timbers of Jasper's home on St. James Street, and the Richmond-Petersburg Turnpike was slightly altered from its course at one spot to spare the Sixth Mount Zion Baptist Church, which was founded by this famous Richmonder.

A little more than a century ago one of Richmond's revered black ministers suddenly became a national celebrity. On the surface of things, the Reverend John Jasper's phenomenal popularity stemmed from one sensational sermon, "The Sun Do Move," which he first preached to an overflow crowd at the Sixth Mount Zion Baptist

Church in March 1878. Although his delivery of this sermon on innumerable occasions in Virginia, Washington, D.C., Philadelphia, and Baltimore won him a national reputation, in Richmond John Jasper's fame and stature long had been secure. Only to a respected preacher would both the *Richmond Daily Dispatch* and the *Whig* give page-one coverage; only a thrilling orator could continuously pack the auditoriums in which he repeated his challenge to Galileo. Following his impressive appearance before a capacity crowd at Richmond's Mozart Hall, Jasper was invited to deliver his sermon before the Virginia General Assembly. "There is no colored preacher in the world," the *New York Times* declared in 1901, "more widely known than the Rev. John Jasper, by reason of his persistent and earnest expounding of the doctrine of 'The Sun Do Move'."

That sermon, the *Times* explained in its article about Jasper's death at age eighty-eight, had been printed in a Richmond paper, and copied in newspapers throughout the country and, later, Europe. Jasper "ministered to the largest colored congregation in the South," the *Times* noted, and "preached his sermon hundreds of times. . . . Up to the time of his death, the bare announcement that he would preach from the old familiar text . . . was sufficient to fill the church to overflowing."

An amazing aspect of "The Sun Do Move" was that Jasper's sermon had little to do with the movement of the sun. Jasper electrified his audiences with "the Lord as a defender of his ancient people," and presented majestic Old Testament examples of the all-conquering power of God. Moreover, at the distance of a hundred years, we can see that John Jasper's historical significance did not rest on his most popular sermon. Of even greater importance than his preaching was his enduring leadership in Richmond's black community during the pivotal years of transition from slavery to freedom.

John Jasper was born on July 4, 1812, in Fluvanna County, Virginia, evidently on a plantation owned by Wilson Miles Cary. . . . Throughout his adult life, until emancipation, John Jasper was hired out as an industrial slave. . . .

Despite his labor in the factory, six days a week, from before dawn until after nightfall, Jasper found some free time for himself on Sundays and holidays. [On] one such occasion, on his twenty-seventh birthday, Jasper experienced a deeply emotional religious conversion that he remembered in every detail for the rest of his life. Walking through great crowds of Fourth of July celebrants at Capitol Square in 1839, Jasper suddenly was "deeply convicted on his sins." After several weeks of increasing distress, on July 25, while stemming tobacco leaves, "the light broke." He came to the conviction that God had assured his salvation and called him to preach. The next year he was baptized and received into membership at Richmond's First Baptist Church, where some two thousand black communicants worshipped in harmony with an even greater number of white members, including Samuel Hargrove, the man for whom Jasper worked. By mutual agreement a year later, in 1841, seventeen hundred black Baptists, including John Jasper, withdrew from the First Baptist Church to form the First African Baptist Church of Richmond.

From 1825 when he first had come to Richmond as a thirteen-year-old youth until he joined the church in 1840 as a man of twenty-eight, Jasper had witnessed the growth of Virginia's capital. According to the 1840 census, Richmond's population was twenty thousand: half were white, two thousand were free blacks, and eight thousand were slaves. Urban life was more varied than rural life, and urban slaves tended to be less restricted by traditional plantation slave codes than their rural counterparts. While the majority of urban slaves worked as domestic servants, many, like Jasper, were hired out as factory hands, draymen, carpenters, stevedores, or common laborers. Others were owned outright by the city or by corporations such as the Tredegar Iron Works. Some factories provided barracks-like buildings for their slaves, others provided hired-out slaves with allowances for living expenses, and others maintained traditional slave quarters on their premises. Apparently John Jasper lived with Samuel Hargrove for about twelve years, until his responsibilities as a husband and father required that he be provided with a separate house. . . .

Beginning in 1828 the Virginia Baptists began to exert greater control over their black churches, while laws passed in 1831 by the General Assembly prohibited slaves and free blacks from assembling for instruction in reading or writing. To become familiar with the Bible, Jasper resorted to underground instruction. He studied a speller for about seven months in 1840 with a slave named William Jackson, and from this limited schooling, he educated himself. So diligently did he study the Bible that, in time, he was said to be able to recite it from memory.

Having successfully educated himself, Jasper was equally determined to preach, despite the state's restrictions. . . . Laws, of course, are not always uniformly enforced, and by 1840 the law prohibiting slaves from preaching frequently was circumvented in special circumstances. When a slave preacher enjoyed the respect and confidence of white civil and religious authorities, he was permitted to participate in religious gatherings, and particularly at funeral services. It was primarily as a funeral preacher that John Jasper exercised his oratorical powers for the quarter of a century before 1865, when the restrictive laws were lifted. . . .

Apparently Jasper's religious work was not limited to funerals. During quiescent times the white minister in charge of a black congregation was present only as a supervisor; the black preacher conducted the service. Jasper preached occasionally at his church in Richmond, and for several years just before the Civil War he served the Third African Baptist Church of Petersburg. He had first preached there when he had been sent by the Richmond African Missionary Society to present the Richmond society's donations to the annual meeting of the society's Foreign Mission Board in Petersburg. After hearing Jasper's sermon his listeners urged him to arrange to be hired out in Petersburg so that he could preach every Sunday. This was not feasible, but he was able to travel to Petersburg to preach on two Sundays each month. In Petersburg he was in great demand as a funeral preacher. He also continued to work actively in his home church as a personal evangelist, religious counselor, and an occasional preacher.

In 1859 Jasper was transferred from the tobacco factory to the rolling mills on the James River just above Richmond. He worked there until Richmond fell in 1865 and frequently preached to the other mill hands. During the war white authorities encouraged Jasper to preach among the sick and wounded in the Chimborazo Hospital. Throughout the war he ministered to the physical wounds and spiritual needs of Confederate soldiers.

With the defeat of the Confederacy in the spring of 1865, slavery was abolished. The Thirteenth Amendment legalized the de facto emancipation initiated by the victorious Union army. Free at the age of fifty-three, John Jasper was determined to achieve his life's ambition to become a fully independent minister and to found a church. But Jasper realized that his dream had to be deferred a little longer while he attended the immediate exigencies of providing for his family. With seventy-three cents in his pocket, but forty-two dollars in debt for house rent, Jasper was desperate to earn a living for his wife, the former Mary Anne Cole, whom he had married in 1863, her daughter, and the nine children of his first marriage.

From April until July 4, 1865, Jasper worked for the city of Richmond cleaning mortar from old bricks in order to rebuild the war-ravaged city. In July he accepted a full-time pastorate at the Third Baptist Church of Petersburg. A year later he went briefly to Weldon, North Carolina, to organize a black Baptist church. Finally, in December 1866, he returned to Richmond to work as a missionary among those in need of practical as well as spiritual guidance in their transition from slavery to freedom. . . .

In the winter of 1867 Jasper began to organize the church that he long had felt was his mission in life. He was the first black minister to form a church in postwar Richmond, but it was an unpromising beginning. At first he held services for nine followers on Brown's Island in the James River in a decrepit stable that had once belonged to the Confederate government. Many of the recently emancipated but unemployed Negroes had taken shelter in abandoned shanties along the river and canal. Drawn by the message of his sermon and his example, these people flocked to Jasper's church, which was officially organized on September 3, 1867, as the Sixth Mount Zion Baptist Church. To accommodate his growing congregation the meeting place successively moved from the stable, to a cabin, to a carpenter's shop at Fourth and Cary streets, to a large room on Cary between Third and Fourth streets. When the congregation became too large for this room, on March 15, 1870, the members bought for two thousand dollars a small brick chapel on the corner of Duval and Saint John streets which had been occupied by the African Methodist Episcopal Zion Church since 1865. The congregation almost immediately outgrew this new home, so the members constructed a substantial annex at the back of the church. In 1870 a Sunday school was organized. Membership grew due to the contagious enthusiasm of John Jasper, and over the years Sixth Mount Zion Baptist Church became the center of religious life in the section of Richmond known as Jackson Ward. By 1887 the original structure had been razed and a large Norman-Gothic edifice of red brick and gray stone had been constructed on the site.

. . . The church's ministry became a monument to the dynamic leadership and oratorical gifts of John Jasper. He became an institution in postwar Richmond, as with regal dignity week after week he led the repentant to be baptized in the James River. On one occasion he baptized more than three hundred converts in four hours. According to the Reverend William Asbury Christian's history of Richmond, the Sunday after the old James River Free Bridge at Ninth Street had been completed in 1873, its endurance was tested as thousands stood on the bridge to watch Jasper baptize fifty-five persons. Meanwhile, Sunday after Sunday, the capacity of his church was tested as hundreds of Richmonders, black and white, crowded into the pews long before the appointed hour to hear his wondrous sermons.

So it was that in March 1878 when Jasper announced that he would preach upon the topic, "The Sun Do Move," the good people of Richmond, even the doubters, knew they would be moved even if the sun stood still. Crowds began to gather several hours early in the streets leading to the church. Well before the service began not even standing room was available as the congregation waited silently and expectantly. "If I do not prove by Bible authority that the sun do move," Jasper proclaimed, "I will never preach again." According to a reporter who had gone as a confirmed skeptic, however, the sermon had little to do with the movement of the sun.

Taking as his text Exodus 15:3 ("The Lord is a man of war. The Lord is his name"), Jasper's greatness as an orator pealed forth in "unmeasured splendor" as he portrayed the power of God to deliver His people. In his triumphant conclusion Jasper polled the congregation, asking everyone who believed that the sun had moved to raise his hand. In what appeared to be a unanimous affirmation, the reporter observed that "the curious result of it all was that Jasper didn't convert me to this theory, nor did he convert me to his religion, but he did convert me to himself. . . . My vote was in favor of Jasper's logic, his genuineness, his originality, his philosophic honesty, and his religion. . . . I felt his greatness."

For more than thirty years the congregation of Sixth Mount Zion Baptist Church had felt their minister's greatness. His sermons drew people to his church, but John Jasper was much more than a great preacher. An educator before his people had public schools, he taught in his church. He developed social service programs to care for orphans and the aged, the infirm and the indigent. And in guiding his flock through the wilderness from slavery to freedom, John Jasper's example was more eloquent than his sermons, his vision more inspiring than his lectures, his dignity more edifying than his discourse. After his death in 1901 at the age of eighty-eight, one of Jasper's faithful converts described the message of his life: "When he went in the streets he was so stately and grave like, that he walked different from all the people. . . . You felt the ground got holy where he went 'long. Some of them say it was equal to a revival to see John Jasper moving like a king 'long the street. . . . Oh, it made us proud just to look at him."

Bratton, "John Jasper of Richmond," *Virginia Cavalcade* 29 (Summer 1979): 32–39

"He Is a Man Who Would Walk into the Jaws of Death to Serve His Race": John Mitchell, Jr.

The late nineteenth and early twentieth centuries have been called the "nadir" period in the history of Afro-Americans—but discrimination and repression could not contain the militant spirit of John Mitchell, Jr. (1863–1929). Born a slave, proud and precocious as a youth, Mitchell for forty-six years served as the outspoken editor of the Richmond *Planet* (the precursor of today's Richmond *Afro-American*). He also enjoyed brief success as a banker and once "was an officer and the sole Negro member of the American Bankers Association." Later, however, he was indicted for illegal business practices; the charges were ultimately quashed, but he died a poor man. From his base in Jackson Ward and as grand chancellor of the Knights of Pythias, he wielded considerable political power and ran for governor in 1921. Because of the commercial enterprise of Mitchell, Giles B. Jackson, Maggie L. Walker (q.v.), and others, Richmond "was considered the most important center of Negro business activity in the world" from 1891 to the 1920s.

Men are brave often from experience with arms and the scenes of war, others because of a recklessness of life and a dare-devil spirit, and still others are born for deeds of bravery and glide as easily to places of danger as if led by unerring instinct; they are bold, aggressive, determined and venturesome. Such a man as the last is John Mitchell, Jr., and it remains yet for history to say for certainty what good July 11, 1863, had in store for the Nation, for on this day he first raised his infant voice. It was when his parents lived in Henrico county, Virginia; they were slaves. His mother was a seamstress and his father was a coach man. From the day of his birth it will be observed that he, too, was a slave. But little does he know of those dark and "cruel slavery days." The sound of cannon, the roar of musketry, the hissing of grape and canister did not go unheeded by his infant ears.

At this time the "Fall of Richmond," the Union sentinels passing back and forward on the streets of the city did not slightly attract his attention. Little fellow that he was, their presence had as much terror for him as they had for the rebels. The "blue coats" mission, however, he could not then understand.

As he grew older, he coupled with his school duties that of the duties of a newsboy, peddling the evening daily papers on the streets of the city, with all the strength of his young life crying "State Journal, here's your State Journal."

He soon became carriage boy for James Lyons, a rich, aristocrat lawyer; he was a typical Southerner who had owned young Mitchell's parents before the war, and consequently had been his "marster." The boy often accompanied him to his farm in Henrico county.

It was here he had the recollection of seeing Jefferson Davis, the ex-President of the Confederate States, and he was reminded that he had a glass eye, a thing that remains fresh in his mind.

He [Lyons] bitterly opposed young Mitchell's being educated, but despite all this his mother kept him at school, taught by Rev. A. Binga, Jr., of Manchester, Virginia. What ability he had, if any existed at that time, seemed latent within him.

In 1876 he entered the Richmond Normal High School. In 1877 he received the silver medal for having stood the highest in a class of thirty pupils.

January 1, 1881, he brought into the school-room a map of Virginia, on which he had spent his Christmas holidays to make it ornamental as well as accurate. His surprise was great when teachers and pupils gathered round and gazed in wonderment upon the production. This he donated to the school upon the suggestion of the principal, and then proceeded to draw another which would render insignificant the work they had taken the pains to praise.

In May, 1871, this production was exhibited. Crowds of pupils gazed thereon; it was taken from him and he heard nothing more of it until at the graduation exercises, Hon. A. M. Riley, who was minister to Austria, and now one of the Judges of the Court of the Khedive of Egypt, saw it and said it was worthy of a special gold medal and he would be the one to present it. This he did June 5, 1881, stating that it was the best production ever executed by any pupil, white or black, in the State.

Young Mitchell stood at the head of his class and won a gold medal offered for that accomplishment. In 1881 he won another gold medal in an oratorical contest in which there were five competitors. He has since drawn a map of Yorktown, surrounded by dignitaries of the Revolutionary War. All this was done with lead pencils which usually cost two cents each. The work resembles the finest steel engraving, and would be readily taken for such. Mr. Mitchell has never received any lessons in the work and this makes it the more surprising. So imbued were his friends with the fine character of the work that they endeavored to secure for him an apprenticeship in the Bureau of Engraving and Printing at Washington, District of Columbia.

August 15, 1881, when Hon. Fred Douglass wrote to Mr. J. W. Cromwell, by whom Mitchell had been sent: "I am much obliged to you; I am glad to have the evidence of the talent and skill afforded in the map of Virginia by your young friend, John Mitchell, Jr., with the industry, patience and perseverance which he has shown in this work, I have no fear but that young Mitchell will make his way in the world and be a credit to our race."

In May, 1878, young Mitchell professed religion and joined the First Baptist church, Richmond. He became an active member of Sunday school, and was made chairman of the executive board of the Virginia Baptist State Sunday school convention. In 1883 and 1884, he was the Richmond correspondent of the New York *Freeman*. December 5, 1884, he assumed the editorial charge of the Richmond *Planet*, which in 1939, became the Richmond AFRO-AMERICAN, making it the oldest secular newspaper in continuous publication.

Mitchell was a bold and fearless writer, carrying out to the letter all he says he will. He gave his attention particularly to Southern outrages of the black people. His exposure of the murder of Banks, a black man, by officer Priddy (white) attracted wide-spread attention. The jury brought in a verdict that the deceased came to his death by some unknown disease and no one was to blame.

Mitchell condemned the crime and declared the officer guilty of murder. He was summoned before the grand jury, an attempt being made to indict him for making such a charge. The case was dropped. He discovered that the man had been unmercifully clubbed by the officer; so he consulted four colored physicians in order to have the body exhumed and the head examined.

After much inquiry, he discovered that the body had been sent to the dead-house of the University of Virginia, Charlottesville. He boarded a train for that place and went into the dead-house; he saw portions of a body which were covered over as he entered. He did not know the victim. He was locked in the dead-house himself, by parties present, but got out, and after hunting for the physician in charge without success, hurried back to Richmond to appear at court the next morning. The officer was never punished; this was a specimen of Southern justice.

The lynching of Richard Walker, in Charlotte county, demonstrated Mr. Mitchell's courage again. This black man was lynched by a mob of white men at Smithville, about eighty-six miles from Richmond, Virginia. Mr. Mitchell condemned the affair and declared that his murderers should be dangled from a rope's end.

This occurred in May, 1886. The editorial appeared on a Saturday, and on the following Monday he received a letter containing a piece of hemp, abusing him and declaring they would hang him, should he put his foot in the county. Mitchell replied that he would visit the county, adding: "There are no terrors, Cassius, in your threats, for I am armed so strong in honesty that they pass me by like the idle winds, which I respect not."

Later on he armed himself with a brace of Smith and Wesson revolvers, went to the scene of the murder, which was five miles from any railroad station, and was locked in the jail for the purpose of inspecting the place where Walker had been found, and returned to Richmond and published an account of his trip.

A short account of him appeared in the New York World on February 22, 1887, where these words depict clearly his character. Said this journal:

> One of the most daring and vigorous Negro editors, is John Mitchell, Jr., editor to the Richmond Planet. The fact that he is a Negro and lives in Richmond, does not prevent him from being courageous almost to a fault.
>
> He is a man who would walk into the jaws of death to serve his race; and his courage is a thing to be admired. Mr. Mitchell is one of the intensest lovers of his race. His pen seems dipped in vitriol and his words are hurled with the force of Milton's Satan, whom we find described as having such strength that his spear, to equal which, the tallest pine hewn on Norwegian hills to be the mast of some great admiral, were but a wand.

For 46 years, Mitchell and the *Planet* were a one-man NAACP.

He also founded the Mechanic Savings Bank and became Grand Chancellor of the Knights of Pythias.

He became a national figure as delegate to two Republican conventions and even a candidate for governor.

"John Mitchell," Richmond *Afro-American*,
20–24 January 1976

"Destined to Make an Indelible Impression": Lila Meade Valentine

If the turn of the nineteenth century in Richmond belonged to Justice Marshall (q.v.) and his distinguished male friends, the turn of the twentieth was, if not dominated, at least greatly influenced by a coterie of remarkable women in the capital city. Intelligent, public-spirited, courageous in battling prejudice and vested interests, these Richmonders carried the burden of forcing progress in many a reform crusade. Working either as individuals or in small groups, and not always agreeing on a particular issue, they included the noted authors Ellen Glasgow (q.v.) and Mary Johnston, as well as Grace Arents, Adele Clark, Mary Munford, Maggie L. Walker (q.v.), and the only woman memorialized by a portrait tablet in the Virginia State Capitol—Lila Meade Valentine (1865–1921). The "tributes" below were written in 1931 by two of her friends and coworkers.

§ Mrs. Lila Meade Valentine

Adele Clark

Lila Meade Valentine, leader of the woman suffrage movement in Virginia, and one of a group of leaders in public education and in public health, a discriminating patron of the arts and a spiritual power in her church, is regarded by many people as one of the great Virginians, not only of her generation but in the history of the State. The years of her life—1865 to 1921—comprised a period of dramatic adjustments in the general social order and in the status of women, and in each movement for progress and for the public welfare she participated. The General Assembly of Virginia in 1926, in voting to authorize the placing of a tablet to her in the State Capitol, adopted a resolution which said in part that the tablet would be erected in recognition of her "sacrificial service in the cause of woman suffrage." Mrs. Valentine's interest in woman suffrage was two-fold—she believed in women and she believed in the extension of democratic government.

Born in Richmond February 4, 1865, Lila Meade, daughter of Richard and Kate Fontaine Meade, was an infant at the time of the evacuation of Richmond by the Confederacy, and grew up in the post-war period when the new South was born. She was educated in Richmond and acquired a knowledge of several languages and of music, as well as of the subjects of a general curriculum. Her marriage to Benjamin Batchelder Valentine occurred in her early twenties, and theirs was a partnership of interests—literary, musical and broadly social.

Mrs. Valentine's home on Third and Cary Streets became the center of numerous activities. Early in her public welfare work was the founding of the Instructive Visiting Nurses' Association, that great force for public health. Public education next engaged her interest, and it was in her home that meetings were held to promote the kindergarten in the public schools, the building of the John Marshall High School and the formation of the Richmond Education Association, of which she was at one time president. She was a prime mover in the survey of educational conditions in Virginia and was a leader in the group which asked the Governor to call a State-wide conference on education, out of which grew the Co-Operative Education Association.

Mrs. Valentine's logic led her to the conviction that woman's interest in public affairs and responsibility for a fair social order required that freedom of action and dignity of status possible only to enfranchised citizens. In 1909 she became actively interested in the suffrage movement, and at a meeting of about a score of women interested in woman suffrage she was unanimously chosen to head the Equal Suffrage League of Virginia, affiliated with the National American Woman Suffrage Association. She was the president of the State league throughout the eleven years of its existence, president of the Richmond league for ten years and honorary president of the Virginia League of Women Voters, the foundation of which she laid.

In the storm of public comment which followed the formation of the Equal Suffrage League of Virginia, Mrs. Valentine remained unshaken in her conviction, and exhibited a tact and graciousness, combined with her spirited championship of the cause of suffrage and her brilliant oratory, that made her a welcome speaker in drawing rooms, courthouses, lecture halls, colleges and universities. She toured the State, speaking in practically every county of Virginia, equally at home at a farmers' picnic, a courthouse green, the State Fair Grounds, a church assembly or a street meeting. Not only did she speak for suffrage in places all over Virginia, but she organized local leagues, and administered from headquarters the Statewide work of the Equal Suffrage League. At the annual convention of the league, over which she presided, her presidential addresses were brilliant features and her parliamentary knowledge made her conduct of meetings a model of the technique of presiding.

Mrs. Valentine's activities for suffrage were not confined to Virginia. She spoke for suffrage in several States, including Pennsylvania and South Carolina, in the latter State addressing the legislature in session. She was a member of the executive council of the National American Woman Suffrage Association. Having many friends in England where she frequently visited, Mrs. Valentine was in close touch with the English movement for suffrage and a sympathizer with the conservative branch of the movement.

In 1912, 1914 and 1916 she conducted the legislative campaign for an amendment to the State Constitution to enfranchise the women of Virginia, and from 1918 to 1920 labored for the passage of and the ratification of the national amendment to the Constitution of the United States for woman suffrage. Her patience in interviewing every member of the Legislature won for her the admiration even of the enemies of woman suffrage. She conducted the memorable hearings on suffrage before the Legislative Committee, arranging her speakers in such a way as to develop the argument together with the dramatic climaxes. By pen as well as speech she constantly presented to the public the reasons for the enfranchisement of women, her favorite simile for the ballot being to describe it as a tool for the building of society and good citizenship.

When the United States entered the World War, Mrs. Valentine, as president of the Equal Suffrage League of Virginia, offered her services and those of the league to the Governor of Virginia. Governor Stuart called upon the league to assist in the recruiting meetings, and Lila Meade Valentine was the first person in Virginia to speak on the streets for recruits. Loving humanity as she did, and with a strong feeling for the ideal of peace, the deep sense of patriotic duty which impelled her in her war work lifted her speeches to a high plane of spiritual and sacrificial appeal.

In 1920 when the ratification of the suffrage amendment to the United States Constitution was imminent, Mrs. Valentine, realizing the need for training in citizenship, asked the University of Virginia to conduct an Institute of Citizenship and Government and to place a citizenship instructor in the extension department. The university, acting favorably upon her suggestion, conducted the second Institute of Citizenship held in the United States and was the first university in the country to place on its staff an instructor in citizenship education. Mrs. Valentine organized a committee of 100 citizens in Virginia to bridge the work of the Equal Suffrage League and the League of Women Voters, which was to be.

Always fragile of body, the strain imposed by her arduous work for suffrage made serious inroads upon her health. The loss of her husband in 1919 was a blow from which she never wholly recovered. She directed from her sick-bed much of the campaign for ratification of the suffrage amendment. Although unable to leave her room she was one of the first women to register as a voter, the registrar coming to her home to enroll her. After an illness of nearly a year, during which she fought the good fight for recovery, she died in July, 1921.

§ Remembering Lila Meade Valentine

Mary Holt W. Carlton

Miss Helen Adams, a retired educator with exceptional talents for teaching young children, reminisced recently about her cousin, Lila Meade Valentine, a participant in the parlor-mapped strategy which produced the Richmond Kindergarten Training School and in whose honor the first kindergarten in the Richmond school system was named. A dynamic crusader, Mrs. Valentine became a figure of international eminence for her leadership in the effort to win the right to vote for women. In 1936, fifteen years after her death at age 56, she was commemorated by Virginia for "service to humanity." A memorial plaque with her likeness chiseled in marble was placed in the chamber of the House of Delegates proclaiming her "greatness in mind and soul."

The greatness of Lila Meade Valentine's spirit is implied in Helen Adams' recollection that "Cousin Lila never held it against anybody who felt differently about things." Mrs. Valentine employed "quiet educational propaganda" to approach the uninformed individual. She was compassionate in her regard for the feelings of those who were frightened by any possible change in the traditional status of women.

Miss Adams came to Richmond from New York City as a youngster, with her mother, a recent widow, and her two brothers, and spent several months with Mrs. Adams' aunt, Mrs. Richard Meade, before moving to 123 South Third Street, where she stayed for about a year.

Kate Fontaine Meade lived at 101 South Third Street with two unmarried daughters. The third daughter, Lila, and her husband, Benjamin Batchelder Valentine, lived in the adjoining house. Helen Adams remembers her cousin Lila as a tall, handsome brunette who refrained from mentioning her cause on any unsuitable occasion:

"She was too sensible to argue with those whose minds were closed to reason." Although, like most of us, she didn't want to be unpopular, her convictions were strong and clear and her patience was enduring.

Helen Adams remembers her cousin particularly for her vivid personality and gracious and generous nature. Although her eyes reflected understanding in their alert sensitivity, they could on provocation become fiery. Yet, far from being a raucous-voiced Amazon suffragette, Mrs. Valentine radiated gentle self-assurance. She was endebted to her father, her husband, and her father-in-law for recognizing the needs of her inquiring mind and for stimulating and encouraging her.

Miss Adams loved her "Cousin Lila" and, although she was too young to understand its import, Helen respected all of Mrs. Valentine's social concerns: her interest in the public schools and playgrounds, the Richmond Education Association, the Anti-Tuberculosis Auxiliary, and the Instructive Visiting Nurses Association. Lila Meade Valentine's life was filled with "the fury of doing." Helen Adams felt "very close to her. It was impossible to dislike her."

An old photograph reveals Mr. and Mrs. Ben Valentine at their home, in a formal garden with an ivied wall and pachysandra. He is reading to her as they stand in a walkway bordered by a row of tulips; for she was handicapped by poor eyesight. She and her husband shared many interests. Their living room, a large pleasant place lined with bookshelves and pictures, and furnished with comfortable chairs (some wicker), was the setting for social betterment meetings.

Miss Adams remembers the informal meals in the Valentine home and the pleasure of conversation with a small group. It was "Cousin Lila" who gave Helen the pale blue satin dress and her debutante party at 816 West Grace Street.

Lila Meade Valentine has been destined to make an indelible impression on those like Helen Adams in all future generations.

"Lila Meade Valentine," *Richmond Quarterly* 2 (Fall 1979):
33–37

"Maggie, with a Radiant Disposition, Helped in Any Way She Could": Maggie L. Walker

The axiom that "character must be equal to adversity" could have been the personal credo of Maggie Lena Walker (1867–1934), a pioneer in several fields despite the severe obstacles of sex and racial discrimination and physical affliction. Born on Church Hill to parents employed by former Union spy Elizabeth Van Lew, she shared Miss Van Lew's rock-ribbed determination to follow the course she felt was right, community pressures to the contrary. Perhaps best-known today as the first woman bank president in America, Maggie Walker oversaw the diverse activities of an important black fraternal society, was a crusading journalist, ran for state political office in 1921, and provided leadership in the local NAACP and other organizations. Crippled by an accident in 1906, she became a paraplegic—a stunning handicap but one that scarcely diminished the pace and scope of her remarkable endeavors. Her home, at 110½ East Leigh Street in Jackson Ward, now stands as a memorial to her and has been designated a National Historic Landmark. The portrait below comes from a book on notable black Americans and was written by Professor Benjamin G. Brawley (1882–1939) of Howard University.

On the afternoon of Sunday, November 30, 1924, there was a host of people assembled in the City Auditorium in Richmond, Virginia. The weather was chill and threatening; but as early as one o'clock they began to come, and two hours later the throng was unprecedented. Visitors had come from other cities; civic leaders and ministers gave the support of their presence; and the Governor of the Commonwealth, E. Lee Trinkle, added his word of praise, saying, "If the State of Virginia had done no more in fifty years with the funds spent on the education of the Negroes than educate Mrs. Walker, the State would have been amply repaid for its outlay and efforts."

Who was the woman who was thus so signally honored?

Maggie Lena Mitchell was born in Richmond July 15, 1867, and died December 15, 1934. Her mother, early left a widow, lived in an alley and worked hard at the washtub to support the children in her care. Maggie, with a radiant disposition, helped in any way she could, and in 1883, when not quite sixteen years of age, was duly graduated from high school. Already serious far beyond her age, she became a teacher, but, being drawn to business, left the schoolroom to take a course in this field, and in 1889 became the executive secretary of the Independent Order of St. Luke. Ten years later she became the secretary-treasurer of the organization, a position which she held for thirty-five years. Meanwhile, in 1890, she was married to Armstead Walker, and in course of time became the mother of two sons.

The original idea behind the Order of St. Luke was that of many similar organizations, by small weekly dues to assist a man or woman to provide against sickness in old age and for funeral expenses. There had been many such orders or societies in the South; Virginia seemed to have more than her share; and sometimes they had not been very well managed. The history of St. Luke was to be different. Thanks to the initiative and energy of a consecrated woman, it was to set a new standard and show what at least was possible in all such enterprises.

When Mrs. Walker began her work with the organization, she received as her salary only eight dollars a month, and for this sum she was expected to collect dues, verify cases of illness and death, keep the books, and pay out all claims as they were due. She looked not at the reward, however, but at the opportunity; and she had vision. If the Order could help a thousand persons, why not ten thousand, a hundred thousand? And why should it think only of sickness and death? Why should it not train the people to save and invest their money, to own their homes, and to win their way to independence? Why should it not also teach the children thrift, letting them learn the value of their pennies, and telling them to avoid extravagance or waste?

With such an aim, and with her genius, Maggie L. Walker had the energy of a dozen women, and all who came into her presence felt the inspiration of her character. She seemed to think in big terms, and lived in a realm above things little or mean. Eminently religious, she appealed to the solid, church-going element in the city, and helped in ways innumerable. When she took charge of the Order, it had 3,408 members, but no reserve fund and no home property. At the time of the testimonial in 1924, it had 100,000 members, a building costing $100,000, an emergency fund of $70,000, and a newspaper, the *St. Luke Herald*. Fifty-five clerks were employed in the home office; there were 145 field workers; and 15,000 children were enrolled in the thrift clubs.

As the organization grew and the volume of its business increased, the need of a bank was felt. Accordingly in 1902 Mrs. Walker brought before her council the plan of the St. Luke Penny Savings Bank. Though this bore the name of the order, it was legally to be separate. She was able to convince her hearers, and became the president of the new enterprise. As with insurance, she had to learn the business from the ground up as well as she could; but again her faith and initiative told, and the institution became in time the St. Luke Bank and Trust Company, a depository for gas and water accounts in Richmond, and for city taxes.

"When any of our girls are advanced to making as much as fifty dollars a month," said Mrs. Walker, "we begin to persuade them to buy a home. As soon as they save enough for the first payment, the bank will help them out. There is a woman in the office here who came to us eighteen years ago. She did odd jobs of cleaning, and we paid her a dollar a week, which she was glad to get. But we encouraged her to fit herself for better things. She studied, took a business course at night school, and has worked her way up until now she is our head bookkeeper, with a salary of one hundred and fifty dollars a month. She owns a nice home, well furnished and fully paid for, and has money in the bank.

"Then there was that one-legged little bootblack at Second and Cary Streets. He joined our Order. He had a rented chair out on the sidewalk in the weather. We helped him save, and when he had fifty dollars, we helped him rent a little place with three chairs. That was seven years ago. Now he has a place of his own with twelve chairs. He has bought a home for his mother—paid $1,900 for it—and has it furnished and free of debt. And his bank account never falls below five hundred dollars.

"Numbers of our children have bank accounts of from one hundred to four hundred dollars. They sell papers, cut grass, do chores, run errands, work in stores Saturdays. We teach them to save with the definite purpose of wise use of the money. We do a great deal of the same kind of work with the grown people. Our bank lends money for home-building at six per cent, and we tide the deserving ones over times of trouble. Six hundred and forty-five homes have been entirely paid for through our bank's help."

This same spirit went over into community and interracial work. When Mrs. Janie Porter Barrett, another noble spirit, was founding the home for delinquent Negro girls at Peake, eighteen miles from Richmond, and needed money to pay for the tract of a hundred and forty acres, Mrs. Walker organized a Council of Women with fourteen hundred members, and thus raised the first five thousand dollars necessary for the purchase of the farm. Later she contributed liberally of her own means according as the home had need.

From this service for the unfortunate developed community work in Richmond. "The white women began it," said Mrs. Walker. "You know what some of them have done here—women who stand at the top socially and who are leaders in the church and the club life of the city and state. They had done fine community work for white people, and at length they went to our preachers and asked them to invite their leading women to a conference. As a result we began some forms of community work. Then a philanthropist who gave the white women a house for a working girls' home said that if we colored women would show our interest in social work among our people by raising a thousand dollars for it, he would give us the use of a large house, and if we made good, he would deed it to a board of white and colored women.

"You know we had to make good after that. We raised the thousand dollars, and we have kept right on. The house has been deeded now to our bi-racial board. The white women don't work for us,—they work with us; and they've helped us to connect up with every charitable organization in the city. We have four paid workers, and the Community House is just such a center of influence as we have needed all these years."

Meanwhile Mrs. Walker's influence was widening. A tall, large woman with clear kindly eyes and a firm mouth, she was a marked figure in any assemblage. She became president of the state branch of the National Association of Colored Women, and served on numerous other boards and councils. All the while she was working not for a day or a year but the large future. It was her desire to have the Order of St. Luke and the bank on such a basis that they could still move steadily forward when she was gone. Most admirably did she succeed in her endeavor.

Let no one think that she did not have her trials and sorrows. With all of her generosity there were those who were envious or jealous, and even in the Order itself she more than once had to face intrigue. Then suddenly came the hardest blow of all, one under which any heart, however brave, would have quailed. Her husband, mistaken for a burglar, was shot by one of his sons. Dark days followed, but for the mother it was the breaking of sunlight when the young man was exonerated in court. Later she had a fall, one from which she never recovered; still she gave of her best, never faltering. Thus it was that she became one of the noblest of Negro Builders.

Brawley, "Maggie Walker," *Negro Builders* (1937), pp. 267–71

"Richmond Was . . . a State of Mind": Cabell and Glasgow's Richmond

Richmond was planned as a commercial venture, but it has always been a cultural city as well. Although residents have worked in iron manufacturing, tobacco marketing, and flour exporting, plus scores of other businesses, there have always been those whose interests lay in books and artistic ventures. Perhaps the best testament to Richmond's intellectual life, aside from the continuing lecture series sponsored by various groups, the Richmond Symphony, the Virginia Museum of Fine Arts, and other similar organizations, is its institutions of higher learning. Richmond is the site of four such institutions: the University of Richmond (1832), Virginia Union University (1899), Virginia Commonwealth University (1838), and Union Theological Seminary (1812).

In the following selection Maurice Duke (1934–) traces the history of reading, writing, and theatergoing in Richmond. Although these kinds of activities are often the pursuits of the leisure class, they nonetheless give a community its intellectual uniqueness. Duke is a native Richmonder and professor of English at Virginia Commonwealth University. The author of books and articles on American literature, he was for twelve years book editor of the Richmond *Times-Dispatch*.

Because the history of Richmond parallels so closely that of the country as a whole, a thorough study of the life of the city inevitably leads one to considerations beyond rigid geographic confines. The purpose of this paper is not, however, to chart in detail the growth of the capital of Virginia. That story has already been set forth in a number of books, which, taken together, present in minute detail nearly all the facts one would want concerning the city. Although I do plan to trace the history of the city, placing its story in the overall context of American life in the last century, I want to focus primarily on Richmond's cultural life—the people's reading habits, the theater and the writing tradition, all of which combined to produce a major part of the day-to-day living in the city. . . .

§ The Reading

Although at present Richmond is served primarily by three newspapers, there has been since the beginning of the city an impressive number of such publications. The first great newspaper to be established was the *Richmond Enquirer*, which made its appearance in 1804 and lasted until 1877. The other major newspapers of the nineteenth century were the *Richmond Dispatch*, which ran from 1850 to 1903; the *Richmond Examiner*, from 1847 to 1867; and the *Richmond Whig*, published from 1824 to 1888. While these papers were serving the city during the entirety of the last century, a number of similar but smaller publications came and went, some of them lasting only one or two issues, others living on for a decade or more. Significantly, slightly more than one hundred and fifty newspapers were founded in Richmond between 1804 and the close of the century.

Richmonders of the last century read much more than their local newspapers, however. Since its earliest years Richmond has been a city whose residents have been interested in books. During the early years the majority of books bought and read in the city came from Europe, primarily England and France, but the Greek and Roman classics also played a large part in the forming of many young Richmonders' ideas, with numerous such books being available in the small Richmond library as well as on the local booksellers' shelves and in many private homes. Richmonders also reflected the tastes of the rest of the country, particularly the South, in their interest in the novels of Scott and Cooper, which were avidly read.

Interest in books was evident in the Virginia colony from its earliest days, and records of what the early residents read have been sufficiently preserved so that we are able to compile impressive lists of actual titles. Speaking of eighteenth-century Virginians, one historian has noted that it "is astonishing to find how closely these colonials followed the reading habits of England," and Richmond appears to have been little different from the state at large. Although it must be admitted that most of the extant lists apply to the state rather than to the city, several documents do survive to tell us something about reading habits and tastes in nineteenth-century Richmond in particular.

Early in the nineteenth century, for example, a lady named Maria Martini, who with her husband taught school in various Virginia localities, began keeping a list of the books she had read and where she had read them. The list began with the simple statement "Books read in Augusta County, Va., from May 1806 unto April 1807" and continued until November 1822, the date of the last entry. During these years Mrs. Martini, who had been born in London and who had come to America when she was twelve years old, spent time in Richmond —from September 1813 until January 1814 and then several years later for an undetermined period. One scholar has observed that "books were evidently plentiful in Richmond," inasmuch as during her first stay Mrs. Martini lists eighty-nine volumes which she read while there. When she finally left the city to take up residence in Prince Edward County, where she and her husband accepted teaching posts, she noted having read a total of 628 books while in the city. Whether or not her claims are entirely factual may very well be open to discussion; however, she does list the books by title, indicating that they most probably were available in the city. Among the authors of works she speaks of having read are James Boswell, Edmund Burke, Samuel Richardson, Henry Fielding, Laurence Sterne, Maria Edgeworth, Ann Radcliffe, John Locke, Thomas Love Peacock, François Chateaubriand, and, of course, the current best-seller, Sir Walter Scott, under whose name eleven novels are listed.

Information concerning Richmonders' reading tastes during the nineteenth century can also be obtained from an extant copy of the 1855 *Catalogue of Books in the Richmond Athenaeum Building*. The catalogue is located in the Richmond Public Library. Begun in 1812 as a public library venture in the city, the Christian Library, as the space in the Athenaeum Building which was allotted to the library was called, served Richmond's reading public until about the time of the Civil War. Prior to 1812 there had been—by 1785 to be exact—the Richmond Library, whose records I have been unable to locate. After the closing of the Christian Library there was no public library until Thomas Nelson Page founded the Rosemary Library in memory of his wife in 1890.

The catalogue of the Christian Library is 107 pages long and lists about 1,500 volumes under seventeen different headings. Among them are "Theology"; "Philosophy, Mental and Moral"; "Natural Sciences"; "Philology, including numerous books from the Greek and Roman classics"; "History and Historical Biography," the most numerous holdings of which are in the history of France, of Great Britain, and of America; and "Belles Lettres and History of Literature." The list of books in this last section might almost be a catalogue of primary major works in English literature to 1855, works by most of the standard authors being listed there.

For example, one finds there substantial or complete works in "English and American Poetry" by the following authors: Joseph Addison,

Mark Akenside, Samuel Butler, Lord Byron, Geoffrey Chaucer, Samuel Taylor Coleridge, William Congreve, William Cowper, John Dryden, John Keats, Charles Lamb, James Macpherson, John Milton, Thomas Moore, Edgar Allan Poe, Alexander Pope, Matthew Prior, Sir Walter Scott, William Shakespeare, Percy Bysshe Shelley, Edmund Spenser, the Earl of Surrey (Henry Howard), Jonathan Swift, Edmund Waller, William Wordsworth, Sir Thomas Wyatt, and Edward Young.

English drama is represented in the catalogue of the Christian Library by such playwrights as William Congreve, John Horne, Ben Jonson, Bulwer-Lytton, John Marston, William Shakespeare, and James Shirley, plus a ten-volume work, being "a collection of successful modern plays as acted at the theatres royal, London."

Under the category of English and American Novels and Translations one finds in the catalogue such titles and names as *Arabian Nights*, Boccaccio, Miguel Cervantes, Fanny Burney, John Esten Cooke, James Fenimore Cooper, Daniel Defoe, Alexandre Dumas, Maria Edgeworth, Henry Fielding, Oliver Goldsmith, James Hogg, Dr. Samuel Johnson, Washington Irving, John Pendleton Kennedy, *The Lamplighter*, Bulwer-Lytton, Henry Mackenzie, Captain Frederick Marryat, a fifty-volume set of British novelists "with an essay and Prefaces biographical and critical by Mrs. Barbauld," James Kirke Paulding, François Rabelais, Mrs. Radcliffe, Clara Reeve, Samuel Richardson, Sir Walter Scott, Miss Sedgwick, Tobias Smollett, Laurence Sterne, William Makepeace Thackeray, and Horace Walpole. Present also are some thirty-two titles on the history of English and American literature plus substantial collections titled "French Writers in Verse and Prose," "Italian Literature and History of Literature," "Spanish Literature," "German Literature," "English and American Classics, In Prose, Essayists," and so on. How much this collection was actually used is not possible to determine. Obviously, however, a number of free library books were available to residents of the city.

During the time that the Christian Library was in full operation, the State Library, which was then housed in the Capitol building in Richmond, held some 14,000 volumes. Although we do not know its exact contents, there is little reason to assume that this collection differed significantly in character from that of the Christian Library, with, of course, the exception of including numerous state papers.

§ The Theater

In addition to having available numerous newspapers and books, nineteenth-century Richmond was also the site of a very active theater. The date of the founding of the first theater in Richmond is unknown, but it is most probable that the colonial acting companies, who usually traveled by water, began to come to the city shortly after it became the capital of Virginia in 1779. At any rate, we do know that there was a theater in operation in the early 1780s, although where it was located is not known. Most of what went on the boards in Richmond during the decade of the 1780s was typical eighteenth-century fare, complete with numerous Shakespeare plays, which were popular at the time.

As the eighteenth century gave way to the nineteenth, Richmond theater gained in importance, with a major playhouse being built on Shockoe Hill, now the site of the business district but at that time one of the prominent residential areas in the city. Numerous companies with varied repertories began coming regularly to town, and so important did the theater become that there have been recorded "the initial performance of twenty-four English plays which were produced in Richmond before they are known to have appeared elsewhere in America." As the new century began moving forward, the theater in Richmond gained significantly in importance until 1811, when, on December 26, the Richmond Theater burned, claiming the lives of seventy-two persons. Among the victims were some of Richmond's leading residents, including the governor of the state, who initially escaped the fire but lost his life when he returned to the burning building in an attempt to save a child who was his ward.

Following the tragic theater fire, the city was without a playhouse for eight years. But in the early summer of 1819 the Marshall Theatre was opened, and once again Shakespeare, the eighteenth-century standard fare, and American plays, and later the talented vocalist Jenny Lind, vied for favor in the city. Theatergoing in Richmond remained quite popular even through the dark years of the Confederacy, at which time the city's largely transient population still looked forward to the nightly performances. Following the war, the city continued to enjoy the performances of the "leading actors of the time —including the Booths and lovable Joe Jefferson," who came to the city even while it was undergoing the throes of Reconstruction. By the summer of 1870, the noted Edwin Forrest was in the city to present Shakespeare's *Othello*. Indeed, throughout the century, the well-known actors from the United States and abroad continued to visit Richmond, where they apparently always found receptive audiences.

In the summer of 1874 Joe Jefferson returned as Rip Van Winkle, perhaps his most famous role, and the same year saw the appearance of Charlotte Cushman, Lawrence Barrett, and Janauschek. In 1877 Adelaide Nelson appeared in *Romeo and Juliet*, followed by Kate Claxton in *The Two Orphans*. In 1879 Sir Law Barrett did *Hamlet* and T. C. Bangs did *Julius Caesar*. Toward the end of the century, in January 1896, Sir Henry Irving was lavishly entertained in the city and afterwards appeared in *The Merchant of Venice*. Besides the major figures who regularly included Richmond on their tours, there were regional and local troupes who supplied the city with dramatic entertainment during the whole of the nineteenth century.

§ The Writing

In addition to the drama, writing played a significant role in Richmond during the last century, but when one begins to compile a list of the writers of that era he runs the risk of indulging in what H. L. Mencken, in the "Sahara of the Bozart" essay, called "curious sidelights upon the ex-Confederate mind!" Richmond writers of the last century numbered, as well as I have been able to determine, somewhere around fifty, but either they were unknown beyond the confines of the areas in which they lived or their reputations have declined so markedly that even few specialists in American literature would recognize them. A number of the better-known authors from the city deserve mention, however.

Among the earliest Richmond writers whose reputations survive on the national level are such figures as William Byrd, Thomas Jefferson, William Wirt, and Chief Justice John Marshall. Added to these are such names as Dr. George William Bagby, the popular humor writer whose reputation, although modest, was nevertheless nationwide; Mary Johnston, who began publishing her romantic historical novels just before the close of the century; Thomas Nelson Page, the celebrated writer of stories in black dialect; and Father John Banister Tabb, whose poetry, once quite popular, is all but forgotten today.

Without doubt, however, the most significant literary person and the most significant publication associated with Richmond in the last century were Edgar Allan Poe and the *Southern Literary Messenger*. Founded by Thomas Willis White of Yorktown in August of 1834, the *Southern Literary Messenger* during its day was one of the major literary periodicals, publishing works by Southerners and Northerners alike, many of whom were well-known figures of the day. A year after the

Messenger began, White offered Poe, who had been reared largely in Richmond but had been living away from the city for a number of years, a staff position, which he readily accepted. Poe was at this time of his life anxious to gain the experience of editing a magazine, and moreover he wanted to return to Richmond. He had been raised there in the home of the merchant John Allan, after the death of his mother. (She, incidentally, had come to the city in 1811 with her three children after accepting an actress's role at the Richmond Theater.) Poe stayed on with the *Messenger* until 1837, at which time he went north, once again, as was his nature, in search of greater opportunities. Under his editorship, however, the journal prospered. Its name, along with that of Poe, has become a permanent fixture in Richmond literature and culture.

In addition to the native authors, Richmonders during the nineteenth century also had contact with many international writers of the first rank, who often included the city on their agendas when they came touring from abroad. Dickens visited the city in March of 1842 and was lavishly entertained. Thackeray, Matthew Arnold, and Oscar Wilde also visited Richmond over the years of the last century, each in turn speaking to receptive audiences, although Wilde, who arrived in the summer of 1882, was described by Richmond's major historian as "a queer Englishman, who . . . appeared on the stage in knee britches, ruffled shirt, a big sunflower on his coat, and his long hair parted in the middle and falling upon his shoulders." These figures, both from Richmond and abroad, made the city a kind of center for literature below the Potomac during the whole of the nineteenth century. It would not be until the decade of the 1920s, however, that the city would come to be known nationwide for such writers as Ellen Glasgow and James Branch Cabell and for another literary publication, *The Reviewer*, together bringing to town such people as H. L. Mencken, Joseph Hergesheimer, Carl Van Vechten, Hugh Walpole, and Burton Rascoe. (It was also the site of one of the annual meetings of the Modern Language Association.)

§ Conclusion

From the vantage point of time one can see how a viable and readily functional myth came to grow and be accepted by Richmonders who were born in the decades following the Civil War. To many of these people Richmond was perhaps as much a state of mind as it was a geographic locale, and Richmond's former days represented a time during which, because idealized, the city seemed somewhat larger than life. Richmond of the past had witnessed the American Revolution, the War of 1812, the coming and passing of the Confederate government, military defeat, and Reconstruction. Moreover, Richmond, basically a commercial city, had a tradition of at least some interest in books, the theater, and the arts in general. Taken together, all of these various facets of Richmond's past, unified by the city's longevity, often led Richmonders of the post-Reconstruction era, rightly or wrongly, to view themselves as unique. . . .

Duke, "Cabell and Glasgow's Richmond," *Mississippi Quarterly* 27 (Fall 1974): 375–85

"Georgian Morality, Victorian Prudery, and Post-Civil War Neuroses": Ellen Glasgow and James Branch Cabell

Raised by a strict Presbyterian father, of whom she once wrote, "he never committed a pleasure," Ellen Glasgow was a self-styled early feminist who became a major force in American literature around the turn of the century. Attractive and precocious, she spent most of her life at the family home at One West Main Street in Richmond. As a child, Glasgow was given no formal education, but she more than compensated for its lack by wide reading. Owing to personal tragedies, coupled with her unhappy ventures in love, she early adopted a cynical and fatalistic view of society. Couched in the realistic mode of fiction made popular by the influential William Dean Howells, her female characters are generally stronger than are her males, who are sometimes dissolute, sometimes boorish. Although strongly tinged with an aura of romantic idealism, Glasgow's novels are models of a new kind of Southern fiction, making her one of the major writers of her time and one whose influence was wide and lasting. She received a Pulitzer Prize in 1942 for *In This Our Life*. Her autobiography, *The Woman Within* (1954), was published posthumously.

Born at the site of the present Richmond Public Library—near where the rare book room is located, he once wryly remarked—Cabell was a contemporary and friend of Ellen Glasgow. Their fiction, however, is quite different; his is in the vein of fantasy, hers is in the more conventional realistic mode. Cabell was graduated from the College of William and Mary and worked for a time as a newspaper reporter, both in New York City and in Richmond. Around the turn of the century he began publishing romantic stories, which were in vogue in the magazines of the era. Soon, however, he began to infuse the delicately wrought tales with strains of irony and sexual innuendo. Largely ignored in his early years, Cabell published *Jurgen* in 1919, and immediately his name and that of the title of the book, taken from the name of the main character, became household words. *Jurgen* was seized by the New York Society for the Suppression of Vice on the charges that it was "a lewd, lascivious, indecent, obscene and disgusting book." Such advertisement insured Cabell overnight fame, and when the book was cleared, a call for a collected edition of his works was answered by his publishers with the eighteen-volume Storisende Edition. Cabell wrote a total of fifty-two books, most of them in the ironic fantasy mode, but he never again achieved the fame brought by *Jurgen*. He married twice, the first time to Priscilla Bradley and upon her death to Margaret Waller Freeman, who, with Emily Clark, was one of the founders and editors of the *Reviewer*.

In the following selection, Edgar E. MacDonald (1919–), a Richmond native and a scholar of both authors' works, places Glasgow and Cabell in context against the city in which they lived most of their lives.

§ I

When Henry James visited Richmond in the winter of 1906, he expected to find still vibrant in the air some of the tragic glamor that had been associated with the name of the capital of the Confederacy. He had envisioned a "ghost-haunted city," but to his dismay it appeared to him "simply blank and void." True there was ice on the streets so that the populace kept close to their grates and the sweet gardens lay symbolically dormant. For James, there were no "references" in the romantic tradition apparent; then he realized that "the large, sad poorness was in itself a reference." He surveyed the desolate scene and wrote mournfully of the low aesthetic level, antedating the sage of Baltimore by some years. As he wandered about the White House of the Confederacy, he mused on the sorry objects of veneration. "It was impossible . . . to imagine a community, of equal size, more disinherited of art or of letters. . . . The social revolution had begotten neither song nor story—only, for literature, two or three biographies of soldiers, written in other countries." While James composed this dirge in the solid, Edwardian comfort of the Jefferson Hotel, he seemed remarkably unaware that scarcely more than a block away on Main Street a thirty-two-year-old Ellen Glasgow had already published six novels, three of which were to merit prefaces for later editions—prefaces, ironically enough, compared with his own for excellence. The social revolution that James in 1906 felt was neglected and therefore so unproductive of song and story was the very soul and theme of the six-year-old *The Voice of the People* and the two-year-old *The Deliverance.* If James was ignorant of these "social histories" and their author, Miss Glasgow was nevertheless aware of Henry James. In 1906, James was also unaware of the twenty-seven-year-old James Branch Cabell, who had enjoyed a modest success with his first attempt at a comedy of manners, *The Eagle's Shadow* (1904), and whose short stories were appearing in respectable magazines. While James's assessment of the cultural scene in Richmond appears unflattering to the two embryonic writers, they both echoed his judgment in their later assessments.

After their attainments were recognized, both Ellen Glasgow and James Branch Cabell commented at some length on the absence of a great literature in the South prior to their day. In her preface to *The Miller of Old Church,* she cited the apology of John Esten Cooke in his "Virginia Literature in the Nineteenth Century": "It may be said of it with truth that it is notable for its respect for good morals and manners; that it is nowhere offensive to delicacy or piety; or endeavors to instill a belief in what ought not to be believed." Ellen Glasgow more forthrightly suggested that the South, Virginia in particular, produced no great works because of its complacency, its blind contentment, its moral superstition, resulting in a literature of evasion. Inasmuch as the region produced great men, if not great writers, she went on to suggest "that the creative art of the South was not a substitute for experience but experience itself, circumscribed and intensified." In short, the art of life was in living, not in contemplation. In his turn, James Branch Cabell, in his "Mr. Ritchie of Richmond," cited Agnes M. Bondurant's *Poe's Richmond.* " 'It was not the planters'—that is, the landed aristocracy of Virginia—'but the professional and businessmen of Richmond who were responsible for the promotion of literary culture in the city. These were the people who showed enough appreciation for Dickens and Thackeray to give them pleasant receptions.' " Mr. Thomas Ritchie was the toastmaster at the *petit souper* which some ninety of Richmond's merchants and tobacconists tendered Charles Dickens on his visit to the city. Mr. Ritchie admitted that he, a semiretired editor of the *Richmond Enquirer*, was the only one present who might qualify as being literary. He explained that "the *forte* of the Old Dominion [was] to be found in the masculine production of her statesmen . . . who have never indulged in works of imagination, in the charms of romance, or in the mere beauties of the *belles lettres*." Oratory, richly elegiac, served the literary hungers of most southerners. Cabell went on to reflect that even in his day the businessmen ran Virginia's colleges, its symphonies, its museum of fine arts, "while the culture of Virginia, as thus comfortably conducted, has proved to be sterile in every field of aesthetics—except only, as I have suggested elsewhere, in the superb and philanthropic romanticizing of Virginia history and in a free-spirited invention of priorities and relics." Though Cabell made these observations over twenty-five years ago, today he could still observe that "throughout all Virginia, Mr. Thomas Ritchie, under one or another alias, is still talking."

If the literary tradition was oral, the great theme, infinitely embroidered during the early years of both writers, was the war. In "Almost Touching the Confederacy" and "As to Childish Matters of Long Ago," Cabell gives us two charming insights into the Richmond of his childhood. In the former essay, he marveled at the creation by his elders of the noble myth "of the Old South's perfection," of their "half-mythopoeic and half-critical frame of mind" which allowed them to talk one way upon a platform and another way "in your father's drugstore." Ellen Glasgow, in her preface to *The Battle-Ground*, also comments in some wonder on the "chanting chorus of male and female voices" which during her childhood recounted the heroic legends of the Lost Cause. A grimly realistic Ellen Glasgow would observe, "A War in which one had lost everything, even the right to own a doll with real hair, was not precisely my idea of romance." Much later, after she had written *Virginia*, Ellen Glasgow recounts the visit she received from the elderly widow who reproved her for not "writing about the War." " 'If only I had your gifts, I should devote them to proving to the world that the Confederacy was right. Of course, I know that even the best novelists are no longer so improving as they used to be; but I have always hoped that either you or Annie Cabell's son would write another *Surry of the Eagle's Nest*.' " Significantly, while both authors eschewed the historical and sentimental romance that might have appealed to the tastes of Richmonders, it was those same sentimentalists who served the two writers as the basic model for their fictional "heroes."

§ II

In his treatise on *The American Novel and Its Tradition*, Richard Chase sees the distinction between British and American as essentially the novel of manners versus the romance, the former realistic and "staunchly middlebrow," the latter abstract, probing the extreme ranges of experience. The history of the American novel also marks the rise of realism, but Chase does not equate the realistic novel with the novel of manners. The latter

> is distinguished from the novel in general because it concentrates so calculatedly on manners, because it focuses on a particular social class or group of classes above the lower economic levels, and because it has an affinity in tone and method with the high comedy of the stage. Most important of all, such moral standards as are advanced by the author are those of a society . . . or have, at least, a concrete social sanction and utility.

He goes on to add:

> Only in Cooper's New York and Westchester, in old New England, in the Old South, in Mrs. Wharton's New York, in Ellen Glasgow's Richmond, and perhaps one or two other places, like G. W. Cable's New Orleans, have there been momentarily settled social conditions involving contrasting classes with contrasting manners.

Ellen Glasgow's *Romantic Comedians* and *They Stooped to Folly* are prime examples of the novel of manners in America, but even her sociological studies of the rising lower and middle classes in such early works as *The Voice of the People* and *One Man in His Time* are predicated on a social structure that recognized class distinctions. While the Civil War destroyed a multiple class structure in the South—slave, free Negro, poor white, merchant, planter—the fifty-year hiatus between that war and World War I was marked by an accompanying economic stagnation that essentially prolonged black slavery and retarded the evolution of class structures among the whites. In addition, Richmond as a symbol of the defeated South, a city which had known the vicissitudes of war including occupation, enjoyed its own heightened sense of fallen grandeur. It was Troy, it was Rome. It was a mythic city along with Charleston and New Orleans. In time, its myths became salable products, like its antiques.

Georgian morality, Victorian prudery, and post-Civil War neuroses combined to give Richmond its defined class structure and its social

attitudes, attitudes sharpened by the general poverty of the Reconstruction period. Both Ellen Glasgow and James Branch Cabell commented at various times on the strictures of the accepted mores; they
permeate the Glasgow opera and are reflected in much of Cabell's
work. Ellen Glasgow wrote, "Even in the Richmond of my childhood
certain imponderables were more precious than wealth," but went on
to add that gradually "imponderables might be respected, but possessions were envied." Like most older cities that did not change too
rapidly, Richmond had its distinctive criteria as to social rank, and the
people whose names were known fell into three general classifica-
tions: the old families, the old citizens, and the old merchants. The
old families were those whose ancestors had been prominent office-
holders in colonial times, whose forebears traced to the younger sons
of the English landed gentry and minor nobility. The old citizens
were the respectable, pious yeomanry, whose antecedents had also
been landholders but on a smaller scale and who had not known the
glories of office. The old merchants included the Scottish tobacconists,
the few but highly respected Jewish shopkeepers, and other German
and Irish tradesmen, all of whom were addressed with respect. There
was a rapport among these three "old" categories, a mutual observance of the distinctions very much like British acceptance of class.

An example of class-consciousness in Richmond, albeit one of
democratic coloring, was occasioned by a visit to the city by the Prince
of Wales, later Edward VII. When he visited in October 1860, as Lord
Renfrew, he was accompanied around the city by a delegation of
prominent citizens which included the leading merchants, among
them a Mr. MacFarland, who owned a shoe store down on Main
Street, and a Mr. Dooley, an Irish hatter, the proprietor of an establishment next to Mr. MacFarland's. The prince mentioned in the
hearing of his civic hosts that he needed a pair of shoes, and all Mr.
MacFarland's fellow citizens looked expectantly toward him. The gentleman said never a word, however, not about to divulge to royalty
that he was in trade. A little later, the prince mentioned that he needed
a hat, whereupon Mr. Dooley spoke up. "Your Grace, I have a little
hat business and would be honored if you would accept whatever
may be to your liking. It's down on Main Street, right next to Mr.
MacFarland's shoe store."

While the older citizens of Richmond felt in accord with its social
structure, new people, whatever their financial status, were received
with reserve; they were on probation. But if you had ancestors, why
there you were! Nobody could take ancestors away from you, no matter what you did. But if you had no known ancestry, what else could

one judge except the conduct of the person? It was very simple and in no way snobbish; only new people who had to worry about their position were ever snobs. But careful social deportment, very public respect for the late Confederacy, commendable industry leading to wealth, these could mitigate social distrust of the new, and by judicious intermarriage with the daughters of the old families (everyone knew the flower of Southern manhood had perished in the War), one could acquire ancestry, or at least cousins who had it. Another way, after industry had proved worth, was to discover ancestors by means of genealogical research. Mrs. Archibald in Ellen Glasgow's *The Sheltered Life* does a delicious job of translating the family of her new brother-in-law, Joseph Crocker, a carpenter, from "plain people" to "quiet people" and finally, with the aid of a genealogist, to an "old family."

Ellen Glasgow both accepted Richmond and rejected it, refusing to take any of its inherited notions as the Gospel. Socially and financially, her family was as secure as any in Richmond. One of the younger children in a large family, her self-confessed "morbid sensitivity" made her side with a delicate mother exhausted from childbearing, frequently not rational in later life, a condition common in that era. A father who enjoyed remarkable bodily vigor, one who could reconcile his Calvinistic stoicism with his physical pleasures, would incur her defiance. Her mother would die when Ellen was twenty, a traumatic experience for the sensitive girl. Her father remained an enduring enigma until she was forty-three. Even then the gentleman required a tumble down the stone steps of 1 West Main at the age of eighty-seven before he could be sufficiently impaired physically to hasten him to his spiritual reward. In the disparity of parental temperaments, the resulting stress for Ellen Glasgow would give her the double vision of life which results in protest, in art. The code of chivalry as practiced in Virginia, more immediately in Richmond, would become the focus of her attack. The church, which upheld the code, would be the first institution openly rejected.

But Ellen Glasgow's hostility to the enslaving notions of her native culture in no way lessened her social standing in Richmond. Lila Meade Valentine, Mary Branch Munford, Mary Johnston, and other forward-looking Richmond ladies were enlightening the Southern male that his chivalrous pose was a subterfuge long overdue for public exposure. Ellen Glasgow's iconoclasm had resulted in a novel by a twenty-two-year-old young woman being published by a Northern press, and if the financial reward was not consideration enough, there was her considerable personal charm. Charm in Richmond was, as elsewhere, proof of breeding. Ellen Glasgow continued to enjoy close friendships with her childhood friends. Even in later life, she did not play the role of authoress for Richmonders that she played so successfully for visiting critics. Her closest personal friend was Carrie Coleman Duke, a vivacious woman whom many thought scatterbrained, even superficial, but one who told anecdotes well, who brought into Ellen Glasgow's life the easy laughter of one who lived on the surface. She was Ellen Glasgow's ears for the hard-of-hearing writer, especially on her flights from Richmond into the surrounding universe. James Anderson, a faithful Glasgow house servant, observed of Mrs. Duke, "Miss Carrie wears life like a loose garment." In the latter half of her life, Ellen Glasgow's closest companion was her nurse-secretary, Anne Virginia Bennett, who had been in attendance at the death of two sisters and Glasgow père. Of her companion, Ellen Glasgow wrote:

> Few persons have ever felt less interest in, or respect for, the profession of letters; and, as with the other inhabitants of Richmond, some of them almost as dear to me as Anne Virginia, she has always looked with suspicion upon "the people who write." But I have always done both my reading and my thinking alone. I have known intimately, in the South at least, few persons really interested in books more profound than "sweet stories." My oldest and closest friends, with the exception of James Cabell, still read as lightly as they speculate, and this description applies as accurately to the social order in which I was born. . . . Nevertheless, as I had discovered in New York and in London, the social levels are very much the same everywhere.

While Ellen Glasgow's two earliest works were set in New York, her best work was inevitably of her native state. As she observed, "I could write only of the scene I knew, and this scene had been furnished, however inadequately, for the past three hundred years." When she came to write of Richmond specifically, she "saw a shallow and aimless society of happiness-hunters, who lived in a perpetual flight from reality, and grasped at any effort-saving illusion of passion or pleasure."

In *A Certain Measure*, Ellen Glasgow confessed that at the beginning of her career she was meticulous in describing real places in setting the scenes of her novels; "my realistic conscience sternly forbad me to turn a maple into a mulberry tree." Later, when her artistic purpose was served, she did not hesitate "to make two trees grow in my Queenborough where only one was planted before me in Richmond." Richmond as a setting was used extensively; its houses, parks, gardens, and streets serve exclusively as background for seven of her novels,

The Romance of a Plain Man, The Builders, One Man in His Time, The Romantic Comedians, They Stooped to Folly, The Sheltered Life, and *In This Our Life.* Richmond also provides settings for *The Voice of the People, The Battle-Ground, The Deliverance, Life and Gabriella,* and *Vein of Iron.* In addition, characters in other novels make trips to Richmond. Ellen Glasgow first utilized Richmond in *The Voice of the People;* its Jeffersonian capitol and her own house at 1 West Main are described. Eugenia Battle Webb, the heroine, rides down Franklin Street; then "presently the carriage turned into Main Street, halting abruptly while a trolly car shot past. 'Please be very careful,' called Miss Chris, nervously gathering herself together as they stopped before a big gray house that faced a gray church on the opposite corner [Grace]." In *The Sheltered Life,* a mature Ellen Glasgow sat in her garden at 1 West Main and poured her hard-won stoic philosophy into the mind of General Archbald. Even today, over forty years later, the garden is much as she described it, with its wall, its stone birdbath, its old sycamore. "In the garden, which was reached by stone steps from the back porch, splendor flickered over the tall purple iris that fringed the birdbath, and rippled like a bright veil over the grass walks and flower beds. A small place, but it held beauty. Beauty, and that deep stillness through which time seems to flow with a perpetual rhythm and pause."

Of *The Romance of a Plain Man,* Ellen Glasgow wrote, "All the opening scenes on Church Hill are faithfully rendered," and she lovingly recounts the details of the scenes and the names of the people who lived there. All the changing mores that many of the Glasgow characters will regret are echoed in the changes that take place in geographical Richmond. *Life and Gabriella* opens in an old house on Leigh Street in what was termed the Court End in earlier days, an area now almost totally razed by city planners. When Gabriella returns from New York (c. 1912), her brother-in-law Charley, prefiguring Babbitt by at least ten years, boasts of the new Richmond rising from the ruins of the old. "We haven't left so much as an old brick lying around if we could help it. If you were to go back there to Hill Street [read *Leigh*], you'd scarcely know it for the hospitals and schools we've got there, and as for this part of the town—well, I reckon the apartment houses will fairly take your breath away. Apartment houses! Well, that's what I call progress—apartment houses and skyscrapers, and we've got them, too, down on Main Street."

Charley drives up Franklin to show Gabriella the unnamed Monroe Terrace, Chesterfield, Gresham Court, the latter two still occupied by residents living in them when Charley drove past sixty years ago. He drives up Monument Avenue, "the handsomest boulevard south of Washington. It's all new, every brick of it." Gabriella misses the gardens, the shrubs, and flowers. She asks, "But where are the old people —the people I used to know?" Besides the apartment houses, Charley exults over the hospitals. He names the physicians; "they've all got their hospitals." The rootlessness of apartment living does not enter Ellen Glasgow's novels as a significant motif, but the loss of the individual in the collective environment is clearly implied. In later works, Monument was given the derogatory pseudonym of Granite Avenue. With its memorials to the heroes of the Confederacy, its mansions built by the nouveaux riches, and later its apartment houses, Monument obviously symbolized for Ellen Glasgow the vulgarization of the free spirit into the mass conformity of external show; it was a realtor's conception of the capital of the Confederacy, prefiguring the press-agent commercialism of latter-day chambers of commerce. As Ellen Glasgow moved away from naming specific places in her later works, she still saw her characters acting out their dramas in scenes explicit enough to be recognized by native Richmonders; the scenes evoked certain moods within the writer, and they served the psychological and philosophical ambience of her novels. If Richmond was primarily a social attitude for Cabell, it was, as she said of her Queenborough, "the distilled essence of all Virginia cities."

In the last year of her life, Ellen Glasgow sent a New Year's greeting to a young soldier who had been raised on Third Street on Gamble's Hill. "As soon as I am well again, in April perhaps, I shall call my little white dog and set out for the terrace on Gamble's Hill. When you were a child, did you roll down those steep terraces? And do you remember, as I do, the gold of the buttercups?" Ellen Glasgow died the following November in the big gray house which Richmond had swept past, leaving it a lonely relic among the antique shops. But the spirit of an older Richmond was still at work in the house; for three days after her death her sister Rebe and her brother-in-law Cabell Tutwiler closeted themselves in Ellen's study, destroying every last scrap of paper that would not redound to the glory of family and writer.

§ III

While Ellen Glasgow's social relationships in Richmond were not literary nor intellectual, they were in general pleasant enough. She could look on her fellow citizens with an amused, even affectionate, tolerance. James Branch Cabell, on the other hand, was early subjected to subtle social pressures that further inhibited an already intensely shy youth. His relationship with Richmond requires a more detailed recounting of family history. If the influence of Richmond on Cabell demands *biography*, let us recall that the word was chosen by Cabell to describe his major work.

Cabell's maternal great-grandfather, Mr. Thomas Branch of Petersburg, of obscure parentage and fired with Methodist zeal, flourished in unpropitious times and became the patriarch of a large and prosperous family. He moved to Richmond and established the Merchants' Bank; his sons and sons-in-law were the leading reestablishers of Richmond's economic life after the fall of the Confederacy. His oldest living son, James Read Branch, married into an old family, the Pattesons, but Cabell would write "that Grandmother did not ever weigh the fantastic notion of the Branches' being the social peers of the Pattesons." During the latter days of the war, Grandmother had brought her children to live with her father, Dr. Patteson, in Richmond, as her husband was serving in the Confederate army. Colonel Branch died in a tragic accident soon after the war, but the dynamic Martha Louise Patteson Branch saw that the children of this union married well. The second daughter, born in Petersburg but raised in Richmond, married Dr. Robert Gamble Cabell, Jr., on November 14, 1877. Unlike the Branches, the Cabells were old family. Annie Branch, protected from the poverty of Reconstruction by Branch money and raised in the home of an adoring and aristocratic grandfather, could never have suspected that she was socially vulnerable.

When Cabell returned to Richmond from William and Mary in 1898, he found an alteration in his parents' domestic relationship. Dr. Cabell, with no word of explanation to his three teen-age sons, and apparently little to his wife, had elected to move out. Whatever the private disagreements between husband and wife may have been, the personality of Cabell's mother must have had a bearing on the separation. Anne Harris Branch, child of the "newly arrived" Branches and "old family" Pattesons, had married at the age of eighteen a man twelve years older than herself. Numerous reports would have her beautiful and pleasure-loving. Her open nature made her disregard the more rigid strictures of society. Presbyterian Calvinism was still a meaningful part of Richmond's social fabric, but young Mrs. Cabell, freed from Branch Methodism by Patteson Episcopalianism, would dare to smoke and drink cocktails before other ladies freely confessed to these pleasures. Unlike her Patteson mother, Annie Cabell was not given to the pleasure of reading; her pleasure was agreeable company. Cabell confessed that he modeled the charming Meloir in *The High Place* on his mother's personality. If "this bright light creature's very diverting chat" does not savor of the intellect, the hero reasons, after all "he had not married her in order to discuss philosophy." Among those that Annie Cabell found agreeable company was her amusing, man-about-town cousin John Scott, only one year older than herself. Mrs. Cabell either did not care what people thought of her social attitudes or else was unaware of the censure her conduct provoked in the upper levels of Richmond society. Judging from a number of intangibles, and certainly in the eyes of her oldest son, she may be credited with a large amount of innocence. Innocence in a girl might be overlooked by an indulgent husband, but it seemed out of place in a woman approaching forty, so that Robert G. Cabell, Jr., no prude but raised in the Presbyterian church, found his position as compromised husband, even if only in talk, intolerable.

The fifth child of the patriarch Thomas Branch of Petersburg was Sarah Frances Branch, and she married an Irishman, Frederic R. Scott. They were the parents of six sons and three daughters, and they too moved from Petersburg to Richmond. Their first child, John Walker Scott, was born January 19, 1858. He attended the University of Virginia and Harvard University. He traveled widely and he spent some years in Albemarle County as a gentleman farmer. In his forty-fourth year he began to give some thought to settling down to the practice of law. His younger brothers were already a part of that financial structure that Branch industry was rebuilding. His brother Frederic William Scott was a successful stockbroker and, with the death of their father, was looked upon as the head of the Scott family.

On Wednesday afternoon, November 13, 1901, John Scott went riding at the Deep Run Hunt Club. He dined with his family in their commodious mansion at 712 West Franklin Street, across from Monroe Park, later called on a young lady, and then proceeded to the Commonwealth Club at 401 West Franklin Street, some four short blocks from the Scott residence. He left the Commonwealth at 1:45 A.M. of the fourteenth, after ascertaining from a friend that he was in walking condition. He walked west on Franklin Street and passed the residence of his first cousin, Anne Branch Cabell, 511, where her widowed sister Elizabeth Branch Bowie lived on the third floor. It was the house that Dr. Cabell had quitted three years before, but young Mr. James Cabell was there, recently returned from employment in

New York and now employed as a reporter for the Richmond *News*. Scott passed the iron gate of 515, the residence of Major E. T. D. Myers, on the corner of Belvidere and Franklin streets. There he met his death. An unknown assailant fractured his skull.

For some ten days the four Richmond newspapers speculated on every aspect of the murder, in particular the motive. Revenge soon emerged as the accepted theory, and in the rumors of arrest, "a very important person," "a well-known citizen," or "a society man" were widely referred to. In the minds of many Richmonders, there were no doubts; the evidence pointed to the one man who had the strongest motive: James Branch Cabell had murdered his mother's lover. In less than two weeks after the murder, with rumors and speculation at their height, all four newspapers lapsed into total silence. People could air their opinions behind closed doors, but the Scotts had effectively ended any public discussion of the scandal. Cabell would later attempt to clear his name in the court of public opinion, but he ran into the adamant opposition of his cousin Fred Scott, who was determined to protect the Scott family's reputation even at the expense of an innocent man. Cabell never forgave his cousin.

Cabell's reaction to this period of stress in his life was in marked contrast to his earlier trial in the court of public gossip in Williamsburg. His painful separation from Gabriella Brooke Moncure and his intense unhappiness at the injustice of the homosexual rumors at college left him without direction, with no vent for his feelings. This time, however, the acceptance of three of his short stories by *Harper's*, *Smart Set*, and *Argosy* in the same year as the murder, 1901, served to allay his sensibilities, and writing would prove the needed outlet for his suppressed emotions.

Just when Cabell learned of the role assigned him in this scandal we cannot be sure until new evidence comes to light. Biographical details seeded in his fiction make it appear that he was aware of his being credited with murder before he learned of the slander against his mother. Perhaps he thought at the time that proximity and the old Williamsburg gossip would naturally accord him a role in public speculation. His mother could observe with one of his characters in *The Cords of Vanity*: "People talk of course, but it is only on the stage they ever drive you out into the snow-storm. Besides, they don't talk to me." Cabell was absorbed in his writing during this period, and Townsend in *Cords* most likely echoes Cabell's attitude toward the gossip. "I did not greatly care what Lichfield said one way or the other. I was too deeply engrossed; first, in correcting the final proofs of *Afield*, my second book . . . ; secondly, in the remunerative and uninteresting task of writing for *Woman's Weekly* five 'wholesome love-stories with a dash of humor.' "

The third son of Mr. Thomas Branch of Petersburg was John Patteson Branch. He married the daughter of a Methodist minister in Petersburg, and he remained a zealous Methodist. He established his family in Richmond in a large remodeled house at 1 West Franklin Street, and upon the death of Thomas Branch was looked on as the head of the family and its growing empire. The Branches and their in-laws were now among the "economic royalists" of Richmond, to use a term applied to them by one of their own. They married well, but it was generally understood that the Branch contribution to marriage was money rather than family background. The separation of Robert Cabell, Jr., from Annie Branch and the sensational publicity surrounding the murder of John Scott had further impaired their social standing. The Cabell family had been handsomely memorialized in a monumental work that had appeared in 1895. A similar volume recording the virtues of the Branch forebears would do much to repair their social estate. And who could be more appropriate as its compiler than the scholarly victim of that society which was to be placated? Thus Mr. John P. Branch commissioned and financed the son of his maligned niece to produce *Branchiana*. Genealogical research was congenial work for James Branch Cabell, and he duly traced the ancestry of Thomas Branch back to its immigrant, Christopher Branch, who had arrived in Virginia commendably early, in 1619. As luck would have it, however, no one truly illustrious was to be found in the Branch line, and they fell into that middle category of respectable and pious good people, the counterpart of the "old citizens" in Richmond. Cabell's findings appeared in 1907, and the Compiler's Foreword to *Branchiana* is amusingly both an apology for the plainness of the Branch ancestry and a virtuous advertising of their marital fidelity. Implying that the noble connections of more illustrious families were frequently the result of extralegal bed-play, he added: "Shuffle over it as you may, the authentic forebearer of this family was merely an honest and God-fearing yeoman whose reputation is not attestedly enhanced by even the tiniest infraction of the Decalogue." Cabell later had better luck when he went abroad for research in England, where he found an illustrious Branch ancestor, who was proudly offered to the local gods in 1911 as *Branch of Abingdon*.

The year 1907 recorded another stage of the events that kept alive the gossip surrounding Cabell's name. His mother determined upon a divorce, a step not lightly taken at that time. Dr. Cabell's desertion of his wife had undoubtedly played a large role in appearing to give verity to the slander of the John Scott case. Perhaps Anne Branch Cabell felt that a divorce could harm her name no further, that indeed a divorced woman stood better than one abandoned. There may also have been some thought that a divorce would cause embarrassment for Dr. Cabell, a husband who had treated her cruelly. The divorce was a simple matter of depositions recorded in a lawyer's office and presented to the chancery court.

At about the time his mother was granted a divorce, Cabell decided he would take his revenge on Richmond society by satirizing it in a "novel" that would expose its multiple hypocrisies. Its "hero," significantly named Townsend, would daringly be the philandering cad that gossip made of the reticent Cabell, and though called Lichfield, its setting would clearly be Richmond. *The Cords of Vanity* was begun early in 1907, and, following his usual penchant, Cabell reworked some of his short stories into the appearance of a very episodic novel. Thus the highly romantic stuff of magazine fiction is cemented together by a protagonist who is Cabell's age and who speaks in the first person. Much of the cement is thinly disguised autobiography. But Cabell's sentimentalism kept interfering with his irony. In the middle of the novel, he observed: "When I began to scribble these haphazard memories I had designed to be very droll concerning the provincialism of Lichfield; for, as every inhabitant of the place will tell you, it is 'quite hopelessly provincial,'—and this is odd, seeing that, as investigation will assure you, the city is exclusively inhabited by self-confessed cosmopolitans." He went on to add that "comprehension [is] the grave of gusto," and confessed, indeed touchingly, "For the rest, Lichfield, and Fairhaven also, got at and into me when I was too young to defend myself. Therefore Lichfield and Fairhaven cannot ever, really, seem to me grotesque."

Though exemplifying the cad, Townsend deplores the decline of romance and a race of heroic men (example: Col. James Read Branch, C.S.A.). Yellow journalism now records our vices; "in real life our peccadillos dwindle into dreary vistas of divorce cases and the police court." Townsend's uncle observes, "Blow, bugle, blow, and set the Wilde echoes flying!" And Cabell affects the style of that author. Undisguised biography comes to the surface:

> Depend upon it, Lichfield knew a deal more concerning my escapades than I did. That I was "deplorably wild" was generally agreed, and a reasonable number of seductions and murders and sexual aberrations was, no doubt, accredited to me.

But I was a Townsend [Cabell], and Lichfield had been case-hardened to Townsendian vagaries since Colonial days; and, besides, I had written a book which had been talked about; and, as an afterthought, I was reputed not to be an absolute pauper, if only because my father had taken the precaution, customary with the Townsends, to marry a woman with enough money to gild the bonds of matrimony. For Lichfield, luckily, was not aware how near my pleasure-loving parents had come, between them, to spending the last cent of this once ample fortune.

For Bulmer through the novel read Branch. Townsend's mother is clearly Cabell's mother . . . , and her witticism "James and I just live downstairs in the two lower stories and ostracise the third floor" is given to Mrs. Townsend. The character of Stella Musgrave too appears modeled on a younger Annie Branch Cabell, and her description of her Methodist grandfather is patently a portrait of Thomas Branch of Petersburg. The psychoanalysts will note that Cabell kills off both Stella and Townsend's mother.

Cabell intended following *Cords* with a candid account of life in Richmond to have the punning title *Townsend of Lichfield*, but for his "comfort's sake" he gave up the idea. "I had looked forward to a liberal dealing with real persons—presented under such pseudonyms as would ward off libel suits, without ever becoming in the least impervious—and to some salutary loosing of long-pent-up malice." He went on to observe that for Lichfield "immoral conduct did not exist until some open mention of it was printed in the local newspapers." Cabell never wrote his uninhibited exposure of Richmond society; however, its attitude of self-mockery, delight in subterfuge, rigid adherence to the outward proprieties despite the damning evidence would enter into every subsequent work from his pen. He would indulge in more thinly disguised biography in *The Rivet in Grandfather's Neck* and *Something about Eve*.

Another biographical detail is relevant here. While Cabell's literary efforts met with some modest success, he was far from being in a position to support himself from his earnings. When his brother married a wealthy heiress from North Carolina in 1911, Richmond gossip has Cabell remarking, "I suppose I too will have to marry money like my brother." When the essentially shy and reserved author met the well-to-do Mrs. Shepherd, mother of five children, at Rockbridge Alum Springs in 1912, he tells us it was not a matter of falling in love. It was a feeling of wholly dear contentment being near this older, maternal woman who appeared unaware and unconcerned with what

Richmond people might think of her. Her light, engaging talk revealed no fear of censure. Her pleasure in meeting and being with people was totally unrelated to the restrictive dictates of Richmond's reigning social arbiters. Here was another defenseless Annie Branch. She really needed someone to protect her from her innocence, someone to prove she was "old family," in a book to be entitled *The Majors and Their Marriages*. Their first and only child would be named Ballard Hartwell, two of the happy genealogical discoveries in Priscilla Bradley Cabell's ancestry. Percie Cabell wore her newly brought-to-life honors with aplomb, and her preoccupation with the important things in life, such as good meals, a well-run house, and loving attention to one's family, was largely responsible for the healing of Cabell's neuroses concerning Richmond's social attitudes. With his acceptance as a respected householder, discreetly amusing himself with gullible Yankee critics, he could in time write his Comedy of Redemption.

In *The Cords of Vanity* and *The Rivet in Grandfather's Neck*, however, Cabell set out to write the social comedies that Ellen Glasgow produced in her three best novels of Richmond life. But sentiment intruded on his irony. Allegory and Poictesme were later to give him a remove from his subject matter that would allow him to maintain his ironic pose. While Ellen Glasgow's tragic despair occasionally intruded on her irony, she could look on Richmond with amused detachment. Her neuroses lay elsewhere, with her father and her deafness, but Cabell could not write of Richmond objectively until after his major work was accomplished. In his cosmic comedies, Cabell appears to stand outside of time and place, but it would be difficult to find an American writer whose environment played a larger role in creating those stresses which result in literature.

§ IV

Whatever esteem Ellen Glasgow and James Branch Cabell won in American letters, their works were not widely read in Richmond. Numerous stories are told of the indifference of their friends to their writings. Richmonders loved to recount anecdotes about the families, foibles, and affairs of the two, but references to the novels brought shrugs. Hers were reputed to be high-minded and dull. "I hear they're depressing, and I certainly don't need that," would be a response accompanied with laughter. His were supposed to be risqué, but how could one tell, with all that make-believe? "I honestly can't make any sense out of it," would be admitted with engaging candor. But just as

Henry James came to realize on his visit to Richmond that "the large, sad poorness was in itself a reference," perhaps we too should see in Richmond's "indifference" to Glasgow and Cabell as artists a deeper significance than the easy attribution of superficiality so frequently implied. The story-telling tradition throughout the South was primarily oral, allowing infinite variation, responding to the needs of varied auditors, coloring the basic myths of patriarch, quest, apotheosis. The tradition served in kitchen and parlor; it served as the pasturage of the lesser sentimentalists such as Page and Cooke as well as of the academically revered Warren and Faulkner. And despite their truly prestigious centenary celebrations, are Nebraskans devoted readers of Willa Cather?

The careers of Ellen Glasgow and James Branch Cabell reaffirm the observation that art is preeminently provincial, that it springs from a certain age and a certain locality. Richmond's class structure allowed Ellen Glasgow to write "English" novels, and when World War I accelerated the evolutionary into revolutionary changes, the results were her novels of manners, wherein her ironic gifts came to fruition. Cabell's pre-World War I work was flawed by its reflection of Richmond's ambivalent attitude toward itself, a mixture of public sentiment and private derision. World War I liberated Cabell, allowing him to be openly satirical in his philosophical comedies of disenchantment, and it provided a mundane society ready for sophisticated innuendo. The duality of Richmond's penchant for "Queen Anne façades and Mary Ann behinds" had become the national allegory of the American Dream versus the Gopher Prairie reality. As Cabell wrote Theodore Dreiser, "You and I regarded, as it were, the universe from very much the same point of view, and have been honored with, through many years, the same opponents." Earlier, the temperamental disparity of Ellen Glasgow's parents had provided conflicting visions of life for a child who would dedicate her efforts to an attempt to bring them into a single focus, a "wholeness of perception." And young James Cabell had looked on in wonder at a society that could propound a comforting myth in public while admitting to a painful awareness of reality in private, a schizoid behavior that would obsess the young man, driving him to philosophical quests for an ultimate unity. That which troubled them in youth they came to accept in age as the universal experience of the human heart. "When she was born," Ellen Glasgow asked herself late in life, "were ideas any more free in Oxford or Bloomsbury than in Richmond?"

If Richmond was a state of mind, a social attitude, a mythic symbol, it was also a geographical place, still recognizable despite the changes.

One suspects that basically both writers felt comfortable there; they mocked it, they enjoyed its intimacy, they felt lonely there, it was home. After all, they were born there, but more significant, as far as Americans are concerned, is the fact they died there. Its literary flowers are few, but it's still a place with roots. And we still find talk about the people we grew up with vastly diverting.

MacDonald, "Glasgow, Cabell, and Richmond," *Mississippi Quarterly*, 27 (Fall 1974): 393–413.

"This Quiet Man, Whose Tireless Pen Traced the Marches [of] . . . Great Captains": Douglas Southall Freeman

Pulitzer Prize-winning biographer, distinguished editor of the Richmond *News Leader* (1915–49), lecturer at Columbia and other universities, radio commentator, prominent Baptist layman—all are apt labels for Douglas Southall Freeman (1866–1953). The holder of a Ph.D. degree in history awarded by Johns Hopkins University in 1908, he lived by the axiom that "time alone is irreplaceable" and earned the designation, "the most efficient Virginian since Jefferson." His extraordinary energy and other qualities are illuminated in the sketch below by Dumas Malone (1892–), longtime biographer-in-residence at the University of Virginia, one of the premier scholars of his generation, and recipient himself of a Pulitzer Prize for his definitive, multivolume series, "Jefferson and His Time."

When death came to Douglas Southall Freeman in Richmond on the thirteenth day of June, 1953, he was sixty-seven years old. He delivered his regular radio broadcast on the morning of the day he died, speaking like a father to his fellow Virginians in his familiar drawl, and, almost at the end, he finished the last chapter in this volume. Lying on his desk in his third-floor study at "Westbourne" was a framed quotation from Tennyson's "Ulysses" which included these words:

> Something ere the end,
> Some work of noble note may yet be done,
> Not unbecoming men that strove with gods.

This quiet man, whose tireless pen had traced the marches and described the battles of so many great Captains, did not have quite time enough to finish his own last work of noble note. He lacked several months of living as long as George Washington did, and his own labors ended before he could carry that hero through his second term as President and bring him home to Mount Vernon for the rest and peace he so richly deserved and had so vainly sought. Douglas Freeman himself had long ago found the peace of an ordered life, but rest was the last thing on earth he wanted. Almost certainly he would have finished another and final volume and attained another major goal had he been permitted to fill out the biblical span of three-score years and ten. To his friends it is an even more important consideration that he would have been deeply happy in these continued labors.

Yet, if we disregard the mere tale of years and apply the measure of labor and achievement, he had lived several lives already. He himself gave no sign of a split personality, but for purposes of description we will say that he lived at least two lives—as an editor and as a historian. Either one of these would have been far too full for most mortals, but this incredibly effective man serenely proceeded from task to task with unhurried step. No one can fully explain how he did all that he did, for inner springs of power are invisible to the observer, but unquestionably he pursued clear-purposed goals through the tangles and perplexities of daily existence, and by mastering himself made himself the master of his destiny. He revealed a quality that he assigned to young George Washington: "the quenchless ambition of an ordered mind." Also, he was a living illustration of certain truths that Thomas Jefferson proclaimed to his young daughter: "No person will have occasion to complain of the want of time who never loses any," said that incessantly active Virginian. "It is wonderful how much may be done if we are always doing."

The major clue to his extraordinary accomplishments must be sought in the man himself, not in environmental influences that he shared with others; but his remarkable career cannot be understood or even viewed outside of its distinctive setting. Theodore Roosevelt in his *Autobiography* quoted a bit of homely exhortation from a rural Virginian which is pertinent in this connection, for Lee's biographer found the same philosophy in the General and was himself an exemplar of it: "Do what you can, with what you've got, where you are." Douglas Freeman liked to speak of himself as a "tramp newspaperman," but actually his career as an editor was wholly confined to Richmond. He was never a foreign correspondent, and only as a lecturer or consultant did he ply the journalistic trade in other cities. No one would think of describing this author of vast military volumes as provincial, but the fact is that he dealt first and primarily with the great chieftains of his own State. He stayed where he was and started with what was there. This exhaustive investigator eventually sought materials from everywhere, but, because of the physical necessities of his professional life, he had these materials brought to him as a rule—in books and photostats and microfilm—and he surveyed them in his own study. Long before his career ended he was traveling many thousands of miles every year, but there never was a time when his life did not center in Richmond, and neither in spirit nor manner did he ever cease to be a Virginian.

Virginians are not all alike, to be sure, and some of them did not lay the emphasis on the same things that he did. He did not romanticize the past and the first families. Once in private conversation I remarked to him that he was the most efficient Virginian since Jefferson —a charge that he smilingly denied. I still regard this particular parallel as close, but I doubt if this Richmonder got his major inspiration from Jefferson, even in matters of industry and order. If he consciously modeled himself on anyone it was on Robert E. Lee, whose statue he saluted every day as he drove to and from his office. Also, by right of his own surpassing knowledge, this man of the pen who never drew sword became the literary embodiment of the historic tradition which Lee personified and which George Washington had symbolized before him.

§ I

Douglas Freeman was born in Lynchburg, but his family moved to Richmond when he was only a little boy, and he grew up in the former seat of the Confederacy. In stories he often referred to the "Jeems" River, which flowed by both these small cities. Even Richmond was small in his boyhood, and his own talk always retained the flavor and humor of the countryside. His father, Walker B. Freeman, was a Confederate veteran who had served in the ranks throughout the War and was at Appomattox at the surrender. In later years he was known as "General" Freeman but he gained this title as an officer of the United Confederate Veterans, not as an officer in Lee's army. In Virginia very little notice seems to have been taken of the fact that the "General" came of *Mayflower* stock, and it made little difference in those days that he was not conspicuously prosperous in his insurance business. Hardly anybody in that locality at that time was prosperous in any business. It was more significant in his son's life that he came of a long line of devout Baptists. Douglas Freeman was a deeply religious man, and in his youth he gave serious thought to becoming a minister. It was highly significant, also, that the boy heard stories of the Army of Northern Virginia at his father's knee. He himself attended Confederate reunions, where he saw gnarled and wounded men, and from an early age he cherished the ambition to tell their full story. He was born and bred a Confederate, though there is no sign that he was ever a bitter one.

In the old Confederate capital above the James the boy received all of his formal education through the college stage. He attended the University of Richmond, a Baptist institution, and was always loyal to it, serving it afterwards for many years as head of the Board of Trustees. At all stages he was a good student and his interest in history may almost be described as innate, but this was quickened by Professor Samuel Chiles Mitchell, an inspiring teacher, who encouraged him to pursue the subject further. While an undergraduate he began to be a newspaper correspondent, besides contributing to the college literary magazine, and once having got printer's ink into his veins he never could get it out. For the moment, however, history had the priority. He gained a fellowship at the Johns Hopkins University, where he studied history and economics, and at the unusually early age of twenty-two received the Ph.D. degree. Throughout the rest of his life the title "Doctor" was fastened on him. Incidentally, he picked up a good deal of medical knowledge in Baltimore—from medical students he associated with and from his elder brother, Allen, who became a doctor in the more usual meaning of the term. The only copy of the young graduate student's dissertation—on the Virginia Secession Convention—was destroyed by fire before ever it was published, but his *Calendar of Confederate State Papers* appeared in the same year (1908) that he took his degree.

Leaving Baltimore, where the atmosphere may have seemed Southern but was not quite Confederate, he returned to Richmond. There, before embarking irrevocably upon a newspaper career, he served as secretary of the Tax Commission of the state and drafted its report. For a time he was on the staff of the *Times Dispatch*, but his enduring connection was with the afternoon paper, the *News Leader*. This began when he was twenty-five. At the age of twenty-nine (1915) he became the editor, and he held this post until he was sixty-three. It was also when he was twenty-nine that his edition of *Lee's Dispatches* appeared in print and that he signed a contract for a biography of the great

Captain, but nearly a score of years were to pass before he could publish that.

Of Dr. Freeman's journalistic career I can speak with no special competence and I make no pretense of describing it with any adequacy. Being the editor of a paper with a small staff was no sinecure. One of his associates on the *News Leader* estimated at the time of his death that during his service of more than a third of a century he wrote at least 600,000 words every year—that is, the equivalent of about three books the size of this one and perhaps a hundred altogether. Yet his associates remembered him as one who always emphasized the virtue of brevity in a newspaperman. With this went an emphasis on restraint. "Don't gush, and don't twitter," he told his juniors. "Play it straight." In the course of his career he championed many changes which may be described as "reforms" while opposing others which he regarded as backward steps, but the predominant impression he gave was not that of a crusading editor. He was too judicious for that, and, while liberal in spirit, he could hardly have embodied the Lee tradition without being conservative in the true sense of that much abused term. He sought to safeguard old and enduring values and was wholly unsympathetic with demagoguery of any brand.

He was fully aware of the ephemeral nature of his own writing for a newspaper—"writing in sand" he called it—and as an editor he was relatively a local figure. During the First World War he won his spurs as a daily commentator on military events. He himself never served in the armed forces, since he was incapacitated by hernia, but long before he achieved national fame he was recognized in Virginia and the South as an authority on military matters and on the Confederacy. Some wag remarked that the Confederate flag might as well be flown from the masthead of the *News Leader*, and during the Second World War he vivified his comments on terrain and movements by drawing analogies from the Virginia scene and Lee's battles.

Most of the stories about him as a newspaperman that are still current relate to his later years, when he had become a legend. He worked behind an uncluttered desk and under a sign which read: "Time alone is irreplaceable . . . Waste it not." He answered his letters immediately, wasting no words in his replies, but during his office hours he gave his visitors no impression of being hurried. His junior colleagues spoke of his daily editorial conferences as "pow-wows" and described themselves as "carrying wampum to the great white father." No pipe of peace was circulated, however; nobody smoked at these conferences because he did not, and in his presence everybody guarded himself against profanity, which he did not use because of his respect for the English language. Perhaps the publisher, John Stewart Bryan, sometimes called him "Douglas" in private but he did not do so in public; and Dr. Freeman never called his long-time friend anything but "Mr. Bryan." Both of them antedated the first-name era, and were heirs of a tradition of politeness which avoided excess of familiarity. Like Mr. Bryan, however, Dr. Freeman was characteristically genial; he told a good story, and there was plenty of laughter at his staff conferences.

No small part of his local and regional reputation before the appearance of his great historical works was owing to his frequent appearances as a speaker. Besides considering the ministry as a calling, he had flirted in his youth with the idea of becoming an actor, and he soon made himself at home on the public platform. In later years he often described speaking as a waste of time, but until the end of his days he engaged in it, and it might almost be described as his third life and third career.

The first time I ever saw the versatile and indefatigable young editor was when he was making a speech. It was at a convocation at the University of Virginia, whither I recently had come to teach American history, and as I remember, he delivered a challenging and inspirational address, such as everybody expected. He was about thirty-seven at the time, and stories were current about the incredible number and variety of things he did. Obviously he was a well-informed, a high-minded and a public-spirited man—just the sort of person one would turn to for a challenging speech in behalf of a good cause, such as the advancement of Southern education. But I wondered at the time if he were not spending himself too freely, if he were not scattering his fire too widely; and no external observer could have anticipated at this stage that, while still performing his manifold editorial tasks and making his innumerable public appearances, he would gain enduring fame as a writer of history. Nor could one who listened to his spoken words have anticipated the quality of his formal writings. Rarely did he write out his speeches and rarely did they represent him at his best; he simply took them in his stride. He had to take an enormous number of them before he was through: in the year 1937, when he seems to have been at the peak, he spoke eighty-three times to various audiences, besides delivering ninety lectures on journalism in Columbia University.

Long before then his radio talks had made his name a household word in the Old Dominion. Beginning in 1925 he was a daily commentator, and on Sunday he delivered what amounted to a lay sermon. I speak of these programs chiefly from hearsay, for I had no radio during the years that I was a resident of his State and I never had much chance to hear them. Those that I did hear were just what I had expected from the common account of them. His radio performances were highly distinctive, if not unique. He made no special preparation for them, except such as he had already made in going over the news of the day and writing his editorials, and he spoke from the briefest of notes. On a local station, without a nation-wide hookup, he talked to his fellow Virginians, and he was just as relaxed as he was in his weekly current-events class or in his office at the *News Leader*. This was homely fare every day, and on Sundays it was inspirational. Everybody knew who Dr. Freeman was. Even before his great books came out he was the local authority on the Confederacy, on Richmond's past and present, and on everything military; and until the end he was to his own people a combination of lay pastor and family physician.

§ II

The local celebrity became a national literary figure and gained a sure place in American historiography with the publication of *R. E. Lee* in 1934–1935, when he was forty-eight. The one-volume work he had contracted for in 1915 had grown to four large volumes, and the calendar showed that it had been a score of years in preparation. To those who were unfamiliar with the slow processes of research and writing this seemed a long time, no doubt, but to the initiated who were also aware of this author's other tasks it was a notable performance by any reckoning. Probably it would have been impossible if he had not firmly regularized his own procedure and advanced with steady and unflagging step toward the distant goal of his high ambition.

It was in 1926, when he was forty, that he began to follow his now-famous schedule. It is now impossible to believe that he was ever unsystematic; and while soaking up Confederate lore as a young editor he must have done a vast amount of work on the life and campaigns of the great Confederate chieftain. But as his original plan expanded and his canvas lengthened, he became convinced that he must make a second vocation out of the historical research and writing which was his first love anyway. This necessitated a careful apportionment of his precious hours, and as rigid an observance of his historical as of his editorial schedule. At first he set himself a program of fourteen hours a week, and to make sure that he would attain it he began to keep books on himself. He did more than maintain a balance. He amassed credits—"s.c.o." or "special carry over" of hours he called them—and he made up for lost time before he lost it. From the day in 1926 when he began to keep these records until December 10, 1933, when he finished *R. E. Lee*, he spent 6100 hours on that work.

This impressive total could not have been attained in that period unless he had exceeded his original weekly allowance. This grew from fourteen hours to twenty-four, and his working day was lengthened by making it start sooner. Sometimes his doctor intervened—he was dangerously ill in 1929—but as a rule his day dawned at 2:30. He always regarded these undisturbed morning hours, when the world was still asleep, as the best ones, but actually he did his newspaper work first. Through with that, by the time that most people are only at the halfway point, he went home for luncheon, rested briefly, worked in the garden for a bit, and then turned to history in the afternoon —as he always did on Sundays. He rigidly restricted his social engagements, and in the evening, after listening to some music, he retired very early. He gave no impression of being hurried and he made light of the rigors of his schedule, but he was doing more than time and a half by ordinary human standards and was wasting no moment of it.

Eventually the story of his working habits became widely known and helped make him a legendary character on the national as well as the local scene, but when his first major work was published reviewers and readers judged him by results without much knowledge of processes. I shall never forget the impression his *R. E. Lee* made on me at the very first reading. By that time, although I had no such acquaintance with the man as I gained later, I had first-hand knowledge of his scholarship, for I had seen the articles on Lee, Stonewall Jackson, and others that he had prepared for the *Dictionary of American Biography*. He afterwards told me that he found the writing of these sketches, under sharp restrictions of space, a cruel task. These were miniatures, and to paint them he had to turn aside from the vast canvas on which he was then working and to which he had become accustomed. But they left no doubt of his historical craftsmanship and his skill in portraiture, whatever the scale might be, and I awaited with confidence the appearance of his long-heralded life of Lee. Great as my personal expectations were, the realization far surpassed them, and never did I devour a major historical work with such insatiable appetite and more unalloyed satisfaction. The book reached the full stature of the man, in my opinion, and to say this was praise enough for Douglas Southall

Freeman, who had so often saluted the greatest of Southern soldiers and so long lived in spiritual companionship with that supremely great gentleman.

Having grown up in the shadow of the Lost Cause, I could not wholly divest myself of sentiment when I read this book, and, besides having an honored place on my shelves, it has retained a special place in my affections. For that reason I may be giving it greater relative emphasis than the author himself would like. As he perfected his craftsmanship in later years, he saw faults in his earlier work which he regretted. That often happens with good workmen, however, and if there were any accusing voices when *R. E. Lee* appeared these were drowned in the chorus of praise which rose spontaneously. Northern and Southern accents were undistinguishable, and the public response showed unmistakably that Lee was a national and not merely a Southern hero. He had long been that, to be sure, but to everybody it seemed fitting that he had been most fully described and most adequately portrayed by a son of the Confederacy who lived in Richmond.

This work, like all the major works of Freeman, is a blend of biography and military history, and it has the qualities of exhaustiveness and judiciousness which became his hallmark. The author himself never expected that all of his military judgments would be accepted without question, and some of them may be disputed, no doubt, after the lapse of a score of years. In the interval the style of writing about what he called the War Between the States has taken on a somewhat more Northern tinge and General Ulysses S. Grant, for one, has gained new admirers. To this Lee's biographer would raise no objection whatsoever. He would say now as he did then: "Circumstance is incommensurable: . . . why invoke comparatives?" Recognizing that Lee, like every other leader, must be judged "by what he accomplished, where he was, with what he had at his command," he indulged in no extravagant utterance and purposely avoided historical controversy. He gave the record of deeds and events with unexampled fulness and can be safely controverted only by students of comparable diligence, of whom there never can be many. Some have objected to his story on the ground that he always viewed the scene through the eyes of Lee and kept the reader at Confederate G.H.Q. That, however, was a matter of method, and a wise method it was, for this was intended as no history of the War Between the States. It is a biography of the Confederate Commander and a story of the war as he waged it. Gettysburg was a Federal victory as well as a Confederate defeat, but Freeman sought to show, in terms of military circumstances and personalities, why Lee lost it, leaving to others the task of describing it from Meade's headquarters.

As military history this story requires supplementation, and nobody realized that more than its author, but as the biography of a great soldier it approximated completeness so nearly as to be virtually unchallengeable. By comparison, other accounts of Lee—neglecting important phases of his earlier and later life, and emphasizing battles to the exclusion of problems of management and supply—seem pale and meagre. There is vast leisureliness in this narrative and at times its flow is impeded by detail which may seem unnecessary, but trivial items may assume crucial importance in battle and the texture of this tapestry is provided by its richness of detail. From this carefully wrought and slow-moving story Lee emerges in full glory. This is not to say that he was impeccable in judgment; Freeman describes his mistakes with complete candor at the times he made them and sums them up in a final critique—the chapter entitled "The Sword of Robert E. Lee." Also, he underlines the General's chief temperamental flaw, his excessive amiability at times in dealing with his commanders. But the balance is heavily on the credit side, and fresh and needed emphasis is laid on the intellectual quality of Lee's generalship. In his great ability as an administrator and his genius as a commander there was more of the infinite capacity for taking pains, more of the clear thought of an orderly and penetrating mind, than had been previously supposed. It took the orderly and penetrating mind of a Freeman to discern this.

The man who is shown is essentially the Lee of legend, far more fully pictured and far better explained. He is made more real by being made more human, but in life as in legend he was heroic—a knight *sans peur et sans reproche* and the *beau idéal* of the Christian gentleman. If there be those among us who have repudiated this ideal, or those whose vanity is flattered when human idols are shown to have feet of clay, they will find scant comfort in this book. But as most Americans rejoiced a score of years ago they can still rejoice that the painstaking labors and fair judgment of scholarship served to provide a firm foundation for one of the noblest of our symbols. Lee may still seem almost too good to be true, but his memory inspires no jealousy— since his life was set on a background of dark tragedy, just as Lincoln's was. It seems safe to predict, therefore, that this classic portrait of him, done in the grand manner by patient and skillful hands, will be cherished as long as the ideals of the Republic shall endure. . . .

Two weeks after his fifty-eighth birthday, Freeman finished *Lee's Lieutenants*, and he began outlining the first chapter of another major work six months later—on January 7, 1945, to be precise. This was his biography of George Washington, and he was engaged on it the rest of his life, spending 15,693 hours on it according to his own records. In the midst of this period of eight and a half years (June 30, 1949) he retired from the editorship of the *News Leader*. He continued his radio broadcasts and many other public activities, but more nearly than ever before he became a full-time historian. That is, he worked at history fifty-six hours a week as a rule. His labors on *R. E. Lee* and *Lee's Lieutenants* were spread over a period of twenty-nine years, and he did not keep exact records during the first of these. It is impossible to make exact mathematical comparisons between the time spent on these two works and on *George Washington*, but, roughly speaking, the third major undertaking may be compared to the two others in bulk and in the hours directly devoted to it. Against the seven volumes of Confederate biography may be set the five volumes on Washington that he published before his death. . . . In sum, he embarked at the age of fifty-eight on a literary and historical task which was roughly equivalent to the one he had performed already.

The question naturally arises, why did he do it? He did not then lack for useful and interesting employment. Besides doing his editorial work, he was serving on many boards; he belonged to all the major historical and literary societies, and in them could have consorted even more than he did with his brethren in letters and learning; he was traveling on the average 20,000 miles a year and could have had endless speaking engagements. He had fame enough, being now indisputably recognized as one of the first military historians of the world. Also, it might seem that he had won the right to rest, or at least to modify a schedule that most men would have found intolerable.

He made his decision after some pressure. To many it seemed desirable, even imperative, that his powers be employed in something fully worthy of them. No minor task would do; it had to be a major undertaking. Stephen Vincent Benét summed the matter up when he said that Douglas Freeman ought to be "chained to his desk" and forced to write a life of George Washington. There was logic in this, beyond a doubt. Materials on Washington that were now available had not been fully exploited; an authoritative military estimate of him was needed; and Washington was the fountainhead of the tradition which had been inherited by Lee as a man and soldier. The first great American hero clearly deserved and seemed now to require full-length treatment, and the finger of destiny pointed to America's greatest military biographer. Freeman never considered anything less than a spacious study of the whole man and his whole life. The work he planned was to be more extensive than any that had ever been written on this subject. Indeed, it had no real parallel in American biography, and in sheer bulk the task was enough to deter any but the most indefatigable workman. What was more, it fell within another century, which Dr. Freeman had never explored as a scholar and in which he had not lived in spirit—as he had lived so long in Lee's Virginia and the Southern Confederacy.

His acceptance of this challenge may be attributed, perhaps, to the "quenchless ambition of an ordered mind," which he was soon to perceive in Washington. In Freeman himself this took the form of eagerness to match his talents and skills against an immense task while there was yet time. There were grave risks but these were calculated risks, and he assumed them fully confident of his demonstrated powers and his tested methods. He viewed this gigantic undertaking with the eye of an engineer; he counted the time and concluded that he could perform it, relying on his unequalled craftsmanship. A notable aspect of his treatment of Lee was his emphasis on that General's ability in organization and administration, and this was to be even more notable in his treatment of Washington. Native ability and high character are not enough; industry and system are indispensable to those who would achieve greatly. He counted on them in his own case, and if there have been other American historians who have matched him in industry (which is doubtful), no one of them seems ever to have matched him in system.

> Malone, "The Pen of Douglas Southall Freeman," in Freeman,
> *George Washington* (1954), 6:xi–xxi, xxiii–xxiv

"Everywhere There Is the Aura of a Gently Cultivated Intellect": Clifford Dowdey

Clifford Dowdey (1904–79) was born in Richmond, where he graduated from John Marshall High School. After attending Columbia University, he returned to the city of his birth and worked briefly as a reporter on the Richmond *News Leader*, gaining the experience that would later see him through a decade as an editor of various magazines in New York City. During his ten-year stay there, he also contributed westerns and romances to popular magazines, and at night he did extensive research into the Civil War and its background. Dowdey became a major force in the world of letters with the pub-

lication of *Bugles Blow No More* (1937), which recounts the story of
Richmond during the Civil War. Heavily based on original research,
the novel won for its author a Guggenheim Fellowship, which in turn
led indirectly to Dowdey's becoming an important historian of the
South. Shortly after the publication of the book, Margaret Mitchell,
author of *Gone with the Wind*, wrote to Dowdey, saying:

> Never in my life have I read a book that held me as "Bugles"
> did. . . . There were times, in the battle chapters, when my
> mouth grew so dry from the dust the soldiers' feet kicked up that
> I all but choked but I wouldn't go get a drink to ease myself for
> fear of losing the spell.

> How wonderfully you made Richmond your heroine—she *was*,
> wasn't she? At least the city was the heroine for me and when you
> had finished with her I felt that I knew her mind and her heart
> and could find my way about her streets blindfolded.

Bill Millsaps (1942–), the author of the following newspaper
feature story, is a native of Daisy, Tennessee, and attended the University of Tennessee. He has been the sports editor of the Richmond
Times-Dispatch, which he joined in 1966, since 1977, having previously
worked as a reporter on the Knoxville, Tennessee, *Journal*. Millsaps
is a former president of the Associated Press Sports Editors.

While city traffic burns its way past the Jefferson Davis Monument,
only two blocks away the town house at 2504 Kensington Avenue
seems quiet, tranquil and subdued as the late afternoon heat shim-
mers off the street.

Inside, the air is cool, almost crystalline as shadowed corners and
dark objects subtly appear and disappear with changes in the angle of
the sun.

Books are literally everywhere—in the living room, in the study, in
the bedrooms, even stacked in the bathroom. They range from a
three-volume collection of the letters of James Joyce to the complete
roster of all the North Carolinians who fought in the Civil War.

Everywhere, there is the aura of a gently cultivated intellect, the
sense of a time and age preserved, the electric sweat of creativity, the
atmosphere of freedom. And everywhere in the house is the presence
of Clifford Dowdey.

At the age of 65, Dowdey is a vigorous, vibrant man with a storehouse of bittersweet memories, an abiding interest in professional

football (especially the Baltimore Colts), psychology, philosophy, Impressionist art, and eighteenth- and nineteenth-century music.

Behind him in a 43-year career as a writer are 17 novels. Seven dealt with the military and political history of the Confederacy. A native Richmonder, Dowdey is regarded as the outstanding living authority on the Army of Northern Virginia and its super-legendary leader, Robert E. Lee, about whom he wrote a 781-page biography published in 1965.

Dowdey works amidst the graying, dusty evidence of The Lost Cause. In his second-floor study, light streams through two windows onto ceiling-high bookshelves, a huge desk, an old typewriter, stacks of yellow foolscap paper, and a gold watch that his great-grandfather carried through the Civil War.

Among the hundreds of books in the study are biographies of both great and obscure military leaders as well as studies on the military activities of foot soldiers. One wall is almost completely covered with lithographs. There are vivid battle scenes that speak of death on both a great and small scale, counterpointed by grainy representations of the Sweet Life of Old Virginia prior to 1861.

If Dowdey has made the far-distant past a great portion of his life's work, he hardly lives in it. He began his writing career in the rough-and-tumble newspaper era of the 1920s, starting as a reporter with The News-Leader in 1925. (Virginius Dabney, the retired editor of the Times-Dispatch, was one of his co-workers).

Then in 1926, Dowdey went to New York and began turning out pulp fiction. Dowdey once said that, for a while, he " . . . killed a thousand men . . . for a penny a word." In 1934, he went to Delray Beach, Fla., and began work on his first novel, "Bugles Blow No More," a study of the citizens of Richmond during the Civil War. Published in 1937, it was an instant best seller and made Dowdey a writer of high reputation in one swift stroke.

Following were Dowdey articles in all the leading magazines, Dowdey critiques for various journals, and Dowdey screenplays for Hollywood motion pictures. And always, there were the novels.

On the bookstands now is Dowdey's "The Virginia Dynasties." Currently, Dowdey is finishing a sequel to it: "The Golden Age: A Climate for Greatness," a story of the governmental technicians who came out of the Virginia General Assembly and stirred the colonists to revolutionary ardor in the 1760s.

Dowdey is in his 11th and final year as a teacher of creative writing at the University of Richmond. And he reads current novelists with a great deal of interest and a great deal of dismay.

Dowdey, is, of course, much more than football fan, music lover, writer, and teacher. He is a complex, intelligent, civilized man driven by a high sense of his own talent weighted down by a personal tragedy and shoved into each new day by what can perhaps best be called a sheer desire to survive.

Dowdey's survival mechanism has an almost unvarying daily routine.

"I am up by seven almost every morning," he said. "Then I have breakfast, and I go to the typewriter around 8, then do research from 2:30 to around 5 p.m. Then we (he and daughters Patsy, 18, and Sarah, 15) have dinner. The next morning, it's the same all over again."

Dowdey's stature as a writer is high enough that what he writes, sells. And there have been enough sales over the years that Dowdey, while not enormously wealthy, is economically comfortable.

Yet he would like to become known once again as a fiction writer, to get away from the non-fiction, historical milieu. "Now that I have been acknowledged as the outstanding living historian on the Army of Northern Virginia, I have made a discovery: nobody cares anymore," he contended.

But at this late stage, it may prove difficult for Dowdey to break his ties with history. "Publishing techniques have changed drastically," he said. "The emphasis now is on the single-shot best seller. They (the publishers) don't rely on a stable of nine or 10 good writers anymore. Novels are a gamble, a very big gamble. Enormous amounts of money are spent on promotion."

Asked who among the current top novelists he admired, Dowdey quickly shot back. "None, although I must admit I was greatly impressed with Norman Mailer's 'Armies of the Night' (which recently won the Pulitzer Prize for non-fiction)."

What about John Updike's "Couples" and Philip Roth's "Portnoy's Complaint?"

"I can't believe that those books are truly honest pieces of work. You know, a few years ago there was a book published called 'My Secret Life.' It was written in the nineteenth century, and the life of the main character was virtually dominated by his sexual impulses. When that book came out, people thought of that type of man as a freak. Now, Updike and Roth have made him a hero."

Among the prominent writers of the age, Dowdey rates Fitzgerald, Joyce, and Proust at the top of the list.

"Fitzgerald was a really skilled writer. He was a genuine craftsman, but I think he was a dreadful man. I was in Hollywood when he was there at one time, and we were introduced. He remarked that I had an Irish name. I said, 'Yes, my ancestors were the O'Dowda's from County Galway.' Well, he sneered at me and said, 'Gentry people. My ancestors were potato famine Irish' and he walked away. I was stunned.

"John O'Hara? He's dated, still writing about the 1920s. Hemingway? I liked his early short stories very much, but I didn't care for some of his later work. He was a strutting egomaniac. He seemed to be primarily concerned with making a public figure of himself. Other writers disliked him very much for that."

Dowdey, who chain smokes from two packs of cigarettes at once— (this day it was Chesterfield and Salem), talks much like he writes: everything flows in a soft, candid conversational stream.

The subject of Hollywood brings a smile and a pause as he enjoys the memory.

"What a marvelous time we had. We lived in great grandeur in a small hotel named the Garden of Allah. It had four small rooms and a garden in the back, with bungalows all around it."

He did not discuss the screenplays, but he remembered the people. "There were screen writers like Philip Wylie and Harold Lamb, and at one time, Humphrey Bogart was there with us. We all had set hours. We wrote from 8 a.m. until noon, then the parties began. And they never seemed to stop until it was time to write again the next morning.

"A glorious time it was. Yes, I have closed a few bars in my day."

There was obviously more to being a Hollywood writer than the warm California sun, parties, and a host of intelligent friends or Dowdey, possibly, might still be there. "Nobody wants to work there. A writer never gets to work on anything that really interests him. The movie industry is geared solely to money-making. There was really no satisfaction in working there, so I left."

Dowdey, however, missed the ready and plentiful cash the movie industry provided him. But he never discussed the subject of a possible return with his wife, the former Frances Gordon Wilson, also a native Richmonder. One day, the problem came out into the open, quite by accident.

"It was very early in the morning," said Dowdey, "and the mailman woke us up with a special delivery letter from Paramount. I opened it and saw that they wanted me to do a screenplay for $2,500 a week. I was so excited, I rushed into the bedroom (in the Dowdey house the sleeping quarters are downstairs, the living quarters upstairs) and blurted out about the offer and all the money that we could have again. My wife just sat there in bed and very calmly told me, 'The epitaph of too many of your friends is "Just one more picture." ' Well, I was just devastated. I turned them down, and I have never had the desire to go back again."

Dowdey has lived in Florida, New York, Connecticut, Arizona ("my favorite"), and Mexico ("I can remember when Acapulco was a marvelously cheap place"), but here in Virginia, where his family roots penetrate to the Blounts who settled in Jamestown in 1609, Dowdey is home.

Like many others of the monied and/or educated class, Dowdey likes the Old Dominion's life style. Mass Culture has yet to take a strong foothold here, and Dowdey, like many thousands of other Virginians, is happy that it has not.

"When the colony was founded," Dowdey said, "the settlers brought with them a social structure and adapted it to Virginia. It was satisfactory to them, and it remained virtually unchanged until the war and the end of slavery.

"The war brought poverty and dislocation, and the two combined to keep out any appreciable influx of new citizens until the 1920s. There was some infusion of new blood into the state after World War I, and the pace of movement into the state really picked up after World War II. Yet from 1750 until the 1950s, there was really very little change in the way Virginians lived and enjoyed their environment.

"This perpetuity of culture also had some unfortunate side effects. There was a very bad tendency toward complacency.

"But in my books, I emphasized the good values of the past. There was a high sense of personal honor, a sense of duty toward humanity. Senator Harry Byrd personified this sense of personal honor. But now things are changing. And I think that Virginians are becoming more aware of their involvement with the problems of today and the future."

As a man of long experience with all stratas of American society, Dowdey sees the current upheaval in our culture as affecting every class but one—the very rich.

"Outside of a general social revolution," he said, "the very rich will remain the same. The young men will go to the same schools: Groton, St. Mark's, Harvard, and Yale. They'll go on the same stag lists for the deb parties where they will meet girls of their same economic status. They'll marry and produce children that go to the same schools and so on and so on. It has been that way for years, and I don't see it changing."

Dowdey has always been conscious of the rich, what he calls "the privilege" that money affords. "When I was going to John Marshall High School back in the 20s, I can remember boys from rich families being delivered at school in Pierce-Arrows, which were absolutely the finest automobiles of the time. I saw then what money could do, and I wanted to be able to do that type of thing for my children some day."

And, to an extent, Dowdey does. "When I take my girls to New York, we stay in the best hotels. We may stay a shorter period of time, but we have the best. When we eat, I have taught them not to look at the price. They order what they want, regardless."

Dowdey is very, very close to both Patsy and Sarah, both of whom exude an air of quiet beauty and quiet emotional strength.

"I have told Patsy (a graduating senior at Collegiate)," said Dowdey, "that when she finishes her college training she can spend a year at the Sorbonne. The money is there for her education. It's hers anyway. She wants me to go with her to Paris, take a flat, and enjoy Paris with her."

Dowdey smiled as he discussed the prospect of a year in Paris, but in five years he may be ready to take that trip. He has, in short, come to a stopping place. The words don't come easy any more.

Dowdey said he knows what it was like for Hemingway when the words came hard. When Hemingway could no longer write up to his own high standards and when he found it difficult to maintain the hedonistic image he had created for himself, he loaded a shotgun, put it to his forehead, and pulled both triggers.

Hemingway, said Dowdey, came to the frightening end to which Somerset Maugham brought Rev. Davidson in "Rain." "Rev. Davidson had convinced himself and others that he was a man above human passion, above lust. Sadie Thompson changed all that for him. It totally destroyed his self image. He had to kill himself, and he did."

Dowdey was asked what he would do if he became as profoundly dissatisfied with his own work as Hemingway became with his.

There was a long pause and Dowdey said, "I think I am at the stage right now." It was a brutally candid answer.

But Dowdey is not a poseur, not a man for whom a false image has been necessary. He has been honest with himself and his work, and he can go on.

"I have other plans. This book on the Golden Age is real physical work. I plow through it, struggle with it and now the end is in sight."

What next?

With obvious effort, he said, "Frances was found to have incurable cancer two-and-a-half years ago. With cobalt treatment, the cancer was arrested. But now she is subject to periods of extreme depression. My daughters are resilient, but I am not. I had thought of doing a book on the effects this type of depression can bring on a family. But now I'm not so sure. I may try something completely new, something totally divorced from the subject."

The disease and the depression have torn at Dowdey's emotions. For years he was a devout communicant of St. Paul's Episcopal Church. No more. "The church gave me nothing at a time when I most needed its help," he said.

Without the church, Dowdey has gone to great length to attempt to live with the nearness of death, what he called "the great senselessness, the great lack of purpose in it all."

"I began reading the existentialist philosophers and theologians like Paul Tillich. He spoke in terms of the Eternal Now, the idea of surviving for the day, the hour, the minute. My God is Tillich's Ultimate Concern, the human devotion to duty, personal honor, and finally our mechanism for survival. The Authentic Self survives."

After so many contributions to our culture, Dowdey has reason to be a proud man.

"Write it down that I am a professional writer. I am, I guess, proudest of that. I am my own man, I always have been, and on my own terms, too. Some time ago, I was feeling very depressed, very down. And Patsy said to me, 'Don't worry. When Richard Strauss died, he said "I was my own man." You are too.' It was just what I needed. I like that. I like that very much."

Millsaps, "Clifford Dowdey," Richmond *Times-Dispatch*,
8 June 1969

"Publicist for a Liberal South": Virginius Dabney

For many of the years that Douglas Southall Freeman (q.v.) edited the Richmond *News Leader*, his counterpart at the *Times-Dispatch* was Virginius Dabney (1901–). Like Freeman, Dabney had several concurrent and full careers—as a Pulitzer Prize-winning journalist; as a historian of Richmond, the Old Dominion, and the South; as a patron of higher education and a lecturer at Princeton and Cambridge universities, and elsewhere—to mention only some of the most conspicuous. But unlike Freeman, the courtly and gracious Dabney was a southerner of liberal instincts, well before such sentiments became fashionable or legally mandated. Though his liberalism was not all-encompassing and might seem modest by the standards of the 1980s, he nonetheless took stands in earlier decades that were both courageous and controversial, as discussed below by historian Morton Sosna (1945–).

Any list of white Southern liberals between 1920 and 1950 would reveal a high percentage of newspapermen; almost every major city in the South contained white newspapermen who campaigned against racial intolerance. Men such as Louis I. Jaffe of the *Norfolk Virginian-Pilot*, Julian LaRose Harris of Georgia's *Columbus Enquirer-Sun*, Grover Hall of the *Montgomery Advertiser*, John Temple Graves II of the *Birmingham Age-Herald*, Barry Bingham and Mark Ethridge of the *Louisville Courier-Journal*, Hodding Carter II of Greenville, Mississippi's *Delta-Democrat Times*, Jonathan Daniels of the *Raleigh News and Observer*, W. J. Cash of the *Charlotte News*, and Ralph McGill of the *Atlanta Constitution* were the publicists for a liberal South and frequently took an active role in the major liberal organizations. Prominent among these men was Virginius Dabney, frequent contributor to many national magazines and from 1936 to 1969 editor of the influential *Richmond Times-Dispatch*.

Dabney's background was patrician; he was born into one of Virginia's leading families, including in its ranks numerous planters, lawyers, doctors, and college teachers. His mother was a collateral descendant of no less a Virginian than Thomas Jefferson. His father, Richard Heath Dabney, was a long-time history professor at the University of Virginia, where from 1905 to 1923 he also served as dean of graduate studies. The elder Dabney was a highly respected historian who wrote books on John Randolph of Roanoke and the French Revolution, and who for many years carried on a close personal correspondence with Woodrow Wilson. After his death in 1947, a eulogizer wrote that Heath Dabney had "embodied all that was most admirable and pleasing in the Old-School Virginia gentleman, with whom honor came first, and human kindness close behind." Virginius's paternal grandfather, for whom he was named, was a well-known literary critic and the author of two novels. But probably the most famous Dabney of all was Virginius's great-grandfather, Thomas Smith Gregory Dabney, who in 1835 had moved his family and slaves from Virginia to Mississippi where he established Burleigh, a cotton plantation running to more than 40,000 acres and ultimately holding over 500 slaves.

Thomas Dabney was a model planter, the kind from whom legends are made. He was progressive both in the way he ran his plantation and in the way that he treated his bondsmen. A deeply religious man, he encouraged his slaves to learn to read and write, recognized the sanctity of black families, and whenever possible purchased spouses of his own slaves who were owned by another master. Until the Civil War Burleigh flourished. Dabney was a Whig who opposed secession and even considered migrating to England once the conflict began, but since this would entail parting with his beloved servants and leaving them to some unknown fate, he rejected the idea. The saga of Thomas Dabney, including his travails during the Civil War and Reconstruction, was recorded by his loving daughter Susan Smedes in her 1887 *Memorials of a Southern Planter,* which she wrote specifically to counteract the malevolent image of the slaveholder popularized by such works as Harriet Beecher Stowe's *Uncle Tom's Cabin* and Fanny Kemble's *Journal of a Residence on a Georgia Plantation.* The book was a success; seven editions were published within a space of twelve years. An English edition appeared in 1890, and another American one in 1914. Though biased, *Memorials of a Southern Planter* stands out as a first-rate historical source, undoubtedly one reason why it was reprinted again in 1965.

It was to such a heritage that Virginius Dabney was born in University (now Charlottesville), Virginia, in 1901. Growing up in the intellectually congenial atmosphere of a college community, he received an excellent education. Dabney was an outstanding student. He was graduated Phi Beta Kappa from the University of Virginia in 1920 and went on to receive his master's degree in 1921. After teaching French for a year at a high school near Alexandria, Dabney became a reporter with the *Richmond News Leader* in 1922. He remained with the *News Leader* until 1928, when he joined the editorial staff of the *Richmond Times-Dispatch,* a position he would hold for the next forty-one years.

There was little in his early years to indicate that Virginius Dabney would eventually concern himself with the problems of Southern blacks. Dabney's father, though his education set him apart from most white Southerners, had been conservative and entirely orthodox. Virginius's own comfortable background insulated him from many of the blatant racial injustices of the era, and not until much later in his life did he fully comprehend them. Even at the height of his fame as a progressive-minded newspaperman, Dabney's racial liberalism never quite moved beyond a highly articulate—and undoubtedly sincere— separate-but-equal position. However, what distinguished him from his father was a willingness to criticize openly members of Virginia's political and ecclesiastical establishment. For example, in 1926 his coverage of the trial of a Negro woman sentenced to thirty years in prison for stealing less than $200 led to public indignation against the ruling judge.

In taking periodic whacks at the Southern status quo, Dabney unquestionably reflected the great impact that H. L. Mencken had upon young, educated white Southerners whose views matured during the 1920s. Illustrative of his intellectual debt to Mencken was Dabney's long interest in one of the more enigmatic figures of Southern history, Bishop James Cannon, Jr., a Virginia Prohibitionist and one of the driving forces behind the Anti-Saloon League's successful effort to secure passage of the Eighteenth Amendment. The anti-clerical Mencken once described Cannon as "the most powerful ecclesiastic ever heard of in America." Dabney undertook a probing investigation of Cannon's life and work, beginning in 1929, that culminated in the 1949 publication of a scathing biography appropriately titled *Dry Messiah*. Though Dabney showed a grudging admiration for Cannon's high-handedness and efficiency, the book was devastating; Dabney was brutally frank about his distaste for the hypocrisy he thought his subject represented. He characterized Cannon as "one of the most significant and most ominous figures of his time, a man whose tempestuous career holds lessons for us all."

By exposing men such as Cannon, Dabney showed his willingness to acknowledge the South's seamier side, but like other Southern liberals, he did not believe that Bishop Cannon truly represented the region. Dabney had his own vision of a Silent South. For him it consisted of the spiritual descendants of Thomas Jefferson—an elite of educated humanists who exercised a liberalizing influence far out of proportion to their numbers. It was a radically different kind of Silent South from the noble white yeomanry perceived by Howard Odum.

In 1932 Dabney outlined his views in *Liberalism in the South*, a four-hundred-page volume dealing with enlightened white Southerners since the eighteenth century. Dabney believed that the defense of slavery had retarded the development of the region's otherwise liberal impulses, but that once the trauma of the Civil War era was over, the South's liberal heritage reasserted itself. The book chronicled the work of native Southerners such as Jabez Lamar Monroe Curry, who from the end of the Civil War until his death in 1901 had continuously campaigned for greater educational opportunities for both white and black Southerners. Dabney asserted that the influence of men like Curry was increasing and making the South a better place in which to live. "The South may rejoice," he wrote, "that the social attitudes of its leaders and its people are coming to be more and more shot through with liberalism." According to Dabney, Southern white men with liberal proclivities were chiefly responsible for the progress that had occurred since antebellum times and their continuing activities could bring about the "future greatness" of the region.

Though it focused on numerous nonracial areas, *Liberalism in the South* tried to show that advances had also been made in black-white relations. Despite the demagoguery of some Southern politicians and the activities of the Ku Klux Klan, Dabney insisted that there was "a growing awareness on the part of the dominant race that the Negro is not a serf or a helot, but a human being with legitimate aspirations . . . which are slowly being realized." Dabney even detected a "growing conviction" on the part of a "substantial body of Southerners" that Jim Crow laws were excessively severe. However, he made it a point of noting that the prevailing view among the white majority was that segregation should be strictly maintained.

Liberalism in the South demonstrated the young man's yearning to find a liberal tradition in his region's turmoiled past. At times he strained to prove his thesis. Arthur Raper thought well of the work but pointed out that Dabney tended to label almost anything "liberal." Clarence Cason, an Alabama writer, was more blunt. He thought the book "entirely too long, because there simply never had been that much liberalism in the South." At any rate, in his own way Dabney had tried to prick some holes in the idea that the South was a blight upon the rest of the nation. Its past was not totally dark; its future was bright. These were the book's principal contentions.

Like other liberals, Dabney pointed to the futility of Reconstruction. In a 1936 article for the *American Mercury*, he speculated that if the South had won the Civil War it would have at least been spared the "ordeal to which it was subjected at the hands of thieves, cutpurses, and picaroons from the North." Only white Southerners, implied Dabney, could solve the region's problems. Yet he did not lament the Confederacy's demise. According to Dabney, if the Confederacy had been successful, the poor whites might have risen to power sooner and more assertively than they ultimately did, with the end result a South ruled by some "Führer Huey Long." It was an unusual point for a Southern liberal to make; such a view, for example, would have been unthinkable to Howard Odum.

During the mid-thirties Dabney's reputation as an outspoken Southern liberal continued to grow. Particularly daring were his editorials denouncing the 1933 conviction in Atlanta of a nineteen-year-old black Communist, Angelo Herndon, who received a sentence of 18–

20 years at hard labor for having organized a demonstration of unemployed white and black workers to protest the inadequacy of Fulton County's relief programs. Though the lily-white court considered its judgment merciful (the obscure Georgia insurrectionary law under which Herndon was tried could have demanded the death penalty), the case would become second only to Scottsboro as an example of "Southern justice." Yet in openly criticizing the outrageous verdict, Dabney was only one of two white Southern journalists, the other being W. T. Anderson of the *Macon Telegraph*. Moreover, after attending a May 1936 meeting of the Southern Policy Association, the predecessor of the Southern Conference for Human Welfare, he publicly denounced the poll tax and began to write editorials against it in the *Times-Dispatch*. It was a bold move for the editor of Virginia's leading newspaper to take, for Virginia in the heyday of the Byrd machine was probably the most tightly run and narrowly ruled of the Southern states. The political scientist V. O. Key characterized it as a "political museum piece," so much under the control of an oligarchy that its politics resembled those of England prior to the Reform Bill of 1832 more closely than they resembled those of any other American state.

The following year Dabney again went out on a limb. In February 1937, after an NAACP-sponsored antilynching bill was introduced in Congress, Dabney wrote a strongly supportive editorial in the *Times-Dispatch*. Only federal action could wipe out lynching, he insisted, while urging other Southern liberals to support the measure. He later wrote additional editorials as well as an article for the *Nation*.

Walter White was elated. "Like a pebble dropped into a still pond," he told Dabney, "the repercussions of your superb editorial stand." White sent reprints to every member of Congress and to the press. He believed that Dabney would deserve much of the credit if the antilynching bill passed and told Carl W. Ackerman, the dean of Columbia's journalism school, that the *Times-Dispatch* editorial marked "one of the most significant positions taken by an American newspaper since the Civil War." According to White, Dabney deserved a Pulitzer Prize. White wrote to each of the thirteen members of the Pulitzer committee, a move that made even Dabney suspect that he was carrying things too far. Nevertheless, for almost a year White kept up his one-man campaign to get Dabney the Pulitzer. In the end, he failed, and he also lost his fight for federal antilynching legislation.

White's lionization of Dabney showed how desperately the NAACP director wanted Southern liberals to support his efforts. For the most part, he was unsuccessful. Committed to protest and legal action,

White wanted federal help to deal with Southern racial issues, which conflicted with the aim of the majority of Southern liberals. Moreover, as the Pulitzer Prize episode demonstrated, White's attempts at influence were at times heavy handed, and he made numerous enemies, black as well as white. Although White was in reality a cautious leader who fulfilled an important and necessary role, his style, plus his visibility as head of an established organization, made him seem more radical than he was. Walter White, to many Southern liberals, was the archetypal black agitator. Eventually, Dabney would join the chorus of White's critics. In 1939, to White's great disappointment, Dabney opposed the NAACP's attempts to integrate Southern professional and graduate schools following the Supreme Court's decision in *Missouri Ex Rel. Gaines* v. *Canada.*

In November 1938 Dabney expressed a desire to participate in the Birmingham meeting of the Southern Conference for Human Welfare. But when he discovered that known Communist party members would be included in the conference, he refused to go to Birmingham or have anything further to do with SCHW. Yet he generally shared most of the group's early goals. This was particularly true of the organized campaign against the poll tax. Dabney lent his name and prestige to the anti-poll tax movement with editorials, articles, and speeches. "From the crags above Harper's Ferry to the mesa fringing the Rio Grande, a revolt is brewing against the poll tax," he happily reported for the *New York Times* in 1939. Dabney argued that the poll tax was a relic from the Reconstruction era and that universal white manhood suffrage had been a tradition in Virginia ever since 1619. Moreover, since the measure disfranchised many more whites than blacks, Dabney did not hesitate to call for its immediate repeal in Virginia as well as elsewhere in the South.

Dabney's outspoken views on such controversial matters aroused the ire of many white Southerners. When in 1941 he called upon defense industries to hire Negroes and pay them equally with whites, one outraged reader referred to the "BLITZKRIEG" that Dabney had started against the "decent white worker." The following year he waged practically a one-man campaign in the state to save Odell Waller, a convicted black Virginia sharecropper, from a death sentence for the murder of his white landlord. Dabney later remembered having "caught hell all over the place" for maintaining that Waller, whose landlord had been cheating him, should not be executed.

In 1942 Dabney published his second major work, *Below the Potomac,* a book about the status of the South on the eve of the United States' entrance into World War II. As he had done in *Liberalism in the South,*

Dabney once again defended the region from its image and tried to demonstrate that it was making substantial progress in many areas. "It should be emphasized," he wrote, "that the demagogues are distinctly in the minority here. . . . They merely make the most noise, and consequently are the recipients of the most publicity." Dabney also asserted that portrayals of the *Tobacco Road* type did not do justice to poor Southern whites. Only a few were as "filthy and depraved as Jeeter Lester and his libidinous entourage." Dabney assured his readers that they would not necessarily find such people every time they traveled South.

Predictably, much of the book was devoted to race. Dabney had extensive praise for the Commission on Interracial Cooperation. He contrasted Will Alexander's group with what he termed the divisive "pugnacity" of the NAACP, which he considered detrimental to the interests of the vast majority of Southern Negroes. Dabney called lynching "the greatest of all blots on the good name of the South," but he modified his own position regarding a federal antilynching law, arguing that a decline in lynchings and actions on the state level made such a measure less necessary than it had been a few years earlier. Dabney believed that any new attempt to present Congress with an antilynching bill would trigger Southern filibusters rather than reduce mob violence. He insisted that a federal law should be enacted only as a last resort. In general, Dabney maintained that Southern race relations were not as terror-prone as people would think from reading newspapers. Tuberculosis, he pointed out, was a more serious threat to Southern blacks than lynching. In the traditional manner of a Southern liberal, he also noted that blacks were still discriminated against and segregated in areas outside the South. "Obviously the Negroes of Mississippi suffer under serious disabilities," he wrote, "but how much worse is their condition than that of their racial kinsmen in Harlem or the Chicago Black Belt?"

Dabney was particularly enthusiastic about the progress in black education in the South and impressed with what he saw as the increasing tendency of whites to facilitate rather than hinder efforts in this area. He called for federal funds to help Southern states advance black education. Unaided, the South could not upgrade Negro schools to a level of substantial equality with white ones, and this had to be done in order to rid education of discrimination. The alternative would be to admit blacks to white schools. However, since only an "infinitesimal minority" of white Southerners would agree to an abolition of the dual school system, Dabney surmised that such an approach was unlikely in the foreseeable future. In fact, he did not favor admitting blacks to white Southern educational institutions under any circumstances, even on the graduate level. Despite the Supreme Court's ruling in the *Gaines* case, Dabney believed that the time was not yet "propitious." He maintained that the one or two blacks in a state who sought to exercise their undoubted legal right for an equal education might endanger the lives and welfare of hundreds of Negroes in the violent white reaction that would almost certainly follow. Given the situation, the most positive step would be for several Southern states to pool their resources and establish quality regional institutions for black higher education. But he admitted that the Supreme Court's possible refusal to sanction such a program presented a major obstacle.

Dabney, though not a hard-core opponent of Supreme Court decisions against racial discrimination, was a middle-of-the-road Southern liberal. He believed in justice for blacks but insisted that proponents of change still had to recognize the racial sensitivities of the vast majority of white Southerners. "Americans must candidly admit that the democratic ideal is at war with the thesis that American citizens can be placed in separate pigeonholes and given varying educational and social advantages, depending upon the color of their skin," he could write in one sentence, while in the next: "Yet sight must not be lost of the fact that the modern South inherited a problem of tremendous complexity and difficulty at the close of the Civil War." For Dabney and for Southern liberals in general, such a position proved increasingly difficult to maintain.

Like other Southern liberals, and despite his own genteel heritage, Dabney denounced traditional white paternalism. He regarded the racial outlook of William Alexander Percy, a Mississippi planter and poet who was an articulate exponent of paternalism, as unfit for the twentieth century. "Mr. Percy was led into the unfortunate error," said Dabney, "of assuming nearly all other large Southern plantations were like his 'Trail Lake' and that other Southern landlords were like himself. Would that they were!"

But, in his own way, Dabney still asserted that the future of Southern blacks lay in the hands of an elite group of Southern whites. "In that great future which awaits the South," he wrote somewhat self-righteously, "its alert and uninhibited editors may be expected to join with its colleges and universities, its public-spirited professional men, its socially conscious women, and its articulate and progressive business and labor leaders in building below the Potomac and the Ohio a grander civilization than that storied land has ever known." The *Times-Dispatch* editor made it clear that he regarded the press as vital to this heretofore Silent South:

> How, for instance, would Louisiana have got rid of the Huey Long machine, and its assorted crooks and thieves, without the courageous New Orleans newspapers? Who but the Atlanta press is leading the opposition to Talmadge in Georgia? Where in the South does one find a more insistent and effective advocate for fairness and justice for the Negro than in the white press? Where have the better schools, better roads, better health, and better penal institutions had more tenacious champions than among Southern publishers and editors? . . . The press of the South frequently is the spearhead leading the advance to new frontiers, the panzer division which breaks a path for the slogging infantry. There is at least one large, influential, and forward-looking newspaper in every Southern state.

Below the Potomac, though it defended the theory behind segregation, inveighed against any further browbeating of Southern blacks. Dabney argued that the education and uplift of Negroes created useful citizens without leading to that "oft debated, and somewhat nebulous concept," social equality. White Southerners who still clung to what he described as "out-moded ante-bellum notions" of race relations would have to give them up. Dabney's argument was a familiar one to white liberals: "Ultraconservative Southerners whose chief thoughts on the race problem revolved about the business of 'keeping the Negro in his place' seem unable to explain how the white population is ever to be reasonably healthy and prosperous if for every two white persons there is a diseased, poverty-stricken and illiterate, if not criminally inclined, Negro."

The entrance of the United States into World War II changed the racial situation throughout the nation so dramatically that the views expressed in *Below the Potomac* seemed outdated even as the book was being released by its publishers in 1942. The wartime militancy of American blacks and their sympathizers, plus the resulting white anxieties, particularly in the South, severely tested the racial liberalism of Virginius Dabney. He soon became one of the leading critics in the country of what he regarded as the excesses in Negro demands. Dabney applauded the statement of FEPC chairman Mark Ethridge to the effect that the white Southerner would never countenance the abolition of legal segregation. "You are dead right, and I am glad that you said it," he told Ethridge. He railed against those who he felt were misleading blacks. "My considered judgment," he informed John Temple Graves, "is that Mrs. Roosevelt, Pearl Buck, Herbert Agar and a few others are doing tremendous harm. In fact, I believe that they have had as much to do with stirring up the Negroes as anybody." Dabney took special umbrage at the militant tone of such leading black news-papers as the *Chicago Defender, Pittsburgh Courier, Baltimore Afro-American,* and New York's *Amsterdam News.* "I believe that it will be obvious to you," he wrote the editor of *Reader's Digest,* "that when supposedly responsible Negro opinion compares Mark Ethridge to Gene Tal-madge that things have come to a pretty pass, and we are in danger of wholesale race riots." And Southern blacks, Dabney added, would be the major losers in any confrontation.

Dabney hoped that his reputation as a liberal would enable him to speak freely and influentially on wartime racial tensions. In Janu-ary 1943, he outlined his views in an *Atlantic Monthly* article entitled "Nearer and Nearer the Precipice." "A small group of Negro agitators and another small group of white rabble-rousers," he wrote, "are pushing this country closer and closer to an interracial explosion which may make the race riots of the First World War and its after-math seem mild by comparison." Dabney severely criticized A. Philip Randolph for his intention to lead a Negro protest march on Wash-ington, D.C. and Roy Wilkins of the NAACP for remarking that American blacks did indeed desire social equality with whites. Such militancy, insisted Dabney, only inspired the South's demagogues to new mischief. He once again had harsh words for the "radical ele-ment" of the black press, particularly concerning the harm done through attacks on Southern liberals. The Richmond editor did not believe that Southern blacks could make progress unless they had the support of men like himself. Dabney hoped that to relieve the South's current sense of racial crisis and avert bloodshed, both the Randolphs and the Talmadges could be silenced for the duration of the war.

"Nearer and Nearer the Precipice" received wide attention and caused an immediate outcry from blacks and some of their white sup-porters. The distinguished black writer Langston Hughes wondered whether the American dream for which the nation was fighting was just for whites. "Mr. Dabney's article as a whole," said Hughes, "im-plies that Negroes, segregated, Jim-crowed, and lynched as we are, should still not seek to disturb the *status quo* of racial oppression." Criticism of Dabney was not confined to Northern blacks. P. B. Young, the editor of the relatively moderate *Norfolk Journal and Guide,* told his long-time Richmond friend that the *Atlantic Monthly* piece had failed to point out that Negroes were under tremendous pressure and had to fight bitterly for every bit of humane treatment they received. Said Young: "You seem to fail to realize that what is actually going on is a determination on the part of many that the Negro shall have no part in this war, and subsequently no part in the fruits of victory. . . . You fail to see that the Negro is being reduced to a menial or common laborer; that organized labor is excluding him from any skilled work —except what it has been forced to by a presidential executive order." Young also took strong exception to Dabney's assertion that no black man in the South could win election to Congress in the foreseeable future. He informed Dabney, "It is the same thing that Messrs. Rankin, Talmadge, Bilbo and others say with the difference that their language is always coarse and their attitude brutal, while your language is always cultured and your attitude dignified. The result is the same."

Dabney's views, which a great many other Southern liberals shared, contributed to a growing chasm between Southern and non-Southern liberal blocs. *The New Leader*, an organ of the non-Communist left, ran an article entitled "What's Happened to the Southern 'Liberals'?" Cy Record, the author of the piece, said that wartime changes in the South bewildered Southern liberals more than any other group. According to Record, white Southern liberals—he mentioned by name, in addition to Dabney, John Temple Graves, Mark Ethridge, Jonathan Daniels, and Jennings Perry—had been "caught woefully offguard, unprepared to measure the impact of the war . . . and unable to channel their general humanitarian impulses into the stream of rapid social and economic change." *The New Leader* also took Southern liberals to task for insisting that only they could bestow progress upon poor whites and blacks. "The thought . . . that Negroes, organized and led by their own leaders, might make immediate demands for certain rights and prepare to implement such demands is shocking to the liberal temperament, not to say terrifying," wrote Record.

Dabney did not take such criticism lightly. He regarded himself as a sincere friend of Southern blacks and did not argue, as John Temple Graves did, that blacks had to drop all their wartime demands. He vigorously endorsed the Durham statement, and he played an instrumental role in the formation of the Southern Regional Council. Only the controversy resulting from his *Atlantic Monthly* article caused him to decline to serve as chairman of the June 1943 interracial conference in Richmond. If for no other reason than to quell Negro militancy, Dabney thought it absolutely essential to establish a dialogue between blacks and liberal Southern whites. "I am sure you can see that if our group keeps on manifesting relative indifference in the face of the

Negroes' great eagerness to cooperate," he wrote to one wavering Regional Council supporter, "they will become convinced that we are not serious . . . and will conclude that Southern whites are a hopeless lot." Dabney feared that the end result of such inaction would be that Southern blacks would increasingly look up to the "radical Northern leadership of the Walter White caliber."

During 1943 Dabney worked hard to promote a coalition between blacks and white Southern liberals. In October he wrote of the "Dynamic New South" for the *New York Times*, arguing that, rather than following Tobacco Road to its logical end of misery, disease, and poverty, the former Confederacy was on "a broad highway which may well lead to the greatest prosperity it has ever known." A month later, writing in *Survey Graphic*, Dabney addressed himself more directly to the issues raised by the newly created Southern Regional Council. He noted that the white South still had plenty to answer for in its treatment of blacks and that segregation constituted a tremendously thorny problem. The principle of racial separation, according to Dabney, could only be defended if "absolutely equal" facilities were provided for both races, and such was obviously not the case in the South. Segregation had instead come to mean "discrimination and a whole series of hateful oppressions." Dabney insisted that the Southern Regional Council recognized this fact and meant to deal with it. He added that if he himself were a Negro, he would wish segregation abolished, but would realize that to do so in the face of the overwhelming hostility of white Southerners would do more harm than good. In Dabney's view many white Southerners were prepared to make reasonable concessions to some black demands, particularly if they came from the black South rather than from sources above the Mason-Dixon Line. However, he detected "a deliberate conspiracy of northern extremists to picture the entire South as the abode of lantern-jawed lynchers, tobacco chewing hillbillies, and bigoted ignoramuses with no humane instincts or decent sensibilities." He regarded this as the single greatest obstacle to racial progress.

Dabney believed that Southern liberals had to come up with some dramatic gesture to demonstrate that their empathy with blacks was not confined to rhetoric. He envisioned something both symbolic and substantive and decided to take a bold step. In November 1943, in two *Times-Dispatch* editorials, Dabney urged that Virginia repeal its segregation laws in regard to servicing blacks on streetcars and other common carriers. His chief argument was that enforced segregation on public conveyances was an irritant to both whites and blacks and, especially when administered by uncouth whites, a source of frequent interracial friction. Furthermore, according to Dabney, Jim Crow streetcar laws defeated their own intention in that they more often than not forced whites and blacks to push their way past each other and thus come into more actual contact than they would if left to sit wherever they pleased. He characterized a statewide abolition of such laws as a "conservative course in race relations," for it would offer tangible evidence to Southern Negroes that their best interests lay in renewed cooperation with their white fellow citizens rather than with outside groups. "We white Southerners," Dabney concluded, "can remedy the evident injustices in the treatment of the Negroes, and thereby win their confidence, respect and cooperation, or we can refuse to do anything, and repeat the old nonsense to the effect that 'the problem will solve itself, if people will only stop talking about it.'"

Despite his labeling of this proposal as "conservative," Dabney's views prompted an outpouring of praise from the militant Negro press, the NAACP, and Northern liberals—the very groups that had so roundly denounced him only a few months earlier. The *Pittsburgh Courier*, one of the papers Dabney usually referred to when he spoke of "sensation-mongering" black publications, ran a laudatory editorial about Dabney's "Sanity in the South." The *Courier*'s executive editor, P. L. Prattis, congratulated Dabney for his stand and maintained that no matter what the *Times-Dispatch* editor chose to call his action, it represented a radical step forward. "You are tampering with the foundation of racial chauvinism," said Prattis. "Should you succeed, the super-structure must of necessity become less secure." Roy Wilkins informed Dabney that Negroes outside the South greeted his proposal with happy amazement and said that the NAACP did not mind being cast in the role of "bogey man" in order to secure such concessions. "It has been more of a tonic than you can imagine," he wrote. Writing in the *Progressive*, Oswald Garrison Villard, an ogre to many white Southerners, called Dabney's position on bus segregation a "statesmanlike and far-seeing stand."

More significant than the accolades was the fact that Dabney's effort to eliminate Jim Crow on buses aroused much more white Southern hostility than support. No other white Virginia newspaper defended his proposal; indeed, the only other white paper in the entire South to agree with Dabney was a small weekly in Kinston, North Carolina. Even Ralph McGill's *Atlanta Constitution* refused to stand with him. Dabney found himself trying to explain his editorials to disbelieving readers and friends. He told one worried Virginia woman that he did not propose abolishing segregation anywhere but on common carriers.

Louis I. Jaffe, an editor for the *Norfolk Virginian-Pilot* who in 1929 had received a Pulitzer Prize for his criticism of the Ku Klux Klan and the Byrd machine, could not understand how his Richmond colleague could call for the abandonment of Jim Crow on public transportation without giving up the entire theory behind segregation. Dabney replied that the war had increased racial tension in the South and that the elimination of segregated buses and streetcars would give Negroes a psychological lift so that they would feel "we are not stalling them off with nothing but fine words." Since the law would be repealed on the basis of its ineffectiveness, Dabney foresaw no major threat to institutionalized racial separation. Nevertheless, no city, county, or state agency in Virginia considered Dabney's plan.

Despite his advocacy of an idea that, by his own admission, "set the whole South on its ear," Dabney felt uncomfortable in the role of militant. R. M. Golightly, coordinator of the Detroit-based National Committee to Abolish Jim Crow Transportation, offered Dabney his group's assistance, but Dabney flatly rejected the suggestion, arguing that Northern interference would only decrease the already slim chance that his proposal had for adoption. Dabney may have been sympathetic to the problems of Southern blacks, but as the urbane and sophisticated scion of one of Virginia's more prominent families, he was also a close associate of Richmond's banker-lawyer-merchant elite. He did not appreciate Richmond women telling his wife, who had a black cook, "If V would stop talking so much we might have some cooks in *our* kitchens."

The truth of the matter was that Dabney, nurtured in a South where segregation was at its peak, was too much a product of Southern gentility to shift his views easily on this touchy issue. Though he represented the best of his tradition, he had limits. Thus Dabney could be "impressed" by the letter of an army major stationed in Washington who complained of the "cocky insolence" of the city's blacks and who wrote that "unless the Negroes are immediately forced out of their Virginia toehold and a stop is put to this equality octopus, Virginia and the whole South . . . will soon be enmeshed in its tentacles." Dabney answered that he did not soft-pedal the importance of maintaining racial separation, and that the *Times-Dispatch* frequently ran editorials criticizing Mrs. Roosevelt and the NAACP. "It seems to me that we must take a stand somewhere," said Dabney, "and unless we take it now, the whole structure of segregation will crumble."

Dabney never could comprehend what blacks thought they could possibly gain by undertaking a militant campaign against Jim Crow. He could not understand why so many of their leaders became immediately incensed when white Southern liberals stated the necessity of segregation even though they offered other reforms and concessions. For Dabney, push was beginning to lead to shove, and that could not be tolerated. "I am entirely sure that the colored people ought to have a good many things that they haven't got," he wrote to one fearful Southern white, "but I am also sure that we ought to maintain the segregation of the races." In June 1943 he heard that blacks were planning to take their cause into the streets. His reaction was total apprehension: "It appears that Negroes are to be told to go into restaurants reserved for whites and take seats, to go into the theatres and do likewise, and to sit in the section set aside for whites on streetcars and buses. Furthermore, they are supposedly being told not to fight back, if there is any trouble, but to emulate Gandhi and his followers in India by resisting non-violently. I do not have to tell you how disquieting this sort of thing is, even when there may be no truth at all in it." Thomas Sancton's *New Republic* articles on racial injustice in the South rankled Dabney so much that he suggested that FEPC chairman Mark Ethridge should use his influence in Washington to have the lid put on Sancton.

A series of exchanges between Sancton and Dabney revealed the differences between a white racial liberal who had left the South and one who had chosen to remain. During the war Sancton, a native of New Orleans who made his home in New York, believed that whites had for too long appeased the "understandably rebellious" blacks with empty promises. "In communication with family and friends," he wrote Dabney, "I see the same old rationalized prejudices and selfishness in full sway and I have a sickening feeling that it is these qualities which win out time after time when the issue of Negro justice comes to a real showdown." Dabney replied that Sancton's position paralleled the ultimately destructive one taken by Northern Abolitionists in the 1830s. . . .

Sancton answered by assuring Dabney that he was not a "white rabble-rouser," but rather a Southerner who loved the South and who had more faith in the mass of whites and blacks in the region than did Dabney. Sancton noted that he got the impression from reading Dabney's books, articles, and editorials that Dabney was "not quite sure lint-heads and ignorant blacks—even though they were deserving of reform measures like the New Deal's—would in the long run turn out any differently; except perhaps a little healthier." Sancton believed that Dabney's argument that Negro and white agitators had the South on the brink of race war was too simple, and that he should instead turn his passion on the majority of Southern whites. . . . He main tained that though gains made by Southern blacks with the encouragement of white liberals might look impressive on paper, they had not raised most Negroes from almost "complete social and economic serfdom," and that in general Southern whites did not intend to give black people a thing unless forced to by external pressure.

Dabney respected the sincerity of Sancton's views but thought him thoroughly misguided. He admitted that Southern whites were overwrought, antagonistic, and not very anxious to talk about the rights of blacks. Yet, as Dabney saw it, this was precisely the point. In such a charged atmosphere it would be difficult to achieve small advances for Negroes, let alone a complete breakdown of Jim Crow. He expressed astonishment over Sancton's assertion that Southern whites never did anything for blacks. Though indifference toward the plight of blacks was no doubt the feeling of the vast majority of Southern whites, according to Dabney, many "prominent white Southerners" did care, and their prestige and influence had helped Negroes achieve genuine advances in education, health, and economic well-being.

Like Thomas Jefferson, whom he admired greatly, Dabney was an upper-class Virginian who celebrated the virtues of democracy. He was more willing than most white Southerners to extend the fruits of democracy to blacks. He thought that this could be done through the activities of people like himself without unduly shocking white Southern sensibilities, and he devoted himself to publicizing liberal trends in the South. But Dabney's way failed to alter significantly the status of black Southerners. Not only did Southern Negroes, assisted at first by white and black Northerners, begin demanding their own version of racial justice, but they did it without consulting Virginia gentlemen. Dabney's genteel heritage, the source of many of his views about the necessity for change in the South, was undoubtedly one of his greatest strengths. But for a white liberal striving to comprehend the meaning of genuine racial justice in the South, it was also a major weakness. Dabney believed too strongly in the wisdom of his white elite. Despite his brief campaign against segregated public transportation, Dabney's wartime stand against black militance tarnished his reputation as a liberal. In continuing to insist that separate could be made equal, he would not win it back.

Sosna, "Virginius Dabney," *In Search of the Silent South*
(1977), pp. 121–39

"His Favorite Topic of Conversation Was Simply People, High and Low, Good and Bad": Lewis F. Powell, Jr.

The first Virginian appointed to the United States Supreme Court since well before the Civil War, Lewis F. Powell, Jr. (1907–), brought to the bench in 1972 a career marked by a distinction in the law which few if any attorneys could hope to match. In addition to his leadership in a prestigious Richmond law firm, the Suffolk native had served at various times as president of the American Bar Foundation, the American College of Trial Lawyers, and the American Bar Association. All the while he was active in civic affairs, perhaps most constructively as chairman of the board of the Richmond public schools in the difficult days of early integration. The insightful portrait below—by one of his former law clerks, the author-editor J. Harvie Wilkinson III (1944–)—provides a perceptive look at both Powell the lawyer-jurist and Powell the man.

It is now 8:30 A.M., and Sally Smith's car pulls up promptly. We spy in the distance a tall, trim figure in a dark suit, carrying a briefcase, walking a confident, punctual gait toward the car. Thirty seconds later the car door opens, the briefcase is handed me, Justice Powell slides in, breaks into a very quick, relaxed grin: "Good morning, chillier than I thought," or, if it is warm, "Sally, why don't we all go down to the beach today?" followed by a round of knowing laughs.

The ride to the Supreme Court will last ten minutes, through the high-rise and public-housing culture of southwest Washington, then a brief stretch of gas-shortaged stations, next the prim townhouses of Capitol Hill, and last the Supreme Court, in the Capitol area itself, ruled by the traffic whistle and the construction roar. But the ride is a time of cheer, of nonbusiness, often an occasion for ribbing. "Sally, where are you hiding those gloves we gave you for Christmas?" he might ask, or "Jay, you look like you've been awake now for all of five minutes." Conversation might range from moon landings to shopping in the southwest Safeway, but the Supreme Court greets us all too soon, and a day's earnest business begins.

Justice Lewis F. Powell, Jr., had perhaps as extensive and high-placed experience in the American legal profession as any man ever appointed to the Supreme Court. Since 1937 he had been a partner in the illustrious Virginia law firm of Hunton, Williams, Gay, Powell and

Gibson. In 1964–65 he had been president of the American Bar Association, and in 1969–70 president of the American College of Trial Lawyers. He had served as a member of important national commissions, some of which, such as President Johnson's Crime Commission, involved an inevitable acquaintance with the Supreme Court and its work. He had circulated, both socially and professionally, with Justices, judges of all levels, lawyers, former law clerks, and government officials who had studied, worked, or practiced before the Supreme Court and knew its business well. Yet such relationships, important as they were, never really prepared him for his new position. It took a while, he once chuckled, just to learn the Court's etiquette. "I was told, I think on about the second day, when somebody caught me in one of the corridors with my coat off . . . that Justices don't walk the corridors in their shirt sleeves." . . .

What I admired was his calm, a quality of quiet and reflection that underlay his judgment, a philosophic turn of mind that almost never lapsed into resignation or indifference. Shortly after his nomination, his friends undertook to explain what would make him a great Justice. A *Richmond News Leader* editorial may have put it best: "How does one describe him? One searches for the proper adjectives. Reflective, yes. Scholarly, yes. Judicious, certainly. Incisive. Quiet. Kind. A man about whom, in Emerson's phrase, there is 'a certain toleration, a letting be and a letting do, a consideration and allowance for the faults of others, but a severity to his own.'" One feature was missed—his sense of humor, especially toward himself. He salvaged many a moment with humor, without which the business of Court might have seemed unleavened and grave. He even brought his law clerk out of spells.

One day I recall being particularly frustrated, and as we rode home together, I sat silent, deep within myself, still banging against the day's problems. Suddenly, I noticed he was talking and asking what jobs I'd held before turning to law. He recalled a college summer of his own, when he had gone to work for the Department of Public Works in Richmond, which tried to use him in an engineering capacity, since he had had such a course at college. "I didn't know what in the world to do," he laughed. "My supervisors were confounded. They kept putting me on simpler and simpler jobs, and I was still helpless. Finally, they had the bright idea to stick me on ditches, where they thought it impossible to foul up. But you know, Jay, there are ditches in Richmond where the water still flows the wrong way."

This poking fun at himself extended to public occasions. In one speech, he recalled the tribulations of confirmation:

I was cornered in the corridors of the Senate Office Building
by half a dozen or more Women's Lib people who ambushed me
as I came out of a Senator's office late one afternoon and I had
a rough experience. I started off on the wrong foot and was
completely defeated. I tried to be agreeable and I said, "Ladies,
I've been married 35 years, I have three daughters and two
granddaughters, and I've got to be for you." And a spokesman
for the group looked at me without the slightest twinkle of
humor and said, "That's what all you men say!"

A good laugh may be the best and sometimes the only escape from
a hard day. He reached the Court each morning between 8:30 and
9:00 A.M. and generally left between 6:30 and 7:00 P.M. He left at no
set hour, only when his work reached a convenient break. As his first
spring at the Court wore on, he began to depart at gradually later
times, staying longer with the light, until by May he was leaving well
past 7:00. I told him one evening riding home that among the many
things he had successfully taught me was that no honest day's work
ever ended before sundown. Some undertakings at the Court absorbed him so completely that he seemed momentarily oblivious of
time and occasion. Riding to work one morning, he expressed sudden surprise at the absence of traffic. "You're forgetting George
Washington's birthday," Sally kidded.

His work week routinely extended to evenings and to weekends.
He always worked six full days a week, more often seven. During the
Court's term, he came to his chambers three Sundays out of four.
Monday mornings often found a memorandum on my desk, evi-
dencing thorough weekend attention to a case. Four, sometimes five,
evenings a week were also devoted to the job. He would return home,
and after dinner and a catchup on the evening news, spend two or
three hours at work before retiring. He generally reserved for the
day his sustained efforts on difficult opinions and used his evenings
mainly for reading, either certiorari petitions, briefs, or opinions circulated from other Justices. I remember him walking to and from the
Court, briefcase always in hand. Once he left without it, and I asked if
he had forgotten anything. "No," he smiled. "But I look strangely
dismembered, don't I?" . . .

At Hunton, Williams, he had been basically a corporate lawyer,
specializing in matters of securities law and corporate mergers, acqui-
sitions, and reorganizations. He had served on the boards of directors
of many national corporations, Squibb, Philip Morris, and Ethyl Corporation among them. More than most corporate lawyers, he had also

been something of a generalist in the field of law and public policy, serving as chairman of the Richmond Public School Board and later the State Board of Education. He was on numerous national commissions, including the Blue Ribbon Defense Panel appointed by President Nixon to study the Department of Defense and the National Advisory Committee on Legal Services to the Poor. But the shift from Hunton, Williams to the Supreme Court was still primarily one from corporate to constitutional law. And, contrary to some views, constitutional law was not simply a broad and unformed policy field to be roamed and understood at will. . . .

During the time I worked for him his favorite topic of conversation was simply people, high and low, good and bad, in all the astonishing states into which life had thrown them. There was a tolerance in his description of others. He traced the hopes and disappointments of his characters, almost as if he were one of them and lived along with them in his stories. He told laughingly of a salty hunting guide on the eastern shore of Maryland giving the Supreme Court "the dickens," and admiringly of a man who found in an auto graveyard a spare part for two dollars that would otherwise have cost fifty, and very sadly of a lifelong garage attendant who found the screeching and wheeling of the cars so intolerable, he finally had to quit and rest his nerves. He asked about people, if my friend had yet made it into law school, if a child of the elevator operator at the Court had recovered from the flu. He spoke of the change in fortunes of people he knew, of a shy boy who became a great philanthropist, of a college standout whose potential failed to flower. He relished human uniqueness, the whole rich tapestry of life, and the characters that moved therein. He often pondered the kinds of fates and forces that placed "John" here and "Jim" there. Mostly, he treated me to a wealth of feeling observation on human nature such as I had not seen before.

Among his best opinions were those where an individual injustice seemed uppermost, and to this he responded warmly. Both the lawyer and the humanist went to work—to allow an alien the right to practice law in our country, an illegitimate child to recover benefits for the death of his father, a Mississippi black to tell his story in court, or to allow a one-time indigent defendant the protections under Kansas garnishment law "needed to keep himself and his family afloat." These opinions seemed effective, not only because they were compassionate but because they were reined in by his lawyer's instinct, his feeling disciplined by the vigor of structure and thought, as a Mozart symphony is the more moving because it is restrained. I recalled again the words of Jean Camper Cahn—"to respond with humanity

to individualized instances of injustice and hurt"—and thought them
realized.

Like so many others at the Supreme Court, Justice Powell had long
been a fan of the Washington Redskins, an informed but unfanatic
follower who knew the names of the linebackers, but not the offensive
linemen. The Redskins traditionally repaid their fans with a long
string of losing seasons, and the Justice was among the sufferers. He
occasionally relived those losses—in agony only a Redskin fan would
know—telling of Sonny Jurgensen and his golden arm bringing the
Redskins last-minute rallies, falling desperate inches and seconds
short. "Sonny is always the showman," he told me. "He keeps your
hopes going right up to the bitter end." The Justice had been for
years a Redskin season ticket holder, but he surrendered his tickets on
arrival at the Court, then decided to retrieve them. When Jurgensen
injured his ankle at the beginning of the 1972 season, the Justice
added to the athlete's fan mail, wishing him a speedy return to action.
But even without Jurgensen the Redskins enlivened the Justice's first
fall on the Court with a successful season and an eventual trip to the
Super Bowl. Yet, win or lose, the Justice was not without coaching
suggestions as we rode to work the next morning. I once told him
that Monday-morning quarterbacking wasn't cricket. He smiled, remarking quizzically that since everyone could second-guess his own
decisions, wasn't he entitled to do some of the same?

He relaxed with sports. He was a determined athlete in his school
days, once even a semipro baseball player. A friend remembers him at
McGuire's prep school as a first baseman. "I can see him now with the
same lanky frame . . . stretching off first base, and there was always
a damn gap between the bottom of his trousers and the top of his
socks." As he grew older, he turned from baseball and basketball to
occasional hunting and tennis. But he spent endless hours coaching
his son, watching him progress from the neighborhood team, the
Rothesay Rebels, to a standout starting quarterback at his own alma
mater Washington and Lee. Once he mentioned that, given his choice
of careers, there was nothing he would rather have been than a professional athlete. Every contest, he said, had a quick and indelible
outcome. Athletes, moreover, were the real idols of a nation craving
for visible, physical heroes and frustrated over the ambiguities and
complexities of national problems. Few things, he thought, were more
satisfying than watching a drama of physical coordination and grace.
I remember objecting, more earnestly than his tone required. "Mr.
Justice, you're not injury-prone, you don't have to negotiate an annual

contract, you never get booed coming off the field. And, besides, think of what a Supreme Court Justice can accomplish."

"Maybe so," he laughed. "But nobody ever retires your number."

Upon occasion, the Justice and Mrs. Powell invited the staff to their apartment for cocktails or dinner. These gatherings were great fun and offered us all the chance to put office frustrations in a more jovial perspective. Invariably, the occasions were enlivened by Mrs. Powell, a woman with a remarkable talent for decor and furnishings and the gift of putting guests immediately at ease. She was always a favorite of mine because we laughed at the same things. One evening she and the Justice invited me for dinner, and one of the items served was fresh asparagus. I made what I now know was the horrendous mistake of eating only the tips and leaving the stalks on my plate. To this day she won't let me forget it.

"You may have passed up your chance for fresh asparagus for a while," she once teased.

Though his work as a Supreme Court Justice was even harder than his previous work had been, at least, she said, he was more frequently at home. His diversions were few. Judging on the Supreme Court can be a solitary occupation, more lonely for one such as the Justice who kept an active schedule prior to coming on the bench. His had been a life of friendship and travel, seeing clients, attending directors' meet-ings as well as conventions and seminars of the organized bar. He worked often in concert with the country's upper echelons of lawyers and businessmen. He saw himself as activist and partisan, in behalf of clients' causes, political candidates, ABA programs, and community projects. He spoke vigorously and emphatically on national issues that included civil disobedience, the necessity for the control of crime, and a strong national defense.

Suddenly this had changed. The excitement of competition and partisanship was replaced by an obligation of detached and neutral judgment. The collegial associations of the prominent lawyer yielded inevitably to the pressure for aloofness on the judge. The hours of travel became long hours at the desk, alone in thought and in his reading. Much of judging on the Supreme Court is solitary and in-tense intellectual labor, one of the world's great intellectual and philo-sophical experiences, but one for which the Justice sacrificed much in the vigor and variety of his life-style. "The truth is," he once said, "that I'd rather be a lawyer than a judge. I was never in any doubt as a lawyer as to which side I was on."

Though I worked for him as judge, it is impossible not to remember him as a lawyer. He had a banking friend who always used to call him "the barrister," the title that seemed to fit him best. He saw lawyering as an artisan trade, perhaps because he began it in the Depression and had once offered his services to a Richmond firm for nothing, explaining simply that "I just wanted somewhere to practice law."

He pronounced the word "lawyer" with particular care and pride. "Bill is a fine lawyer," he often said, if he admired the job a clerk had done. He had learned life's lessons from the law, lessons he related to his clerks in timely anecdotes, best called "lawyerisms." Once, in a memorandum for him, I had overlooked an important and elemental issue and sat red with embarrassment when he informed me of this. He, however, seemed unruffled and recalled the time when he had just arrived at Hunton, Williams, as a young attorney eager to make a first impression. It was nearly his first case; he had researched it exhaustively, he thought, and found a Virginia precedent, right on point, holding for his side. But disaster awaited. His brief had been sent to a New York law firm with whom Hunton, Williams had been working on the case, and the law firm had returned it promptly to his senior partner with the notation that the precedent had been completely overruled by a recent Virginia statute. He had been mortified. "There's not a lawyer in the country who hasn't occasionally missed things," he explained. "I still dream about that mistake."

Another "lawyerism" rescued me from an even more delicate situation. We had had differing views on a particular case, one about which I felt strongly. I had argued my side one afternoon, researched it further that evening, and appeared early next morning armed with books and rhetoric to which he listened and responded patiently for almost an hour. At the end he said, "I'm sorry, but I simply disagree." When I rose to leave, it suddenly dawned on me that my remarks had been unusually heated and persistent and had carried somewhat beyond the bounds of civil discussion. I felt sickened that, for the first time, he would think me disrespectful. But he spoke before I reached the door. "There's absolutely nothing to worry about," he assured me. "You wouldn't be worth much as a lawyer if you weren't contentious."

The Justice never thought of himself as holding a regional seat or being a regional representative to the Supreme Court. In fact, he mentioned once that carefully balanced sectional representation was not essential to the Court's proper functioning. What he did hope was that Justices would come to the Court from a broad range of backgrounds, from government service and political life, from prior state and federal judgeships, from the great law schools, and from the practicing bar. Amidst the praise and support for his appointment, the most he would say was, "It seems a wise thing to have some practicing lawyers appointed to the Court."

Perception of a lawyer's working habits almost invisibly conditioned his conduct as a judge. Lawyering required a "patience with detail," he might say, or, when work was heavy, "the best lawyers have never worked by the clock." The frequent comparisons between Justice Powell and the late Justice Harlan stemmed from the fact that both were "lawyer's judges," with backgrounds of thorough and precise articulation in the best traditions of the private bar. It has been observed often that legal training and professional legal attitudes and associations have a conservative impact, that they inculcate a preference for stability and a view of reform only as a properly channeled and slowly evolving process. Professor [A. E. Dick] Howard saw this legal training as the formative force in Justice Powell's philosophy:

> Legalism tends to conservatism in the sense that law is a conserving force, one that looks to rules and accepted modes. No man has spent his life more squarely in this legalistic tradition than Lewis Powell, who comes to the Court, at age 64, with habits and attitudes that cannot fail but be shaped by conspicuous success and recognition at working within these accepted legal modes.

The most succinct expression of the Justice's philosophy of the Court's role confirmed this:

> (1) I believe in the doctrine of separation of powers. The courts must ever be mindful not to encroach upon the areas of the responsibilities of the legislative and executive branches.
> (2) I believe in the Federal system, and that both State and Federal courts must respect and preserve it according to the Constitution.
> (3) Having studied under then Professor Frankfurter, I believe in the importance of judicial restraint, especially at the Supreme Court level. This means as a general rule, but certainly not in all cases, avoiding a decision on constitutional grounds where other grounds are available.
> (4) As a lawyer I have a deep respect for precedent. I know the importance of continuity and reasonable predictability of the law. This is not to say that every decision is immutable, but there is normally a strong presumption in favor of established precedent.
> (5) Cases should be decided on the basis of the law and facts before the Court. In deciding each case, the judge must make a

conscious and determined effort to put aside his own political
and economic views and his own predilections and to the extent
possible to put aside whatever subtle influences may exist from
his own background and experience.

And, finally, although all the three branches of Government
are duty bound to protect our liberties, the Court, as the final
authority, has the greatest responsibility to uphold the law and to
protect and safeguard the liberties guaranteed all of our people
by the Bill of Rights and the 14th Amendment.

The caution and restraint of that statement were, in the last analysis,
not so much a product of the lawyer as a part of the man himself. He
taught, by example, a serenity in the face of ambiguity and uncertainty, something I found it difficult to achieve. "We shall see," he
would sometimes say, when I rushed to ask if such and such would
occur. His caution made him believe that careless and ebullient op-
timism could be a dangerous state. Occasionally, he chided me as
being too hopeful an evaluator of the progress of work in his chambers and once circulated a memorandum to his staff to dispel "the
euphoria of my friend Jay, who keeps telling me that we are in 'great
shape.' "

His reserve may have owed something to the reigning ethos of his
state and region. Virginia had, for most of his lifetime, been governed
by the Byrd organization, a clique of gentlemen aristocrats who, in
their finer hours, imparted a tone of civility and tolerance to life in
the Old Dominion. One notable exception was that of "massive resistance," where the Byrd organization in the late 1950s chose to close
public schools rather than accept racial integration. That was not
the aim of the then Mr. Powell, who from 1952 to 1961 had been
Chairman of the Richmond Public School Board. In the words of one
prominent observer, "His primary concern was to keep the schools of
Virginia open and to preserve the public education system for all
pupils." That a poisonous racial climate did not envelop Richmond
was "in large measure due to the calm leadership, the perceptive
judgment, and the open-minded and fair attitude which exemplified
Mr. Powell's school board incumbency." . . .

As my time with him drew to a close, I was undecided whether to
teach or to practice law. He became during the moments of decision
something of a career counselor, exploring all paths but dictating
none. "What you really need to do, Jay," he said, "is to get married."
He thought me sadly incapable of caring for myself. My apartment,
he had heard, was in a state of disarray, and he had learned, with

incredulity, that I had been cooking for myself. Jay "tried spaghetti last night with disastrous results," he once wrote a mutual friend. "It reminded him of glue."

The day came—I got engaged. We set the wedding for June 30, 1973, shortly after I thought the term of Court would end. My fiancée came to Washington each weekend, and the Justice could not resist the chance for fun. "Lossie," he would say, with his very gravest look, "I'm not at all certain the Court will adjourn in time for the wedding. If I need Jay here with me in the closing moments, I know you'll understand." Lossie looked very concerned, whereupon the Justice broke out laughing. "We'll get you married somehow," he promised. "If worst comes to worst, I'm empowered to perform the ceremony here in my chambers."

He enjoyed the wedding's approach. "Grooms are only incidental to a wedding ceremony," he warned. "Don't insert yourself in any arrangements. The ladies will always outmaneuver you because they'll devote full time." During May and June, the closing months of the term, I was kept much too busy even to think about marriage. New projects appeared faster than the old were done. Finally, the term ended, several days before the wedding, and I headed quickly home. The departure seemed rushed and fatigued, a strangely emotionless end to an experience that had meant so much. Driving home, I regretted leaving the Justice without one good, final conversation, to relive old moments and express my thanks. But there had been no complete good-bye, I thought; getting married seemed to have caught me up before the clerkship had let go.

Saturday evening of the reception: a gay, spinning, half-remembered affair. Snapshot smiles and faces, distant laughs, and spilling champagne. But my two co-clerks, Bill Kelly and Larry Hammond, were there, and Sally Smith, too, letting the good times roll. Suddenly, I caught the Justice walking over from across the room. He was grinning broadly as he shook my hand. "Well," he said, "we all made it, didn't we?" For just a moment, I tried to be serious and grateful. Don't mention it, he seemed to be saying. "Go have fun."

Wilkinson, *Serving Justice* (1974), pp. 69–70, 76–81, 110–19, 121–23

"The Times Change": The City's First Black Mayor and Black Majority City Council

A turning point in the city's history was reached on 8 March 1977 when Henry L. Marsh III was sworn in as mayor, thus becoming Richmond's highest locally elected black official. Moreover, the City Council over which Marsh began that day to preside was for the first time in history predominantly black. Marsh's victory concluded a seven-year period during which by federal order no local elections could be held to select council members. That order was the result of the city's earlier attempt to annex a portion of neighboring Chesterfield County, an action that was challenged in court under the federal Voting Rights Act. At the end of the litigation the Justice Department ruled that the voting strength of Richmond's black residents had been diluted by the annexation, thus paving the way for the implementation of a black majority on the council. Marsh's tenure as mayor lasted until 1982, when he was succeeded by Roy A. West, principal of Albert H. Hill Middle School.

The selections that follow, comprised of three newspaper stories centering on the occasion of Marsh's installment, give evidence not only of the new mayor's hopes for his native Richmond, but also that Richmond, once again, was scheduled for social and political change.

§ Dishwasher Makes Good

By Steve Clark

An Only-in-America story? Here's one that has all the ingredients of a good one:

A black youngster grows up in the days of segregation in a Southern city which once was the Capital of the Confederacy.

When it comes time for him to go to high school, one of the best schools in the city is the closest high school to the house where his family lives. But he can't go to that school because of the color of his skin. Instead, he rides in the back of a city bus past the all-white school everyday to attend an all-black school in another section of town.

The youngster's father is a clergyman and doesn't have a lot of money, so the youngster works at a number of jobs to earn spending money. He carries newspapers in the afternoon. At nights, he is a busboy and a dishwasher at an ice cream parlor which is popular with the white residents of the city. He holds a number of other odd jobs, including parking cars in the garage of a large downtown hotel.

He makes good grades in high school, even though he sometimes falls asleep in class because of the night jobs. After high school, he goes to college, an all-black university right down the street from the high school he attended. He is graduated from college with honors, then leaves town to study law. He gets a law degree, marries a woman who will become a dentist, then returns to his home town to become a lawyer.

The times change, and the youngster, now a man, gets involved in local politics. He is elected to City Council, and then, several years later, he becomes the first black mayor of the city that was the Capital of the Confederacy.

It's an interesting story, but it won't sell, you say. It's not believable. It couldn't happen.

Well, it did. It happened two days ago when Henry L. Marsh III— former carrier for The News Leader, former dishwasher at the Clover Room, a 1952 graduate of Maggie Walker High School, a 1956 graduate of Virginia Union University—was chosen mayor of Richmond.

Was Bused to Maggie Walker

Marsh sat behind the big desk in the mayor's office at City Hall yesterday morning, and talked about his formative years.

"My mother died when I was 5 years old, and for a while we (his two brothers, his sister and he) were raised by an aunt and uncle in Smithfield," he said.

When Marsh was 11 years old, the Marsh children returned to Richmond to live with his father, who preached at African Methodist Episcopal Zion churches in several towns near Richmond.

"I came back to town in the fifth grade and went to George Mason School," he said. "We lived on 29th Street (Church Hill) right across the street from the school."

If there had been no segregation, he would have moved on to John Marshall High School, which in those days was downtown, where the new John Marshall Courts Building now is located.

"I was bused," Marsh said with a grin. "I rode the city bus right past John Marshall to go to Maggie Walker."

"It was obvious that the schools were not equal, and we were all aware of it," Marsh said. "For example, several foreign languages were not available to us at Maggie Walker, and we had to take physics in the back of a chemistry class."

Even so, the 43-year-old Marsh has fond memories of his days at Maggie Walker, where he was editor of the school paper and vice president of the senior class.

"The teachers were extremely dedicated and that made the difference," Marsh said. "School was an exciting experience and I hope we can instill the same excitement that I felt in each child in the school system today."

Proud of His Family

Maybe the black schools in the days of segregation were inferior, but Marsh said any black student who wanted to could learn. His family provides a good example. All four of the Marsh children earned undergraduate and post-graduate college degrees.

"I am extremely proud of the academic achievements of my family. Actually, I'm the dumbest one in the group."

He is especially grateful to his sister, Mrs. Marian Jones, the oldest child, who is head medical technologist at Ft. Bliss Army Hospital in El Paso, Tex.

"My sister could have been a doctor, or maybe a surgeon, but she sacrificed herself for me," Marsh said. "Before my senior year at Virginia Union, she took a job as a medical technologist. She said she wanted me to have one year in college when I wouldn't have to hold a job to earn money. So that year, I made nine A's, three B's, was president of the student government, and went out for the tennis team. I consider that the turning point of my life. It proved to me that I could perform if I had the time."

At the same time, Marsh doesn't regret and isn't ashamed of the time he spent at odd jobs such as dishwashing.

"I never felt sorry for myself," he said. "I wouldn't trade any of the experiences I've had. They made me what I am—whatever that is."

What he is is mayor of Richmond, a city in which he grew up a "second-class" citizen. Only in America.

Richmond *News Leader*, 10 March 1977

§ All the Marsh Family Turns Out for New Mayor's Election

By Joy Propert

The family of the new mayor of Richmond turned up at the city council meeting today but not for his election.

"It is a moment in city history, having a black majority on council, and I did not want the children to miss it," said Henry L. Marsh III, the city's first black mayor.

Marsh, vice mayor since 1970 and a member of council for 11 years, was elected mayor this morning. The new nine-member council has five black and four white members.

At the Marsh home at 3211 Q St. the pre-election scene was filled with excitement and a need to keep one eye on the clock. The family had to reach City Hall by 10 a.m. and three children were being decked out in their favorite outfits for the occasion.

Mrs. Marsh, known to her dental patients by her maiden name, Dr. Diane Harris, had chosen a white blouse, brocade skirt, and a matching brocade coat trimmed in fur for the occasion.

The Marshes' two daughters, Nadine, 13, a seventh grader at Henderson Middle School, and Sonya, 11, a fifth grader at George Mason Elementary, were dressed in identical pantsuits with turtleneck shirts. Only the colors were different—Nadine had chosen green and gold; Sonya, navy blue and burgundy.

Stuffed Animal

Their younger brother, Dwayne, 7, a second grader at Reid Elementary, also was dressed up for the occasion. He was lugging a giant stuffed rabbit, Peter, from room to room as the family hurried to complete last-minute arrangements.

"Mommy should be at work now," volunteered Dwayne.

The Marsh family is used to juggling four careers. Marsh has his law practice in addition to his council duties and other civic responsibilities. Mrs. Marsh combines a nine-hour day as a dentist with her role as wife and mother.

Additional help with the house and the children comes from the family's housekeeper, Mrs. Viola Riley, who works for the Marsh family four and one-half days per week.

Skipping School

The children, said Mrs. Marsh, seemed to be more excited about being allowed to skip school, or, at least, part of a school day, than the possibility of seeing their dad elected mayor.

Mrs. Marsh, daughter of a physician, met her future husband in college although both grew up in Richmond. She was graduated from Virginia Union University and the couple became engaged during their graduate school years at Howard University.

Little change in family life is expected by the new mayor's wife.

"I told him before the election that if we won I would give him a sympathy card and a road map home," she said.

The children are more understanding of the hours Marsh must spend away from home now that they are older, said Mrs. Marsh.

"The middle child had a particularly hard time adjusting to his absences when she was very young," she said. "He would be gone in the morning when she woke up and gone when she went to bed at night.

"There were times when she thought he had run away from home."

The years have brought an appreciation of their father's community responsibilities, she said.

A couple of weeks ago the oldest child, Nadine, had to write a composition on a famous black American. Her choice: her father.

Even on the day of his election as mayor, Marsh made a trip to his office before the family photo session at 9 a.m. and the council meeting at 10.

More Responsibility

Despite his experience on council and as vice mayor, Marsh sees his responsibilities increasing with today's election.

"I think the mayor has to set the tone for the community," he said, as his wife adjusted the back of his vest and Dwayne held his dad's coat aloft.

The children, particularly Nadine, have been taking some teasing from their classmates since their dad became a likely choice to be Richmond's new mayor.

"They kept asking me, 'How come your picture isn't in the paper like Amy Carter's?'" she said.

Richmond's new first lady, who believes she is still the only female dentist with a full-time practice in the city, expects little change in her life with her husband's new title.

"Life will still be a big juggling act for me, just as it was when we were first married," she said.

The only family celebration planned for today was a family lunch after the election, probably at a local restaurant.

Then Mrs. Marsh would see patients in the afternoon and the two girls would go to school.

Only Dwayne would miss a full day of school because he has to travel farther than his sisters.

"I still will be going to work each day at 8:45 and finishing up at 5:45," said the First Lady of Richmond.

Richmond *News Leader*, 8 March 1977

§ City's First Black Mayor Offers Goals for Action

The following is the text of the address by Henry L. Marsh III, delivered after he was elected mayor of the city of Richmond yesterday morning.

I am highly honored by the confidence you have shown me by your votes and generous expressions. I thank you for your support, and I pledge to you my best efforts in the months ahead.

On a personal note, I am extremely grateful to all those individuals who believed in me and who supported me over the years. To my wife and children—who inspire and comfort me—and who permit me to donate much of their family time to public service—I am especially grateful.

To the members of my law firm—who cover for me when I'm absent and who provide me with counsel on a regular basis—I am particularly grateful.

To the small band of campaign workers and the thousands of voters —who were responsible for my successful reelection—I am also grateful.

To all who have supported me or wished me well, I will strive to be worthy of your trust.

I am fully aware of the significance of this occasion. Never before in the history of the city of Richmond has a majority of the City Council been black. Never before has the highest local elected official been black. This election also signals a return to a regularly elected council after a seven-year court struggle and this election has produced the first council with a majority of members who were not supported by the organized business community.

Because of the special nature of this election victory, it is appropriate for me to pause and to share my thoughts with you and the people of our city.

First, I would like to publicly express my appreciation to the three retiring members of council. I would publicly express a special thanks to Mayor Bliley. During the past few years, there has been a sharing of power by the majority of council with the minority faction. I understand that the mayor was largely responsible for this. Moreover, during the past seven years, I can't recall a single instance when the mayor was discourteous or rude to me or to any member of council. And he was provoked on numerous occasions. Tom, you have set a standard which will indeed be difficult to meet.

Second, I would like to say a word about the new majority on council. During recent months, I've repeatedly indicated how much I have appreciated the efforts of Mrs. Dell. I am equally enthusiastic over the three new members of council. Each is unusually well-equipped to render effective service. Each is committed to making government more effective, especially for the individual citizens. Because of the diverse but wide community involvement of these council persons, Richmond can rest at ease because I am confident the ship of state is in good hands.

Third, I would like to set forth for the new council my notion of the goals and suggestions for action for the city. I must emphasize that these are my personal goals and suggestions. The new council or the people of the city may reject them—in whole or in part.

First, I will caution all who expect miracles that miracles are rare indeed, and that the problems that confront us have existed for years and have been reinforced by generations of neglect and discrimination.

Similarly, I will warn those who expect that we will maintain the status quo that we can do better than we have in the past, and that although we can't solve all of the tough problems, we can begin.

As a first priority, we should make an attack on the widespread poverty which affects a sizable segment of our people. Unless we begin to make inroads on the condition, all else that we do may be in vain.

Secondly, we should seek to achieve greater racial understanding in our community. Here in Richmond, where free government had its foundations, we should make our city a place where racial justice abounds.

Our city can be and ought to be a model for the nation in demonstrating how a city government can operate free of discrimination on the basis of race, religion, or sex.

We offer the hand of friendship and cooperation to the business community. Our interdependence is obvious. We recognize the vital role that business must play if our city is to realize its potential. If we are to obtain the resources to satisfy our human needs, we must expand our economic base and create the jobs needed by our citizens for dignity.

We similarly offer friendship and cooperation to our friends in the labor movement. Our cooperation is essential if our city is to prosper.

The racial polarization which stifles progress in our community must be eased.

To foster racial understanding, we must facilitate greater communications between the different segments in our community and we as a council should do this.

We must strengthen our commitment to excellence in education. Needed resources should be provided. But the primary ingredients needed are involvement and attitude. In cooperation with our school board and Dr. Hunter, who made a great start, we shall work to instill in each child that thirst for knowledge which is essential to a great school system.

Finally, our system works best with maximum involvement of the people and with greater access to the government.

To achieve this goal, we should, one, encourage all of our citizens to register to vote. Secondly, we should appoint to boards and commissions persons from all geographic areas and from all segments of the population.

On the question of access, as mayor, I plan to establish hours where I will be available at City Hall to hear from the people on a regular basis. I hope to establish, and will talk to the city manager about this, a periodic mayor's report to the people on radio and television. I will establish in my district an office where citizens may come to discuss their problems and will assist other council persons to establish offices in their districts.

On last Tuesday, the people of this city achieved a great victory. But that victory—as Winston Churchill said of another triumph for freedom—"is not the end. It is not even the beginning of the end. But it is perhaps, the end of the beginning."

In Richmond, we have made that beginning and with your prayers and cooperation we can make Richmond the type of community where each person can enjoy the dignity and respect which God intended.

Richmond *Times-Dispatch*, 9 March 1977

Appendix
Historic Richmond: An Annotated Bibliography
by Daniel P. Jordan

The titles with an asterisk (*) are especially recommended.

Akin, Warren. *Letters of Warren Akin, Confederate Congressman.* Edited by Bell I. Wiley. Athens: University of Georgia Press, 1959. The letters of 1864–65 provide insight into wartime Richmond attitudes and life, as depicted by a Georgia politician.

Allen, Hervey. *Israfel: The Life and Times of Edgar Allan Poe.* 2 vols. New York: George H. Doran Co., 1926. Contains some readable, useful sections on Richmond; journalistic and overly romantic.

Alley, Reuben E. *Frederic W. Boatwright.* Richmond: University of Richmond, 1973. A brief biography of Boatwright (1868–1951), longtime president of the University of Richmond.

———. *History of the University of Richmond, 1830–1971.* Charlottesville: University Press of Virginia, 1977. An affectionate, general recounting of the university's origins and subsequent development.

Ambler, Charles H. *Thomas Ritchie: A Study in Virginia Politics.* Richmond: Bell Book & Stationery Co., 1913. A scholarly yet pedestrian biography of Ritchie (1778–1854), arch-Democrat and notable editor of the Richmond *Enquirer.*

[Anburey, Thomas]. *Travels through the Interior Parts of America.* 2 vols. 1789. Reprint. London: W. Lane, 1791. This perceptive British officer visited Richmond on parole in early 1779; see volume 2, pages 300–322, for his descriptive letters.

Baker, Leonard. *John Marshall: A Life in Law.* New York: Macmillan, 1974. A massive biography with numerous references to Richmond and an extended account of the Burr trial, but less than first-rate scholarship.

Beirne, Francis F. *Shout Treason: The Trial of Aaron Burr.* New York: Hastings House, 1959. A spirited account of the famous trial that rocked Richmond in the spring and summer of 1807.

Berkeley, Edmund, and Berkeley, Dorothy Smith. *John Beckley: Zealous Partisan in a Nation Divided.* Philadelphia: American Philosophical Society, 1973. Chapter 2 covers the Richmond story of Beckley (1757–1807), an early mayor who gained fame after leaving the city.

Berman, Myron. *Richmond's Jewry, 1769–1976: Shabbat in Shockoe.* Charlottesville: University Press of Virginia, 1979. A reliable survey of America's sixth-oldest Jewish community, based in part on personal interviews and manuscript material; contains some rich biographical information.

Beveridge, Albert J. *The Life of John Marshall.* 4 vols. Boston: Houghton Mifflin Co., 1916–19. Scholarly and detailed with numerous contemporary quotations about the man and his times; read selectively for the Richmond portions of this magisterial biography, the standard source on Marshall.

Bill, Alfred Hoyt. *The Beleaguered City: Richmond, 1861–1865*. New York: Alfred A.
    Knopf, 1946. A lively, generally sound, "popular" history; a bit longer but less
    authoritative than Emory Thomas's *The Confederate State of Richmond*, listed
    below.
*Bondurant, Agnes M. *Poe's Richmond*. Richmond: Garrett and Massie, 1942. Excellent;
    a competent and detailed description of the largely cultural environment of
    Richmond in the early nineteenth century and of Poe's relationship to the city;
    topically organized; available in a new paperback edition (1978).
Boney, F. N. *John Letcher of Virginia*. University, Ala.: University of Alabama Press, 1966.
    A scholarly biography of Letcher (1813–88), Virginia's governor, 1860–64.
Bontemps, Arna. *Black Thunder*. New York: Macmillan, 1936. Fictionalized version of
    Gabriel Prosser's Revolt in 1800.
Brandon, Edgar Ewing, comp. and ed. *Lafayette, Guest of the Nation: A Contemporary
    Account of the "Triumphal Tour" of General Lafayette*. 3 vols. Oxford, Ohio: Oxford
    Historical Press, 1950–57. Lafayette's gala visits to Richmond in 1824 and
    briefly in 1825 are recounted in volume 3.
Brewer, James H. *The Confederate Negro: Virginia's Craftsmen and Military Laborers,
    1861–1865*. Durham, N.C.: Duke University Press, 1969. Much of this schol-
    arly and well-researched monograph is about Richmond.
Brown, Henry Box. See Stearns below.
Bryan, John Stewart. *Joseph Bryan . . . A Memoir*. Richmond: N.p., 1935. An affectionate
    biography of Bryan (1845–1908), who rode with Mosby and later became a
    leading Richmond entrepreneur, newspaper magnate, and public benefactor.
Cabell, James Branch. *As I Remember It*. New York: McBride, 1955. Memoirs of Cabell
    (1879–1958), a distinguished Richmond literary figure.
Calendar of Virginia State Papers. See Palmer below.
Calisch, Edward N. *Three Score and Twenty*. Richmond: Old Dominion Press, 1945.
    Biographical sketch (by Edith Lindeman Calisch), selected sermons and ad-
    dresses of the versatile Rabbi Calisch, of Congregation Beth Ahabah.
Caravati, Charles M. *Major Dooley*. Richmond: Maymont Foundation, 1978. A brief,
    admiring, illustrated biography of James H. Dooley (1841–1922), Confederate
    veteran, lawyer, successful businessman, and one of the city's greatest philan-
    thropists whose legacy—with his wife's—includes the Richmond Public Li-
    brary, Maymont Park, and the Crippled Children's Hospital.
———. *Medicine in Richmond, 1900–1975*. Richmond: Richmond Academy of Medicine,
    1975. A heavily factual, topically arranged monograph, published under the
    auspices of the Richmond Academy of Medicine.
*Cate, Wirt Armistead. "A History of Richmond, 1607–1861" (3 vols.). A major source,
    massive and detailed, yet unpublished; available in typescript in the library of
    the Valentine Museum.
Cavada, Frederic F. *Libby Life: Experiences of a Prisoner of War in Richmond, Va., 1863–64*.
    Philadelphia: King & Baird, 1864. Called by one authority "the best source for
    the human interest side of Libby during its period of heaviest use"; includes
    some pen-and-ink sketches.
Chastellux, François Jean, marquis de. *Travels in North America in the Years 1780, 1781,
    and 1782*. Edited by Howard C. Rice, Jr. 2 vols. Chapel Hill: University of
    North Carolina Press, 1963. Volume 2 has material of interest on Richmond as
    seen by this perceptive French officer; Rice's is the best of several editions of
    this travel account.

Chesnut, Mary Boykin. *Mary Chesnut's Civil War.* Edited by C. Vann Woodward. New Haven: Yale University Press, 1981. Chesnut spent much time in Richmond as the wife of a prominent Confederate official from from South Carolina; in many ways a masterwork based on wartime notes later revised and then published posthumously in two flawed editions as *A Diary from Dixie* (1905; 1949).

*Chesson, Michael B. *Richmond after the War, 1865–1890.* Richmond: Virginia State Library, 1981. A judicious, scholarly monograph offering fresh insights on a wide variety of topics; nominated for a Pulitzer Prize.

Christian, W. Asbury. *Richmond, Her Past and Present.* Richmond: L. H. Jenkins, 1912. A long, undocumented narrative, moving from date to date and drawing heavily from newspaper accounts; a storehouse of factual information.

Clark, Emily. *Ingenue among the Lions: The Letters of Emily Clark to Joseph Hergesheimer.* Edited with an introduction by Gerald Langford. Austin: University of Texas Press, 1965. A number of literary figures of the 1920s in Richmond and elsewhere are portrayed, often in a biting and sarcastic manner, in this series of letters from the editor of the *Reviewer* to one of the leading novelists of the day.

———. *Innocence Abroad.* New York: Alfred A. Knopf, 1931. Recounts the story of the *Reviewer,* an impressive Richmond literary journal of the early 1920s, and of its supporters, including Ellen Glasgow and James Branch Cabell.

———. *Stuffed Peacocks.* New York: Alfred A. Knopf, 1927. Literary essays and stories largely about local personalities.

Cromwell, Giles. *The Virginia Manufactory of Arms.* Charlottesville: University Press of Virginia, 1975. An accurate, well-illustrated history of the manufactory established in the late 1790s and active from 1802–21 and 1861–65.

Cunningham, Horace H. *Doctors in Gray: The Confederate Medical Service.* Baton Rouge: Louisiana State University Press, 1958. This scholarly monograph contains considerable material on Richmond topics.

Cutchins, John A. *A Famous Command: The Richmond Light Infantry Blues.* Richmond: Garrett and Massie, 1934. A highly descriptive account of a notable unit whose history parallels that of the city.

———. *Memories of Old Richmond, 1881–1944.* [White Marsh, Va.: McClure Press, 1973]. Amusing and strongly anecdotal recollections of the city and its people, by a retired lawyer who was born in 1881.

Dabney, Virginius. *Across the Years: Memories of a Virginian.* Garden City, N.Y.: Doubleday & Co., 1978. Exceptional memoirs of the longtime editor of the Richmond *Times-Dispatch*; engagingly written and good for recent social and political history.

*———. *Richmond: The Story of a City.* Garden City, N.Y.: Doubleday & Co., 1976. Immensely readable, a storehouse of informative anecdotes, with coverage from 1607 to the present; this is the best history of Richmond, by one of her most distinguished citizens.

———. *Virginia: The New Dominion.* Garden City, N.Y.: Doubleday & Co., 1971. This comprehensive, gracefully written survey contains some excellent material on Richmond.

Dabney, Wendell P. *Maggie L. Walker and the I. O. of Saint Luke: The Woman and Her Work.* Cincinnati: Dabney Publishing Co., 1927. Suggests the remarkable contributions of Walker (1867–1934), a talented and versatile Richmonder.

Daniel, Frederick S. *The Richmond Examiner during the War; or, The Writings of John M. Daniel with a Memoir of His Life, by His Brother.* New York: N.p., 1868. Daniel

(1825–1865), acid-tongued, outspoken editor of the *Examiner*; selections here include his notorious "Parliament of Beasts" (the Secession Convention meeting in Richmond in early 1861).

Davis, Joe Lee. *James Branch Cabell.* New York: Twayne Publishers, 1962. A brief but sound study of Cabell and his works.

Davis, Varina Howell. *Jefferson Davis, Ex-President of the Confederate States of America: A Memoir by His Wife.* 2 vols. New York: Belford Co., 1890. Read selectively for some instructive material on the Confederate capital, as presented by Mrs. Jefferson Davis.

Davis, William C., ed. *The Image of War, 1861–1865.* 3 vols. to date of a projected six volumes. Garden City, N.Y.: Doubleday & Co., 1981–. This stellar series will surely rank as *the* photographic collection about the Civil War and will be of interest to students of the capital of the Confederacy.

DeLeon, Thomas C. *Belles, Beaux, and Brains of the 60's.* New York: G. W. Dillingham Co., 1909. DeLeon was a journalist, novelist, and Confederate officer; his books provide some first-rate descriptions of Richmond political and social life, but some inaccuracies as well.

———. *Four Years in Rebel Capitals.* Mobile: Gossip Printing Co., 1890.

Dennett, John Richard. *The South As It Is: 1865–1866.* Edited with an introduction by Henry M. Christian. New York: Viking Press, 1965. A collection of articles originally published in the *Nation* and based on the eyewitness reporting of a Yankee journalist who traveled widely in Virginia and other Southern states; three chapters are about Richmond sentiments and conditions in July 1865.

*Dew, Charles B. *Ironmaker to the Confederacy: Joseph R. Anderson and the Tredegar Iron Works.* New Haven: Yale University Press, 1966. A model business history about a key Richmond—and Rebel—industry.

Dickens, Charles. *American Notes for General Circulation.* 2 vols. London: Chapman and Hall, 1842. For Dickens's mixed verdict on Richmond, see volume 2, pages 195–99.

Dodson, E. Griffith, comp. *The Capitol of the Commonwealth of Virginia at Richmond: Portraits, Statuary, Inscriptions, and Biographical Sketches.* Richmond: N.p., 1937. A handy reference for information about the Capitol and Capitol Square.

Doherty, James L. *Race and Education in Richmond.* Richmond: N.p., 1972. The focal point of this general account is the significant year of 1970.

*Dowdey, Clifford. *Bugles Blow No More.* Boston: Little, Brown & Co., 1937. Likely the best selling novel ever written about Richmond; covers 1861–65 in an evocative fashion.

———. *Experiment in Rebellion.* Garden City, N.Y.: Doubleday & Co., 1946. Although focusing on the Confederate high command, this readable narrative has much on wartime Richmond.

*Dulaney, Paul S. *The Architecture of Historic Richmond.* 1968. Rev. ed. Charlottesville: University Press of Virginia, 1978. This fine guide begins with an extended analysis of the city's architecture and then provides a closer look at each of Richmond's historic areas; contains helpful maps and numerous illustrations; the 1978 edition updates the original architectural inventory of over 750 items, describes current preservation efforts, and contains over 200 photographs of local buildings.

Dunaway, Wayland F. *History of the James River and Kanawha Company.* New York: Columbia University, 1922. A scholarly history of the great canal.

Edmunds, Pocahontas Wight. *Virginians Out Front.* Richmond: Whittet and Shepperson, 1972. These eleven biographical sketches include Richmonders Virginia Randolph Ellett, Ellen Glasgow, John Powell, and Douglas Southall Freeman.

Ellyson, Louise. *Richmond on the James.* Sante Fe and Richmond: Press of the Territorian, 1970. Brief; pen-and-ink illustrations and "a short history."

Ely, Alfred. *Journal of Alfred Ely, a Prisoner of War in Richmond.* Edited by Charles Lanman. New York: D. Appleton and Co., 1862. A relatively objective view by a New York congressman accidentally captured at First Manassas and confined for five months in a Richmond prison.

Ezekiel, Herbert T. *The Recollections of a Virginia Newspaper Man.* Richmond: Herbert T. Ezekiel, 1920. A collection of humorous anecdotes about Richmond and Richmonders generally of the late nineteenth century.

———, and Lichtenstein, Gaston. *The History of the Jews of Richmond from 1769 to 1917.* Richmond: Herbert T. Ezekiel, 1917. Lengthy and detailed, with numerous primary sources and lists of names; superseded by Berman above.

A Full Account of the Great Calamity. . . . Richmond: Ellyson and Taylor, 1870. Contemporary pamphlet on the Capitol disaster of 27 April 1870.

Garmon, Gerald M. *John Reuben Thompson.* Boston: Twayne Publishers, 1979. Thompson (1823–73), Richmonder, author, editor of the *Southern Literary Messenger,* etc.

Gavins, Raymond. *The Perils and Prospects of Southern Leadership: Gordon Blaine Hancock, 1884–1970.* Durham, N.C.: Duke University Press, 1977. A scholarly study of racial attitudes and leadership in the person of Hancock, a Richmond minister and a professor at Virginia Union University.

Gay, Thomas B. *The Hunton Williams Firm and Its Predecessors, 1877–1954.* Richmond: Hunton Williams, 1971. An account of the notable Richmond law firm and some of its major cases; by a senior partner.

Glasgow, Ellen. *The Woman Within.* New York: Harcourt, Brace, 1954. Glasgow's autobiography.

Godbold, E. Stanly, Jr. *Ellen Glasgow and the Woman Within.* Baton Rouge: Louisiana State University Press, 1972. A sound biography with some revelations about Glasgow's personal life and some critical insights into her writings.

Godwin, Katherine. *Living in a Legacy: Virginia's Executive Mansion.* Richmond: Virginia State Chamber of Commerce, 1977. Includes historical and personal commentary, illustrations, and recipes; written from the authoritative perspective of a two-time "First Lady."

Goldfield, David R. *Cotton Fields and Skyscrapers: Southern City and Region, 1607–1980.* Baton Rouge: Louisiana State University Press, 1982. A premier urban historian, Goldfield offers many scholarly observations on Richmond in this volume and in the one below.

———. *Urban Growth in the Age of Sectionalism: Virginia, 1847–1861.* Baton Rouge: Louisiana State University Press, 1977.

Grigsby, Hugh B. *The History of the Virginia Federal Convention of 1788.* Edited by Robert A. Block. 2 vols. Richmond: Virginia Historical Society, 1890–91. Reprint. New York: Da Capo Press, 1969. Grigsby's volumes on these famous conventions in Richmond are valuable for their numerous personality sketches.

———. *The Virginia Convention of 1829–30.* Richmond: Virginia Historical Society, 1854. Reprint. New York: Da Capo Press, 1969.

Hale, Thomas F., and Ford, Barbara. *Maymont Park*. Richmond: Hale Publishing, 1973. Features color photographs by Hale, narrative by Ford.

———, and Jones, Bob, Jr. *Richmond Today*. Richmond: Hale Publishing, 1978. Photography by Jones.

———, and Manarin, Louis H. *Richmond: A Pictorial History*. Richmond: Hale Publishing, 1974. State Archivist Manarin wrote the text for over two hundred photographs chosen by Hale from the Valentine Museum and Dementi collections, covering from 1865 to modern times.

———, and Westbrook, Bill. *The Fan*. Richmond: Hale Publishing, 1972. A lavish photographic essay in color by Hale, with text by Westbrook.

Harris, William C. *Prison-life in the Tobacco Warehouse at Richmond*. Philadelphia: G. W. Childs, 1862. Written largely "within prison-walls" by a Federal lieutenant incarcerated early in the war; reflects the somewhat relaxed circumstances then prevailing for Union officer–prisoners of war in Richmond.

Harrison, Constance Cary. *Recollections Grave and Gay*. New York: Charles Scribner's Sons, 1911. Says much about social and economic conditions, and leading personalities in the Confederate capital.

Hatcher, William E. *John Jasper*. New York: F. H. Revell Co., 1908. A general treatment of the noted black preacher-orator, with some of his sermons, including his legendary "The Sun Do Move."

Hening, William W., comp. *The Statutes at Large . . . of Virginia. . . .* 13 vols. New York: George Cochran, 1819–23. Volumes 10–13 (1779–92) contain much of the social, economic, and political legislation that enabled Richmond to grow as a young capital city; indexed.

Henley, Bernard J. "Richmond, Virginia, 1607–1963." A typescript chronology giving major events by date from 1607 to 1963; conveniently indexed; available in the Virginia State Library.

Hibbs, Henry H. *A History of the Richmond Professional Institute*. Richmond: Whittet & Shepperson, 1973. A detailed account of the evolution of RPI by its founder and longtime head.

Hoehling, A. A., and Hoehling, Mary. *The Day Richmond Died*. New York: A. S. Barnes, 1981. A popular, dramatic, but not always accurate account of the fall of Richmond in early April 1865; built around lengthy quotations but undocumented in general.

Hoge, Peyton H. *Moses Drury Hoge: Life and Letters*. Richmond: Presbyterian Committee of Publication, 1899. Hoge was a staunch Presbyterian clergyman; this family account contains material on wartime Richmond and religion.

Hunter, Robert, Jr. *Quebec to Carolina in 1785–1786. . . .* Edited by Louis B. Wright and Marion Tinling. San Marino, Calif.: Huntington Library, 1943. This diary of a young London merchant contains scattered observations on Richmond.

Jackson, David K. *Poe and the Southern Literary Messenger*. Richmond: Dietz Printing Co., 1934. A concise but scholarly account of Poe's relationship with Richmond's leading literary journal, with two appendixes of letters from publisher T. W. White.

Jackson Ward. See Richmond, City of.

James, Henry. *The American Scene*. New York: Harper & Brothers, 1907. James's impression of Richmond is given in chapter 12.

Jeter, Jeremiah Bell. *The Recollections of a Long Life*. Richmond: Religious Herald Co., 1891. Jeter, 1802–80, a prominent Baptist minister-evangelist-educator and editor of the *Religious Herald*; read selectively for material about Richmond, including information on the origins of what is now the University of Richmond.

Johnston, Isaac N. *Four Months in Libby, and the Campaign against Atlanta.* Cincinnati: Methodist Book Concern, 1864. Describes the famous tunnel escape of early 1864.

Jones, Benjamin Washington. *Under the Stars and Bars: A History of the Surry Light Artillery; Recollections of a Private Soldier in the War Between the States.* Richmond: E. Waddey Co., 1909; facsimile with introduction by Lee A. Wallace, Jr., 1975. Jones's letters to his wife-to-be; good for camp life in and around Richmond.

Jones, John B. *A Rebel War Clerk's Diary.* Philadelphia: J. B. Lippincott & Co., 1866. Another famous and colorful diary with important daily insights—but one noted for its author's strong prejudices and after-the-fact editing.

Jones, Katharine M., ed. *Ladies of Richmond, Confederate Capital.* Indianapolis: Bobbs-Merrill, 1962. A fine documentary, chronologically arranged and containing the eyewitness accounts of dozens of upper-class women.

Jones, Virgil Carrington. *Eight Hours before Richmond.* New York: Holt, 1957. A lively narrative of the abortive cavalry raid on Richmond by Yankees Kilpatrick and Dahlgren in March 1864.

Kean, Robert Garlick Hill. *Inside the Confederate Government: The Diary of Robert Garlick Hill Kean.* Edited by Edward Younger. New York: Oxford University Press, 1957. Revealing on the inner workings of the Confederate government; by the head of the Bureau of War.

Kimball, William J. *Starve or Fall: Richmond and Its People, 1861–1865.* Monograph Publishing on Demand, Sponsor Series. Ann Arbor: University Microfilms International, 1976. A brief general survey, better researched than the paucity of footnotes would suggest.

Kimball, William J., ed. *Richmond in Time of War.* Boston: Houghton Mifflin Co., 1960. Snippets from a large variety of mainly primary sources, organized by years and covering all aspects of city life, 1861–65.

Kimmel, Stanley P. *Mr. Davis's Richmond.* New York: Coward-McCann, 1958. Basically a pictorial account, combining a readable narrative with scores of well-chosen illustrations.

Klein, Maury. *The Great Richmond Terminal: A Study in Businessmen and Business Strategy.* Charlottesville: University Press of Virginia, 1970. An important case history of what is now the Southern Railway Company.

Kocher, A. Lawrence, and Dearstyne, Howard. *Shadows in Silver: A Record of Virginia, 1850–1900, in Contemporary Photographs.* New York: Charles Scribner's Sons, 1954. Features some admirable photographs of Richmond scenes and citizens—as chosen from the Cook Collection and taken mostly by George and Huestis Cook; topically organized, with accompanying text.

Lafayette, marquis de. See Brandon above.

La Rochefoucauld-Liancourt, François, duc de. *Travels through the United States of North America . . . 1795, 1796, and 1797.* 4 vols. London: R. Phillips, 1799. Volume 3 contains extended remarks on Richmond's social and economic life.

Latrobe, Benjamin Henry. *The Virginia Journals of . . . , 1795–1798.* Edited by Edward C. Carter II et al. 2 vols. New Haven: Yale University Press, 1977. These splendidly edited and lavishly illustrated volumes contain much of value on Richmond, including detailed physical descriptions and social commentary from Latrobe, a pioneer architect and designer of several structures in the early city.

Lee, Robert E. *The Wartime Papers of R. E. Lee*. Edited by Clifford Dowdey and Louis H. Manarin. Boston: Little, Brown & Co., 1961. An ably edited selection of Lee's most important war papers, illuminating for Richmond history in several respects and including correspondence with family members residing in the city.

Little, John P., M.D. *History of Richmond*. Richmond: Dietz Printing Co., 1933. Reprinted from articles in the *Southern Literary Messenger* (1851–52); covers through 1851 and is social as well as political history.

Lutz, [Francis] Earle. *A Richmond Album: A Pictorial Chronicle of an Historic City's Outstanding Events and Places*. Richmond: Garrett and Massie, 1937. Selective illustrations, in rough chronological order, with commentary.

Lutz, Francis Earle. *Richmond in World War II*. Richmond: Dietz Press, 1951. Detailed, and one of the better of several accounts of Virginia cities in World War II.

[McCarthy, Carlton]. *Walks about Richmond....* Richmond: McCarthy & Ellyson, 1871. Anecdotal tour of historic sites; billed as "A Story for Boys, and a Guide to Persons Visiting the City."

McGuire, Judith White [Brockenbrough]. *Diary of a Southern Refugee, during the War*. New York: E. J. Hale & Son, 1867. McGuire was a clerk in the Confederate commissary department; good on the Richmond homefront.

MacKay, Alexander. *The Western World: or, Travels in the United States in 1846–47*. 2 vols. Philadelphia: Lea & Blanchard, 1849. Volume 1, chapter 17, contains some descriptive and informative comments about Richmond.

Macon, T. J. *Life's Gleanings*. Richmond: W. H. Adams, 1913. Anecdotal; covers from the Civil War through the early 1900s.

Manarin, Louis H., ed. *Richmond at War: The Minutes of the City Council, 1861–1865*. Chapel Hill: University of North Carolina Press, 1966. Merits attention for its superior illustrations and its official record of the domestic side of the war.

_____, and Wallace, Jr., Lee A., comps. *Richmond Volunteers: The Volunteer Companies of the City of Richmond and Henrico County, Virginia, 1861–1865*. Richmond: Westover Press, 1969. A convenient reference for unit names, histories, and rosters.

Marshall, John. *"My Dearest Polly:" Letters of Chief Justice John Marshall to His Wife . . . 1779–1831*. Edited by Frances Norton Mason. Richmond: Garrett and Massie, 1961. A sentimental narrative built around forty-three of Marshall's letters; contains items of political and social interest.

_____. *The Papers of John Marshall*. Edited by Herbert A. Johnson, Charles T. Cullen, William C. Stinchcombe, and Charles F. Hobson. Chapel Hill: University of North Carolina Press, 1974–. 3 vols. to date. Volume 1 in this scholarly edition takes Marshall through his youth, Revolutionary duty, legal training, and early political and professional career to 1788, and it has some illuminating material on Richmond in the 1780s; volume 2 contains Marshall's correspondence, papers, and account book, 1788–96.

Maury, Betty H. *The Confederate Diary of . . . 1861–1863*. Edited by Alice M. Parmelle. Washington, D.C.: N.p., 1938. Maury, the daughter of famed naval officer Matthew Fontaine Maury, wrote of daily life in Fredericksburg and Richmond.

Meagher, Margaret. *History of Education in Richmond*. Richmond: N.p., 1939. Short but informative; heavily factual.

Merriman, Paul R. *Flora of Richmond and Vicinity*. Richmond: Virginia Academy of Science, 1930. A lengthy nontechnical guide published by the Virginia Academy of Science; illustrated.

Moeser, John V., and Dennis, Rutledge M. *The Politics of Annexation: Oligarchic Power in a*

Southern City. Cambridge, Mass.: Schenkman Publishing Co., 1982. Focuses on the controversial Richmond-Chesterfield case of 1970.

Moore, Samuel J. T., Jr. *The Jefferson Hotel, a Southern Landmark*. Richmond: N.p., 1940. A brief account of the origins and early years of the Jefferson Hotel, with an extended sketch of its founder, Major Lewis Ginter.

_____. *Moore's Complete Civil War Guide to Richmond*. 1973. Rev. ed. Richmond: N.p., 1978. A handy source for finding "what was where" in Confederate Richmond; privately printed by one of the city's premier Civil War buffs.

*Mordecai, Samuel. *Virginia, Especially Richmond in By-Gone Days*. Rev. ed. Richmond: West & Johnston, 1860. Highly recommended; this classic provides a chatty and informative tour of the principal homes and landmarks of Richmond, with descriptions of its citizens, high and low; first published in 1856.

Munford, Beverley Bland. *Random Recollections*. New York: De Vinne Press, 1905. Munford, 1856–1910, was a prominent Richmond lawyer, politician, and author of the conservative school.

Munford, George Wythe. *The Two Parsons. . . .* Richmond: J. D. K. Sleight, 1884. Amusing and revealing stories about two eminent divines—the Reverends John Blair and John Buchanan—and about other Richmond notables and events in the Jeffersonian era.

Munford, Robert B., Jr. *Richmond Homes and Memories*. Richmond: Garrett and Massie, 1936. As stated in the foreword, it provides "a fair picture of the Richmond of the eighties and nineties"—with emphasis on the city's upper-class people and places; detailed and affectionate.

Mustian, Thomas F. *Facts and Legends of Richmond Area Streets*. Richmond: Carroll Publishing Co., 1977. After several short and delightful chapters, this handy little guide gives the name origins of "Richmond Streets from 'A' to 'Z' "—that is, from Accomac Street to Ziontown Road.

The Negro in Richmond, Virginia: The Report of the Negro Welfare Survey Committee. Richmond: Richmond Council of Social Agencies, 1929.

Olmsted, Frederick Law. *A Journey in the Seaboard Slave States*. New York: Dix & Edwards, 1856. Read selectively for the Richmond portions of this classic travel account by a famous northerner known for his keen observations and hostility to slavery.

O'Neal, William B. *Architecture in Virginia*. New York: Virginia Museum, 1968. This superb guide contains an admirable section on Richmond, with maps, photographs, and a succinct, lucid, and authoritative commentary.

Palmer, William P., and Others, eds. *Calendar of Virginia State Papers*. 11 vols. Richmond: N.p., 1875–95. For the trial record for Prosser's Revolt (1800), see volume 9, pages 140–74, of these official records of the Commonwealth.

Patrick, Rembert W. *The Fall of Richmond*. Baton Rouge: Louisiana State University Press, 1960. Interesting and informative published lectures about the three days (April 2–4, 1865) when the Rebels departed and the Yankees arrived; recommended.

Pember, Phoebe Yates. *A Southern Woman's Story: Life in Confederate Richmond*. Edited by Bell I. Wiley. Jackson, Tenn.: McCoward-Mercer Press, 1959. Excellent, especially on her experiences in Richmond's Chimborazo Hospital; Wiley adds a helpful introduction and notes; first published in 1879.

Perdue, Charles L., Jr.; Barden, Thomas E.; and Phillips, Robert K., eds. *Weevils in the Wheat: Interviews with Virginia Ex-Slaves*. Charlottesville: University Press of

Virginia, 1976. Contains numerous Richmond items, as recorded in interviews originally conducted by the Federal Writers' Project in the 1930s.

Picturesque Richmond. Richmond: J. L. Hill Co., 1891. Consists of commercial advertisements, photographs, essays on largely economic and political topics, and numerous sketches of major Richmond businessmen and businesses.

Poe, Edgar Allan. . . . *Letters Till Now Unpublished in the Valentine Museum, Richmond, Virginia,* with introductory essay and commentary by Mary Newton Stanard. Philadelphia: J. B. Lippincott Co., 1925. Reprint. New York: Haskell House, 1973. Most of the letters are from Poe to his foster father, the Richmond merchant John Allan.

Pollard, Julia Cuthbert. *Richmond's Story.* Richmond: Richmond Public Schools, 1954. A low-key, descriptive narrative prepared by the Richmond School Board, presumably for school children; almost entirely on pre-twentieth century topics.

*Putnam, Sallie A. [Brock]. *Richmond during the War.* New York: G. W. Carleton & Co., 1867. Reprint. New York: R. M. McBride Co., 1961. Some scholars argue that this source is more valuable than Mrs. Chesnut's celebrated diary, noted above.

Quinn, Arthur Hobson. *Edgar Allan Poe: A Critical Biography.* New York: Appleton-Century-Crofts, 1941. A long, scholarly analysis, with some sound and illuminating material on life in Richmond; the definitive Poe biography.

Rabinowitz, Howard N. *Race Relations in the Urban South, 1865–1890.* New York: Oxford University Press, 1978. Richmond is one of several cities featured in this scholarly monograph; well researched and comprehensively indexed.

Randolph, [Reverend] Peter. *From Slave Cabin to the Pulpit.* Boston: J. H. Earle, [1893]. Chapters 6–7 relate this black minister's experiences in Richmond after the Civil War.

Raper, Julius Rowan. *Without Shelter: The Early Career of Ellen Glasgow.* Baton Rouge: Louisiana State University Press, 1971. A serious study of Glasgow's formative years and influences; also analyzes her first six novels.

Reardon, John J. *Edmund Randolph: A Biography.* New York: Macmillan, 1975. This large, scholarly biography contains scattered information about Richmond, long the home of Randolph (1753–1813), patriot, governor, eminent lawyer, first U.S. attorney general, etc.

Reid, Whitelaw. *After the War: A Southern Tour.* Cincinnati: Moore, Wilstach & Baldwin, 1866. The insightful observations of a northern Republican journalist who was anti-South *and* antiblack; contains a chapter on Richmond; covers 1865–66.

Revolutionary Virginia: The Road to Independence. See Van Schreeven below.

Rhodes, Marylou. *Landmarks of Richmond.* Richmond: Garrett and Massie, 1938. A brief, illustrated guide to key Richmond sites.

Richmond, City of. *The Jackson Ward Historic District.* Richmond: City of Richmond, 1978. An invaluable, comprehensive reference work on the single largest black historic district in America; includes maps, photographs, and a catalog of buildings; text by Robert P. Winthrop, photography by John G. Zehmer, Jr.

Richmond: Capital of Virginia. Richmond: Whittet & Shepperson, 1938. A useful, general, topical history written "by various hands" (all reputable) to commemorate the city's bicentennial; handsomely printed, it surveys fifteen subject categories, such as "Industry and Trade," "The Church," "Art and Architecture," "Medicine," "Politics and Government," and "Music and the Theatre."

Richmond Portraits. . . . See Valentine Museum below.

Richmond, Virginia: The City on the James. See Sanford below.

Robertson, James I., Jr., comp. *Civil War Sites in Virginia: A Tour Guide.* Charlottesville:

University Press of Virginia, 1982. This handy paperback has a useful section on Richmond and its environs.

Ross, Capt. Fitzgerald. *Cities and Camps of the Confederate States.* Edited by Richard B. Harwell. Urbana: University of Illinois Press, 1958. Contains numerous references to life in Richmond as seen by this touring, pro-Southern British officer in late 1863 and early 1865: originally published in 1865.

Rouse, Parke, Jr. *Richmond in Color.* New York: Hastings House, 1978. Over thirty color plates of Richmond scenes and sites, with an informed narrative by Rouse; brief and marred by a few typographical and other errors.

Royall, William L. *Some Reminiscences.* New York: Neale Publishing Co., 1909. An episodic, conservative view by Royall, 1844–1911, soldier, lawyer, essayist; includes material on the Civil War, dueling, economic questions, and Richmond personalities and politics.

Rubin, Louis D., Jr. *No Place on Earth: Ellen Glasgow, James Branch Cabell, and Richmond-in-Virginia.* Austin: University of Texas Press, 1959. Short, suggestive, biographical-literary essays about two famous Richmond authors.

Ryan, David D. *The Falls of the James.* Richmond: N.p., 1975. A fine photographic album; the commentary by Newton H. Ancarrow covers the past and present.

———. *Harvest of a Quiet Eye: A Portfolio of East Main Street.* Richmond: Doryan Press, 1969. A slender volume of contemporary photographs.

Sanford, James K., comp. and ed. *A Century of Commerce, 1867–1967.* Richmond: Chamber of Commerce, 1967. Produced and distributed by the Richmond Chamber of Commerce and drawn in part from its records; richly illustrated; provides "a published record of the commercial life of Richmond" for the century covered; supersedes, with the volume below, an earlier Chamber of Commerce publication, *Richmond, Virginia: The City on the James* (Richmond: George W. Engelhardt, 1902–3).

———. *Richmond: Her Triumphs, Tragedies, and Growth.* Richmond: Whittet & Shepperson, 1975. Expanded version of *A Century of Commerce,* above, to add 1607 to 1867, and 1967 to the present.

Sanger, William T. *As I Remember.* Richmond: Dietz Press, 1971. This brief volume, by a former president of the Medical College of Virginia, covers Richmond health services in the modern era.

———. *Medical College of Virginia before 1925 and University College of Medicine, 1893–1913.* Richmond: Whittet & Shepperson, 1973.

Schöpf, Johann D. *Travels in the Confederation, 1783–1784.* Translated and edited by Alfred J. Morrison. 2 vols. Philadelphia: William J. Campbell, 1911. The impressions of this German traveler are given in volume 2, pages 48–68.

*Scott, Mary Wingfield. *Houses of Old Richmond.* Richmond: Valentine Museum, 1941. Scott's books are invaluable for both their informed narratives and their useful photographs, many being of structures no longer standing.

*———. *Old Richmond Neighborhoods.* Richmond: Valentine Museum, 1950.

Shockley, Martin S. *The Richmond Stage, 1784–1812.* Charlottesville: University Press of Virginia, 1977. Thorough and detailed, with numerous illustrations, covering from the first appearance of a professional acting company in the city through the aftermath of the great theater fire of December 1811.

Simcoe, Lieut. Col. John G. *Simcoe's Military Journal.* New York: Bartlett & Welford, 1844. Includes British Ranger Simcoe's account of the military action in and around Richmond in 1781.

Smith, William. *Memoirs of Governor William Smith, of Virginia. . . .* Edited by John W.

Bell. New York: Moss Engraving Co., 1891. Read selectively from these reminiscences of Virginia's last Civil War governor; also includes other Smithiana—documents, speeches, and the like.

Smyth, John F. D. *A Tour in the United States*. 2 vols. London: G. Robinson, J. Robson, and J. Sewell, 1784. Volume 1, pages 30–59, record this traveler's view of the city as it looked in the early 1780s.

Stanard, Mary Newton. *Richmond: Its People and Its Story*. Philadelphia: J. B. Lippincott Co., 1923. An undocumented, somewhat nostalgic history, blending social and political topics and covering to 1870 (except for a brief epilogue); organized by major eras; well illustrated.

————. See also Poe above.

Stearns, Charles. *Narrative of Henry Box Brown, Who Escaped from Slavery Enclosed in a Box 3 Feet Long and 2 Wide. Written from a Statement of Facts Made by Himself. . . .* Boston: N.p., 1848. Brown's spectacular escape from Richmond is the highlight, but the book also touches on industrial slavery in antebellum Richmond; in the genre of abolitionist literature.

*Thomas, Emory M. *The Confederate State of Richmond: A Biography of the Capital*. Austin: University of Texas Press, 1971. A brief but scholarly and clearly written narrative by a native Richmonder; offers a convenient overview of the city during the Civil War; see also Bill above.

Trowbridge, John T. *The Desolate South, 1865–1866: A Picture of the Battlefields and of the Devastated Confederacy*. Edited by Gordon Carroll. New York: Duell, Sloan, and Pearce, 1956. A Yankee journalist's vivid account of his travels through Dixie after the war; includes Richmond and several Virginia battlegrounds; a longer version was published in 1866.

Valentine Museum. *Fifty Years in Richmond, 1898–1948*. Richmond: Miller and Rhoads, 1948. An eclectic but interesting photographic record of a half-century's notable people, places, and events.

————. *Richmond Portraits in an Exhibition of Makers of Richmond, 1737–1860*. Richmond: Valentine Museum, 1949. Features 156 portraits of prominent Richmonders, with biographical sketches of both subjects and artists.

Van Schreeven, William J.; Scribner, Robert L.; and Tarter, Brent, comps. and eds. *Revolutionary Virginia: The Road to Independence*. 6 vols. to date. Charlottesville: University Press of Virginia, 1973–. This fine documentary covers from 1763 to 1776 and contains Richmond material; volume 2, for example, has a superb editorial note and the proceedings for the Second Virginia Convention, which met in the city and featured the emotional oratory of delegate Patrick Henry.

Wagenknecht, Edward C. *Edgar Allan Poe: The Man behind the Legend*. New York: Oxford University Press, 1963. A short but serious study of the "character and personality" of Poe, with little on Richmond as such.

Wallace, Charles M. *The Boy Gangs of Richmond in the Dear Old Days*. Richmond: Richmond Press, 1938. Humorous recollections, in capsule segments, of youthful days and doings in late nineteenth-century Richmond.

Walthall, Ernest T. *Hidden Things Brought to Light*. Richmond: Dietz Printing Co., 1933. Offers a quick, quaint, anecdotal tour of the city's places and people known to businessman Walthall (1848–1912); first published in 1908.

*Ward, Harry M., and Greer, Jr., Harold E. *Richmond during the Revolution, 1775–83*. Charlottesville: University Press of Virginia, 1977. A highly useful survey, with handy maps and illustrations and as much social and economic history as political and military history; a publication of the Richmond Independence Bicentennial Commission.

Weddell, Alexander W. *Richmond, Virginia, in Old Prints, 1737–1887*. Richmond: Johnson Publishing Co., 1932. Dozens of prints, handsomely presented, with a text by Weddell and a foreword by Douglas Southall Freeman.

Weddell, Elizabeth W. *St. Paul's Church, Richmond, Virginia*. 2 vols. Richmond: William Byrd Press, 1931. Recounts the history of a famous Episcopalian church; illustrated; with numerous lists and a lengthy section on "Memorials and Thank Offerings."

Weld, Isaac, Jr. *Travels through the States of North America . . . 1795, 1796, and 1797*. 2d ed. 2 vols. London: J. Stockdale, 1799. Volume 1 features brief but interesting observations on Richmond by this Irish traveler.

Wessells, John H., Jr. *The Bank of Virginia: A History*. Charlottesville: University Press of Virginia, 1973. Gives the story of a major financial institution, the former Morris Plan Bank, and of its leaders, notably Thomas C. Boushall and Herbert C. Moseley.

Wiley, Bell Irvin. *Confederate Women*. Westport, Conn.: Greenwood Press, 1975. Short, readable, with some material on wartime Richmond.

Williams, Frances Leigh. *Matthew Fontaine Maury: Scientist of the Sea*. New Brunswick: Rutgers University Press, 1963. A thick, detailed biography of the famed "Pathfinder of the Seas."

Williams, Jay Killian Bowman. *Changed Views and Unforeseen Prosperity: Richmond of 1890 Gets a Monument to Lee*. Richmond: N.p., 1969. A privately published, award-winning senior thesis from Yale University; uses a Richmond milestone to offer insight into an era.

Winthrop, Robert P. *Architecture in Downtown Richmond*. Edited by Virginius Dabney with selected photographs by Richard Cheek. Richmond: Historic Richmond Foundation, 1982. Based on a comprehensive recent survey; features 150 photographs by Cheek, as well as about 1,000 other pictures.

———. *Cast and Wrought: The Architectural Metalwork of Richmond, Virginia*. Photographs by Katherine Wetzel and foreword by Margot Gayle. Richmond: Valentine Museum, 1980. Offers an informed photo-narrative tour of one of the town's "greatest civic treasures."

Wirt, William. *The Letters of the British Spy*. Edited with an introduction by Richard Beale Davis. Chapel Hill: University of North Carolina Press, 1970. Ten stylish and engaging essays, largely on Virginia themes and personalities, including some Richmond material of significance; also features a sketch of Wirt, a notable Richmond lawyer, politician, biographer of Patrick Henry, and later U.S. attorney general; first published in 1803.

Wise, John Sergeant. *The End of an Era*. Edited by Curtis Carroll Davis. New York: T. Yoseloff, 1965. Originally published in 1899; provides a vivid, often humorous view of Richmond in the late 1850s and Civil War years when Wise (1846–1913) was a youthful member of a family prominent in local affairs.

Sources

Bagby, George W. "Canal Reminiscences." In *The Old Virginia Gentleman and Other Sketches*, ed. Thomas Nelson Page, chap. 9. New York: Charles Scribner's Sons, 1910.

———. *John M. Daniel's Latch-Key.* . . . Lynchburg, Va.: J. P. Bell & Co., 1868.

Berry, James, et al. *The Richmond Flood . . . of June 22, 1972.* Lubbock, Tex.: C. F. Boone, 1972.

Bondurant, Agnes M. *Poe's Richmond.* Richmond: Garrett and Massie, 1942.

Brandon, Edgar E., comp. and ed. *Lafayette, Guest of the Nation: A Contemporary Account of the "Triumphal Tour" of General Lafayette.* . . . Vol. 3. Oxford, Ohio: Oxford Historical Press, 1950–57.

Bratton, Mary J. "John Jasper of Richmond: From Slave Preacher to Community Leader." *Virginia Cavalcade* 29 (Summer 1979): 32–39.

Brawley, Benjamin. "Maggie L. Walker and Her Enterprise." in *Negro Builders and Heroes*, chap. 38. Chapel Hill: University of North Carolina Press, 1937.

Brown, Henry Box. See Stearns below.

Bryan, J., III. *The Sword over the Mantel: The Civil War and I.* New York: McGraw-Hill, 1960.

"The Burning of the Richmond Theatre, 1811." *Virginia Magazine of History and Biography* 51 (July 1943): 297–300.

[Burr Dines with Justice Marshall]. Richmond *Enquirer*, 10 April 1807.

Byrd, William, of Westover. *The Prose Works of.* . . . Edited by Louis B. Wright. Cambridge, Mass.: Harvard University Press, Belknap Press, 1966.

Caperton, Helena Lefroy. "Mellow Days: A Sketch of Mid-Victorian Richmond." *Reviewer* 1 (May 1921): 206–11.

Chesterman, Evan R. "The M'Carty-Mordecai Affair Near Oakwood." Richmond *Evening Journal*, 19 November 1908.

Christian, Joseph. "The Capitol Disaster, April 27, 1870: A Letter of . . . to his Wife," ed. William M. E. Rachal. *Virginia Magazine of History and Biography* 68 (April 1960): 193–97.

Christian, W. Asbury. *Richmond, Her Past and Present.* Richmond: L. H. Jenkins, 1912.

Clark, Emily. *Stuffed Peacocks.* New York: Alfred A. Knopf, 1927.

Cutchins, John A. *Memories of Old Richmond, 1881–1944.* [White Marsh, Va.: McClure Press, 1973].

DeLeon, Thomas C. *Four Years in Rebel Capitals.* . . . Mobile: Gossip Printing Co., 1890.

Dickens, Charles. *American Notes for General Circulation.* 2 vols. London: Chapman and Hall, 1842.

Dowdey, Clifford. *Bugles Blow No More.* Boston: Little, Brown & Co., 1937.

Duke, Maurice. "Cabell and Glasgow's Richmond: The Intellectual Background of the City." *Mississippi Quarterly* 27 (Fall 1974): 375–91.

"The Fall of Richmond." ["The Evacuation," by Clement Sulivane, Captain, C.S.A., and "The Occupation," by Thomas T. Graves, Aide-de-Camp to General Godfrey Weitzel, U.S.A.] In Robert U. Johnson and Clarence C. Buel, eds. *Battles and Leaders of the Civil War.* . . . , 4:725–28. 4 vols. New York: Century Co., 1887–88.

"Gen'l [Joseph Reid] Anderson Dead." Richmond *Times*, 8 September 1892.

Glasgow, Ellen. *The Romance of a Plain Man*. New York: Macmillan, 1909.

Grigsby, Hugh B. *The Virginia Convention of 1829–30*. Richmond: Macfarlane and Fergusson, 1854.

Harrison, Constance Cary [Mrs. Burton]. *Recollections Grave and Gay*. New York: Charles Scribner's Sons, 1911.

Harwell, Richard, ed. *Margaret Mitchell's "Gone with the Wind" Letters, 1936–1949*. New York: Macmillan Co., 1976.

Hening, William W., comp. *The Statutes at Large . . . of Virginia*. . . . 13 vols. New York: George Cochran, 1819–23.

High, Stanley. "By Their Bootstraps." *Reader's Digest* 32 (March 1938): 73–77.

"The Home Life of Chief Justice John Marshall." *William and Mary Quarterly* 12 (January 1932): 67–69.

Irving, Pierre M. *The Life and Letters of Washington Irving*. 4 vols. New York: G. P. Putnam, 1862–64.

Jefferson, Thomas. *Papers*. Edited by Julian P. Boyd. 21 vols. to date. Princeton: Princeton University Press, 1950–.

Jeter, Jeremiah Bell. *The Recollections of a Long Life*. Richmond: Religious Herald Co., 1891.

Joel, Joseph. "My Recollections and Experiences of Richmond, Virginia, U.S.A., 1884–1892," ed. Myron Berman. *Virginia Magazine of History and Biography* 87 (July 1979): 344–56.

"John Mitchell, Jr." Richmond *Afro-American* (magazine section), 20–24 January 1976.

Jones, Plummer F. "The Negro Exposition at Richmond." *American Review of Reviews* 52 (August 1915): 185–88.

La Rochefoucault-Liancourt, François, duc de. *Travels through the United States of North America . . . 1795, 1796, and 1797*. 4 vols. London: R. Phillips, 1799.

"The Lee Monument at Richmond." *Harper's Weekly* 34 (June 1890): 470.

"Lila Meade Valentine: Two Tributes." *Richmond Literature and History Quarterly* 2 (Fall 1979): 33–37.

Lutz, Francis Earle. *Richmond in World War II*. Richmond: Dietz Press, 1951.

MacDonald, Edgar E. "Glasgow, Cabell, and Richmond." *Mississippi Quarterly* 27 (Fall 1974): 393–413.

MacKay, Alexander. *The Western World; or, Travels in the United States in 1846–47*. . . . 2 vols. Philadelphia: Lea & Blanchard, 1849.

Malone, Dumas. "The Pen of Douglas Southall Freeman." Foreword to Douglas S. Freeman, *George Washington*, vol. 6, pp. xi–xxiv. New York: Charles Scribner's Sons, 1954.

[Marsh, Henry L., III, as Richmond's First Black Mayor]. Richmond *News Leader*, 8, 10 March 1977; Richmond *Times-Dispatch*, 9 March 1977.

Millsaps, Bill. "Clifford Dowdey and the Sweet Life." Richmond *Times-Dispatch*, 8 June 1969.

Mitchell, Margaret. *See* Harwell above.

Moeser, John V. "What's Ahead for Our City?" *Richmond Lifestyle Magazine* 3 (March 1981): 56–59.

Moore, Samuel J. T., Jr. *The Jefferson Hotel: A Southern Landmark*. Richmond: N.p., 1940.

Mordecai, Samuel. *Virginia, Especially Richmond, in By-Gone Days*. . . . Rev. ed. Richmond: West and Johnston, 1860.

Munford, George Wythe. *The Two Parsons*. . . . Richmond: J. D. K. Sleight, 1884.

Palmer, William P., and others, eds. *Calendar of Virginia State Papers.* 11 vols. Richmond: N.p., 1875–95.

Perdue, Charles L., Jr.; Thomas E. Barden; and Robert K. Phillips, eds. *Weevils in the Wheat: Interviews with Virginia Ex-Slaves.* Charlottesville: University Press of Virginia, 1976.

[Putnam, Sallie A.]. *Richmond during the War: Four Years of Personal Observation.* New York: G. W. Carleton & Co., 1867.

Randolph, [Reverend] Peter. *From Slave Cabin to the Pulpit.* Boston: James H. Earle, [1893].

[Richmond Black Code]. In *The Charters and Ordinances of the City of Richmond*, pp. 193–201. Richmond: Ellyson's Steam Presses, 1859.

Robbins, Tom. *Even Cowgirls Get the Blues.* Boston: Houghton Mifflin Co., 1976.

Rubin, Louis D., Jr., "Railway Tunnel's Collapse Twenty-four Years Ago Sealed-in Engine and Crewmen." Richmond *Times-Dispatch,* 8 May 1949.

Schöpf, Johann David. *Travels in the Confederation* [1783–1784]. Translated and edited by Alfred J. Morrison. Philadelphia: William J. Campbell, 1911.

Sosna, Morton, "Virginius Dabney: Publicist for a Liberal South." In *In Search of the Silent South: Southern Liberals and the Race Issue*, chap. 7. New York: Columbia University Press, 1977.

Stearns, Charles. *Narrative of Henry Box Brown, Who Escaped from Slavery Enclosed in a Box 3 Feet Long and 2 Wide. Written from a Statement of Facts Made by Himself. . . .* Boston: N.p., 1849.

[Tobacco Festival, 1949]. Richmond *News Leader,* 14 October 1949; Richmond *Times-Dispatch,* 9 April, 15, 17 October 1949.

[Washington's Statue Unveiled]. Richmond *Enquirer,* 24 February 1858.

Weddell, Alexander W. *Richmond, Virginia, in Old Prints, 1737–1887.* Richmond: Johnson Publishing Co., 1932.

Wilkinson, J. Harvie, III. *From Brown to Bakke: The Supreme Court and School Integration, 1954–1978.* New York: Oxford University Press, 1979.

———. *Serving Justice: A Supreme Court Clerk's View.* New York: Charterhouse, 1974.

Wise, John Sergeant. *The End of an Era.* Edited by Curtis Carroll Davis. New York: T. Yoseloff, 1965. Originally published in 1899.

Index

Names of fictionalized characters do not appear in this index.

Acknowledgments

Agnes M. Bondurant. *Poe's Richmond*. Richmond: Garrett and Massie, 1942. Reprinted by permission of Agnes Bondurant Marcuson.

Julian P. Boyd, ed., *The Papers of Thomas Jefferson*, Vol. 8: *25 February 1785 to 31 October 1785*. Copyright 1953 by Princeton University Press, © renewed 1981 by Princeton University Press; and Vol. 9: *November 1785 to June 1786*. Copyright 1954 by Princeton University Press. Reprinted by permission of Princeton University Press.

Edgar E. Brandon, comp. and ed. *Lafayette, Guest of the Nation: A Contemporary Account of the "Triumphal Tour" of General Lafayette. . . .* Vol. 3. Oxford, Ohio: Oxford Historical Press, 1950–57. Reprinted by permission of Grace M. Glasgow.

Benjamin Brawley. "Maggie L. Walker and Her Enterprise." In *Negro Builders and Heroes*, chap. 38. Chapel Hill: University of North Carolina Press, 1937. Reprinted by permission of The University of North Carolina Press.

J. Bryan III. *The Sword over the Mantel: The Civil War and I*. New York: McGraw-Hill, 1960. Reprinted by permission of Harold Ober Associates Incorporated.

"The Burning of the Richmond Theatre, 1811." *Virginia Magazine of History and Biography* 51 (July 1943): 297–300. Reprinted by permission of *Virginia Magazine of History and Biography*.

Joseph Christian. "The Capitol Disaster, April 27, 1870: A Letter of . . . to His Wife," ed. William M. E. Rachal. *Virginia Magazine of History and Biography* 68 (April 1960): 193–97. Reprinted by permission of *Virginia Magazine of History and Biography*.

Emily Clark. *Stuffed Peacocks*. New York: Alfred A. Knopf, 1927. Reprinted by permission.

Clifford Dowdey. *Bugles Blow No More*. Boston: Little, Brown & Co., 1937. Copyright 1937 by Clifford Dowdey. Reprinted by permission of Harold Ober Associates Incorporated.

Maurice Duke. "Cabell and Glasgow's Richmond: The Intellectual Background of the City." *Mississippi Quarterly* 27 (Fall 1974): 375–91. Reprinted by permission of *The Mississippi Quarterly*.

Stanley High. "By Their Bootstraps." *Reader's Digest* 32 (March 1938): 73–77. Reprinted from the March 1938 *Reader's Digest* by permission. Copyright © 1938 by The Reader's Digest Assn., Inc.

"The Home Life of Chief Justice Marshall." *William and Mary College Quarterly Historical Magazine*, 2d ser. 12 (January 1932): 67–69. Reprinted by permission of *The William and Mary Quarterly*.

Joseph Joel. "My Recollections and Experiences of Richmond, Virginia, U.S.A., 1884–1892," ed. Myron Berman. *Virginia Magazine of History and Biography* 87 (July 1979): 344–56. Reprinted by permission of *Virginia Magazine of History and Biography*.

"John Mitchell, Jr." Richmond *Afro-American* (magazine section), 20–24 January 1976. Reprinted by permission.

"Lila Meade Valentine: Two Tributes." *Rich...ond Literature and History Quarterly* 2 (Fall 1979): 33–37. Reprinted by permission of *The Richmond Quarterly*.

Francis Earle Lutz. *Richmond in World War II*. Richmond: Dietz Press, 1951. Reprinted by permission of The Dietz Press.

Edgar E. MacDonald. "Glasgow, Cabell, and Richmond." *Mississippi Quarterly* 27 (Fall 1974): 393–413. Reprinted by permission of *The Mississippi Quarterly*.

Dumas Malone. "The Pen of Douglas Southall Freeman." Introduction by Dumas Malone to *George Washington, Planter and Patriot*, Vol. 6, by Douglas Southall Freeman is reprinted with the permission of Charles Scirbner's Sons. Copyright 1954 Charles Scribner's Sons; copyright renewed 1982.

John V. Moeser. "What's Ahead for Our City?" *Richmond Lifestyle Magazine* (March 1981): 56–54. Reprinted by permission of *Richmond Lifestyle Magazine*, now a part of *Commonwealth, The Magazine of Virginia*.

Charles L. Perdue, Jr., Thomas E. Barden, and Robert K. Phillips, eds. *Weevils in the Wheat: Interviews with Virginia Ex-Slaves*. Charlottesville: University Press of Virginia, 1976. Reprinted by permission of The University Press of Virginia.

Tom Robbins. *Even Cowgirls Get the Blues*. Boston: Houghton Mifflin Co., 1976 (reprint by Bantam Books). Reprinted by permission of Tom Robbins and the publisher.

Morton Sosna. "Virginius Dabney: Publicist for a Liberal South." In *In Search of the Silent South: Southern Liberals and the Race Issue*. New York: Columbia University Press, 1977. Reprinted by permission of Columbia University Press.

J. Harvie Wilkinson III. *From Brown to Bakke: The Supreme Court and School Integration, 1954–1978*. New York: Oxford University Press, 1979. Copyright © 1979 by Oxford University Press, Inc. Reprinted by permission.

J. Harvie Wilkinson III. *Serving Justice: A Supreme Court Clerk's View*. New York: Charterhouse, 1974. Reprinted by permission of J. Harvie Wilkinson III.

Material from the Richmond *Times-Dispatch* and the Richmond *News-Leader* is reprinted by permission.